Three Civilizations, Two Cultures, One State

Three Civilizations, Two Cultures,

One State: 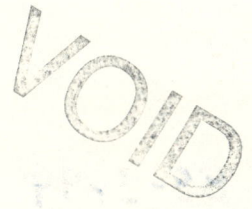 Canada's Political Traditions

Douglas V. Verney

Duke University Center for International Studies Publication

Duke University Press   Durham 1986

© 1986 Duke University Press
All rights reserved
Printed in the United States of America
on acid-free paper ∞
Library of Congress Cataloging-in-Publication Data
appear on the last printed page of this book.

For Francine
whose loving encouragement
made this work possible

Contents

Tables ix

Preface and Acknowledgments xi

Introduction 1

1 American in Civilization, Canadian in Culture 9
2 Pragmatism and Canada's "Philosophical Federalism" 35
3 The Americanization of the Social Sciences: The Canadian Response to Scientific Empiricism 58
4 Taking Tradition for Granted: English Canada's Attachment to Westminster 112
5 The "Reconciliation" of Parliamentary Supremacy and Federalism 149
6 From Conquest via Rebellion to Dualism: French Canadian Perceptions before 1867 172
7 Dualism versus Majority Rule 210
8 French Canada and the Triumph of Majority Rule 252
9 Quebec and the Rest of Canada: The Limitations of Philosophical Federalism 300
10 Options Canada: Options Quebec 346
11 Conclusion: Toward a New State Structure? 391

Notes 405

Bibliography 435

Index 445

Tables

1 Tentative Estimate of Relative Rankings of the Four English-speaking [sic] Democracies according to Strength of Pattern Variables   83

2 Canada's Constitutional Development: 1949 in Historical Context   291

3 Liberal Members of Parliament from Quebec in the House of Commons, 1957-68   315

4 Synthesis in the Seven Dyads   342

5 Liberal MPs Representing Western Provinces   358

Preface and Acknowledgments

A question that has puzzled many foreign observers is: How has Canada avoided becoming a miniature replica of the United States? This study explains its success by distinguishing between Canada's civilization, which it shares with the United States, and its two indigenous cultures, which it assiduously protects and promotes. Three civilizations have left their mark on Canada: those of France, Britain, and now the United States. But Canadian intellectuals demonstrated their cultural autonomy first by resisting the American philosophy of pragmatism, and have continued to do so by responding critically to the methodologies of the American social sciences.

Despite the problems presented by having both an English-speaking and a French-speaking culture, Canada has managed to retain a single political system. The country has been transformed from a British Dominion into an independent and officially bilingual state. To understand the emergence of modern Canada, it is necessary not only to look to the impact of successive civilizations, but also to examine Canada's own political theory.

The book interprets this domestic history not in terms of two cultural solitudes—of "English Canada" and Quebec—but as the interaction of different political traditions. The majoritarian viewpoint of English-speaking Canadians, committed to the Westminster doctrine of parliamentary supremacy, is contrasted with the dualism of most francophones, with their preference for a truly federal Constitution that would protect the rights of the minority community. The vast majority of Canadians are neither United Empire loyalists nor Quebec separatists: they are committed to the idea of one state with two cultures. And they are still resolving the relationship between the two language groups.

Perhaps the most significant feature of the analysis is the insistence that the problems facing Canada, from Americanization to bilingualism and separatism, cannot be treated in isolation. They are intertwined. It is the resolution of Canada's problems that is leading to the emergence of a unique and vital entity, one that is different from the usual nation-state but which nonetheless has many lessons for other countries today.

A large number of colleagues and friends have read drafts of one or more chapters over the years. In Canada I am particularly indebted to Claude Bissell, Hartwell Bowsfield, Ramsay Cook, Robert Cox, C. Brough Macpherson, Kenneth McRoberts, Peter Hogg, Peter Newman, Thomas Goudge, Donald Smiley, Reg Whitaker, and Jack Granatstein.

In the United States I have been helped by Henry Bienen, Walter Murphy, the late Walter Kaufmann, and several colleagues at the Institute for Advanced Study, notably David Hollinger, John Rawls, and Quentin Skinner.

In the United Kingdom, W. H. Morris-Jones and later James Manor were good enough to publish my articles on Canada in the *Journal of Commonwealth and Comparative Politics* in 1974, 1978, and 1983. The most recent article was based on Chapter 5 of this book.

I am indebted to a succession of graduate students who were of help to me as research assistants: Mark Bartholomew, Alan Rossman, Alex Stewart, Helen Robinson, Virginia Brisbin, Scott Sinclair, Malcolm Brown, Donald Wallace and Vandana Chauhan.

When preparing a draft of the concluding chapter, I was able to use a York University Minor Research Grant to interview several of those persons in Ottawa, Montreal, and Quebec City who were associated with the various options presented to the people of Canada from 1978 on. I would like to thank all those who gave me their time.

I am also grateful to the Rockefeller Foundation for enabling me to sketch a first draft of the book at the Villa Serbelloni, Bellagio, Italy; and to Clifford Geertz and the Institute for Advanced Study for the year in which I was able to draft the early chapters. York University was good enough to grant me research leave, and later put at my disposal its impressive Secretarial Services headed by Doris Rippington. D. C. Gupta typed the final corrections.

The study seemed almost finished on a number of occasions, but it proved impossible to put it all together until Canada ratified its Constitution and the Trudeau era came to an end. A word of congratulations is in order to those many politicians and intellectuals who devoted so much time and energy to doing what they thought best for their nation.

York University gave me sabbatical leave, and the Canada Council a

Leave Fellowship, when I began this enterprise in 1974–75. I received sabbatical leave again in 1983–84. I wish to thank the Social Sciences and Humanities Research Council of Canada for a Leave Fellowship and the Jules and Gabrielle Léger Fellowship for 1984–85, and the Shastri Indo-Canadian Institute for a Senior Long-Term Fellowship. Together they made a second year's research leave possible. I was thus able to revise and complete the manuscript and to undertake a comparative study of the problems of parliamentary federalism.

I am indebted to the staff of Duke University Press for their encouragement, and for their gentle suggestions of ways to improve the presentation of the argument and in particular to clarify the distinction between culture and civilization.

Finally, I must thank my wife, Francine Frankel Verney, for her incisive comments on earlier drafts and patience throughout. When she completed a manuscript of comparable size on India in 1978 she remarked in her preface that during the three years since we met (at Bellagio) I had only known her as bearing the burden of an unfinished work. She, however, has borne uncomplainingly ten years of unfinished business on my part.

Douglas Verney

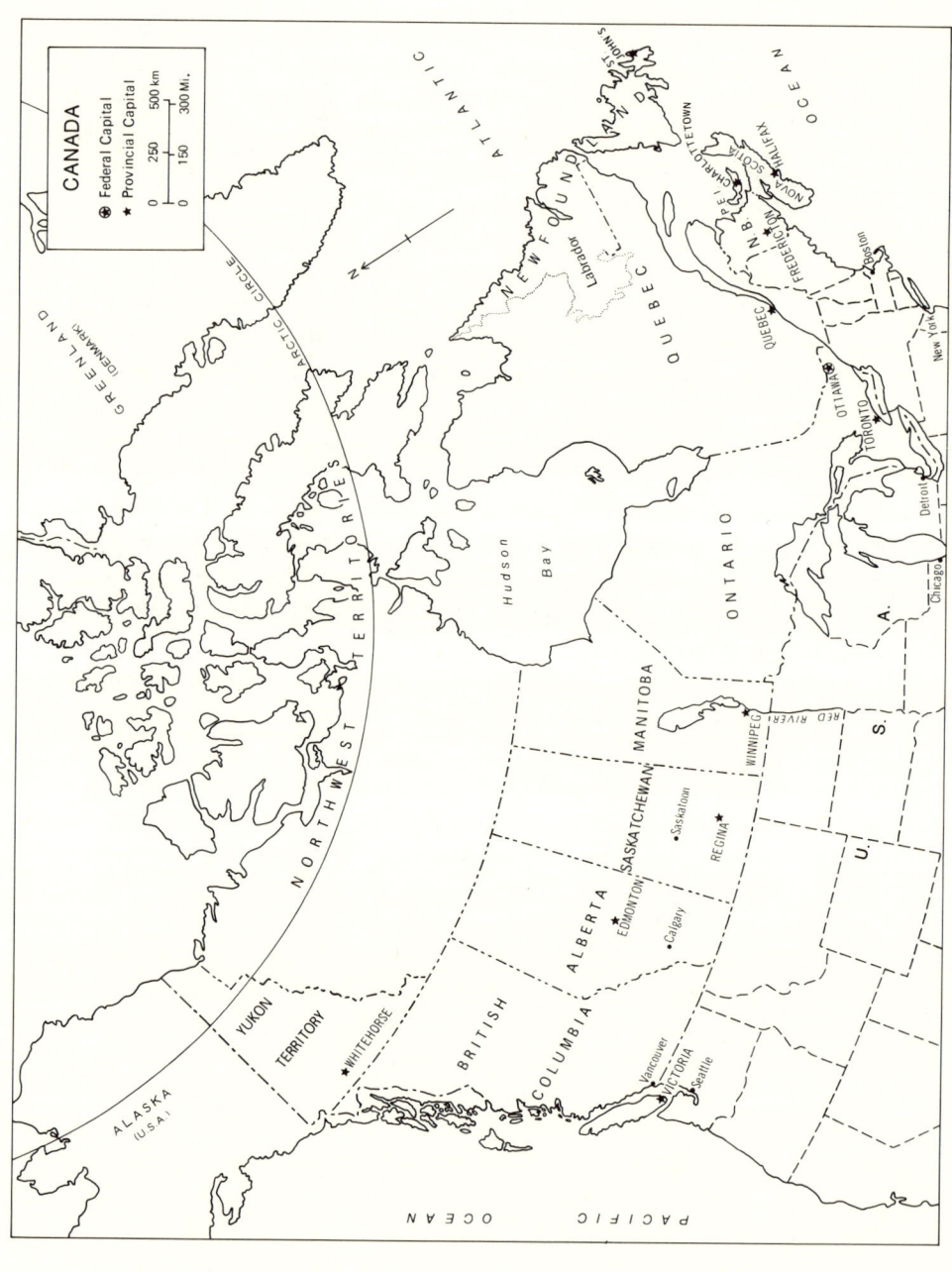

Introduction

It is safe to predict that Canada will become less and less British and more American. The best we can wish for—a wish that may well be realized—is that she may become quite simply Canadian.—André Siegfried, *The Race Question in Canada* (1907)

When Canada celebrated its first centenary in 1967, many thoughtful observers were worried about its future as a country. Could it remain independent of the United States? Only yesterday, or so it seemed, Canada had emancipated itself from British colonialism—for example, by appointing the first Canadian to the office of governor general (in 1952). But now, instead of being able to relax and enjoy its new freedom, Canada appeared in danger of becoming an American satellite with no distinctive identity of its own. Writers like George Grant (in *Lament for a Nation*) and Donald Creighton (in *Canada's First Century*) asserted that although now free from British *political* control, Canada was threatened by a much more ominous—because permanent—form of imperialism, the economic and cultural penetration of the United States.

It was to take a resurgence of Canadian nationalism, inspired in part by the passion of authors such as Grant and Creighton, to bring this era of ideological pessimism to a close. Fresh perspectives emerged, and these in due course aroused attention both in Canada and in the outside world. Symbolic of this new interest in Canada's development was the formation of an Association of Canadian Studies in the United States in 1971. This was followed by similar associations in Europe and Asia. The tenth such association was established in China in 1984 and the eleventh in India in 1985.

The pages that follow offer an explanation of Canada's struggle to have a distinctive political culture. They ask the following questions: How was it that some writers, particularly foreigners, were persuaded that Canada was, after all, very similar to the United States ("a miniature replica")? And how was it that other authors, especially Canadians, were equally convinced that Canada was very different from its neighbor?

To explain this seeming contradiction, a distinction is drawn between the concept of a *civilization*—something imported into Canada and shared with others—and the notion of *culture*—something that was indigenous and unique. Civilization was brought to Canada from France in the seventeenth century. Although there were peoples native to the subcontinent in Canada, Indian tribes (like the Hurons and Iroquois) and scattered Eskimos (now termed Inuit), the land was sparsely populated. There was nothing in North America comparable to the great Indian civilizations in Central and South America, established before the Europeans arrived by the Aztecs in Mexico and the Incas in Peru. When the French brought their civilization to the St. Lawrence River and built Quebec City and Montreal, they did not have to deal with an urban society already in place.

This first (French) civilization was in due course challenged by the British Empire, with its powerful Royal Navy. Following the Conquest of New France in 1760, Quebec became part of an expanded Canada that was a colony of the British. Throughout the nineteenth century the British stamped their civilization across the whole subcontinent, extending their influence westward via the transcontinental railroad. Yet Canada remained thinly populated, a slender thread of settlement strung out along the famous forty-ninth parallel, the endless boundary with the restless United States. There were simply not enough people in the United Kingdom to populate Britain's vast possessions, of which Canada was but one.

The outbreak of war in 1914 marked the beginning of Britain's decline as an Empire. The period after the end of the Second World War in 1945 saw the transformation of the Empire into a Commonwealth of independent nations. Entering the latter part of the twentieth century, Canada came within the orbit of yet another dynamic civilization, the American. The trade that had once flowed between Canada and the United Kingdom now tended to move from Canada to the United States. The east-west axis on which Confederation had been based in 1867 was replaced by a series of north-south axes with the United States.

Each of the three civilizations brought in turn to Canada was the dominant (western) civilization of its time. The French civilization under Louis XIV and the British under Queen Victoria were the equiva-

Introduction 3

lent of the United States today. Canada was the beneficiary not only of civilizations that were in their heyday, but also of the cultural legacy each of them left. This legacy provided the foundation on which Canada built its own indigenous culture.

In some respects there were in fact *two* Canadian cultures, the one English-speaking and the other francophone. Today Canadians are proud of their officially bilingual society and of the two cultures that form its base. It is now doubtful whether anyone who has failed to master both official languages can expect to become prime minister. Indeed a premium seems to be placed on the possession of a feeling for the two cultures, not just a technical mastery of the other language.

There is in addition a growing awareness that Canada not only is officially bilingual but also is committed to developing a multicultural society where immigrants (increasingly from countries and continents very different from Britain and France) are encouraged to retain their traditional culture. But only English and French are official languages, and so this has tended to give the cultures of "the two founding peoples" a much greater significance, particularly in politics, than the diffuse multiculturalism of the "New Canadians."

Despite the experience of successive civilizations, and the increasing awareness of being a society based on two indigenous cultures, Canada has managed to remain politically in one piece. There is widespread acceptance of a political culture that has developed out of the British tradition of parliamentary government and the American example of federalism. Yet this accepted *governmental* culture has not prevented the emergence of a number of different political traditions (or world views) within both English-speaking and French-speaking Canada. These traditions cover a broad spectrum of ideas, from those of the pro-British United Empire loyalists of nineteenth-century Upper Canada (Ontario) and the Maritime provinces, to the proposals for sovereignty-association put forward by the Quebec separatists in the 1970s.

The title of this book in effect summarizes its contents. It notes the impact of three successive dominant civilizations: those of Bourbon France, the British Empire, and the American "Republic of Technology." It indicates the importance of Canada's two languages and cultures in creating a dualist society: of English-speaking Canadians and francophones. It explains how despite the conflicts between the three civilizations and the two cultures, Canada has remained one state. Finally, in describing the interaction of the various political traditions, it shows how profound at times have been the disagreements over the nature of Canada as a society and as a state. The persistence of these disagreements made it difficult until recently for Canadians to articulate the nature of their identity except negatively or elliptically (as in the expression: "Canada is different from the United States because of Quebec").

Canada *is* different from the United States—and also from Britain and France. Part of this difference is due to the presence of Quebec. But it is also due to the interaction of the two cultures over a long period of time—and to Canada's ability to adapt to successive dominant civilizations.

Canadian nationalists question Canada's ability to adapt to a dominant civilization, particularly its capacity to resist American economic imperialism. Despite many attempts to diversify its trade, Canada has become increasingly dependent on the United States for both exports and imports. To many students of political economy, Canada's economic (and military) dependence is enough to make any assertion of political independence questionable.

It is certainly true that there are severe limitations to Canada's assertiveness. But to some extent this is a matter of choice rather than necessity. Canada chose to be a part of NATO and later NORAD—but chose not to accept in toto the nuclear weapons policy of the United States. Canada chose to integrate its automobile industry with the American—but did not accept free trade across the board. Because Canada is not totally free, it does not follow that it is totally dependent.

It is the argument of the first part of this book (Chapters 1-3) that political control and economic penetration are not the only forms of imperialism. There is also a *cultural* imperialism that, if successful, can be completely devasting to a society, for it stifles competing modes of thought. It is at the level of culture, or the realm of ideas, that the ultimate battle lines are drawn, as the religious wars throughout history, and the ideological confrontation of the superpowers today, amply demonstrate.

By drawing a distinction between civilization and culture it is possible to ask whether, despite the massive influence exerted by American civilization, especially at the popular level, there remains a culture that is essentially Canadian. It is because Canada is now seen to possess an interesting and distinctive literature, history, political system, and even society that Canadian studies have attracted an increasing number of scholars in an ever-growing number of countries.

It is one thing boldly to assert that although Canada forms an integral part of a North American civilization it is distinctive in its culture. It is quite another to be able to demonstrate that Canadian intellectuals have shown the capacity to resist being overwhelmed by American cultural imperialism. For example, the philosophy of pragmatism was from its beginnings a distinctively American phenomenon, having begun to take shape in the thought of C. S. Peirce shortly after America's own first centenary (in 1876, a hundred years after the Declaration of Independence). Pragmatism drew attention to the difference between the American world view and European philosophy. Had Canadians been American rather than European in their outlook, they would presumably have been attracted to the world view of pragmatism, rather than to the legacy of European philosophy, during pragmatism's heyday in the half century before the outbreak of the Second World War.

It is possible to argue that in those days Canada was still colonial in its attitudes, especially in scholarship. But the period after World War II was different, for by now Canada had fully established its independence from Britain. It was then that a second wave of American ideas struck Canada: this one more universal in its appeal than a school of philosophy. The new incursion consisted of the methodologies of the social sciences, particularly political science.

The peak of American cultural penetration occurred in the 1960s when the universities were expanding and paying particular attention to the social sciences. American books, journals, research methods, students, and professors flooded into Canada. The dominant position that philosophical pragmatism had failed to achieve after the First World War was easily occupied by the social sciences with their scientific, value-free, and universal methodology. In political science, new fields such as comparative politics and empirical theory gave expression to this "behavioural" approach to the study of political change. For a time it seemed that resistance to the "behavioural revolution" (including the British spelling) was simply the reaction of extreme nationalists or committed Marxists.

However, as the first flush of enthusiasm for a science of politics waned, Canadian scholars began to ask whether it was really value-free—that is, whether it was actually based on an implicit—and American—

philosophy. As we shall see, the world view of Talcott Parsons was similar to that of the philosophical pragmatists. There was an interesting contrast between the polite response to an American political sociologist (S. M. Lipset) by a Canadian Marxist political theorist (C. B. Macpherson) in 1954 and the critical reception given by a Canadian political sociologist (John Meisel) to an American colleague in the same field (Robert Presthus) twenty years later (see Chapter 3).

To understand Canada's political tradition we need to do more than examine the challenge to the country's political identity from without. We need also to look for an explanation from within the country itself.

Traditionally, Canada was thought of in terms of a dominant political tradition, the British. The Westminster parliamentary system was transported to Canada and flourished not only in Ottawa but also in every provincial capital, including Quebec. (The French *ancien régime* had left nothing comparable.) Until the Second World War, Canada was viewed as Britain's senior colony or dominion, loyal in its support of the empire. It is true that there were occasional French Canadian nationalist outbursts in Quebec against the British connection, but these were regarded by English Canadians as the work of a disgruntled minority of Quebecois. (A leading political science textbook, first published in 1947, dealt with the 1837–38 Rebellions in one sentence.) By and large Canada's history was regarded as an evolutionary progress "from colony to nation." Autonomy was the goal on which most Canadians, Conservatives as well as Liberals, were agreed. As one wag put it, the Liberals believed in the autonomy of Canada and the unity of Empire, the Conservatives in the unity of Empire and the autonomy of Canada. When Canada finally made clear that it was an independent member of the Commonwealth in the late 1940s, this traditional political history, which dealt with Anglo-Canadian relationships, no longer attracted scholars. "Memorable history," as one anglophile put it, came to an end.

"Memorable history" was, of course, not over. It was given a new lease on life in a different form barely a decade later when the so-called Quiet Revolution took place in Quebec. Then it began to seem as though Canada might disintegrate under the impact not only of American domination but of internal dissension as well. With the British political tradition in decline and American economic and cultural penetration in the ascendant, it was difficult for more pessimistic Canadians to see how Quebec nationalism, with its call for an independent State of

Quebec, could be resisted—any more than the Irish nationalism of the 1920s by England or the Algerian nationalism of the 1950s by France. Yet Canada was different. It could not have survived as one state unless there had been more than "the British political tradition." As far back as the 1840s, English-speaking Canadians had resisted the pressures of the British government and the United Empire loyalists to make Canada wholly British and to assimilate the francophones. Faced by a choice between support for the British government and cooperation with the French Canadians, English-speaking Canadians chose the latter. It was partly because they thought of themselves as Canadians as well as British that the union of the two Canadas in 1840 survived. Lord Durham's famous description of Canada as "two nations warring in the bosom of a single state" may have applied to the Rebellions of 1837–38, but it was a caricature of the country after 1842.

Nor was the French-Canadian position simply that of a disgruntled and oppressed national minority dominated by an English-speaking imperialist majority. After all, the first of Canada's First Ministers, Louis-Hippolyte LaFontaine, was a French Canadian from Montreal. From 1840 to 1867, Upper and Lower (Quebec) Canada were equally represented in the Legislative Assembly. There was always lively debate among the francophones about the future of Quebec. The separatist movement of the 1960s had its origins in the discontent of the 1830s. The "federalists," like Pierre Elliott Trudeau, could trace support for Canada back to LaFontaine in the 1840s.

But few francophone federalists supported the British doctrine of majority rule, especially after the 1851 census, which showed French-speaking Canadians to have become a minority. They insisted on being treated as a *community,* one that was equal in status to *les anglais*. To them, Canada's political tradition was not majoritarian on the British model but dualist as depicted in the 1840 Act of Union (of Upper and Lower Canada). A century later, when constitutional reform became an issue in the 1960s, French Canadians continued to display their autonomy. Whereas most English Canadians continued to favor incremental reforms, francophones pressed for "structural" change.

Clearly, from the vantage point of the mid-1980s there were several world views, not a single "British" political tradition. There was an English-speaking Canadian "majoritarian" view and a French-speaking "dualist" interpretation. Within the English-speaking framework little remained of the loyalist tradition. Among the francophones the number of *indépendantistes* had also declined. Increasingly there seemed to be acceptance of one state and one political culture, despite (or perhaps because of) the recognition of French as an official language. There was no possibility of a return to the British tradition: the Constitution Act of 1982 saw to that.

With the rise of national consciousness and pride, it seemed unlikely that Canada would be enveloped by the United States and possible that Quebec would be able to coexist with the rest of Canada in a new federal system.

We shall see that there is a sort of historical logic to the events that since 1960 have shaped a new Canada. It is a logic that stretches back to the Quebec Act of 1774, the act that made the continuation of a French cultural presence in North America possible, and to the Constitutional Act of 1791, whereby Roman Catholic French Canadians, like their English Canadian counterparts, were enfranchised. Once the Legislative Assemblies of Upper and Lower Canada, established in 1791, were united in a single Province of Canada in 1840, the opportunity to build a common political culture and a single Canadian state presented itself.

If we are to trace the emergence of Canada's present identity, we must, therefore, look first outside Canada to an assessment of the impact of the great civilizations on its political development. Then we must examine Canada's own remarkable history, a history that encompasses far more than the traditional treatment of Canada as an emerging British Dominion or, more recently, of a turbulent, nationalist Quebec.

It is true, as André Siegfried predicted in 1907, that Canada has become less British and more American—but chiefly in its civilization. In the interaction of its various political traditions and ideologies, from loyalism to federalism, conservatism to socialism, and dualism to separatism, it has in its culture become "quite simply Canadian."

1
American in Civilization, Canadian in Culture

Let us begin with that cliché of Americans who view Canada: that Canadians are basically like Americans. . . . At bedrock, Americans think, the Canadian experience is not all that different from the experience of the United States.—Robin W. Winks, *The Relevance of Canadian History: U.S. and Imperial Perspectives*

1 Continentalism versus Nationalism

If any country in the 1960s seemed indistinguishable from its neighbors in civilization, that country was Canada. Its apparent status as a miniature replica of the United States was aptly symbolized in the construction of the world's tallest freestanding building, a communications tower by means of which Torontonians were said to be able to broadcast more TV channels—American as well as Canadian—than any other Canadian community. Toronto, along with Boston, Montreal, Detroit, and Chicago, formed the northern arc of the twentieth century's most dynamic civilization.

That civilization was set in a world increasingly brought together not only by improved communications (Canadian Marshall McLuhan's "global village"), but also by the growing power of transnational corporations.[1] It was the "global reach" of such corporations that led one IBM executive to say that national boundaries were of limited significance: "For business purposes the boundaries that separate one nation from another are no more real than the equator. They are merely convenient demarcations of ethnic, linguistic and cultural entities."[2]

Implicit in this assertion was an important assumption: that there was a distinction between civilization and culture. Certainly at any time there tends to be a dominant civilization whose technology is acknowledged to be superior. That civilization requires considerable organizational skills and these help to give its society, government, and economy a distinctive character that has widespread appeal as a model. At various times such civilizations as those of Greece and Rome, France and Britain, have offered such an appeal. More recently it has been the United States (and to a limited extent, the Soviet Union) that has provided the pattern for other peoples.

To many foreigners it has seemed that North America forms a single civilization dominated by the United States, and that Canada is merely part of this civilization. As the opening quotation from Robin Winks indicates, at bedrock Canada has not seemed all that different from the United States (though perhaps the United States of yesterday) and any differences between the two countries have been thought to be of minor significance. Yet countries like Canada, which feel themselves threatened by a hegemonic civilization, are only too conscious that there is a difference between the attributes they share with their powerful neighbor and those that are peculiar to themselves. With noteworthy exceptions, it is the shared attributes, for example the science, technology, and economy, that form the common civilization. It is the distinctive characteristics, for example the literature, history, and world view of a people, that on the whole delineate the separate culture.

The term "civilization" is often used synonymously with "culture," particularly in dominant civilizations where the culture is assumed to be universally acceptable. But in comparing Canada with the United States it makes sense to draw a distinction between what the two countries have in common, namely their North American civilization, and what they do not share. Canada, after all, has its own literary tradition and its own philosophical assumptions, in a word, its own culture. In a dominant civilization like that of which the United States is the center, the political system is taken for granted as an integral part of the civilization. It is partly through its political power that the civilization is able to extend its influence. In a peripheral society such as Canada, where a people is attempting to preserve and promote a distinctive cultural identity, the political system plays a different role. There, the government is expected to defend the culture against the dominant civilization.

To thus differentiate between civilization and culture may seem somewhat arbitrary to someone brought up in the English or French tradition, where the terms are used interchangeably. Thus Fernand Braudel has written, "The mark of a living civilization is that it is capable of exporting itself, of spreading its culture to different places. It is impossible to imagine a true civilization which does not export its people, its ways of thinking and living."[3]

But it is common to find such a distinction drawn by German writers (though not by Freud). Norbert Elias has written, "The French and English concept of civilization can refer to political or economic, religious or technical, moral or social facts. The German concept of *kultur* refers essentially to intellectual, artistic, and religious facts, and has a tendency to draw a sharp dividing line between facts of this sort, on the one side, and political, economic and social facts, on the other."[4]

For our purposes it is useful to distinguish between the two terms and to give them more precise, if perhaps arbitrary, definitions. In doing so, we may on occasion take for granted the conventional contrast drawn by many social scientists between "modern" (often meaning "superior") civilization and "traditional" (often meaning "backward") culture. Nevertheless, this convention can be very misleading. A modern civilization is usually superior only to an older civilization that it has replaced: technology is, after all, obsolescent. But a traditional culture may be a superb culture that no modern civilization can replace, let alone surpass. Civilizations rise and fall. It is cultures that, unless destroyed by a powerful alien civilization, persist indefinitely. What is traditional, i.e., a culture, may prove to be long lasting: what seems new and modern, for example, the technology of a contemporary civilization, may turn out to be obsolescent and even transient. Consequently, the humanist scholar who is concerned with a great culture may be taking a longer view of the future as well as of the past than the social scientist whose primary interest is the analysis of a contemporary civilization. For example, in India the civilizations of the Mughal Empire and the British Empire have come and gone. The Hindu culture, which in their heyday both the Muslim rulers and the British denigrated, remains.

It is worth bearing this in mind when viewing Canada's complex relationship with the United States. To view Canada solely as part of North American civilization, as most Americans do, is to emphasize those characteristics that Canada shares with the United States. On the other hand, to note Canada's culture is to become aware of the differences between Canadians and Americans.

Canada has been in the front line in the conflict between civilization and culture. Each of its three successive civilizations has left a different residue. France left its language and literature, its customs and civil law, and, above all, its religion. It did not leave much in the way of political institutions, advanced technology, a scientific spirit, or economic organization. Thus France's legacy for Quebec was largely its culture, not its civilization; and it was the culture that survived. Britain brought not only its culture, particularly its literature, but its civilization as well. This included commerce, industry, and modern agricultural techniques; it also included the Westminster parliamentary system and the concept of the Crown. It is possible for some Quebecois to view Canada's political system, at least in its parliamentary aspects, as a leftover from the once dominant British civilization. But it is also possible to regard the British political tradition as a permanent element of Canada's culture and part of the British cultural legacy that will continue to be treasured long after other features of British civilization have disappeared.

It is too early to say what the legacy of the United States will be. Its science, technology, and multinational corporations have brought many of the benefits of American civilization to Canada. However, Canada's parliamentary system of government remains British in its inspiration, despite the injection of the federal principle first adopted in the United States. At the popular level, American culture as purveyed on television and in popular magazines sometimes seems all-pervasive, much to the chagrin of Canada's intellectuals.

These intellectuals have long differed in their attitudes toward the three civilizations (particularly the American) that have successively dominated Canada; and this, combined with their concern for Canada's own identity, helps to explain the intensity of the conflict between the "continentalists" who see Canada primarily as a participant in North American civilization, and the "nationalists" whose main concern is the preservation of Canada's cultural identity and who believe that the main threat to Canada as a culture emanates from the United States. The humanists among the nationalists have been particularly concerned about the threat they perceived from the social sciences in the United States with their emphasis on "modern civilization" rather than "traditional culture."

Such concern could only be heightened by the writings of someone like Daniel Boorstin, a noted historian and, since 1975, Librarian of Congress. An American scholar, inspired by the Bicentennial celebrations in the United States, Boorstin argued that the old select Republic of Letters had given way to the more democratic Republic of Technology, "largely a creation of American civilization in the last century." According to Boorstin ours is a world of obsolescence ("the great library is apt to seem not so much a treasurehouse as a cemetery") and convergence ("the tendency for everything to become more like everything else"). Moreover, "the Republic of Technology, ruthlessly egalitarian, will accomplish what the prophets, political philosophers and revolutionaries could not."[5] Boorstin was contrasting the New World with the Old. He did not refer to Canada. We may presume that he took it for granted that Canada was too new and too American to have been part of the old Republic of Letters and was therefore destined to become part of the Republic of Technology.

From the perspective of contemporary civilization Canada would seem destined to be not only part of the "Republic of Technology" but part of the universal "Republic of Science" on which that technology depends. Together with what was once called the "military–industrial complex," science and technology formed the basis of the American civilization that became dominant after the Second World War. With the development of survey research and a new computer technology that made the sampling of public opinion possible on a large scale, many of the social scientists in the United States became enthusiastic participants in the Republic of Technology as well as the Republic of Science. They took for granted the American civilization to which they themselves were making important contributions. It was customary in the age of science for social scientists to examine the characteristics of a dominant civilization, whether the France of Comte; the England of Marx, Mill, and Herbert Spencer; or the United States of John Dewey and Talcott Parsons, and to assume that its characteristics were of universal significance. It was a cliché, that the world was moving toward a common civilization, one that would be based on the advanced technology of tomorrow.

Just as important for Canada as the notion of an American Republic of Technology and a universal Republic of Science, was the widespread assumption that North America formed a single market economy into which Canada was fully integrated. This economy extended the common civilization into the field of culture through the mass communications of radio and television, of magazines and paperback books. By the late 1960s many Canadians feared that their country was slipping inexorably and totally into the American orbit, in its culture as well as its civilization. But it was at this point, when there appeared to be a real threat to Canada's distinctive culture, that the willingness of Canadian social scientists to espouse American ideas was severely tested. Having so recently emancipated themselves from British influence, they had little desire to become part of an American cultural empire.

Instead there was a search for an alternative analysis of socioeconomic trends that examined Canada's integration into the American market economy from a different perspective. The choice between continentalism, with its acceptance of close Canada–United States relations, and nationalism, with its ties to conservative humanism, seemed too limited for those social scientists whose natural preference was for a universal scientific interpretation of phenomena. A third option was more attractive than conservative nationalism. This consisted of the neo-Marxist ideas of thinkers who owed more to the European tradition of political economy than to the sociological analysis of Talcott Parsons and his American colleagues with their notion of an evolving social system. Marxism, with its universal application, with its European origins, and with its broad interpretation of history and philosophy, proved more attractive than conservative nationalism to many intellectuals. In addition, the Marxists' concern for the problems of the poor and their traditional rejection of colonialism and imperialism made a great appeal to political activists. Instead of being studied *sui generis,* Canada could be compared with other dependent states in the Americas, and Latin American dependency theory could be incorporated into the Canadian tradition of political economy that had flourished since Innis. The neo-Marxists also attempted to incorporate the modern state into their economic analysis.[6]

Marx himself had stressed what we have called "civilization" with its broad influence on societies. He was fascinated by the big industry of the nineteenth century that had "universalized competition," by the new industrial civilization that had "produced world history for the first time," and by the achievements that had made "natural science subservient to capital." Indeed, to Marx the United States was "the most perfect example of the modern State," though he concluded that the bourgeoisie "transcends the State and the nation."[7]

American social science was able to offer Canadians only associate membership, as it were, in the Republics of Science and Technology and in the American market economy. Marxism, on the other hand, in principle offered full membership for all in a socialist society. This society Marx identified with a universal civilization transcending particular states and cultures. This was the civilization that all advanced industrial societies were asumed to have in common.

Marxism has less to say about particular cultures such as that which distinguished Canada from the United States. Like the bourgeoisie itself, Marx was primarily interested in promoting a dynamic civilization. Though he was not unconcerned about the importance of promoting culture in general terms, he tended to be averse to particular cultures, since these tended to be backward. Marx referred disparagingly to the Germany described by Hegel, and was critical of its metaphysical speculation, its religious obscurantism, and its entailed landed estates. He was particularly critical of the Orient, especially the "undignified, stagnatory, and vegetative life of India" with its "brutalizing worship of nature." As Shlomo Avineri has observed, "Marx unequivocally prefers industrial, liberal, and bourgeois Britain to underdeveloped autocratic Russia, as Britain's level of economic development guarantees the integration of India within the world market and the universalization of European culture."[8]

Clearly Marx was more interested in universal (or Western) civilization (which he identifies here with a universal European culture) than in any particular culture. Indeed, he opposed Hegel's State because of its defense of what he thought were outmoded social formations. Doubtless, had he examined the relatively backward colonial Canada—and still more the Quebec—of his day, he would have welcomed the industrialization of its developing economy, and wouldn't have been too concerned about the preservation of Canada's national identity.

Yet to Canadians, the State (in Quebec, the Province) has been seen as an instrument to nurture Canadian culture. Only through something identifiably Canadian, not British or American, could Canada's national identity be assured. Canada's independence, in the most fundamental sense of the term, depended on the assumption that despite the influence of successive external civilizations, its own culture would persist and would develop gradually over time.

It is true that a civilization powerfully influences a culture, but from the Canadian perspective there has been the hope that its distinctive culture would influence the way in which Canada would ultimately develop as a civilization in its own right. It is the culture which produces a way of thinking, or a world view. This in turn shapes the manner in which social conflict, including class conflict, is articulated and resolved. As anthropologists A. L. Kroeber and Clyde Kluckhohn observed, "the essential core of culture consists of traditional (i.e., historically derived and selected) ideas and especially their attached values; culture systems may, on the one hand, be considered as products of action, on the other as conditioning elements of further action."⁹

Marx seems to have found the persistence of culture through time difficult to explain in the light of his assumptions about its relationship with the changing mode of production. He argued, "The mode of production in material life conditions the general character of the social, political, and spiritual process of life."¹⁰ Elsewhere he recognized the uneven development of material products relative to artistic development, adding, "But the difficulty lies not in understanding that the Greek arts of epic are bound up with certain forms of social development. The difficulty is that they still afford us artistic pleasure and that in a certain respect they count as a norm and as an unattainable ideal."¹¹

Not all neo-Marxists have subscribed to the dependency theory. Others have stressed the relative autonomy of the State. Marx, it must be remembered, was preoccupied with the worldwide extension of the industrial revolution. He was not concerned, as Canadian neo-Marxists have been concerned, with Canada's development in the context of successive civilizations. One Canadian Marxist found little to admire in Canada's own bourgeoisie, whom he regarded primarily as compradors, middlemen who learned to cooperate with all three commercial empires of the St. Lawrence: ". . . Canada's remarkably inert and inept ideological elites are being forced increasingly to admit that Canadian history is the history of a French, British, and an American colony."¹²

This interpretation of Canada as merely the dependent of an external civilization offered no alternative vision of Canada and provided no assurance that Canadians as a people could create their own cultural identity. There was no explanation of how they were able to survive, and even to surmount, the impact of successive civilizations. The perspective remained colonial.

> The contradiction of continuity in change resolves itself in disintegration. A Canadian capitalist state cannot survive because it has neither the material base nor the will to survive, the former contributing substantially to the latter. It remains to be seen if it can survive in some other form.
>
> Yet in a very real sense Canada has fulfilled the dreams and aspirations of its founders. A few years before Confederation, when territorial expansion westward was being considered, George Brown peered into his crystal globe and declared perceptively, "If

Canada acquires this territory it will rise in a few years from a position of a small and weak province to be the greatest colony any country has ever possessed." History has been kind to George Brown and his northern vision.[13]

It was on this note of pessimism that R. T. Naylor concluded his analysis of the commercial empires of the St. Lawrence.

The Marxist perspective has both its insights and its limitations. It helps us to appreciate the complexity of the Canadian political tradition, and it offers us an alternative interpretation of the transformation wrought by civilization. The older perspective saw Canada emerging as an independent state, from colony to nation, but it was flawed by a failure to comprehend the full magnitude of Canada's economic (and presumably political) dependence. The socialist interpretation recognized the seriousness of Canada's economic dependency, but until recently underestimated the extent to which Canada had, in fact, achieved political independence. It is arguable that Canadians themselves determined the degree to which it seemed advantageous to remain a dependent economy. Unwilling to sacrifice the high standard of living relative to most nations of the world, which resulted from their economic dependence, they nevertheless were content to enjoy a somewhat lower standard of living than their American neighbors, if this was the price to be paid for political independence.

By concentrating on Canada's position as an economic dependency, some scholars downplayed Canada's problems of cultural identity, and in particular the problem of attaining its bicultural and multicultural goals. Had Canada's political independence been of little importance, Canadians would hardly have struggled so hard to retain what independence they had. Nor would they have been troubled by the demands of Western and Quebec separatists for some form of sovereignty association. Some of the Marxist analysis tended to underestimate the complexity and subtlety of US–Canada relations as illustrated by the evidence of American restraint in negotiations with Canada on matters of mutual concern.[14] If we ask ourselves why Canadian governments over the years have acted to defend Canada's interests, the conclusion must be that they did so to protect Canada's autonomy as a country with an identity, presumably a cultural identity, of its own. It may well be, as Marx posited, that generally speaking, "the ideas of a ruling class are in every epoch the ruling ideas" and that these ideas are "nothing more than the ideal expression of the dominant material relationships grasped as ideas,"[15] but this does not explain how Canadians have retained much of British political culture even though an interlocking North American bourgeoisie has become "the ruling class."

Canadian problems, then, are not too similar to those of the developing dependent nations. There is general recognition that there is a degree of political independence and autonomy in Canada. This enables the country to discriminate against foreign corporations and to pursue a policy designed to reduce regional economic disparities by transferring money from some provinces to others and to do this by taxing corporations as well as individuals. The people of Quebec have been able, through language and other legislation, to replace the Montreal anglophone ruling class with a French-speaking elite.

Canada, like the United States, has often been unfairly criticized for the absence of a deep indigenous culture. The earliest foreign observers of North American society tended to be critical of these "young" countries, dismissing their culture as imported from Europe and somehow derivative rather than original. One consequence of this rather narrow approach to North American society was that American thinkers were not included in works of political theory. It was true that in the deepest sense of theory as philosophy, the Americans had produced no counterpart of Aristotle or Machiavelli, Plato or Hegel, Locke or Mill. But there was a respectable tradition of political thought by men active in American politics, for example, Jefferson's Declaration of Independence, the American Constitution, the decisions of the Supreme Court and Lincoln's Gettysburg Address. These had been an inspiration to people everywhere and deserved more recognition by political theorists than they received.

Alexis de Tocqueville was one of the first visitors to sense that America was a great and innovative civilization. But it was not until after the Civil War and particularly after the reconciliation between North and South, starting in 1876, that Americans began to reappraise their own assumption that there were very few lessons to be learned from American civilization and that students should be made to concentrate on the study of European culture.

Canada suffered even more from the criticism of North American society as largely derivative. To some extent this was justified, because British North America remained a colony even after Confederation and because its derivative character was more obvious. Even as a civilization it was much less impressive than the United States. Important events comparable to those in the United States tended to occur a generation or two later in Canada and to be less significant when they did take place. The Rebellions of 1837–38 were hardly comparable to the stirring events of the American Revolution sixty years earlier. The passage of the British North America Act of 1867, eighty years after the framing of the Constitution of the United States, was barely noticed outside Canada itself.

Canada also suffered from having no Tocqueville in the nineteenth century. The classic account of Canada equivalent to Tocqueville's *Democracy in America* was Lord Durham's *Report on the Affairs of British North America,* published four years later, in 1839. Trenchantly written, and destined to be known as the Magna Carta of the British colonies, the Durham Report had a very different significance from that of Tocqueville's work. It was a response not to the success of democratization in Canada but to its failure, and it was a response directed particularly to the Rebellions of 1837 and 1838. As governor general for a brief period following the Rebellions, Lord Durham was acutely conscious of Canada's ethnic divisions. There seemed, as he put it in words repeated ad nauseam in the history books, "two nations warring in the bosom of a single state." Durham returned to England in 1839 after a brief tour of duty and died the following year. But thanks to his recommendation for a united Canada, a new era opened with the establishment of a Union government in which French and English at last learned the art of political cooperation.

Durham's recollections of 1837–38 even today are widely quoted and read in Canada. The very different atmosphere of the 1840s is almost ignored except by specialist professional historians. Yet the style of government established in the 1840s formed the basis of the English–French dualism that became the hallmark of Canada before Confederation added the further element of "regionalism." Both dualism and regionalism were then subsumed under the broad rubric of federalism, Canada's experiment in continental government after 1867. By then, Canada's civilization, in the sense of its political system, appeared to be far more advanced than those of several European countries. After all, France in 1867 was experiencing the closing years of Napoleon III's autocratic Third Empire.

If, then, we distinguish civilization from culture, we have to acknowledge the great contribution that these two polities, the American and the

Canadian, made to the theory and practice of government before many European countries had settled on their own modern political systems. Parliamentary government was not firmly established in France until 1875. In Sweden the breakthrough occurred in 1917. But presidential government had of course flourished in the United States since the eighteenth century, while parliamentary government in British North America dated from 1848.

Faced at Confederation with a choice between the Westminster political tradition based on parliamentary supremacy and the congressional system of American federalism, the British North American provinces opted for a new system they called "parliamentary federalism." As a parliamentary system, Canada was to make the House of Commons supreme, but was to acquire both a Senate and a Supreme Court. In the absence of a comprehensive comparative study of the two political systems, it is difficult to assess the similarities between the United States and Canada. But what is clear, at least to Canadians, are the many differences between Canada and the United States.

The practical significance of the establishment of the Dominion of Canada in 1867 was considerable. It seemed at the time that Canada, without a revolution, was to some extent following in the footsteps of the United States in 1787, and establishing a modern federal system that could accommodate new provinces as the Dominion extended its jurisdiction westward. At last Canada seemed to be giving itself a distinct identity as a nation. There was talk of a new political nationality and of "Canadian citizens" replacing "British subjects." Clearly Canada was different, being neither American nor British, but something different—Canadian.

While the practical significance of Confederation has to be recognized, its theoretical importance must not be exaggerated. Canada retained its British parliamentary institutions intact. The much-vaunted "responsible" or Cabinet government, copied from the United Kingdom, was already nearly twenty years old. There seems to have been little serious examination of any alternative system except in Quebec, and there the effort to introduce an "Assembly" form of government had been finally defeated by force of arms during the Rebellions. If there was any innovation it was the grafting of federalism onto the parliamentary system, but this was not done as a consequence of any theoretical analysis, nor was there any awareness that in principle the British and American systems of government were incompatible. Not for the first time, Canadians imagined that they could have the best of both worlds.

It can be argued that in 1867 Canada was going further than combining American federalism with British parliamentary government. It was taking its first important steps away from Westminster in the direction of a North American political system. Not only was there a division of powers between the federal and provincial governments, but there was now a Senate instead of the traditional colonial Legislative Council, and within a decade, a Supreme Court. But it was not until 100 years later that the gradual sloughing off of the British political heritage led to a direct challenge to the Westminster political tradition.

It was one thing for Canadians to accept the replacement of British civilization by one that was North American, but it was another to accept American culture in all its manifestations. Frank Underhill, a University of Toronto historian, was once suspected of disloyalty to the Crown when he frankly admitted that Canada's destiny lay in North America and that in the end geography would be a more powerful influence than history, "for we are inescapably North American. In the long run our Canadian civilization will be a North American one. It is foolish to hope for anything else. If we are eventually to satisfy ourselves that we have at last achieved a Canadian identity it will be only when we are satisfied that we have arrived at a better American way of life than the Americans have. A better *American* way of life, not just a better life."[16]

Like Underhill, English Canadians were willing to give up their preoccupation with the contribution of British civilization to Canada, and to study Canada's own contribution to modern civilization, particularly parliamentary federalism. But they were not eager to study American culture or to give up their interest in British culture and especially English literature, one of the great literatures of the world. Their universities long remained repositories of the English cultural heritage. They were more strongly committed to the humanities with their European tradition than to the newer social sciences, which owed more to the research output of American universities. Indeed, Canada's greatest contributions to the social sciences had a historical orientation. The most significant work in political theory was C. B. Macpherson's Marxist interpretation of English thought in the seventeenth century as based on "possessive individualism." In economics the emphasis was on the economic history of Canada.[17] Even a Chicago-trained social scientist like Harold Innis, who recognized the limitations of European experience for North America, made his greatest contribution to economic history by stressing Canada's east–west lines of communication with their European connection. As he insisted, "The present Dominion emerged not in spite of geography but because of it."[18] Two economists who believed that the direction of trade, and with it influence, was shifting after 1945 to north–south between Canada and the United States had found a haven south of the border: Harry Johnson was at Chicago and John K. Galbraith, at Harvard.

In the decades following the Second World War, English Canada's attempt to maintain the British connection received shocks on several fronts. The decline of Britain as a world power was made evident by the withdrawal of British forces from Greece and Turkey in 1947. The end of empire was signaled by the futile invasion of Egypt in the Suez crisis of 1956. Britain's preference for a new role in Europe over leadership of the Commonwealth was made clear by the referendum favoring membership in the European Community in 1975. Henceforth countries like Canada were abandoned to their own devices. No longer could a Canadian (unless he had direct family connections with the United Kingdom) freely take up employment in Britain. A Frenchman, however, could. Ultimately, Canada might have to reappraise her relationship with Westminster and the Crown.

The second series of shocks for Canada resulted from the Quiet Revolution in Quebec after 1960, with the development of a new secular culture there, wholly French and Quebecois. This soon challenged the once-dominant British culture of the anglophone minority in Montreal with its McGill University and its symphony orchestra.

The third blow to the British connection was the demographic transformation of English Canada. A population once largely descended from emigrants from the British Isles had drawn increasingly on other European countries to meet its manpower needs. In 1901 only 8.5 percent of Canadians were of "European" descent (i.e., had ancestors from neither the British Isles nor France). By 1971 the proportion had risen to 23 percent, and less than half the people of Canada claimed to stem from the British Isles. The cultural implications of this transformation became clear in the late 1960s when the federal government's policies of bilingualism and biculturalism had to be modified, with biculturalism being replaced by multiculturalism. In the 1970s, as the sources of immigration shifted from Europe to other continents, it began to appear that Canada might become a multiracial society, at least in urban areas.

The policy of multiculturalism was in many ways an elaboration of Canada's traditional policy of allowing a cultural mosaic instead of demanding assimilation through the equivalent of the American melting pot. The Government assumed that the French and British, whom it described as the "two charter groups," would continue to enjoy precedence. Little consideration seems to have been given to the probable impact of an increasing proportion of "New Canadians" on the world view so long taken for granted by Canadians who originated in the British Isles, or on the British culture that these charter-group Canadians reflected. It seems to have been assumed that the offspring of New Canadians would be assimilated into the English-Canadian mainstream.

In the United States, perceptions of American society had had to be considerably modified as a result of immigration from the European continent, particularly in the late nineteenth century. The assumption that the newer immigrant groups would be assimilated into traditional American society by a process that has been called "Anglo-conformity" gave way to the "melting pot" hypothesis whereby a new American society was expected to emerge. However, the persistence of different cultures in the United States led to a third theory, that of cultural pluralism. All three approaches have been used to explain the transformation of modern American society.[19] At the same time there developed a pride and confidence in the United States itself and what it stood for. The American Constitution and the political system itself were the main focus of the nation's loyalty.

If American experience is any guide, it seems likely that the "Anglo-conformist" character of Canada will also gradually be altered as a result of immigration. But, whereas in the United States the political system provided a focus of loyalty for all Americans, the British North America Act no longer met the needs of all Canadians. In Canada even the political system remained colonial in form. The Oath of Allegiance was taken not to the Constitution but to the Queen. By the 1980s Canada was faced with a dilemma. There was growing realization that the British political tradition, impressive though it was, was no longer adequate. But there was no agreement on what might replace it. If those English Canadians committed to the British connection were to insist on preserving the Westminster tradition unmodified, the system's resilience would be severely tested. Rather than continuing to identify their traditions with those of Canada as a whole, English Canadians might well have to develop a much greater sense of their own particular identity.

Until the 1950s Canadians were concerned with emancipating themselves from imperial rule and were anxious to be treated as equals of the British. It had been possible to think of Canada as a British and English-speaking Dominion. This picture now needed to be revised. Having achieved their goal of political autonomy without declaring their independence, English Canadians had to reckon with the rapid decline of British power and influence, the cultural revolution in Quebec, and the changing ethnic and racial composition of English-speaking Canada as patterns of immigration altered. They also had to come to terms with the price to be paid for being part of American civilization and for sharing the Americans' standard of living. That price included not only economic but cultural penetration, a penetration made easier by Britain's withdrawal and Canada's own uncertainty about its future.

2   The Canadian Interpretation of Culture

These various blows to the English-Canadian tradition resulted in an increasing concern for the protection of Canada's own culture. But just what was this Canadian culture that the federal government was expected to preserve? There were many educated Canadians who remained dubious about the existence of a truly indigenous Canadian way of life. Opinions were particularly divided over the policies that should be pursued to enhance Canada's cultural identity. One symbol of Canada's ability to participate in the Anglo-American cultural tradition had been the establishment of the annual Shakespeare Festival in Stratford, Ontario, in 1953 under the British director Tyrone Guthrie and with distinguished visiting British actors. It was expected that ultimately the festival would become fully Canadian with a Canadian director and Canadian actors in leading roles. But in the 1980 season the director was still an Englishman, Robin Phillips, and British actors and actresses still played important roles.

Late in 1980, when a successor to Robin Phillips was being considered, Canadian actors refused to perform in the 1981 Stratford season unless greater efforts were made to find a Canadian director. They were supported by the governments of Canada and Ontario. But by no means did all Canadians concur in the federal government's refusal to grant a visa to the Englishman who was the choice of the Stratford festival's board of directors to succeed Phillips. There were many who thought that since the festival was founded to celebrate the works of an English playwright, this was not an issue primarily involving Canadian culture.

Still, the debate had clearly shown that Canadians felt it important to indicate that Canada possessed a distinctive culture. The traditional notion of "culture" identified it with what is now often called "high culture."[20] This interpretation of culture as refinement of taste is still common in the humanities and it is quite helpful in explaining Canada's uniqueness. On the one hand, high culture includes the visual and performing arts, both areas in which Canada has made distinctive contributions. On the other hand, high culture includes the literary tradition of a country, using the term "literature" in the broadest sense. *The Literary History of Canada,* which surveyed writing in philosophy, history, and the social sciences, as well as in belles-lettres, offered proof of the development of a Canadian perspective on the world.

Canada's creative writers, with conspicuous exceptions, have lived apart from writers abroad, many of them directing their attention to the Canadian scene. Yet not all of them by any means would consider themselves nationalistic. Claude Bissell has noted that "there is not among the major writers a strong strain of anti-Americanism." He goes on to say, "This might seem unusual, since Canadian writers, unlike academics, do not enjoy an easy and familiar relationship with their American contemporaries and they are more immediately aware than the academics of the American domination of the whole field of popular culture."[21]

In other words, both high and popular culture need to be considered. Social scientists who concern themselves with a distinctive Canadian culture have to remember that to understand the country's high culture they must read Canada's poets and belletrists and not just conduct opinion surveys.

A more recent definition, and one which has had considerable influence, extended "culture" beyond the traditional high culture to embrace the sciences. C. P. Snow detected two cultures, the one humane and the other scientific.[22] His distinction was in some ways analogous to our distinction between culture and civilization. But Snow's analysis was based on his experience of the two traditional and separate streams of education that characterized the British school system of his day: the classical and the scientific. It is therefore too sharp and too narrow a classification for our purposes. For civilization is more than science: it involves technology and organizational capability. And culture is more than humane culture as defined by Snow, and may include some of the social sciences, particularly history and political philosophy. Indeed, it is arguable that Snow's dichotomy takes no account of the fact that there have been, especially in North America, not two but three divisions of learning: the humanities, the natural sciences, and the social sciences.[23]

A third and even broader approach to culture has become common in the social sciences. Social scientists usually interpret culture as something much broader than high culture. Thus the Canadian Royal Commission on Bilingualism and Biculturalism distinguished two other meanings in addition to "culture in the humanistic sense of the term." The Commission's report says, "In the broadest sense of the term "culture," the sheer fact that men came from elsewhere to take part in building the country has contributed to our cultural enrichment. . . . In a narrower sense Canadian culture has been the richer for the knowledge, skills, and traditions which all the immigrant groups brought with them. . . ."[24]

The Commission went on to eliminate the usage that embraced within the term "culture" every aspect of a group's existence as quite unsuitable for their purposes:

> It [the common definition of the word "culture"] suggests that all North Americans, if not most of the people of the Western world, live in highly industrialized societies within the Judaeo-Christian tradition, and consequently possess a common culture. This conclusion is true, but it is too broad to help us much.
>
> The same can be said of the traditional humanistic sense of the word "culture," but for the opposite reason: it is too restricted.

The Commission preferred the definition of culture as ". . . a way of being, thinking, and feeling. It is a driving force animating a significant group of individuals united by a common tongue, and sharing the same customs, habits, and experiences. Clearly the two cultures designated in our terms of reference are those associated with the English and the French languages in Canada. But as there are the two dominant languages, there are two principal cultures, and their influence extends, in greatly varying degrees, to the whole country." The Commission admitted that cultures borrow from each other as they evolve:

However, the culture of a group must not be confused with a particular system of thought, even though there may be correspondence at a given moment between a culture and an ideology; one ideology can be replaced by another, whereas the culture continues to live. Culture does not determine the thoughts or actions of the group; instead it colours the group's manner of thinking and acting. Culture is to the group what personality is to the individual; it is rare for a person to have two personalities or two styles of living at the same time.

Understood in this way, culture is the sum of the characteristics particular to a group and common to its individual members.[25]

This definition of culture as "a way of being, thinking and feeling," and as something that "continues to live" accords very much with the usage in this book. There is a difference between a culture that persists through time and an ideology, which, like a civilization, can be replaced.

The Royal Commission on Bilingualism and Biculturalism went on to discuss acculturation, a matter of some concern not only for those French Canadians who have had to live and work with anglophones and face the problem of adapting to a different cultural environment, but for English Canadians attempting to resist acculturation from the United States. ". . . Canada must also cope with the American influence in all fields, especially those of culture and the mass media, and in economic and military activities. This presence is so strongly felt that it actually dominates some sectors and it constantly threatens the vitality of the Canadian cultures."[26] And, we might add, the threat to one's culture that is detected by both English and French Canadians is felt even more strongly by the indigenous people of Canada, the Indians and the Inuit (Eskimos).

The social scientists working for the Royal Commission therefore extended the definition of culture beyond the traditional high culture of the humanists and the two cultures of C. P. Snow. Political scientists, especially in the United States, have added their own gloss to this definition. A number of them studying new states were concerned lest they intrude their own cultural biases in favor of Western political institutions, and preferred to examine what they call the "political culture." This, too, concentrated on ways of being, thinking, and feeling.

However, because of its dependence on opinion surveys, the political-culture approach at first tended to lack an historical dimension. Moreover it may have more limited applicability to Canada not only because Canada's problems have an important historical context but because in Canada the clash of a new civilization with an old culture (except perhaps in Quebec) is less marked than in developing countries. The criticism of one political-culture approach—the notion of a "civic culture"—was that in their search for a standard of comparison, investigators were tempted to conclude simply that the United States and Great Britain "most closely approximate the model of a civic culture." They concluded that three other countries where public opinion surveys were conducted "deviate from the civic culture."[27] Yet to regard the United States or Great Britain—or Canada for that matter—as models of a civic culture meant ignoring a common problem that each of these countries faced. French Canadians, American blacks, and Ulster Catholics had all come to regard themselves as a permanent minority for whom the traditional "rule of the majority," tempered by "the swing of the pendulum" at election times, was not an adequate safeguard.

The attempt to deal with culture has, then, taken a variety of forms. For our purposes it has been necessary to make a number of assertions:

(1) that it is useful to distinguish between civilization and culture;
(2) that one of Canada's experiences has been that of transferring from one civilization to another;
(3) that Canada has retained the cultural aspects of each of the civilizations it has experienced, but has resisted absorption by each of them, preferring instead to develop its own culture(s).

These in turn lead to a fourth:

(4) that political activity in Canada has been the mediator between not only successive civilizations but between civilization and culture.

For example, the economy, the class structure, and the political institutions may change, but social attitudes and political perceptions may not. The political arena mediates between the changing economy and less rapidly changing social relationships. The art of politics consists of observing both sets of changes and being able to relate them to each other. Since the early 1960s French-Canadian society has had to adapt rapidly to the demands of a technological civilization. That civilization was being established long before 1960, but the old political system had failed to make the necessary adjustments. Consequently, adaptation in the form of a new educational system and a welfare state was overdue. The inability of the Church to do more than preserve the existing culture threw onto the government of Quebec, the task of transforming Quebec's culture. (The federal government had done its share, with limited success, under the previous regime.) Under the Church the French language had been preserved as part of Quebec's culture. Thanks to intervention by the government of Quebec, the use of that language was extended, and more and more French Canadians became part of their province's technocracy. Politics became the flywheel between the common civilization Quebec shared with the rest of North America and the culture that remained peculiar to the province.

Although, as the Quebec case makes clear, politics is the link between civilization and culture, political scientists have tended to be more interested in civilization. In the United States the study of political sociology came to be considered more fruitful than the study of political philosophy. In a sense, through its stress on public knowledge available to all, sociology was a product of industrial civilization. With its mass clientele of students it stood in contrast to philosophy with its relatively small elite. The spread of the sociological approach to the study of politics created division among political scientists, in Canada as elsewhere. Scholars primarily concerned with their cultural inheritance remained philosophers; those more interested in the scientific approach to civilizations became sociologists. This did not encompass all students of politics, however. Increasingly, those who were interested in the transformation of politics by modern civilization stressed the importance of political economy.

The distinction between civilization and culture has two advantages for comparisons between Canada and the United States. On the one hand, it enables the observer to come to terms with the continentalists and to admit the ascendancy of American civilization, at least for the present, without regarding the United States as necessarily superior to the other peoples on the American continent. On the other hand, it supports the nationalists' contention that there is a need to explore the subtle nuances, particularly in culture, that distinguish two cultures as apparently similar as the American and Canadian. Conventional approaches have enabled scholars to discover similarities where previously only differences were apparent, for example, between such diverse countries as the United States and India. The civilization/culture dichotomy enables us to detect important differences in countries like Canada where initially it is the similarities with the United States that are immediately observable. The visitor to North America who sees the expressways, roadsigns, automobiles, and airports may be forgiven for concluding that Canada is merely a photocopy of the United States' original design. This may be true in large measure of Canadian civilization, but it is less true of its culture.

It is one thing to note different interpretations of "culture" and to reach a satisfactory analytical distinction between culture and civilization in principle. It is quite another to make this distinction in practice. For example, is contemporary architecture primarily an example of the trend toward a global civilization that produces similar buildings throughout the world? Or do architects still make individual statements that indicate they belong to different cultures? Do periods of cultural and conservative nationalism succeed decades of cosmopolitanism and the belief in a shared civilization? And to be more specific from the point of view of the Canadian political tradition, is parliamentary government a permanent contribution to world politics? It certainly seemed so for at least a century when British civilization was at its height; but does it, on later inspection, appear to have been the product of a particular civilization, which may remain an integral part of Britain's own cultural heritage but which may elsewhere have to be replaced?

And finally, what will be the impact of American civilization on Canada? Undoubtedly it will provide a considerable portion of the twentieth-century culture that is handed down to future generations in Canada as well as in the United States. Canadian intellectuals who are concerned about the preservation of their country's identity have to filter the latest American ideas. To do so successfully they have to use the appropriate mesh for each discipline. At the level of science, technology and much of what we have termed civilization, the mesh of the filter can be very broad, allowing a great deal to pass through. At the level of culture, where a nationalist stand is more appropriate, the mesh has to be much finer. For the social sciences generally, and political science in particular, the mesh has to be somewhere in between, since these disciplines mediate between civilization and culture.[28] In any event, if they make such a distinction, Canadians may be enabled more easily to chart a course between the extremes of the more strident forms of nationalism and the more bland and complacent tendencies of continentalism.

3 Canada's Distinctive Character

Writing about the Mediterranean in the sixteenth century, Fernand Braudel used language that may be appropriate for Canada today: "A living civilization must be able not only to give but to receive and to borrow. . . . But a great civilization can also be recognized by its refusal to borrow, by its resistance to certain alignments, by its resolute selection among the foreign influences offered to it and which would no doubt be forced upon it if they were not met by vigilance or, more simply, by incompatibility of temper and appetite."[29]

It is of course only proper to acknowledge Canada's debt to France, Britain, and the United States in the spheres of both civilization and culture. But it is also worthwhile to trace what makes Canada unique—and interesting. How many Americans and Englishmen who have compared their two-party discipline with the multiplicity of parties in France have not done so with a tinge of national superiority? Yet few of them are aware that in Canada it has been the French who have showed the capacity to work as a team (called "voting as a bloc") and the English Canadians, especially before 1867, who have been divided. And Canadian politics do have a nice Gallic touch or two: the notion of a regime change, such as characterized the shift from the Third to the Fourth and then the Fifth Republics, has had some influence on Quebec. To many Quebecois the prospect of a new constitution is merely a continuation of the changes brought about by the Constitutional Act of 1791, the Act of Union of 1840, and the BNA Act of 1867. If the French Canadians prove persuasive enough, parliamentary federalism might well be replaced by something equally innovative.

Canada has never been a Protestant country in the manner of the United Kingdom or the United States. The University of Toronto is a federation that has long included the Anglican Trinity College, Victoria College (formerly Methodist), the Roman Catholic St. Michael's College, and the secular University College. Those colleges that were religious foundations remained universities able to grant degrees in divinity, and until the 1960s, the subject "Religious Knowledge" in one form or another played an important part in the university curriculum.[30] Canada has had Catholic First Ministers and a large Catholic-bloc vote in the legislature since the 1840s.

The "isms" of the modern world have all had their impact on Canada, but they have all been given a distinctively Canadian flavor. "Imperialism" meant loyalty to the Empire; "nationalism" meant one thing to early twentieth-century French Canadians and another to mid-century English Canadians. No political party that has held office has officially called itself a Socialist or even a Social-Democratic Party, but the Cooperative Commonwealth Federation, the New Democratic Party and the *Parti Québecois* have all had overtones of social democracy about them. And nowhere else in the world was there a counterpart to Social Credit, the movement originally formed to give money back to the people.

Until recently English Canadians took their political tradition for granted. Now questions being raised may lead to its reinterpretation. It is necessary to deal with the philosophical assumptions underlying the tradition, and to note the unwillingness of Canadians to adopt the world view of Americans.

The problems Canadians have faced in adapting to American civilization without being assimilated by it are particularly acute in the realm of social and political theory. Since the Second World War, many of the social and political ideas influencing Canadian thought have increasingly come from the United States rather than the United Kingdom. It is this development that has caused many foreign observers, especially Americans, to doubt whether the Canadian mind can be distinguished from the American.

To explain the distinctive characteristics of the Canadian tradition, then, we have first to recognize that as part of the American continent and as a neighbor of the United States, Canada—including Quebec—is part of a dynamic American civilization. It shares the science and technology of the United States and, in many ways, has a similar political economy. To those foreigners, notably Americans, whose interest is primarily in contemporary civilization, Canada is remarkably similar to the United States. Such characteristics as the Crown appear to them to be merely relics of an earlier civilization whose influence will continue to wane.

However, we must go beyond contemporary civilization in our analysis and explore the culture of Canada. In doing so we may have to use a framework somewhat different from the conventional modes. What we may perhaps call the "universal science" mode is based on the assumption, often implicit, that the trends visible in the most advanced civilization of the day are of universal application. The scientific mode sometimes also assumes that the world is developing towards a common civilization and culture, one that will be more rational, more secular and possibly even more harmonious than its predecessors. We can agree with only part of this assumption, namely the universal character of civilizations in their heyday. But it seems doubtful whether the various countries of the world will abandon the particular culture of which they are individually so proud.

Of course, many social scientists have drawn attention to the obvious differences between modern science and technology on the one hand and traditional cultures on the other. But because some of them have been tempted to associate the social sciences with science and technology (i.e., with civilization) rather than with culture, which they have perhaps too readily and too pejoratively labeled "traditional," the emphasis has been on the characteristics that advanced industrial civilizations have in common rather than on the cultural characteristics that distinguish even such similar civilizations as Canada and the United States. In the study of political systems there has been interest in those economic and social indicators that lend themselves to quantitative measurement and rigorous comparative analysis, in the belief that statistics provide a practical alternative to the herculean task of studying a variety of often difficult languages and the different history of each country. This form of comparative analysis, in its endeavor to be worldwide in scope, has naturally tended to stress the civilization that countries seem to have in common rather than the particular cultures that differentiate them. One basic assumption has been that there are discoverable uniformities in political behavior, or what David Easton, the Canadian-born political scientist, has called "regularities." It is also true that social scientists associated with dominant civilizations have not always been sensitive to the need to understand other cultures. Nor have they wrestled with the fact that the social sciences straddle both civilization and culture. Too easily, cultures that do not fit the accepted framework, for example the United Kingdom or the American South, are classified as "deviant cases."[31]

In making the distinction between civilization and culture Canadian political scientists face several difficult problems. One is the fact that their discipline is not readily subsumed under either civilization or culture. For while most students of politics are primarily concerned with issues arising out of the concerns of contemporary civilization, they are nevertheless more aware than other social scientists of the roots that political theory has in the beginning of Western civilization and culture.

The other difficult issue involves the very future of English Canada. We have noted the obvious existence of two cultures in Canada, and we have suggested that all Canadians share a common civilization with the United States. But if English Canadians are different from the Quebecois because of their separate culture, and if they nevertheless share a common civilization with the United States, what is it, if anything, that binds them to Quebec rather than to the United States? Historically the common bond between all Canadians was allegiance to the Crown. Until the Second World War, the Dominion of Canada was an integral part of British civilization, going to war alongside Britain against Germany. The replacement of British by American civilization has meant that the former can no longer play a unifying role. Quebec for its part has clearly severed its ties with British civilization, no longer welcoming the Queen to whom allegiance is nevertheless formally still sworn. Even English Canadians increasingly include Britain among "foreign countries."

Obviously some other unifying force is necessary to replace the one imposed by the imperialism of British civilization. No one seriously thinks it can be replaced by an American *political* imperialism. Canadians are free to choose their own destiny as an independent state. This has to be one that both Canadian cultures, the English-speaking culture that dominates in nine provinces and the French-speaking culture that is preeminent in Quebec, freely accept as distinctively Canadian.

In developing a new state structure in recent years, Canadians have had to reexamine the basis of their political system. Unlike the nineteenth-century Americans, they have not resolved the problem of national unity on the battlefield, and they have not devised a single political ideology for the whole country. There is no "Canadian Creed." As we shall now see, it is not surprising that the American philosophy of pragmatism based on the concept of an agreed world view, was not appropriate for the very different Canadian experience where two cultures continued to find political expression within one state.

2
Pragmatism and Canada's "Philosophical Federalism"

The services are not provided to enforce uniformity. In the United Church of Canada there are no prescribed forms of worship, except part of the ordination service . . . liberty is given to each minister to use his own words in any prayer. . . . "Shall" indicates not prescription but preference. . . . "May" suggests some particular act or prayer but without the preference involved in "Shall."—Introduction to the *Service Book* of the United Church of Canada

1 The Search for a Distinctive Philosophy

In the debate over the form that Confederation should take, a debate that began in earnest in the 1970s, Canadians were to demonstrate not only their imagination but their distance from the American political tradition. Though they might participate in North America's common civilization, they did not behave as if this meant acceptance of a similar political system.

However, one of the problems underlying the debate over Canada's future was the realization that while Canadians were not Americans they had not yet resolved the question of their own identity, or even come to some agreement on the type of political system that should replace the one created in 1867. Yet, if Canada were to have a culture of its own, there had to be a distinctive "way to thinking, seeing and believing," in other words, a distinctively Canadian world view.

Fernand Braudel, whom we cited in Chapter 1, was really referring to what we have called "culture" when he said that characteristics of a great civilization include its refusal to borrow, its resistance to certain alignments, and its resolute selection among the foreign influences offered to it. We need to ask ourselves how far Canadian intellectuals have in fact been able to resist the American world view.

A world view has at least two facets. One consists of the self-conscious assumptions made by philosophers. The other comprises the common assumptions of intellectuals generally, including social scientists as they undertake their research. These latter assumptions are often held unconsciously. It is the assumptions of the philosophers that we shall consider first.

The world view of intellectuals is affected to some degree by the philosophical currents of their day. These in turn are influenced by the writings of the great philosophers of the past. Canada and the United States share a common European heritage in which philosophy has played an important part ever since Socrates. Indeed, by defining philosophy as "critical discussion," the type of philosophy most prevalent in the West since the Greeks, and by distinguishing it from "the teaching of sages" that has been traditional in the East, some commentators have felt able to treat philosophy almost as a European preserve.[1]

Those countries that have not produced a notable philosopher of international repute, for example Sweden and Canada, have tended to be somewhat self-conscious about their cultural development, a self-consciousness that sometimes reveals itself in attempts to remedy this deficiency. In Canada such efforts have become a matter of official concern. The Report of the Commission on Canadian Studies asserted that "philosophy has a vital and distinct contribution to make to the study of Canada," and went on to recommend the establishment of one or two centers for the study of Canadian philosophy.[2]

Presumably this recommendation was based on a certain logic: that unless there is a Canadian philosophy it is difficult to conceive of a Canadian world view; if there is no distinctive Canadian world view, it is hard to dispute the argument that Canadian culture is in fact derivative; and if its culture is only derivative, then Canada may in fact not only lack a distinctive national identity but be unable to develop one.

It is true that by "philosophy" the Commission meant philosophy in the sense that the term is employed by philosophers themselves. "Pure" philosophy in the European sense is, as we have seen, widely considered to be the product of critical discussion between learned minds. Nowadays this means for the most part the writings and discussions of professional philosophers. But, underlying the Commission's recommendation for the study of Canadian philosophy was no doubt the hope that such philosophy would, if encouraged and if suitably Canadian in inspiration, influence the philosophical assumptions of Canadian intellectuals engaged in other fields than philosophy proper. The philosophical assumptions of laymen are more appropriately termed a "world view," as distinct from the critical discussion with which philosophers themselves have been primarily concerned. It would be by shaping the world view of thinking Canadians that "Canadian philosophy" would presumably have a "vital and distinct contribution to make to the study of Canada."

The two different meanings of "philosophy"—philosophy as critical discussion and philosophy as world view—need to be analytically separated, even though in practice they may overlap. Professional philosophers tend to be on guard against any attempt to use philosophy for chauvinistic ends: theirs is assumed to be a universal discipline. In any case, they argue, philosophy cannot be officially stimulated: leading philosophers will not emerge from centers for the study of Canadian philosophy. Great minds are few in number and may appear at any time and in any place.

The experience of philosophy in the United States is instructive in this regard. The study of philosophy has flourished there for a long time, so much so that by the beginning of the twentieth century philosophy was not only an established discipline but a discipline for which American universities like Harvard were world-famous. It was in the 1870s that C. S. Peirce began to publish articles that challenged what he regarded as conventional philosophy. Influenced by Peirce, a number of American philosophers questioned the European philosophical tradition. Peirce and his followers called their scientific approach to philosophy "pragmatism." Under the leadership of John Dewey at Chicago (and later at Columbia) and William James at Harvard, pragmatism became, if not the most important American contribution to modern philosophy (as its admirers have contended), then at least the most distinctively American offering.[3]

2 The Emergence of an American World View: Pragmatism's Unproblematic Assumptions

It was the strength, and some would say the weakness, of pragmatism that it expressed in philosophical terms a world view that had come to be characteristic of Americans generally. As early as the settlement of the American colonies the ground was prepared for one of the most important features of pragmatism as a world view—the consensus on the political ideals of American democracy. From the first, the notion of commitment to the political community was a significant characteristic.

As early as November 1620, while still attached to the Mayflower of Plymouth, the settlers pledged themselves to "covenant and combine our selves together into a civill body politick. . . ."[4] Hence Clinton Rossiter's description of Americans as "people of the covenant."

After 150 years the Revolution transformed the colonists from British subjects into full citizens of the American republic, able to proclaim such ideals as liberty, majority rule, equality, justice, and the rule of law, and later to ensure their application. To the notion of commitment to a covenant by the like-minded, born in isolation, was added the messianic appeal of the Declaration of Independence: this social compact became the political covenant of the people of the United States.

The Civil War saw the extension of the principles of 1776 to all Americans, at least in principle, and the century that followed the war witnessed their gradual implementation. Another immediate consequence of the Civil War was the confirmation of national unity. At a time of massive immigration from all over Europe, the Pledge of Allegiance reaffirmed the Americans' sense of being a people of the covenant, committed to the principles of liberal democracy throughout the United States. The Pledge was a peculiarly American institution, first formulated in 1892. Since then, American children have repeated daily the catechism, "I pledge allegiance to the flag of the United States of America, and to the republic for which it stands, one nation under God, indivisible, with liberty and justice for all." Visitors to the United States have long been impressed by what has been called "the American Creed."[5] The daily pledge is simultaneously a renewal of the original covenant, a reaffirmation of the principles of 1776, and a reminder of the successful struggle to preserve the Union intact.

It may be no coincidence that philosophical pragmatism developed where it did at the end of the nineteenth century. By then the United States as we know it was in being. The whole continent was settled; by about 1890, according to Frederick Jackson Turner, the frontier was closed. National unity was assured. The scientific and technological revolutions of the nineteenth century had transformed the United States into a leading world power. Most important of all, there was general consensus among Americans that their ideals provided the best model for a modern polity. This laid the ground for the emergence of a distinctively American world view.

In contrast to the traditional European stress on philosophy with its concern for critical discussion, there was to emerge in the United States an emphasis on activity and on an investigation of society with the methods appropriate to science, or what the pragmatists took to be science.[6] The pragmatists thought they had no need to discuss the philosophical issues that were elsewhere still being debated. The positivists had already decided that certain problems were not worth discussing because they did not lend themselves to verification. The pragmatists insisted that the correct way of handling certain problems of philosophy was to assume that they had been (or could be) solved by the adoption of scientific methods. In 1920 Dewey wrote of science and its methods, "Roughly speaking, the seventeenth century stressed its application in astronomy and general cosmology; the eighteenth century in physics and chemistry; the nineteenth century undertook an application in geology and the biological sciences"; but now "the new ideas and methods should be made at home in moral and social life. . . . When this step is taken the circle of scientific development will be rounded out and the reconstruction of philosophy be made an accomplished fact."[7]

Pragmatism has often been associated with the Progressive movement of American social reformers of the early twentieth century. While few of the philosophers were active in politics, several of the social scientists who adopted pragmatism as their world view lent their names to the movement. Some, notably Charles Merriam, ran for public office. Between them, philosophical pragmatism and the Progressive movement seem to have accomplished, if not a "reconstruction of philosophy" in the traditional sense, at least the establishment of philosophical foundations for the distinctive liberal American world view. As one later American observer has written, "If pragmatism . . . provided American liberalism with its philosophical nerve, Progressive historiography gave it memory and myth, and naturalized it within the whole framework of American historial experience."[8] That "nerve" was the replacement of traditional "formal" philosophy by a world view that encouraged a scientific view of society, in other words, a social science. This was achieved in large measure through the assumption that a number of important issues could be treated as "unproblematic."

According to Charles Morris, the pragmatists believed that "every problem (whether philosophical or not) is specific and occurs in a situation many features of which present no problem, and which as unproblematic are taken for granted in attempts to solve the problem." Morris, a philosopher sympathetic to the philosophical pragmatists and a pragmatist himself, went on to say, "It is believed that there are four main 'unproblematic' features in the historic occasion of which pragmatism is the philosophical voice. . . ."

The four main facets necessary for the development of pragmatic philosophy were the following:

1. the prestige which science and the scientific method enjoyed in the mid-nineteenth century;
2. the corresponding strength of empiricism in the then current philosophy;
3. the acceptance of biological evolution;
4. the acceptance of the ideals of American democracy.

"These four background factors accepted by the pragmatists—scientific method, philosophical empiricism, evolutionary biology, and the democratic ideal—form the 'unproblematic' context in which the philosophical problems of American pragmatism appeared in the framework in terms of which proposed solutions to these problems were judged. It is the combination of these four influences, taken together, which gave the distinctive direction to this philosophical development."[9]

Simply because Morris asserts that the pragmatists accepted these four factors as "unproblematic," it does not follow that they all consistently conformed to his stereotype. The significance of his statement lies less in its application to the views of the well-known pragmatists than in its usefulness as a short summary of the overall world view of the many twentieth-century American intellectuals who have been influenced by pragmatism.

Scientific Method

The pragmatists were no different from many other intellectuals of their day in their admiration of science. Philosophers generally were becoming enamored of the natural sciences and even theologians began to speak of "theological science." Science was becoming the code word, especially in the United States, for research that was admirable (and worth funding): everyone wanted to be scientific.

The pragmatists took their interest in science one step further than other philosophers. They argued that scientific method should lead to purposeful, and possibly profitable, action. Peirce ended his *Lectures on Pragmatism* (1903) with this pronouncement: "The elements of every concept enter into logical thought at the gate of perception and make their exit at the gate of purposeful action; and whatever cannot show its passports at both these gates is to be arrested as unauthorized by reason."[10] William James went even farther with the blunt assertion: "If no practicable difference can be traced, then the alternatives mean practically the same thing and all dispute is idle. Pragmatism represents . . . the empiricist attitude . . . in a more radical and less objectionable form. . . . An idea is true if it is profitable in our lives."[11]

It was Dewey, however, who linked pragmatism with American democracy as well as with the application of scientific method in fields other than science. In the preface to his *Democracy in Education* (1916) he wrote, ". . . the philosophy stated in this book connects the growth of democracy with the development of the experimental method in the sciences, evolutionary ideas in the biological sciences, and the industrial reorganization. . . ."[12]

It was to be the Chicago school, as James called Dewey and his colleagues, that was to have the broadest influence on American thought. Unlike Peirce, the Chicago pragmatists were not scientists. However, they adopted the vision of the role of science propounded by Peirce. They also believed in the practical nature of knowledge, a view held by James. They called their psychology "functionalism" and their philosophy "instrumentalism." The central concept was activity, or Peirce's "purposeful action." Pragmatism at Chicago was distinctively American less as a school of philosophy than as the expression of an important world view. Some of the founders of the new university believed that its goal was to be an "American" institution different from the Europe-oriented universities of the East. Chicago as a city and as a university was thought to embody all that was quintessentially American in the great new civilization that began to influence the world profoundly as the twentieth century got underway.

Some American social scientists reacted against European philosophy to the point of dismissing critical discussion as idle speculation.[13] Many were impatient with the effort of political philosophers to devise precise definitions, regarding such an enterprise as merely hairsplitting. In political science, Charles E. Merriam of the University of Chicago led the way in his enthusiastic support of science, having abandoned his earlier interest in political philosophy. "What we are really striving to achieve is . . . the development of scientific method in the observation, measurement, and comparison of political relations."[14]

Merriam and his colleagues at Chicago were not interested in science for its own sake, but as a means to an end. In several European countries, where there had been more influence from socialism and greater hostility to religion, intellectuals were inclined to support a direct social revolution. In the United States, much energy was spent by the pragmatists in promoting social change indirectly—through a revolutionary application of science and technology. If the pragmatists needed a substitute for religion it was found in science, not socialism. If they had a mission it was the promotion of scientific method, not revolution. Merriam (brought up in Protestant America and married to a Catholic) stated his position forcefully:

> Politics must reckon with . . . a new world of universal leisure; a new world of education; a nontraditional state of mind; a world of scientific methods and results; a race of beings master of nature's forces in greater measure than before dreamed possible; the participation of the bulk of the community in its fundamental conclusions.
>
> What form of government these changes, more revolutionary than any that ever shook France or Russia, will bring, I shall not undertake to predict.[15]

Empiricist Philosophy

The second unproblematic aspect of pragmatism, the acceptance of empiricist philosophy, would at first sight seem to present few problems. After all, empiricism had been the dominant philosophy in Britain ever since Locke. With its assumption that all knowledge was derived from experience, it was a philosophy that appeared to be particularly attuned to the world of science and technology into which England and later the United States so readily moved.

To the empiricist, our knowledge of the physical world consists of a generalization from particular instances and can never reach more than a high degree of probability. While not rejecting all a priori truths, especially those of mathematics and logic, empiricism as a philosophy was opposed to rationalism, that is, it denied the existence of innate ideas. Though not the only tradition in British philosophy, empiricism was far more influential in England than any of the great metaphysical systems, whether Cartesian rationalism, Platonic (and Hegelian) idealism, or the Thomist assumption of the Roman Catholic Church that reason and faith constituted two harmonious realms.

It is certainly arguable that for natural scientists it is feasible, *in the context of science,* to take the philosophy of empiricism for granted as the only philosophy worth serious consideration.[16] (It needs to be remembered, of course, that outside their laboratories natural scientists, like the rest of mankind, adopt a wide variety of social and political philosophies. In their world view, some are even religious fundamentalists.)

Pragmatism, like empiricism, was a method of philosophy. The truth of a proposition could be measured by its correspondence with experimental results, and by its practical outcome. Like empiricism, philosophical pragmatism was opposed to metaphysical doctrines which assumed that the truth could be reached through deductive reasoning based on a priori grounds. It insisted on inductive investigation and the constant verification of hypotheses: according to the pragmatists truth was relative to the purpose, time, and place when an inquiry was made.

Yet for philosophers as such to regard empiricism as unproblematic, as the pragmatists did, was to narrow the concerns of their discipline. It was tempting to regard the works of the great metaphysical philosophers, for example, as for the most part obsolete, products of a prescientific age. One political philosopher associated with the pragmatists did not even exempt the early empiricists from censure, stating, ". . . philosophers of the significance of Locke, Hobbes, Hegel no longer are able to impose their classification and categories upon the human mind in the field of government."[17] Although these thinkers were literate, they were not numerate. "None of the later writers of the major significance of Locke, Montesquieu, Rousseau employs in consideration of political problems any array of figures."[18]

Under the influence of empiricist philosophy generally, and philosophical pragmatism in particular, political theorists came to be divided (especially in the United States) into political philosophers who continued to believe that the great works of the past still merited close scrutiny, and those whose concern was with theory within the context of empiricism and pragmatism. Marx had disdainfully dismissed philosophy as feeding on the immature sciences. The pragmatists sought an empirical theory comparable to the scientific theories of evolution and relativity, theories that had helped to create a separate philosophy of science. The natural scientists had their Darwin and their Einstein, whose roles in transforming the sciences of biology and physics (through what Thomas Kuhn was to call "scientific revolutions") were plain for all to see.

A number of theorists, by no means all Americans, offered similar leadership in the study of social forces. In 1936 John Maynard Keynes published *The General Theory of Employment, Interest and Money*. As a conceptual framework, Keynesian economics in its heyday seemed to be the counterpart to what Kuhn called the "paradigms" of the natural sciences. But it was limited in its application to particular forms of market economics. The economists, intellectuals, and government leaders most influenced by its arguments were those in the advanced capitalist democracies.

A more ambitious attempt to provide a general empirical theory was made by the sociologist Talcott Parsons, who published *The Structure of Social Action* in 1937. Unlike Einstein and Keynes, who were primarily concerned with their own disciplines, Parsons took as his parish the whole of society, and included political science, economics, and psychology within his domain. "Empirical theory" was to become an important field in political science.

Biological Evolution

The third of pragmatism's unproblematic features was the acceptance of biological evolution, an important issue at the end of the nineteenth century. In assuming that plants and animals developed by a process of gradual and continuous change, the evolutionists challenged the traditional religious belief that each individual species was specially created and that the first part of the Book of Genesis was to be taken literally. Ultimately Darwinism was accepted even by those whose religious tenets appeared incompatible with evolution.

In opting for a scientific rather than a religious explanation of Creation, the pragmatists reflected much of the secular thought of their day. The broad acceptance of evolution had owed much to the work of the English philosopher Herbert Spencer, whose synthetic approach to knowledge led him to publish books on the principles of biology, psychology, sociology, and ethics. Spencer helped to establish sociology as a separate discipline, and he was particularly influential in the United States.[19] He explained the ways in which the individual becomes differentiated from the group and acquires greater freedom.

Spencer's books had less influence on his professional colleagues in the sciences than on social thought, where his work gave rise to the notion of social evolution. It was a short step from the idea of social evolution to assumptions about the "growth" (and later the "development") of societies. Indeed, the one value that a pragmatist like Dewey was prepared to admit as ultimate and nonrelative to local and social conditions was growth.[20] In following the example of the evolutionists, the pragmatists therefore committed themselves to the notion of growth, that is, of gradual and incremental change. In this way they distinguished themselves from those socialist thinkers who stressed the importance of revolutionary change.

The pragmatists, like Spencer, were prepared to combine their stress on scientific method and biological evolution with a concern for values. They were interested in the possibility of evolution, through education, toward a better society. They not only emphasized the relation of truth to the time and place of inquiry, they held that knowledge which contributed to human values was real, and that values were as much a part of the means as of the end itself. Implicit in their philosophy was the assumption that the United States had made great progress as a modern civilization based on universal ideals and individual achievement. This contrast between the progressive world view of Americans and the static outlook of more traditional societies where religious belief was still dominant enabled the pragmatists to accept as unproblematic not only the advances of modern science but the very nature of American democracy.

The Ideals of American Democracy

The philosophical pragmatists were not American chauvinists. As Morris put it: "For pragmatism is in no sense the expression or justification of all aspects and phases of history."[21] Several leading pragmatist social scientists, notably Thorstein Veblen and Charles Beard, had indeed been highly critical of the traditional interpretation of American history and society.

Nor were philosophical pragmatists like Dewey rigorous scientific empiricists eschewing value judgments. The general tone of the pragmatic movement, as Morris describes it, seems to have been very different from that of the scientific age that was to succeed it after the Second World War. The pragmatists had a notion of America as a young culture whose pioneers had created a new and more favorable society. They continued the moral tone and ideal cast of the European Judeo-Christian tradition from which they had sprung. They favored an evolutionary explanation of the human person that was compatible with freedom and moral responsibility. Mead's evolutionary treatment of the self was, according to Morris, compatible with the moral interpretation of American democracy offered by Dewey. Morris suggested that, "when Mead wrote, 'in the profoundest sense John Dewey is the philosopher of America,' it is the moral or ideal aspect of Dewey's interpretation of American democracy to which the characterization applies."[22] In other words, the pragmatists shared a profound admiration for the *ideals* of American democracy. Nevertheless, the critics among them did not hesitate to point out that the practice of American democracy often fell far short of these ideals.

The political ideals of American democracy were presumed to be known to all Americans. Certain basic assumptions, such as liberty and justice, were stated in the Pledge of Allegiance. Others, such as the proposition that all men are created equal, were firmly enshrined in the Declaration of Independence. No attempt seems to have been made to separate principles that were universally applicable from those, such as the principles of the Constitution, that applied specifically to the United States. The political ideals appeared *axiomatic:* there was no need or possibility for empirical investigation into their nature; they were self-evident. The principles also appeared to be *factual:* they were contained in such facts of American history as the Declaration of Independence and the Bill of Rights. And finally they were in a very important sense *normative:* they provided the standards by which the actions of individuals and the performance of institutions could be measured. They spanned logic, science, and ethics.

In sum, the fourth unproblematic feature of pragmatism, the ideals of American democracy, started with what Descartes would have called "moral certainty." It offered a clarity and certitude very different from the confused picture presented by the collage of different theories offered in the standard histories of (European) political thought. Together with the other a priori assumptions of scientific method, empiricism and biological evolution, the basic assumptions of the ideals of democracy reconciled the three worlds of reason, fact, and value. These provided the foundations for the hope that a universal theory of political behavior might be achieved.

3 Canada's "Philosophical Federalism"

Canadians did not share the American experience. They were not a people of covenant. There was no heritage of Puritan settlement and no Mayflower. There was no Declaration of Independence: quite the contrary. After the American War of Independence Canada was the destination of many who rejected the principles on which the new republic was founded. The traditional political outlook of the émigrés manifested itself in their title: United Empire Loyalists. The history of Canada was not to include civil war, although it was to involve the dissolution of the united Empire that had inspired the Loyalists (and, more recently, has raised questions about the unity of Canada itself). With such a different set of historical experiences, Canadians tended to be unsympathetic to the world view generated out of the experience of the other American colonies.

Commenting on Clinton Rossiter's notion of the covenant, a conservative Canadian historian noted that it could be taken to mean three things:

> The first is a need for a measure of uniformity; the covenant is among the like-minded. The second is that the covenant to a degree cuts the covenanted off from the uncovenanted. Third, the covenant implies not only uniformity and isolation, but also a mission. America is a messianic country periodically inspired to carry the republic into other lands. . . . If the mission is denied, . . . if the messianic complex is thwarted, then occurs that search for the domestic traitor, the uncovenanted. . . .

By contrast:

> . . . Canada is not the creation of a covenant, or a social compact embodied in a Declaration of Independence and written constitution. It is the product of treaty and statute, the dry legal instruments of the diplomat and the legislator. It is the pragmatic achievement of the little-regarded labours of clerks in the Colonial Office and obscure provincial politicians, still unknown to the world. . . . As America is united at bottom by the covenant, Canada is united at the top by allegiance. Because Canada is a nation founded on allegiance and not on compact, there is no process in becoming Canadian akin to conversion, there is no pressure for uniformity, there is no Canadian way of life.[23]

In other words, while Canadians also prided themselves on being "pragmatic," they did not share the Americans' assumption that certain issues were no longer open to debate, that they were unproblematic.

Perhaps nothing indicates the difference between the United States and Canada in the realm of ideas more clearly than the indifference of Canadians to pragmatism's philosophical assumptions. The pragmatists virtually reduced what was considered acceptable as philosophy to a single school, empiricism. They confined methodology to what they considered to be "scientific method." They identified the evolution of man and society with betterment or growth and regarded the United States as a civilization in the vanguard of progress. In Canadian thought there was no such agreement on fundamentals, and nothing approaching pragmatism's unproblematic features.

One clue to Canada's different world view has been provided by two Canadian philosophers, Leslie Armour and Elizabeth Trott, in their expression "philosophical federalism." They sum up the assumptions of the Canadian philosophers they have studied as follows: "Only rarely is it [English-Canadian philosophy] used as an intellectual substitute for force—as a device to defeat one's opponent, to show his ideas to be without foundation or to discredit his claim to philosophical thought. There is, in short, a kind of philosophical federalism at work, a natural inclination to find out why one's neighbour thinks differently, rather than to find out how to show him up as an idiot."[24]

Armour and Trott confirm the impression of other observers that Canadian philosophers, like other Canadian scholars, share a common approach: the historical. They quote John Irving's description of the philosopher George Brett as the "founder and chief inspiration of the first indigenous philosophical movement to develop in Canada, the Toronto school of intellectual history."[25]

The Canadian historical approach was not the same as pragmatism's evolutionary interpretation. Philosophy in Canada remained to some extent outside the mainstream of Canadian thought. For example, when faced with the demand for a science of society, philosophers elsewhere might respond in different ways, but at least they reacted. They could choose to support the new social sciences, they could retire into the study of formal logic, or they could extol the virtues of the useful.

> Thus one might become a Moore, a Frege, a Dewey or (like Russell) a little of the three. . . .

In Canada, however, none of these movements caught on. Older views of the function of reason, more traditional accounts of human dignity, a culture which had never been exposed to revolution and valued continuity still managed to assert itself. Watson flourished still. Blewett was still fresh in mind. Rupert Lodge was yet to come.[26]

It is of course arguable that an important reason for the failure of Canada to respond to the challenge of pragmatism was its colonial status, especially intellectually, until well into the twentieth century. There were very few philosophers before the First World War, and the two leading scholars, John Watson and John Clark Murray, had come to Canada from their native Scotland. Like many Canadians in those days, they remained attached to the Old Country and its traditions. It has been said of Watson, who taught at Queen's University from 1872 to 1924, that he was "consistently on the war path against Tyndall, Nietzsche, Spencer, and the American pragmatists. . . ."[27] John Clark Murray, who taught at McGill from 1872 to 1903, was "unalterably opposed to hedonism and utilitarianism. . . ."[28] Such men were hardly likely to become associates of Dewey, or to share the view of James Harvey Robinson, the American pragmatist historian, that history "was not merely a chronicle of the past, but rather a pragmatic weapon for explaining the present and controlling the future of man."[29] Nor were these Scottish-trained philosophers worried about the "formalism" of British empiricist philosophy. By "formalism" the pragmatists meant the refusal of a man like John Stuart Mill to apply logic to the interpretation of the world around him, and his willingness to accept Aristotle's dualism, i.e., the separation of the world of reason from the world of experience. The pragmatists, like Hegel and Marx, thought that these two worlds (and some included the world of values) should be brought together in what social scientists today would probably call empirical theory. Thus, three American pragmatists, Holmes, Dewey, and Veblen, "found themselves arrayed against three apostles of empiricism—Bentham, Mill and Austin. They weren't empirical enough."[30] Unlike the American pragmatists, philosophers in Canada were not searching for a new North American philosophy that would emancipate them from their European heritage: still less were they concerned about the unity of theory and practice.

To attribute Canadian resistance to pragmatism to the colonial tradition may account for the period up to 1914, but it does not explain the failure of that philosophy to make converts of the interwar generation of Canadian-born philosophers. One of Canada's leading postwar scholars, Thomas Goudge, engaged in an argument with John Dewey while still a graduate student. They debated the inconsistency of Peirce's interpretation of the category of "Firstness" in the pages of *The Journal of Philosophy* in 1935–36. Dewey insisted that Goudge had misinterpreted Peirce but Goudge stood his ground and argued moreover that the inconsistency adversely affected Peirce's theory of knowledge. It was Goudge who in 1950 published the first full-length (360 pages) interpretative study of Peirce.[31] In it he suggested that there was a possible conflict between naturalism and transcendentalism in Peirce's philosophy. In a later work, *The Ascent of Man,* Goudge dealt with biological questions that had exercised the early pragmatists.

In other words, while the older generation of expatriate scholars had persisted in their own Scottish traditions, a new generation of Canadian-born philosophers was among the first to recognize the significance of Peirce and pragmatism. They also showed themselves resistant to its message. Pragmatism came to be treated in Canada as an interesting contribution to Anglo-American philosophy, but not a world view to which, as a Canadian, one should become committed.

Instead there seems to have been a common thread of pluralistic tolerance or philosophical federalism in Canada. There were more doubts about the ability of science to solve fundamental problems.[32] At the same time, philosophy was less secular than its American counterpart, and not only in Quebec where Thomism dominated the philosophical scene. In 1929 the eminent French-Catholic philosopher Etienne Gilson became director of the Institute of Medieval Studies at the University of Toronto, devoting himself to the history of philosophy with a particular interest in neo-Thomism. Emil Fackenheim, who had earned his doctorate at the University of Toronto and had been rabbi of Congregation Anshe Sholom for five years, became professor of philosophy at the University of Toronto in 1945. His books dealt with the relations of Judaism and philosophy.[33]

In a book of essays in English and French, published in 1960 under the auspices of the Social Science Research Council of Canada, both the French-Canadian and English-Canadian contributors to the section on religion and philosophy devoted almost all their attention to religion.[34] By the standards of the 1960s both articles seem curiously out of date: philosophy by then had become largely autonomous from religion in both French and English Canada. Nevertheless the book suggests that the continuing significance of religion as an influence on Canadian thought as late as the 1950s should not be underestimated.

In the 1960s one of Canada's most notable philosophers, George Grant, published two books in which he demonstrated a passionate concern for the future of his country.[35] These, too, now seem dated in their generalizations about Canada's decline. But they are important because they reflect the pessimism of a conservative nationalist in the face of an inexorably advancing technology. Instead of welcoming American technology, Grant sadly assumed that it would overwhelm Canada. While his starting point was very different from that of the socialist nationalists of the 1970s, Grant shared their implacable pessimism. He concluded that there was now a North American civilization into which Canada was being absorbed. Like the president of the IBM World Trade Corporation, quoted in Chapter 1, he was impressed by the technological superiority of the United States and paid little attention to political boundaries or what he called "local cultures." He stated, "Nor is it simply that the United States is the most progressive society on earth and therefore the most radical force for the homogenizing of the world. By its very nature the capitalist system makes of national boundaries only matters of political formality."[36] Later he went on to say, "Modern civilization makes all local cultures anachronistic. Where modern science has achieved its mastery, there is no place for local cultures. It has often been argued that geography and language caused Canada's defeat. But behind these there is a necessity that is incomparably more powerful. Our culture floundered on the aspirations of the age of progress."[37] Grant concluded, "In Canada outside of Quebec, there is no deeply rooted culture" and went on to say that, like that of the American South, the indigenous French culture was doomed to disappear: ". . . Indigenous cultures are dying everywhere in the modern world. French-Canadian nationalism is a last-ditch stand. The French on this continent will at least disappear from history with more than the smirks and whimpers of their English-speaking compatriots—with their flags flying and, indeed, with some guns blazing."[38]

There is an extraordinary contrast between the optimistic liberal nationalism of Dewey, the apostle of a newly dominant civilization, and the pessimistic conservative nationalism of Grant, living on the periphery of a dying empire. Grant's was the nationalism of despair. Unwilling to distinguish between civilization and culture, he was convinced that once a civilization like the British had lost its dominant position in Canada, it would be replaced by the next civilization, in this instance "the American Empire."[39] Yet he also accused the Canadian Liberals of ensuring that Canada would be swallowed up by the United States. To them ". . . Canada's disappearance is not only necessary but good. As part of the great North American civilization, we enter wider horizons; Liberal policies are leading to a richer continentalism."[40]

One can sympathize with Grant's feeling of hopelessness at a time when the future of an independent Canada seemed very much in doubt. One can see why neither of the alternatives he refers to, the emergence of a national leader of the Left, like Castro, or of the Right, like de Gaulle, was feasible at that time. But one can also regret that Grant did not offer any intellectual or spiritual guidance to the "ruling elites" he criticized so harshly for leading Canada to the wrong goals. His attitude was very different from the ebullience of the Quebec liberals and socialists who were arguing about the future of French-Canadian culture in anglophone North America, and different from the approach of earlier conservative nationalists in Quebec, determined as they were to preserve the French presence in North America.

Clearly, the Canadian philosophical tradition, then, has had to be one of tolerance to accommodate such diverse currents of thought as neo-Thomism, Anglo-American empiricism, continental liberalism and George Grant's conservatism. This coexistence of different perspectives has been adroitly defended as "not necessarily evidence of the persistence of error but rather evidence of the malleable relation between reason and experience."[41]

Canadian philosophers have not shared the pragmatists' concern for unified knowledge. Few of them would have made William James's assertion that a philosopher should *"see* things, see them straight in his own peculiar way, and be dissatisfied with any opposite way of seeing them";[42] fewer would have suggested that idealists like Royce or Bradley were "guileless thoroughfed thinkers";[43] nor did Canadians expect their philosophy to "settle metaphysical disputes."[44] Traditional French-Canadian scholars, and those English-Canadian philosophers aware of the need to coexist with them, would have had difficulty in echoing such words as, "He turns towards concreteness and adequacy, towards facts, towards action and towards power. That means the empiricist temper regnant and the rationalist temper sincerely given up."[45] If James had been open-minded in the Canadian sense he could not have asserted that, while pragmatism was only a method, "teachers of the ultrarationalist type would be frozen out."[46] French-Canadian Catholics (and rationalists, too) could not have subscribed to this doctrine, or to the view that "an idea is true if it is profitable in our lives."[47] In an essay entitled *"La religion et la philosophie au Canada français"* written for the Social Science Research Council's volume of essays on Canadian dualism, Louis-M. Regis o.p. rejected the substitution of the market for the kingdom of God, adding, "Pour l'Eglise, les valeurs de contemplation sont demeurées supérieures aux valeurs d'action."[48]

Yet if the Canadian philosophical tradition was very different from the spirit of American pragmatism, it also lacked the originality and incisiveness of the European tradition from which it sprang.[49] While there was often a willingness to express a point of view, there was not always a determination to reach a conclusion through critical discussion. (This willingness to disagree on fundamental issues may explain why Canadians have been successful as diplomatists.)

Does the principle of philosophical federalism add up to a distinctive Canadian philosophy? At least one foreign critic thought it did. In an article on Canadian philosophy, the Soviet scholar V. V. Mshvenieradze accused Canadian philosophers of being bourgeois, and the country's philosophy of being "a mixture of philosophical ideas from other countries, mainly Britain, France, and the USA." However, he went on to say, "But the specific feature of Canadian philosophy, as determined by the country's historical conditions of development, lies precisely in its adaptation to local conditions, with a corresponding unique refraction of the philosophical and sociological ideas borrowed from abroad."[50]

One of the "local conditions" has been the interest in the Social Credit movement, particularly in Alberta where for many years a Social Credit government was in power. Several distinguished Canadian scholars wrote books about Alberta, one of them being Toronto philosopher John Irving, who was particularly interested in the rise of the Social Credit movement. He concluded that

> The functioning of the democratic process in Alberta during the rise of the Social Credit movement provides a much needed corrective to the abstract concepts of the classical philosophers of democracy from John Locke to John Dewey. No interpretation of democracy which ignores the phenomena of collective behavior can hope to stand. In its wider implications this book may therefore be en-

visaged as a contribution to the democratic philosophy of society and the state.[51]

Armour and Trott include a chapter on the role of Canadian philosophy in the development of social science, which they entitle "Reason, History, and Social Sciences: George Brett, John Irving, and Harold Innis." Their conclusion reflects the Canadian approach to ideas:

> Social science is possible but it will have to cope with value, it will have to deal with the particularities of culture, the generalities of biology, the limiting conditions of geography and demography, the mechanics of exchange and the possibilities of coercion.
>
> Through it all, we may yet be reasonable—even if being reasonable is mainly the confronting of our insights with the constraints which inhibit our ordinary actions.[52]

Canadian thinkers, it would seem, transcended the British and French traditions in which they were originally nurtured, becoming aware, as Canadians, that there could be no victory for any one point of view. To a Canadian scholar the tenets of pragmatism amounted almost to a second (intellectual) Declaration of Independence, a Declaration for which Canada was thought to have no need. Canadian thought was not a reflection of the philosophy current in the United States.

In conclusion, then, we can suggest that despite the similarities between the civilizations of Canada and the United States—the sharing of an almost empty continent that was exploited by massive immigration largely from Europe, by the application of modern technology, and by the development of a modern political economy—there was cultural differentiation. The United States reached the point when many of its leading philosophers were determined not only to emancipate themselves culturally from their European heritage, but to teach the past from the point of view of the present, and to interpret the present as this appeared to the American eye. Canada did not experience a similar ferment (or at least not until the 1960s). The Canadian temperament was less confident in its assumptions, less hostile to traditional thought, and less convinced that the example of science and technology would be able to provide solutions to all human problems.

The pragmatists prided themselves on their ability to exclude those issues that were of an "unproblematic" nature. But Canadians for their part continued to believe, like Europeans, that the great issues had not been resolved and that philosophy's main concern was precisely with those issues that remain "problematic." As Northrop Frye put it, "nothing has ever been self-evident in Canada."[53] And, one might add, nothing was unproblematic either.

Canada remained a country lacking the unifying characteristics of the American world view or the traditional patterns of settlement that provided a sense of identity in European countries. Because of its colonial past and its dependence on other civilizations, Canada was slow in becoming self-conscious. Because of its size and sparse population Canada was able to practice a considerable degree of pluralism in its thought. And as it was unwilling to become simply North America's "second new nation," there seemed to be no need for agreement on a Canadian world view.[54] The disinclination to press arguments to their logical conclusion would seem to signify a certain conservatism, a characteristic of Canada that has long been noted. But conservatism is not the same as reaction, and in this instance it represented a desire to preserve the mosaic, intellectual as well as social, that came to be the country's trademark.

At the beginning of this chapter we asked whether Canadian intellectuals were able to resist the American world view. We saw how an earlier generation of British-born and educated philosophers, still self-consciously part of Britain's imperial civilization, had little difficulty in resisting pragmatism. But even the next generation, Canadian-born, showed an unwillingness to be absorbed into the American orbit. Later still, George Grant became well known among the educated public for his defense of Canadian nationalism, though few professional philosophers shared his conclusion that Canada's intellectual independence had been forfeited. They remained part of a worldwide fraternity of philosophers, continuing to practice the tolerant "philosophical federalism" of their predecessors.[55]

It is arguable, however, that George Grant was perspicacious, and that after 1960 a price had to be paid for philosophical federalism, which now appeared little more than a reflection of the incapacity of Canadians generally to agree on fundamental questions. In 1979 a conference was called by the Canadian Philosophical Association to involve philosophers from all parts of the country in discussions concerning Canada's future. The aim of the conference was "to see in what areas of the Confederation debate the special skills and talents of philosophers would be useful."[56] The conference papers expressed a wide variety of views and revealed the limitations of philosophers generally, and of philosophical federalism in particular, in resolving the problem of national unity. Some scholars hoped that a reinterpretation of the classical texts of political philosophy, for example, Hobbes and Rousseau on sovereignty, might provide answers to the country's pressing questions. Others referred to the findings of various disciplines on the subject. But, in general, there was reluctance to come to grips with the fundamentals of the Confederation debate itself and so to demonstrate that "the special skills and talents of philosophers might be useful."

One important question of significance for Canada was raised, however. Bruce Hunter asked, why do States last? The answers he gave included the role of a ruling elite, the need for buffer states, the involvement of economic interests, and a shared ideology or religion. Finally, there was a shared sense of history created over time as the most obvious common denominator. Yet he felt compelled to assent to the view that Canada lacked the sense of shared political community created by a common history.[57]

Indeed, if the "logic" of Canada's history is examined, that is, the insistence on remaining independent of the United States and later the expectation of becoming virtually independent of the United Kingdom, it is hard to see by what "logic" English Canada could restrain Quebec from pursuing its own path towards independence.

The conference reached no definite conclusions and confirmed the impression that philosophical federalism, which for so long had given Canadian scholars the freedom to develop their own identity vis-à-vis not only the United States and the United Kingdom but vis-à-vis one another, had reached a dead end. In some ways this state of affairs merely reflected the malaise of much contemporary Western philosophy with its withdrawal from the broad concern for social issues and its preoccupation with questions of language (but without the missionary spirit of the earlier proponents of logical positivism). As Isaiah Berlin has put it, "one of the *prima facie* hallmarks of a philosophical question seems to me to be this: that you do not know where to look for the answer."[58] Faced not only with questions of language or logic, but with profound questions of existence, Canadian philosophers appear not to have known where to look for an answer. True, they were willing to consider arguments put forward by a variety of thinkers (mostly foreign), but it did not prove possible to integrate these ideas into a distinctively Canadian approach to problems, problems that reflected Canada's unique experience.

We suggested earlier that if there were not to be any distinctive philosophical assumptions on which Canadians could agree, it would be difficult to uphold the notion that there was a distinctively Canadian world view. If critical discussion did not lead to the enunciation of a Canadian world view, then it was hard to dispute the argument that there was nothing identifiable as shared by all Canadians. Indeed, there might in fact be no real national identity, only a despairing lament over the identity that Canadians had once possessed when they were all British subjects.

However, one must question the argument that national identity (or culture) necessarily requires a set of philosophical assumptions emerging from a distinctive national philosophy. Professional philosophers in Canada as elsewhere, including the United States, have long argued that their discipline (unlike, say, history) is universal and not national in focus. This explains why philosophers can be read with profit anywhere, irrespective of their country of origin.

Nowhere has the universality of scholarship been accepted more widely than in Canada itself. Indeed, the belief that theoretical scholarship was universal was held so firmly that it threatened the very independence of Canada in the 1960s when the universities rapidly expanded. The challenge was no longer seen as simply an American culture expressing itself through a philosophy that Canadian humanists could reject, but rather a scientific and technological civilization, apparently universal in scope, with the United States as the vanguard. This civilization expressed itself not so much through an explicit humanist philosophy as through the implicit assumptions of the social sciences.

3
The Americanization of the Social Sciences:
The Canadian Response to Scientific Empiricism

In contrast to pragmatism's self-confident commitment to an American creed, the social sciences in the United States claimed to be value-free. Because they were scientific in their methodology they were considered to be universal in their application. The new science of politics promoted by Charles Merriam after the First World War for the study of American politics was an attractive alternative to socialism.

But if scientific standards were to be extended to include Canada, how was Canadian society to be assessed? With the development of comparative political analysis after 1945, a universal standard, which could include other countries as well as the United States, was imperative. American political scientists were attracted by the pattern variables developed by the sociologist Talcott Parsons. But suppose even these objective standards of measurement, together with those proposed for democratic systems by Robert Dahl and for comparative politics by S. M. Lipset, were—like pragmatism—to be shown to have a bias towards American values?

This became an important issue. In recent decades, American behavioralism has been attacked by Marxists for its incompatibility with the socialist world view, which also claims to be scientific. Behavioral methodology has aroused the envy of humanistic scholars less learned in the use of statistical analysis and the more advanced techniques that have been widely adopted. If the American approach to social science is scientific, then it is universal in scope and as applicable to Canada as to the United States. It can, therefore, replace the older (Canadian) interpretation of Canadian government and politics as qualitatively different from those of the United States.

The question that needs to be addressed in this chapter is: Does the adoption of behavioral methods signify the triumph of modern science over traditional interpretations? Or does it symbolize something else:

an American cultural penetration more successful than philosophical pragmatism—and one that if successful could lead to the absorption of Canada into not only a shared North American civilization but a common culture?

1   The Emergence of Scientific Empiricism as the Successor to Pragmatism

Pragmatism, as we have seen in Chapter 2, did not have much influence on philosophy in Canada. It proved to be primarily an American phenomenon and a reflection not of the broad civilization of the whole continent but of the particular experience of the United States. Because its cultural bias was clear, it did not replace European philosophy by offering an acceptable world view that appealed to the New World as a whole.

By contrast, European-style philosophy with its broad spectrum of ideas retained its capacity to transcend the world view of particular countries and to express a more universal experience. Sensing this, later generations of American philosophers continued their study of philosophy as a universal—or at least Western—discipline, and one that was not so culture-bound as pragmatism. Canadian philosophers in their turn, with some exceptions, remained convinced that philosophy as they understood it knew no national boundaries.

Pragmatism was, however, to exert profound influence outside philosophy itself, and particularly on the emerging social sciences. These disciplines (as their adherents called them), including political science, shared the pragmatists' concern that American problems should be studied within an American conceptual framework.

Nevertheless, political scientists took some time to "Americanize" their discipline. Despite the formation of the American Political Science Association in 1903, students continued to study European political theory, often through the medium of American textbooks about the great thinkers from Plato to Mill, rather than through a perusal of the classical writings themselves.[1] Even for an understanding of American politics they often turned to the writings of distinguished European visitors sympathetic to the American experiment, authors such as De Tocqueville and Lord Bryce (who was elected president of the American Political Science Association).

After the First World War those, like Charles Merriam, who promoted the new discipline of political science, wished to go beyond the description of political institutions, whether European or American, and to escape from a political theory that largely involved a study of the history of political philosophy that was wholly European and made little if any reference to the contributions of the American Founding Fathers or Abraham Lincoln. Now there was to be the option of examining America's own ideals through scholarly works on the American political tradition, with particular reference to the great statesmen who molded it.[2]

The United States might not be a country of great political philosophers, but it had made a distinctive contribution to the practice of politics and was in the vanguard of the development of modern science and technology. Pragmatism, with its emphasis on America's own experience and on the methods of modern science, which Americans so much admired, was able to exercise considerable influence over the way in which American social scientists viewed their own society and its political system.[3] Insofar as political science before the Second World War offered a new perspective, it was in the study of American politics and America's problems.

Among the most significant American innovations was the effort to develop the social sciences in a novel fashion, and to do so independently of European thought. One of the leading social theorists was Harvard sociologist Talcott Parsons. He had studied in Germany and then, together with Edward Shils of Chicago, translated the works of Max Weber for an American audience. But when he came to produce his own great work, *The Structure of Social Action,* in 1937, Parsons insisted that it was not intended to be merely a compilation of the theories of a number of European thinkers. Instead it was to be viewed as a single coherent body of theory, that of social action.[4] His later works were uniquely "Parsonian," although he had several collaborators. Like Dewey, Parsons won an international reputation. Indeed, so successful were American social scientists that by the 1950s scholars from all over the world were coming to the United States to study the behavioral sciences. Now the contemporary writings of American scholars like Parsons were read, not only accounts of the Founding Fathers or of Lincoln, as had been the case for the previous generation.

Talcott Parsons became influential in the 1950s just as American social scientists were beginning to take the whole world as their parish. Political scientists sought a broader, though equally rigorous, scientific conceptual framework than that provided by Merriam and the proponents of pragmatism with their admiration of the United States and all it stood for. This framework was provided by Parsons' famous "pattern variables" and by a methodology that became known as "scientific empiricism." In some ways the methodology appeared to be the natural successor to pragmatism. It reflected three of pragmatism's four main assumptions. It enthusiastically accepted the importance of scientific method; it shared the pragmatists' assumption that empiricism, not metaphysics, was the proper role for philosophy; and it took for granted the evolutionary perspective on the progressive development of mankind.

At the same time, scientific empiricism did not burden these three "unproblematic" assumptions of pragmatism with the fourth—the belief in the superior value of American democracy. Many political scientists had modified their American moralism once the emancipation of the American intellectual from Europe was completed.[5] It seemed a far cry from 1941 when Merriam had offered five postulates of liberal democracy—the dignity of man, his perfectibility, the diffusion of society's gains among the masses, the consent of the governed, and the use of peaceful means in the settlement of disputes. Merriam had at that time reaffirmed the philosophical principles associated with pragmatism, linking together the three worlds of reason, fact, and value. He asserted:

> These postulates rest
> upon 1) reason in regarding the essential nature of the political man,
> upon 2) observation, experience and inference,
> and 3) the fulfillment of the democratic ideal is [sic] strengthened by a faith in the final triumph of ideals of human behaviour in general and of political behaviour in particular.[6]

This third postulate of Merriam's, expressing the fourth of pragmatism's unproblematic assumptions (the American democratic ideal), did not lend itself to empirical verification. It was not universal in its applicability, and with its American content it was qualitatively different from the other three. Although it had been useful in underpinning the study of American politics between the wars, and in providing that study with a standard of judgment, it now seemed to have no place in a comparative analysis based on a scientific approach to world problems.

The study of the various political systems in the world, which now included the socialist states and the new states of the Third World, seemed to require a new approach, and not one modeled on any particular system. Scientific empiricism provided a model that was applicable universally and acceptable internationally.

One of the leading proponents of the new scientific empiricism was David Easton of the University of Chicago. He published his influential *The Political System: An Inquiry into the State of Political Science* in 1953. Easton was a Canadian, educated at Toronto and Harvard; and it was not surprising that he welcomed a more international approach to political science than that of the founder of the Chicago school of political science, C. E. Merriam. Easton's writings were in due course to have a considerable influence on a new generation of political scientists in Canada.

The scientific approach meant, according to Easton and others, the search for regularities and recurring patterns, the verification of hypotheses, measurement whenever possible, the separation of facts and values, the systematic organization of data, the recognition of the demands made on the pure scientists to remain independent of outside influences, and the presentation of one's conclusions as an integrated whole. Scientific method came to be widely regarded as unproblematic not only for the natural sciences but for the social sciences.

The emphasis on a truly scientific approach to the study of political problems, in which the comparison of political systems played a large part, became dominant in the United States by the end of the 1950s. In the 1960s it had considerable influence over scholars in Canada. Unlike philosophical pragmatism, scientific empiricism did not appear to be culture-bound. Even if it was largely the product of scholarship in the United States, that country represented by midcentury the dominant civilization in the world. Moreover, it was a North American civilization in which Canadians fully participated.

As Canadians adjusted to their role as partners of the United States, they became more receptive to the notion of the social sciences as a division of learning separate from the humanities. The stress on the social sciences as separate disciplines employing their own methodology coincided with the rapid expansion of Canadian universities in the 1960s. When York University, Toronto's ambitious new institution of higher learning, started its own American-inspired curriculum in 1964, all students were compelled to take at least one integrated course in the Social Science Division. Because relatively few Canadians had been trained in some of the social science disciplines, York, like other Canadian universities, found itself dependent for some years on American expertise.⁷ Confident that their disciplines were sciences, and certain that future development lay in specialization, social science administrators tended to prefer as teachers graduates of the large American universities where such specialists were available.

Of course there always had been some influence on Canada from the United States. In the nineteenth century, both radicals like William Lyon Mackenzie and Louis-Joseph Papineau and conservatives such as Sir John A. Macdonald were impressed by the American example.⁸ In the 1940s, although the British parliamentary tradition from which the Canadian political system had sprung remained an important influence on the study of Canadian government, several Canadian scholars applied the "brokerage" explanation of the role of American political parties to the behavior of Canadian parties. There was growing interest in what, in the new language of American political science, was to be called Canada's "political culture."⁹

In the 1950s Canada was examined by several American social scientists as part of what they termed "Anglo-American society," a society whose leadership had passed from the United Kingdom to the United States. Insofar as Canada still remained different from its southern neighbor, this could be interpreted as "cultural lag"; in due course Canada would catch up with the leader. In other words, it was assumed that all modern democratic societies were converging, sharing the benefits of a common (American) civilization. Such differences as remained were merely cultural relics of a bygone age. Thus, Seymour Martin Lipset could chide C. B. Macpherson for not having drawn comparisons with the United States in his *Democracy in Alberta* (1954).¹⁰ Many Canadians adopted the new methods and techniques of American social science as part of a shared North American civilization—just as they adopted innovations in American science and technology. Certainly a number of younger Canadian scholars, particularly those trained in the United States, found the English books describing British parliamentary institutions (and still more, the books of their Canadian counterparts of a similar genre) somewhat old-fashioned, part of an outmoded civilization. They were easily convinced that there was a "new paradigm" in the social sciences, and that this paradigm was scientific empiricism. The older political "science" represented a "prescientific" era that was now over. So universal became the use of American books, American journals, American magazines and above all American theoretical frameworks, that there were soon allegations of American "cultural imperialism."

These allegations puzzled American social scientists. They had self-consciously abandoned pragmatism with its Americanism in favor of a more scientific approach based on what they called "empirical theory," which was supposed to be neutral. The more scientific political scientists barely recognized their debt to the pragmatists. In 1976 Heinz Eulau made merely a passing reference to pragmatism in a Bicentennial review of the discipline: ". . . post World War I political science was not unaffected by philosophical pragmatism and realism which provided the foundations for the emergence of scientific empiricism as the dominant mode of studying American politics."[11]

Indeed, scientific empiricism had become the dominant mode for studying politics everywhere by the 1960s, enabling American scholars (and those fortunate foreign scholars who had studied with them in the United States or elsewhere) to claim that the methods used—for example, survey research or aggregate analysis—were scientific and universal. Since they were thought to contain no ideological—or even philosophical—content, the research techniques of American scholars were assumed to present no threat to any other culture.

It is true that, with some exceptions, the older generation of Canadian scholars (like Charles E. Merriam himself) tended to be unsympathetic to many of the new trends. It is also true that the Canadian academic community had never shared the pragmatists' unbounded faith in the possibilities of science. And, as a small intellectual elite of humane scholars, the learned societies were somewhat skeptical of anything American. But times changed. The threat from the Soviet bloc made Canadians realize that they shared certain fundamental ideals with their American neighbors. They were prepared to participate not only in NATO (1949) but in NORAD (1957) for the air defense of North America. American science and technology were dazzling the world by their remarkable feats, from the production of successive generations of intricate computers to precision landings on the moon. More and more Canadian social scientists were American-trained and unable readily to identify with the older humanistic elite.[12] Whereas there had been but a score or so of political scientists in Canada in 1950, there were over 700 by 1970. York University established its Institute of Behavioural Research. For the benefit of researchers needing access to data on American voting behavior and on political attitudes in the United States and elsewhere elicited from opinion surveys, the Institute became a member of the Inter-University Consortium for Political Research based at the University of Michigan. When the graduate program in political science was established at York, empirical theory was one of the fields of study. The time seemed ripe for the replacement of an outmoded European approach to parliamentary government by a new North American political science studying the political process of interest groups and public opinion, and making full use of the available technology.[13]

In Canada, the influence of scientific empiricism was to extend far beyond academe. Canadian intellectuals had long enjoyed relatively easy access to positions in government and administration, and this was to increase when the products of the burgeoning social sciences emerged from the graduate schools of Canada and the United States to encourage governments to develop new techniques of rational decision making. According to two commentators on the rational reform of the political process in Ottawa as it affected public policy, it produced "an excessive uncritical fascination with the superficial trappings of public-policy analysis and rational executive government. There was generally a failure to put developments then in a more sober historical and political context. . . . Yet the questions which emerge . . . are not trivial and they deserve careful analysis."[14]

They certainly were not trivial. No one was more responsive to the notion of rational decision-making based on the lessons of science and technology than Pierre Elliott Trudeau, who became Prime Minister in 1968. Although Canadian scholars considerably modified the exuberance of the 1960s in their approach to scientific empiricism, the Government of Canada remained under the leadership of a Prime Minister who had long been committed to a rational and scientific approach to politics. Indeed, Trudeau rejected Quebec nationalism largely because it appealed to the emotions. He had made his position clear before entering politics:

> . . . nationalism will eventually have to be rejected as a principle of sound government. In the world of tomorrow, the expression "banana republic" will not refer to independent fruit-growing nations but to countries where formal independence has been given priority over the cybernetic revolution. In such a world, the state—if it is not to be outdistanced by its rivals—will need political instruments which are sharper, stronger, and more finely controlled than

anything based on mere emotionalism: such tools will be made up of advanced technology and scientific investigation, as applied to the fields of law, economics, social psychology, international affairs, and other areas of human relations; in short, if not a pure product of reason, the political tools of the future will be designed and appraised by more rational standards than anything we are currently using in Canada today.[15]

The influence of scientific empiricism had therefore a double importance for Canada. It involved the attempt by scholars to restructure the analysis of political systems as a scientific rather than an ideological undertaking, and one conforming to a universally acceptable methodology. It also led to the effort on the part of the Prime Minister (described in Chapter 7) to transform Canada's Westminster-type constitution into a more "rational" political system, complete with a written constitution, an entrenched Bill of Rights, and possibly a system of judicial review like that familiar to Americans.

Scientific empiricism was based on the unity of theory and practice: a proposition had to be verifiable and no theory was scientific if it could not be tested. Democratic ideals generally, and American ideals in particular, were not capable of being tested: they were axiomatic. Only actual political behavior could be subjected to empirical investigation. Much therefore rested on the assumption of the scientific empiricists that they were value-free, universalistic scientists, quite unlike the philosophical pragmatists.

How successful were the scientific empiricists in avoiding the adoption of American political ideals in their research? One way of determining how far they were able to remain faithful to their self-imposed standards in their study of the United States, Canada, and other countries is to analyze the writings of some of the leading empirical theorists.

In searching for the answer to the question whether scientific empiricism was universal and value free, we must consider, among other things, whether the American scientific empiricists owed any debt at all to the pragmatists.

Charles Merriam: The Link Between Philosophical Pragmatism and Scientific Empiricism in Political Science?

It is tempting to assume that there must have been a link between the pragmatists and the postwar Chicago School because of the important part played by Charles Merriam who was professor of political science at the University of Chicago from 1900 to 1940. Certainly, as a longtime colleague of the Chicago philosophical pragmatists he shared many of their concerns. "His attitude towards history was clearly related to the concepts of process then current in the pragmatic philosophy of John Dewey, George Herbert Mead and perhaps most of all T. V. Smith."[16]

Merriam's *New Aspects of Politics* (1925), in which he recommended the establishment of a new scientific political science comparable to the newer social sciences, has been described as "clearly in the spirit of his colleagues at Chicago."[17] But while it is true that Merriam had much in common with the pragmatists and shared Dewey's commitment to the promotion of American democracy, it is difficult to trace a close intellectual relationship between Merriam and the pragmatist philosophers. In fact, Merriam was not really a man of philosophical disposition, although he seems to have shared some of the pragmatists' views: "The essence of the pragmatic theory is that of the relativity of values to their working utility at a given time and place. . . . The question is not whether the pattern has a logical basis but does it operate? If so, it is true and right."[18]

Merriam's influence was largely on American political science. His appreciation of the world outside the United States seems to have been somewhat limited. He recoiled from the horrors of the First World War, during which he worked for the American government in Italy; but neither the writings of Marx and Lenin nor the Russian Revolution seem to have made much of an impression, except perhaps to stimulate his interest in science as an alternative to socialism. In *Systematic Politics*, published in 1945, he was still an admirer of the British Empire and showed little appreciation of the further breakup of empires that was to follow the Second World War.

Over the years, Merriam's concerns had shifted from political theory to the application of scientific method to the study of American politics. In introducing his major work, *New Aspects of Politics*, in 1925, he had written that it was not his purpose to suggest either a new theory of politics or a new system of government.[19] His biographer was to comment that while Merriam's writings appeared to describe new directions of change, these directions were in effect consistent with the traditions of American government and the trends in American politics.[20]

The works of the post-1945 Chicago school of American political science by authors such as Herbert Simon, David Truman, Harold Lasswell, and V. O. Key, had little to say about pragmatism. In his *The Political System,* David Easton made two passing references to the pragmatists. Robert Dahl, whose department at Yale did so much to develop new approaches to the discipline in the 1950s and 1960s, made no reference to the pragmatists in his most important theoretical work, *A Preface to Democratic Theory* (1956). Merriam's relations with the Chicago School of philosophical pragmatists had always been more tenuous than those of, say, the sociologists. Whatever link there may have been between political science and philosophical pragmatism through Merriam would appear to have been broken by the scientific empiricists.

To what, then, did scientific empiricism in political science owe its development? According to Robert Dahl, there were "six, specific, interrelated, quite powerful stimuli."[21] These were:

1. Merriam and the Chicago School
2. Immigrant European social scientists
3. The wartime experience of political scientists in Washington
4. The role of the Social Science Research Council
5. The rapid growth of the survey method
6. The support of the foundations

This is a somewhat heterogeneous collection, and if we are looking for intellectual encouragement it would seem to lie in the first two stimuli. Discussing these, Dahl acknowledged that many of the immigrant social scientists found scientific empiricism, with its antiphilosophical bias, too narrow for their European sensibilities. Much would therefore seem to have depended on Charles Merriam and the Chicago School he inspired.

Merriam himself does not seem to have been particularly impressed by post-1945 American political science, complaining that the new generation was cynical and mechanistic. To him they seemed to be using science to question the very principles from which he himself had derived the necessity of scientific method.[22] Even so, Dahl was not alone in the 1960s in paying tribute to Merriam's role in encouraging scientific empiricism. When he published the *International Encyclopedia of the Social Sciences* in 1968, editor David Sills explained that the number of biographical articles, numbering 4,000 in the *Encyclopedia of the Social Sciences* (1930), had been reduced to 600. Among these were a category of persons, such as Harold Laski, whose influence had been important but limited in scope, and another category of persons whose influence, though considerable, fell short of eminence. Among these were Walter Bagehot, A. D. Lindsay, and Gaetano Mosca. Then there were the key figures in the development of each social science discipline. In political science the editor gave three examples: Aristotle, Machiavelli, and Merriam.[23] In the biographical article itself, Barry Karl acknowledged Merriam's important contribution to political science.

However, a few years later, Karl appears to have had second thoughts after he had completed his biography of Merriam and was writing his Introduction. There one learns that Merriam's contribution was chiefly that of a successful academic entrepreneur, and that his intellectual influence was minimal.[24] Certainly in his lifetime Merriam does not appear to have exerted much influence on European scholars. Neither Michels nor Laski, with whom he corresponded, nor Max Weber, seems to have respected him as a thinker.[25]

It is precisely when one recalls the entrepreneurial aspects of Merriam's career that one begins to understand why Dahl thought that the "six, specific . . . quite powerful stimuli" were interrelated. It was Merriam, after all, who had founded the Social Science Research Council. It was Merriam who had persuaded the foundations, notably the Rockefeller Foundation, to invest heavily in the social sciences. It was Merriam who had encouraged the voting studies that had preceded survey research. And it was Merriam who had worked in Washington for several presidents.

Merriam was not a scientist, although he much admired the scientific approach of his older brother John, who became president of the National Research Council and the Carnegie Institution. He was not a politician, although he unsuccessfully tried to become Mayor of Chicago and was an admirer of both Roosevelts, working for Franklin Delano Roosevelt in the 1930s. That is to say, Merriam's influence on scientific empiricism owed more to his progressive views, his optimism, his connections in New York and Washington, his energy and his encouragement to the new generation, in other words to his personality, than to his intellect. "Indeed, what the process-oriented pragmatism of that generation would share with the behavioral orientation of the generation which followed was a capacity to confuse the meaning of results in the search for ends and the analysis of their achievement. The success or failure of any activity came to be measured too easily by the depth of the psychological experience the activity was supposed to create rather than the objective result of the activity itself."[26]

So long as the primary concern of Merriam and the Chicago School was American politics the impact of American political science on Canadians was relatively slight. Canadian scholars interested in their own political system and their emancipation from Britain were unlikely to be much influenced by new trends in American voting studies. Even those, like J. A. Corry and J. E. Hodgetts, whose concern was with the democratic political systems of Canada, Britain, and the United States, seem to have been little influenced by the changing currents in American political science. They made the traditional distinction between political ideals and actual forms of government.[27]

But as Canadian political scientists extended their horizons, the need for an alternative conceptual framework became more apparent. Whereas Corry and Hodgetts had confined their references to Merriam and Easton to their bibliography, Paul Fox introduced his collection of readings *Politics: Canada* with an excerpt from Dahl's writings, entitled "What is political science?"[28] In their textbook *The Canadian Political System: Environment, Structure and Process,* Richard Van Loon and Michael Whittington adopted Easton's input–output–feedback analysis.[29] Harry Eckstein's introductory essay in *Comparative Politics* (Eckstein and Apter, eds.) became compulsory reading in Canadian graduate programs for students entering the field of comparative politics.[30] Few noted the long footnote in which he admitted treating the British political tradition as a deviant case. Few inquired into the assumptions underlying the behavioral approach that he adopted. Scientific empiricism was assumed by its very nature to be the only valid approach to the comparison of political systems, whether in the United States or elsewhere.

The pragmatists (and Merriam) had taken for granted the superiority of Western—and especially American—liberal democracy. They did not confront the problem that faced a later generation of political thinkers, that of encouraging the establishment in new countries of not only the values of liberal democracy but also the appropriate political institutions.

Shils suggested that neither the study of traditional moral and political philosophy nor the examination of the particular political institutions of the Western world would be helpful. He concluded:

> These Western [liberal values] are all values of universal validity, and regimes that do not find a place for them and similar values

are less good than those that do. . . . Nonetheless, we must not be doctrinaire in our belief about the institutional forms in which these values can be expressed. It would be wrongheaded to think that the institutional arrangements in which these values have attained some measure of realization in Western societies exhaust the human possibilities of creation and contrivance. . . .

Instead, suggested Shils, there should be a genuinely comparative study of the new states in the context of empirical theory: ". . . A genuinely comparative study of the new states, within the context of a general and theoretical analysis of all states and societies, will do more to reveal the possibilities of the organization of human life than all the arguments about the inherent genius of the 'African personality,' the 'Islamic state,' the 'Hindu heritage,' or the 'Western tradition.' " Shils went on to muse on the contribution that such an enterprise might make to political philosophy: "It can contribute to the schooling of judgment and the refinement and enrichment of analysis in political philosophy. Thus, it might, by proceeding along the lines of Max Weber, bring to fruition what was begun at Aristotle and Cicero. It will therewith illuminate our spirits while it disciplines our minds."[31]

It would seem that, like the majority of scientific empiricists, Shils assumed that political philosophy began with that great student of comparative politics, Aristotle, and not with his teacher, Plato. Like Merriam, Shils did not question the ideals of liberal democracy, and especially the American variant with which both were most familiar. Rather, both scholars doubted whether the older institutional approach both to American government and to the study of foreign governments in the United States, treated as they were as subjects separate from each other and from political theory, was at all suitable for the very different problems of the new states. To study the problems of the new states required a more synthetic approach, in which the emphasis should be on comparative analysis linked to value theory, presumably through empirical theorizing.

Not all political scientists were as philosophical as Shils. Sidney Verba posed the problem presented by new states in terms of the need for a new political science, just as Merriam had urged in 1925: "This century has seen rapid changes in both the real world of politics and the study of politics. In the political world new nations appear suddenly at every turn and old ones change or disappear as fast. . . . And in the study of politics one can sense a parallel. New approaches, new methods, new theories proliferate on all sides, in many cases inspired by the rapid changes in the political world. The new politics—politics in new areas, politics of a new type—appear to require a new political science to understand them."[32]

Harry Eckstein concluded that traditional political science—that is, the history of political theory, and the study of American and European political institutions—was inadequate for the study of comparative politics on a world scale: "The theoretical equipment of political scientists, such as it was, generally failed them when they confronted political systems unlike the highly differentiated, formally organized, predominantly democratic or totalitarian systems of the West. For this reason also they went to school with social scientists who offered more appropriate theoretical tools and learnt to use these tools."[33]

There was a reaction against the moralistic writings of previous generations in favor of scientific analysis. Gabriel Almond and James Coleman expressed themselves in the self-consciously scientific language of the time: "Casting our problems in terms of formal theory will direct us to the kind and degree of precision which are possible in the discipline, and will enable us to take our place in the order of the sciences with the dignity which is reserved only for those who follow a calling without limit or limitation."[34] In other words, it seemed possible to proceed without the value-laden assumptions of philosophical pragmatism—but not without an analytical framework that encompassed both the "modern" politics of Europe and North America and the "traditional" societies of Asia and Africa with their newly independent polities.

Comparing Political Systems: Parsons' Pattern Variables

The "search for more appropriate theoretical tools," to use Eckstein's expression, ended for many political scientists with the discovery of the sociological theories of Talcott Parsons, and in particular his four "pattern variables." Parsons' contrast between the "universalism" and "achievement" principles underlying modern societies like the United States, and the "particularistic" and "ascriptive" assumptions of traditional societies, seemed to many political scientists to provide a conceptual framework into which both old and new states could be fitted.

Moreover, Parsons also provided some of the elements of a theory of social change, one that could explain the transformation of traditional societies through a transitional stage of cultural dualism. At this stage, both traditional and modern societies existed side by side in the same state, a state that was characterized as being between traditionalism and modernity. Almond and Coleman explained the nature of "political development" as follows: "We have characterized the 'modern' solution of the problems of cultural dualism as a penetration of 'traditional' styles of diffuseness, particularism, ascriptiveness, and affectivity, by the 'rational' styles of specificity, universalism, achievement, and affective neutrality."[35]

Since these pattern variables had such wide currency in comparative politics, and were used to demonstrate that Canada and the United Kingdom were more traditional than the United States, it is important to suggest some idea of what they meant. "Diffuseness" was contrasted with "specificity." In the Old World, the interaction of employer and servant often involved a *diffuse* familial relationship, not simply the payment of a *specific* wage. Similarly, free spending to provide "Old World" hospitality characterized an *affective* response, as contrasted with modern *affective neutrality,* whereby money was first set aside for mortgage payments, insurance, pensions—and taxes.

The other two pairs of pattern variables were to prove even more important in comparative politics, particularly insofar as a society based on the model of universalism-achievement was seen as "ideal." Most educated people now recognize the distinction between *ascriptive* status, which is based on one's family's position in society, and *achieved* status, which depends on one's own efforts. Americans, priding themselves on being achievers, have generally been thought to treat one another impersonally: "His dollar is as good as anyone else's." This *universalism* distinguished America from the *particularism* that is thought to have characterized the Old World, where so much has depended on personal relationships.

As a conceptual framework, Parsons' scheme of pattern variables appeared to offer something hitherto unavailable in political science, the integration of American theory into Western thought. The discipline had often tended to abstract from European experience. Now as leader of the West, the United States could be taken as the model and its experience integrated with that of the new states, states with which the United States had become deeply involved. The key to the understanding of their political systems was provided by evolution (i.e., development or modernization), since all states were proceeding from the traditional to the modern. According to Gabriel Almond, "The political scientist who wishes to study political modernization in the non-Western areas will have to master the model of the modern, which in turn can only be derived from the most careful empirical and formal analysis of the functions of the modern Western polities."[36] In their *The Politics of Developing Areas,* Almond and Coleman adopted Parsons' pattern variables. But as early as 1953 David Easton had referred to Parsons' suggestive insights into the role of theory and to the notion that "all the social sciences may well have a common body of theory."[37] Easton remarked that he had learned a great deal from Parsons' and Shils' *Towards a General Theory of Action.*[38]

Parsons himself seems to have become ambivalent about the nature of his contribution to empirical theory. It is true that he introduced his *The Social System* (1951) as "a statement of general sociological theory."[39] But he concluded that work with a repetition of his remarks in *The Structure of Social Action* (1937): "We have sound theoretical foundations on which to build."[40] He recognized the limitations of his work, and insisted that *"a general theory of the processes of change of social systems is not possible in the present state of knowledge"* (Parsons' italics).[41] Parsons distinguished between a theory as a system of laws and the paradigm he was offering (in the pre-Kuhnian sense of the term).[42] Later, he concluded that it was too early to present a "system *of* theory" and suggested that his own "theory of systems" was fragmentary and incomplete.[43]

Nor were all political scientists convinced that Parsons' theories were appropriate. Samuel Huntington questioned the assumption that social and economic modernization could be expected to be accompanied by political modernization, for example, by participatory democracy. There was too much evidence to the contrary.[44]

On the whole, however, it was Parsons' pattern variables, together with Almond's typology of the political process and Easton's definition of government as the authoritative allocation of values, that provided a new language of discourse for what had once been a traditional discipline. By adopting the assumptions of scientific empiricism, by employing scientific method, and by using the universalistic-achievement model first elaborated by Talcott Parsons as the goal, it now seemed possible to undertake truly scientific investigations not only within American politics but in the burgeoning field called comparative politics.

The seal of approval to this endeavor seemed to be given by the publication of Thomas Kuhn's *The Structure of Scientific Revolutions* in 1962. Scientific empiricists now accepted three propositions:

1. that the distinction between prescientific and scientific disciplines applied to the social sciences as well as to the natural sciences;
2. that to leave the classics of political philosophy unread was to follow in the footsteps of students in the natural sciences who now read up-to-date scientific texts instead of Aristotle's *Physica* and Newton's *Principia;*
3. and that the new language of political science corresponded to the new world view of science that always followed the acceptance of a new paradigm.[45]

If there was a new paradigm in the social sciences, its creator was Talcott Parsons. Comparative politics therefore came to depend for much of its theoretical underpinning on pattern variables, variables whose empirical origins distinguished them from the philosophical assumptions they replaced. As Parsons put it in his preface to *The Structure of Social Action:*

> This body of theory, the "theory of social action," is not simply a group of concepts with their logical interrelations. It is a theory of empirical science the concepts of which refer to something beyond themselves. It would lead to the worst kind of dialectical sterility to treat the development of a system of theory without reference to the empirical problems in relation to which it has been built up and used. True scientific theory is not the product of idle "speculation," of spinning out the logical implications of assumptions, but of observation, reasoning and verification, starting with the facts and continually returning to the facts.[46]

In view of Parsons' stress, evident in this quotation, on what is now known as empirical theory, it is puzzling that he gave no indication of having attempted any genuine empirical science himself. As far as his dichotomous variables are concerned Parsons seems to have obtained them neither from empirical research nor from philosophical speculation. The distinction between "particularistic" and "universalistic" owed its inspiration to Tönnies' comparison of "community" and "association" in *Gemeinschaft und Gesellschaft* (1877). The terms "ascription" and "achievement" were taken from the work of Ralph Linton. In other words, there *was* an empirical basis of sorts for Parsons' typology: but it was the work of other social scientists.

Parsons examined the four possible combinations of his two dichotomies and related them to actual societies. The illustrations he gave were as follows:

Universalistic-achievement pattern: United States
Universalistic-ascriptive pattern: Germany
Particularistic-achievement pattern: China
Particularistic-ascriptive pattern: Spanish America

These pattern variables and their illustrations present a problem. Just what importance should we attach to the four countries or regions named, to the evidence Parsons adduced for their selection as examples, and to the remarks that Parsons made about them? Before judging Parsons too harshly we must remember that in 1951 he was unaware that his dichotomies would be adopted as the theoretical framework for the comparison of political systems. He was not writing about politics, and the countries selected were neither exemplars nor samples of the world's states. Indeed, in none of the papers he wrote on political science topics, collected in *Politics and Social Structure* (1969), did he make any reference at all to the pattern variables as such.

But we have to be concerned with them because they were adopted by numerous scientific empiricists studying other political systems. Moreover, the pattern variables were sometimes used not only for analyzing developing areas but for explaining differences between Canada and the United States. We therefore need to know whether Parsons' empirical theory was scientific or whether, like philosophical pragmatism, it had a normative component.

In attempting to find the answer, what we first notice is that Parsons' four illustrations highlight the difficulties facing the social scientist whose belief in science compels him to relate his theory to practice. In such circumstances, when illustrating a theory that claims to be universal by referring to specific examples, it is difficult to avoid seeming superficial. For example, what precisely is the empirical referent in his example of "Germany"? Initially he said, "Broadly, the philosophy of 'idealism' and the German cultural ideal seem to conform with this pattern."[47] But later he switched from the German cultural ideal to actual German behavior, and referred to the authoritarian family in which the wife is

" 'kept in her place.' This is notoriously characteristic of the traditional German family structure."[48]

Many of the traits sketched by Parsons would indeed seem to fit a certain German social structure.[49] But one begins to suspect that Parsons was using as evidence his own impressionistic observations of Germany in the 1920s. This seems to be confirmed in the summary of his argument, which appeared in another work published in the same year, where he suggested that the universalist-particularistic variable "fits the pre-Nazi German value system."[50] He made only a single reference to another possible example of this pattern: "There are also certain respects in which Soviet Russia [sic] approximates this type."[51] But that was all he said about the Soviet Union at this point.

The "China" to which Parsons referred is far from being the contemporary China of twentieth-century social science research. In offering it as an illustration of the particularistic-achievement pattern, he wrote, "An excellent example seems to be the classical Chinese cultural pattern, with its concept of a harmonious order for the maintenance or restoration of which men are held to be responsible."[52] In the summary he asserted that the particularism-achievement combination "fits the classical Chinese pattern rather closely."[53]

The countries of what he called "Spanish America" (Brazil presumably being excluded?) were treated as a unit. We may presume that unlike his references to "China" much of his information on South America was of a contemporary nature; he admitted, in a rare footnote, that much of his information was derived from conversations with an anthropologist.[54]

The three pattern variables and their illustrations, which we have just discussed, are dealt with in nine pages. But they followed nine pages devoted to the universalistic-achievement pattern alone. Clearly Parsons was primarily concerned with the universalistic-achievement dichotomy. This was the standard to be used. Parsons prefaced his discussion of the other three variables with: "It will not be possible to take space to treat the other three types of society as fully as was done with the universalistic-achievement type, but since a comparative base line has been established, it ought not to be necessary."[55] This comment would seem to indicate that Parsons had other things to explain that were more important to him than the pattern variables. These filled about twenty pages in a book that totaled over 550 pages.[56]

If, however, there is anything in the pattern variables that has both stimulated and irritated scholars it is Parsons' explanation of universalism-achievement. Here he appeared primarily to have the United States in mind. In his account, Parsons seemed to stress its individualism, its orientation towards success, and its identification of class with occupation. He found ethnic and religious divisions dysfunctional.

> The choice of goals must be in accord with the universalistic values. Therefore promotion of the welfare of a collectivity as such tends to be ruled out. The collectivity is valued so far as it is necessary to the achievement of intrinsically valued goals. This is the basis of a certain "individualistic" trend in such a value system.
>
> In the most general terms it may be said that the basic reward in such a system is "success," defined as level of approval for valued achievement.
>
> Ethnic subdivisions within such a society are not, as such, in harmony with its main structural patterns and hence create strains. . . .
>
> Finally, too closely integrated a religious system would be dysfunctional in such a society. If the orientation of such a religion were other-worldly it would undermine motivation in the central role system—if not this, it would, like Marxism as a "religion," tend to shift the balance over to the universalistic-ascriptive type to be discussed below. The pattern of religious toleration and a diversity of denominations as in the American case seems to be the least disruptive structure.[57]

Parsons categorically stated, "This is the type of structure central to what are often called 'industrial' societies."[58] Nevertheless, from what he says elsewhere, such a pattern clearly has limited application to countries where there is conflict over ethnicity or religion, as in Germany. It has its limitations when applied to Catholic countries like France and Italy and particularly for a country like Canada because of Quebec. In fact, in his nine-page section on universalism-achievement, apart from another passing reference to "Soviet Russia," this time in a reference to nationalism, the only country mentioned is the United States, which is referred to several times. Later he contrasted such a society with that of Latin countries having a Catholic background. These countries "have proved relatively unsusceptible to the development of industrial patterns . . ."[59]

Elsewhere Parsons was quite explicit in identifying the universalistic-achievement pattern with the American ethos. "[T]he Universalistic-Achievement Pattern is best exemplified in the dominant American ethos."[60] In *Toward a General Theory of Action* we find the following summary: "The universalism-achievement combination . . . approximates the dominant American 'achievement complex.' "[61]

It would seem, then, that it is difficult to disentangle the universalistic-achievement pattern from American society. The student of comparative politics, taking Parsons at his word as a general and an empirical theorist, is entitled to assume that the "America" referred to is the empirical American social and political system investigated by social scientists, and not some ideal "American creed."

In his explanation, Parsons nowhere referred to any of the pragmatists, not even to Dewey, who had much to say about America's democratic ideals. Parsons remained a scientific empiricist. However, in his introductory description of the universalistic-achievement pattern variable—the one that has been used most often to explain Canada as well as the United States—Parsons wrote: "The combination of universalism with achievement values puts the primary universalistic accent on process, that is, on means-choice and particular goal-choice, leaving the goal-system fluid. *In some such sense the philosophy of pragmatism epitomizes this orientation*" (italics mine).[62] Since this was Parsons' only reference to pragmatism, we should perhaps not read too much into a single sentence. On the other hand, it had a crucial place in his account since it summed up his initial explanation of the first pattern variable. It suggested that he had an understanding of philosophical pragmatism, and it was hardly a casual remark relegated to a footnote.[63]

If Parsons identified universalism-achievement with the orientation of the pragmatist, then it is difficult to avoid raising the possibility that he himself shared the pragmatists' various "unproblematic" assumptions, including their ideological commitment to American democracy. From the way in which he used the universalistic-achievement variable as the standard for comparative analysis, and from his remarks touching Germany and classical China, which included references to their "ideals," such a notion may not be unwarranted. If there was a commitment by Parsons to the ideals of American democracy, then any theory of scientific empiricism based on the pattern variables that purports to be universal must be examined with care. In addition, there must be cause for concern that Parsons was so casual in his own use of scientific procedures, despite his insistence on the scientific canons of "observation, reasoning, and verification, starting with the facts and continually returning to the facts."

The question that troubles the Canadian political scientist, however, is this: If Parsons' references to actual polities were so vague, superficial, and secondhand, why did his framework retain its plausibility for so many American students of comparative politics? One explanation must be that they shared his instinctive notion of the ideals of American democracy as unproblematic, *and as being both scientific and normative.* The pragmatists' main political legacy was to suggest that American democratic ideals were axiomatic, descriptive, and normative. However hard they tried, none of the empirical theorists seem to have completely escaped the pragmatists' sense of commitment to those ideals.

How then can we sum up the assumptions of scientific empiricism in the light of the four unproblematic features of pragmatism? As their nomenclature indicates, the scientific empiricists accepted the first two unproblematic aspects of pragmatism. They also seem to have adopted an evolutionary approach, the third unproblematic feature, deploying their theoretical framework to explain the modernization of developing areas.[64]

It is the fourth unproblematic factor that presents the most difficulties. In themselves, "the ideals of American democracy," are not necessarily uniquely American in content: these may be ideals shared by large numbers of people elsewhere. But they remain "ideals of democracy" and as such have a normative content. The pragmatists, being philosophers first and scientists second, were not too concerned by this: Dewey's main interest was in uniting the three worlds of reason, fact, and value, not in establishing the differences between them.

The scientific empiricists wanted to relate only the worlds of reason and nature (or fact) and were prepared to consider values only when they appeared as factual statements. However, even in combining reason and fact they found themselves in difficulties when dealing with political systems, for they needed empirical referents. These could not be *ideal* democratic systems; they had to be actual systems themselves. In having to choose between recommending universal ideals or simply noting the example of particular systems, they chose the latter. For example, Almond and Coleman began *The Politics of Developing Areas* with the pattern variables. Toward the end of the book they made reference to actual systems embodying these: "It is clear from this list of attributes that the Anglo-American polities most closely approximate the model of a modern political system described in the Introduction and Shils' model of a 'political democracy.' "[65] This emphasis on actual systems did not, however, prevent them from believing that ". . . our work represents a contribution to the general theory of political systems."[66]

The scientific empiricists seem to have added their own gloss to pragmatism's fourth unproblematic feature. Whereas for the pragmatists the categories of analysis were axiomatic, descriptive, *and* normative, for the scientific empiricists they were assumed to be only axiomatic and descriptive.

But did they rigorously adhere to this procedure? As we have seen, Parsons did not, and at one point admitted that his universalistic-achievement pattern variable was based on the same assumptions as those of philosophical pragmatism, which included the fourth unproblematic factor. Nevertheless, we should be careful not to reach a general conclusion on the basis of the work of a single scholar, however eminent. It could be argued that Parsons was not the best example of a scientific empiricist, that he was not primarily concerned with political questions, and that we should also examine the writings of other empirical theorists.

A review of the major works of certain empirical political theorists suggests that they have found themselves in a difficult position—comparable to that of Parsons—in their attempt to link analytical propositions about the nature of democracy with statements about its actual practice, which was their necessary empirical referent. Despite their very considerable efforts to avoid normative statements, these theorists appear to proceed through four stages or steps:

1. They begin by asserting analytical principles (of democracy) that are assumed to be both axiomatic and *a priori*.
2. They insist that these principles must be related to actual practice by careful, scientific, empirical analysis of political systems.
3. They discover the task of empirical verification to be so difficult that they abandon the attempt at scientific investigation of all the data in favor of impressionistic references to selected countries generally considered to be "democracies."
4. They then find themselves transforming their analytical principles or categories of analysis into normative standards of judgment.

Because of their inevitably limited knowledge of political systems other than their own, the empirical theorists themselves have had difficulty avoiding the impressionistic analysis adopted by the traditional scholars whom they have criticised for falling short of scientific investigation. They too have been tempted to move from the world of rational analysis into the world of normative judgments from which they were so eager to escape. We shall now see how a number of scientific empiricists deal with these four steps.

Lipset's Application of the Pattern Variables to Canada

Our immediate and practical concern is the appropriateness of scientific empiricism for the explanation of Canadian political phenomena and as a method of making comparisons between the Canadian and American political traditions. In this regard it may be appropriate to begin with Seymour Martin Lipset, the American political sociologist who set himself the herculean task of trying to compare the countries within what he called "Anglo-American Society." This he defined (without explanation of the countries excluded) as the United States, Great Britain, Canada, and Australia. Lipset began his analysis with a reference to the importance of the work of Max Weber and of the need to make conceptual distinctions. He was convinced that "one particularly effective method for systematically classifying the central values of social systems is a modification of the pattern-variable approach originally developed by Talcott Parsons."[67] Other students of politics had found Parsons' categories useful for analyzing the differences between developing areas and advanced societies. Lipset argued that they were especially appropriate for "highly comparable systems."

Parsons had introduced a number of other categories in addition to the pattern variables noted earlier, observing, for example, that a society could be affective or affectively neutral. Lipset made two important modifications to Parsons' categories. Instead of the affective/affective–neutrality pattern he substituted elitism/equalitarianism. And instead of using the variables as dichotomies he used them as poles: "Although the value patterns are dichotomous, for purposes of comparative analysis it is preferable to conceive of them as scales, along which nations can be ranked in terms of their relative position on each of the pattern variables."[68]

Table 1. Tentative Estimate of Relative Rankings of the Four English-speaking [sic] Democracies according to Strength of Pattern Variables*

	Great Britain	Australia	Canada	United States
Ascription-achievement	1	2.5	2.5	4
Particularism-universalism	1	2	2	4
Diffuseness-specificity**	1	2.5	2.5	4
Collectivity-orientation-self-orientation	1	2	3	4
Elitism-equalitarianism	1	4	2	3

* Ranked according to the first term in the polarity.
** Parsons used only the first two sets of pattern variables in his account of the principle types of social structure (*The Social System*, 181).

Thus Lipset began with categories of analysis that were axiomatic (Step 1). He next proceeded to apply them inductively (table 1).[69]

Lipset began by suggesting that the pattern variables were useful for "systematically classifying" the four countries. It would therefore not be unreasonable to expect him to make such a systematic classification, as proposed in Step 2. But if there are empirical data to support the rankings in table 1 we are not told where they are. Indeed, Lipset admits that his rankings "are based primarily on impressionistic rather than systematically collected evidence."[70] Thus Lipset finds himself, like Parsons, using the very impressionistic approach that as a scientist he deplores. He has moved from empirical verification (Step 2) to impressionistic references (Step 3).

Does he next go on to transform his analytical categories into normative standards (Step 4)? It is difficult to say. He admits that "nations may be ranged in terms of their relative approximation to the 'pure' expression of each of the polar values," but we are given no indication of just what the scale 1 to 4 signifies. It could be that the maximum score obtainable (for the "pure" expression) is ten or even more; if so, none of the countries at all approximates the pure expression of each ideal type. But it seems reasonable to assume that the scale is what it appears to be: a ranking from the bottom (1) to the top (4). If so, then the United States obtains a nearly perfect score, and the American value system stands as the normative model in nearly every instance.

Lipset's definition of the second term in each of the pattern variables appears to be normatively loaded. Thus the American "treats others in terms of their abilities" (i.e., achievement) instead of treating them in terms of inherited qualities, like the British. The American "applies a general standard" (universalism) instead of responding to some personal relationship. And the American relates to selective aspects of another's behavior (specificity) instead of responding to many aspects. Moreover, he gives primacy not to the defined interests of the larger group but to the private needs of others (self-orientation). Finally, instead of emphasizing the general superiority of those who hold elite positions, the American (and even more the Australian) stresses that "all persons must be respected because they are human beings" (equalitarianism). On the basis of such impressions Lipset concludes, "Canada systematically [sic] differed from the United States on all five dimensions, being less egalitarian, achievement-oriented, universalistic, specific, and self-oriented."[71] Lipset supported his judgment with quotations from two Canadian social scientists. These were scholars who were inclined to be continentalist, somewhat American-oriented in their views, and unsympathetic to conservative Canadian mores and the British connection.

It is clear, however, that in ranking societies according to Parsons' categories, Lipset assumes that the American ideal of individual responsibility is the universal pattern variable. Yet one of the traditional European criticisms of the United States (and to some extent of Canada) has long been that they are "bourgeois" societies that have failed to develop politically powerful working-class movements in contrast to those of, say, France or Britain—or Australia. Lipset's explanation of the difference is interesting:

> The two most class polarized nations, Australia and Great Britain, are those in which working class particularism (group consciousness) sustains a sense of political class consciousness. Conversely the two Northern American polities have been characterized by a stronger emphasis on universalism and achievement orientations. Where these values are emphasized, the lower status person is more likely to feel impelled to get ahead by his own efforts and consequently is less prone to accept political doctrines that stress collective responsibility for success or failure.[72]

In other words, for a working man to be oriented towards his own self-interest and to individualism is to be "universalistic." For him to be oriented towards the welfare of other workers as well as himself is to be "particularistic." One begins to sense that the pattern variables are to some extent culture-bound.

Another criticism of both Canada and the United States is that until recently they have failed to attend to the legitimate needs of certain minority groups, notably the French Canadians and the blacks, who have now demanded to be treated as equals. Lipset makes only a passing reference to French Canadians ("In French Canada the dominant conservative clergy feared and inhibited the liberal doctrines of the American and French Revolutions").[73] No reference is made to one of the most prominent features of American society—race relations. Presumably any inclusion of the blacks would have lowered the American ranking on the various scales.

The American value system, in Lipset as in Parsons, is very much that of the self-reliant Protestant frontiersman of the history books. This is not surprising. Lipset compares the societies by a ranking "based on abstracting ideal-typical aspects of the four societies."[74] He then seeks the sources of the value differences of the four in their origins, religious traditions and frontier experience. By and large he tends to describe the United States in terms of its traditional value preferences, i.e., the *ideals* of American democracy. But he draws attention to those *practices* in other countries that confirm his ranking of them. Canada's respect for order and centralization is illustrated by several references to the Royal Canadian Mounted Police, for whom "the respect . . . far exceeds that ever accorded police in the United States."[75] But no reference is made to the Federal Bureau of Investigation, which seems in the past to have been held in equivalent regard in the United States.

Lipset may have been quite unconsciously selective in his use of empirical data, ignoring data that challenged the conventional picture of the United States. The dominant ethos in that country has had little place for the unique character of the Old South ("a deviant case"), for the inferior position of ethnic groups in the cities, or for the segregation of the blacks. It is easy for Lipset to be selective when the term "society" is interpreted to mean not an empirical analysis of the actual society itself, but the assumed value preferences based on the observer's impressions. And once a theoretical framework has been selected one's main concern becomes that of fitting the data into the scheme: one is deductive rather than inductive.

Lipset admits, "It is extremely difficult to verify the assumptions concerning the rank order differences in value emphasis" and finds himself using information from sources (e.g., literary criticism) that would lay no claim to being scientific.[76]

To be fair, however, one must admit that Lipset finds some support for his ranking in certain economic indicators, and that his description of the four countries seems in many ways to ring true. But the crucial point, in the present context, is that once again we find a scientific empiricist choosing pattern variables because of their scientific character, recommending "systematic classification" rather than impressionistic observations, and then being forced to abandon the rules of scientific method. We now see both a sociological theorist (Parsons) and a political sociologist (Lipset) facing the same dilemma.

Dahl's Empirical Approach to Democratic Theory

It seems appropriate to complete our inquiry into scientific empiricism by examining another scholar, the political scientist Robert Dahl, through his chief theoretical work, *A Preface to Democratic Theory*. We shall see if he can tackle the problem of relating analytical principles to actual political systems without succumbing to normative judgments in the process.

The obstacles Dahl encounters in trying to be empirical are truly formidable and his ingenuity in dealing with them admirable. He takes as his starting point neither the notions of traditional European philosophy nor the example of the American political system. Instead, Dahl chooses the democratic ideal, which, however, he does not identify explicitly with the (normative) American ideal of democracy. Rather, he prefers an examination of two American political theories whose inspiration dates from the foundations of the Republic, one of which he calls "Madisonian democracy" and the other "populistic democracy."

As constructed by Dahl, these are not normative but "maximizing" theories: "Madisonian theory postulates a nontyrannical republic as the goal to be maximized; populistic theory postulates popular sovereignty and political equality."[77] They are maximizing in that they state the conditions necessary to attain the maximum achievement of an assumed goal. In other words, we start by defining our goals and then we devise the means of attaining them. Such a theory could be essentially ethical or normative, or as Dahl prefers, ethically neutral, the goals being accepted as given for the purposes of the theory.

Having taken maximization theory as ethically neutral, Dahl decides that it must be more than an axiomatic theory. He seeks an empirical theory. He believes in observing the real world to discover the necessary conditions for maximizing the postulated goal. In other words, he proceeds by asserting analytical principles (Step 1) and then relating these principles to actual practice (Step 2), though without stipulating the need to be rigorously scientific in one's observations. (As we shall see later, he is somewhat ambiguous on this issue.)

Dahl asserts that Madisonian democracy, because it relates to the real world, fits into his construction better than populistic democracy. The goal of a nontyrannical republic can best be achieved by Madison's notion of the separation of powers and the control of factions. Factions cannot be kept under control simply by having elections. The legislature must play its part through majority vote (the "republican principle") and the electorate itself must act (through the creation of numerous diverse interests).

Dahl's difficulty with populistic theory is that its goals of political equality and popular sovereignty cannot be similarly transformed into an empirical theory. He has no empirical referent and so he prefers Madisonian democracy because "whatever its defects of logic, definition, and scientific utility, the Madisonian ideology is likely to remain the most prevalent and deeply rooted of all the styles of thought that might properly be labeled 'American.' "[78]

By contrast,

> . . . the theory of populistic democracy is not an empirical system. It consists only of logical relations among ethical postulates. It tells us nothing about the real world. From it we can predict no behavior whatsoever.[79]
>
> Populistic theory . . . was found to be formal and axiomatic . . . what we desperately want to know (if we are concerned with political equality) is what we may do to maximize it in some actual situations, given existing conditions.[80]

In other words, like the pragmatists, who took the American ideals of democracy for granted, Dahl tempers his scientific approach to democracy by starting from what he calls "the Madisonian ideology." The pragmatists had been content, as philosophers, to proclaim American ideals, which included a dose of populism, if not Rousseau's general will. Influenced by the prevalent scientific empiricism, Dahl feels compelled to adopt only a theory that has an empirical referent. This rules out populist democracy because it "is not an empirical system. . . . It tells us nothing about the real world. . . . From it we can predict no behavior whatsoever." This is a far cry from the pragmatism of Dewey and Beard, and even of Charles Merriam. These were scholars committed to retaining their American ideals. In principle they promoted the unity of theory and actual behavior, but they did not in practice feel constrained to base their theories on the actual American political system. Dahl himself feels he must link theory with practice. But Dahl also finds himself rejecting Madisonian democracy on the grounds that Madison wanted two incompatible goals: political equality and majority rule. He concludes that neither of these maximizing theories is itself adequate.

He therefore suggests an alternative method of constructing a theory of democracy, which he calls the "descriptive method." This involves considering "as a single class of phenomena all those nation states and social organizations that are commonly called democratic by political scientists, and by examining the members of this class to discover, first, the distinguishing characteristics they have in common, and, second, the necessary and sufficient conditions for social organizations possessing these characteristics."[81]

Presumably this involves empirical investigation, but Dahl avoids the scientific empiricists' insistence on the scientific analysis of political systems (Step 2). He does not use the term "scientific" or even "inductive." One cannot tell whether he feels an obligation to study *all* democracies, a sample of them, or just enough to illustrate his point that there must be actual cases in the real world. He continues: "These are not, however, mutually exclusive methods. And we shall see that if we begin by employing the first method it will soon become necessary to employ something rather like the second as well."[82] He begins by employing the same deductive methods he has used for Madisonian and populistic democracy, explaining the necessary and sufficient conditions for democracy both at the election stage and between elections, and incorporating elements of other earlier theories. However, having noted eight conditions of democracy, he has to admit, "no human organization . . . has ever met or is ever likely to meet these eight conditions."[83]

Nevertheless, Dahl has committed himself to using the descriptive method and somehow he must relate his conditions to the real world.

They must be "more or less observable" and so he has to rephrase his question, even at the risk of making his argument still more complicated: "What are the necessary and sufficient conditions in the real world for the existence of these eight conditions, to at least the minimum degree we have agreed to call polyarchy?"[84] In reply, Dahl admits that it would be necessary at this point to "classify and study a considerable number of real world organizations," thus reaffirming the need to proceed from asserting the analytical principles of democracy (Step 1) to relating these to actual practice (Step 2). He then has to agree that, "to carry out this program rigorously is a task far beyond the scope of these essays and quite possibly beyond the scope of political science at the present time."[85]

Having discovered the task of empirical verification to be too difficult, does Dahl then find himself making impressionistic references to selected countries generally considered democratic (Step 3)? We find that he has already made this move in a previous paragraph when, having found that his eight conditions were unattainable, he considered interpreting each of them as a scale along which any given organization might be measured. He then said he could not assign meaningful weights to each of the eight conditions, but if they could be metricized, "it would be possible and perhaps useful to establish some arbitrary but not meaningless classes of which the upper chunk might be called 'polyarchies.' "[86] It was then that Dahl resorted to impressions of what polyarchies looked like in the external world, although it is not clear whether he is empirically defining "polyarchy" or merely giving us illustrations: "Furthermore, 'polyarchies' include a variety of organizations which Western political scientists would ordinarily call democratic, including certain aspects of governments of nation states such as the United States, Great Britain, the Dominions (South Africa possibly excepted), the Scandinavian countries, Mexico, Italy, and France; states and provinces, such as the states of this country and the provinces of Canada. . . ."[87] There is little here of the rigor that supposedly marks the careful empirical analyst. In contrast to his elaborate technical appendixes suggesting modes of measurement, Dahl is quite casual about defining the systems to be measured. "Democratic" is not, according to Dahl, a term applied only after empirical investigation, but is the label used by unnamed "Western political scientists" who may not have been particularly rigorous in their classification of political organizations (which they would "ordinarily call democratic"). We are not even assured that the political systems of the countries listed *are* democratic, merely that "certain aspects" (unnamed) are. South Africa (a possible exception) is included although four years after the book was published that nation was compelled to leave the Commonwealth for continuing its blatant policy of apartheid in defiance of the basic canons of democracy. Nor does the list make an attempt to be inclusive. There is no mention of Switzerland, the Netherlands, Belgium, Ireland, or Finland, not to say of India or Ceylon. Dahl's picture of politics in the world outside the United States seems as hazy as Parsons'. His list, like Parsons', has the appearance of being illustrative, not definitive. But this does not prevent Dahl from concluding that "the first method of constructing a theory of democracy, the method of maximization . . . merges here with what I have called the descriptive method."[88]

But this was as far as Dahl went in applying his "descriptive method" to democracies other than the United States. Like Parsons and Lipset, he was unable to link his analytical principles (Step 1) with rigorous analysis of empirical data (Step 2). Instead, he had proceeded from Step 1 to Step 3, falling back on impressionistic judgments.

The question remains whether Dahl tries to transform his analytical propositions into normative standards of judgment by proceeding to Step 4. He appears to do just this, when he says, "To begin with, each of the eight conditions can be formulated as a rule, or if you prefer, a norm. For example, from the first condition we can derive a norm to the effect that every member ought to have an opportunity to express his preferences."[89] It would seem that by introducing the notion of "ought" Dahl has indeed made the switch from the analytical to the normative.

Dahl himself is less concerned with this dilemma than with the difficulty of confirming his hypotheses with empirical data. He states, ". . . no one has assembled the empirical data necessary for even a preliminary confirmation of their validity. We do have a reassuring amount of quite indirect evidence that agreement on the eight norms is less in, say, Germany than in England, but it seems to me highly arbitrary to leave our crucial hypotheses in such a careless state."[90] This is the only time that Dahl mentions that there is some evidence for the empirical argument he is advancing, but he never indicates what this evidence is. Indeed, at this point, after three pages of impressionistic references to a number of "democracies" other than the United States, Dahl quietly abandons his attempt to apply "the descriptive method" to "all those states commonly called democratic." In the remainder of the book he discusses his eight conditions of democracy with reference for the most part to the United States. Like Parsons, he feels most at home in familiar territory.

When discussing his home territory, Dahl is primarily descriptive, analyzing the "normal" process of American government. This process he defines as "one in which there is a high probability that an active and legitimate group in the population can make itself heard effectively at some crucial stage in the process of decision."[91]

It is useful to recall that we undertook this study of Dahl as an examination of the work of an American political scientist who in the 1950s was a leading proponent of empirical theory. We wanted to see whether, like Lipset, he found it difficult to obey the canons of scientific method in subjecting the field of comparative politics to the criteria of empirical theory.

It was not until the last chapter of the *Preface,* entitled "The American Hybrid," that Dahl's ingenuity in overcoming obstacles began to falter. It was that chapter which led the Cambridge theorist Quentin Skinner to accuse Dahl of making normative judgments, and in particular of actually commending the American system, with all its defects, as though it were a "genuine democracy" of the sort he earlier offered as a theoretical model.

In defense of Dahl it can be said that his critic may have selected one or two comments without placing them in the proper context. Longer extracts would seem to indicate that Dahl's extended comments can be interpreted as being not only commendatory but critical of the American polity:

> This is the normal system. I have not attempted to determine in these pages whether it is a desirable system of government nor shall I try to do so now. . . .
>
> This much may be said of the system. If it is not the very pinnacle of human achievement, a model for the rest of the world to copy or to modify at its peril, as our nationalistic and politically illiterate glorifiers so tiresomely insist, neither, I think, is it so obviously a defective system as some of its critics suggest.
>
> . . . few Americans . . . can fail, at times to feel deep frustration and angry resentment with a system that on the surface has so little order and so much chaos . . . no doubt the normal Ameri-

> can political system is something of an anomaly, if not, indeed, at times an anachronism . . . it often appears to operate in a creaking fashion verging on total collapse.
>
> Yet we should not be too quick in our appraisal, for where its vices stand out, its virtues are concealed to the hasty eye.
>
> Probably this strange hybrid, the normal American political system, is not for export to others. But so long as the social prerequisites of democracy are substantially intact in this country, it appears to be a relatively efficient system for reinforcing agreement, encouraging moderation, and maintaining social peace in a restless and immoderate people operating a gigantic, powerful, diversified, and incredibly complex society.
>
> This is no negligible contribution, then, that Americans have made to the arts of government. . . .[92]

Certainly Dahl was clearly aware of the difference between democratic theory and the actual practice of democracy in the United States. He was, and was to remain, troubled by the contrast between American ideals and American practice: hence his development of the notion of "polyarchy" to describe the American political system instead of the conventional loaded expression "The American Democracy." In such circumstances it is difficult to convict Dahl, as Quentin Skinner has done, of having insisted "that a *prima facie* elitist and oligarchic political system may be properly described as a genuine democracy."[93] In fairness to Skinner, it should be understood that he was making his remarkable and incisive analysis of Dahl's work in the early 1970s when the practice of American politics had reached its nadir. He felt justified in drawing attention as vigorously as possible to the implications of an empirical theory that linked the practice of politics with democratic theory. But it is perhaps going too far to suggest that Dahl's application of the word democracy to describe the United States would seem "to commend the recently prevailing values and practices of a political system like that of the United States." For one thing, the term "genuine democracy" with all its ambiguity, is not used by Dahl. We have quoted Dahl's various comments on the American hybrid at some length to indicate how balanced was his overall judgment. It is difficult to accept Skinner's view of Dahl as a rigorous scientific empiricist who was trapped by evaluative-descriptive propositions into a "false ideological move," commending what he was describing. Dahl was not one of the more rigorous scientific empiricists and he avoided the temptation to commend American democracy for other countries.

Dahl's main concern seems to have been to find an empirical referent that would make democratic theory truly empirical. It was his failure to obtain adequate empirical data about foreign systems that led him to transfer his attention to the United States and to make the judgments he did. In his *Introduction* he makes no references to the American political system. It may seem puzzling that he should conclude his lectures with remarks about the United States, and especially puzzling that he should make normative judgments generally out of character with his empirical approach. After all, the *Preface* was the result of an invitation to lecture "as representative of the empirical school." However, he was also speaking under the auspices of the Charles E. Walgreen Foundation for the Study of American Institutions. He may have felt it appropriate to remember this in his peroration.

It is interesting that Dahl, having begun with a discussion of democratic theory, should find himself spending so much time on American experience. A traditional theorist, uninhibited by the need for any empirical referent, would have been content to compare the merits of Madisonian and populist democratic theory. A truly empirical theorist, committed to the "descriptive method," would have demanded a classification of a large number of liberal democracies in the light of the theories being compared. (Aristotle, after all, compared 158 city-states.) It would seem that, having attempted to use the "descriptive method" to survey a wide variety of democracies, Dahl decided that the task was too onerous.

This tempts one to ask whether it is in fact possible for empirical theorists in the social sciences to practice what they preach and to link theory and practice. Their theories are intended to be part of a universal civilization and to conform to the canons of scientific method. But the practice of politics, even of American politics, is deeply embedded in the particular culture of the state. Even a theorist like Dahl, who begins analytically, soon discovers that there is no way in which he can apply his principles scientifically solely through an exhaustive empirical analysis of data. In the end he cannot avoid using the case materials at hand, especially the politics of his own country, to meet the minimum requirement of linking social theory with social practice. But these "cases" tend to be of limited number and embedded in a particular culture and world view.

Moreover, such is the complexity of social and political systems that it would appear difficult to theorize about politics and society (except within a single system such as that of the United States) without becoming in some sense philosophical. As we have seen, Shils suggested in his 1963 peroration that empirical theory could refine political philosophy. In 1977, Clifford Geertz ended an article with words that echoed those of Shils:

> Political philosophy has always been more a response to the appearance of novel political arrangements—the Greek city state, the Roman imperium, the Renaissance principality, the Enlightenment republic—than a free exercise of systematic reason. Reflections on government need governments to reflect on if they are not to descend into academic exercises. At a time when general questions of justice, equality, liberty and authority are coming back into fashion in the form of deductive theories . . . not the least contribution the study of the New States . . . can make is to rescue such questions from scholastic answers. Whether or not anything comparable to Aristotle, Cicero, Machiavelli or Madison emerges from it we shall merely have to wait and see.[94]

Eulau's American Science of Politics

It is interesting that both the empirical theorists, as evident in the quotation from Geertz, and the pragmatists, do not always include the whole canon of classical writers under the rubric of "political philosophy." Such writers as Plato, Aquinas, Rousseau, and Hegel, whose interest in empirical observation was minimal, or Marx, whose empiricism is controversial, tend to be excluded. In his *Modern Political Analysis,* Dahl's mentors appear to be Aristotle, Max Weber, and Harold Lasswell. The political philosophy that Shils and Geertz hoped would emerge from the study of new states was also expected to be empirical.

Nevertheless, by even raising the question of political philosophy, Shils and Geertz suggest that the social sciences may not be what empirical theorists have assumed them to be, merely immature sciences: they may be of quite a different genre. Certainly the pragmatists realized that while a more scientific approach was desirable, the social sciences were not wholly analogous with the natural sciences. Normative questions, as the scientific empiricists discovered, were difficult to ignore. It was difficult, when constructing a conceptual framework that involved standards against which the performance of particular political systems were to be measured, to avoid stating—or implying—that these standards were thought to be good ones. It was even more difficult to take a diverse, complex, changing political system like that of the United States—or even of Canada—and find out how far it measured up to these standards.

In any event, we cannot ignore the contribution to our understanding made by those nonscientific but "empirical" observers of actual practice who make no pretence of replication, the belletrists and journalists who exercise their imagination and simply paint a picture of society as they see it. However, the problem of relating such practice to theory has yet to be resolved. For any theory, empirical or otherwise, whatever else it may be, must contain a set of logically related propositions. It was no doubt Dahl's inability fully to enunciate such a set of propositions for an empirical theory that led him modestly to call his study "A Preface to Democratic Theory." And one begins to understand why philosophers with a concern for precision were not anxious to accept Dewey's challenge to get out and study the untidy world of man as a social being. They wisely left that enterprise to sociologists and other empirical theorists.

It is of course possible to discern differences in the practice of democracy. Even a casual visitor can sense the difference between democracy as understood and practiced in the United States on the one hand and in the Soviet Union on the other. But to be able accurately to measure and compare the degree of freedom enjoyed by individuals in the United States and a closed society like the Soviet Union according to scientific criteria is surely impossible.

Just as difficult, as Dahl discovered, is the ranking of democracies against one another. If, as Lipset alleges, Canada is more ascriptive and less achievement-oriented in its social behavior than the United States, is this due to cultural lag? Or may it perhaps be due to a different and carefully thought-out world view on the part of many Canadians? What if Canada's more ascriptive society is considered by Canadians, using their own standards, to be in some respects actually superior to the American? How would one go about proving that Canadian standards were not equal to those of the United States?

It is one thing to find that societies are so complex that they are difficult to measure and compare. It is another thing, and a more serious matter, to discover that in the social sciences standards of judgment, even among democracies, vary considerably. Lipset's standards tended to favor the United States. But an inquiry by a Canadian-born scholar, Anthony King, into the greater importance attached to public enterprise and social services in the democracies of Western Europe and Canada than in the United States, concluded that in many instances the United States emerged as the exception to the rule and was placed at the bottom of the scale.[95] King's starting point was clearly very different from Lipset's, since it assumed that a social sensibility was more important than individual self-reliance.

American scholars, as we have seen, have tended not to use measures involving social policy but to employ other standards, for example, self-reliance, that reflect American values and put the United States at or near the top of any scale. This suggests that after all there may be an "American science of politics," a science that works best within an accepted ideological framework. American scholars, whether pragmatists or scientific empiricists, have taken American ideals (although not always the American system) as unproblematic. Yet, as Habermas has insisted in his discussion of Peirce, the distinctive character of a true science is the existence of an uncompelled and permanent consensus about the nature of the scientific enterprise.[96] There is no such consensus internationally.

All this may explain why, despite the enormous effort expended over several decades on comparative political analysis, so little has been achieved in the way of new theory. In his 1976 survey of the discipline of political science in the United States, Heinz Eulau noted that the study of comparative politics was conducted separately from the study of the United States: "The subfield of 'comparative politics' is only rarely thought to include American politics (which for academically parochial and politically chauvinistic reasons is treated as a separate field of study)."[97]

Eulau quoted judgments he had made some twenty years earlier of the discipline, when he said that if ". . . at midcentury political scientists are agreed on anything, it is probably on the muddled state of their science. Political scientists are riding off in many directions, evidently on the assumption that if you don't know where you are going, any road will take you there." He went on to say of these judgments that they "still hold for the discipline as a whole. In fact, from the perspective which I try to represent, the situation may have worsened." But he made an exception for the field called American politics, which "as a specialization has made the most progress toward valid and reliable knowledge."[98] In assessing that field he observed, "The great bulk of these contributions meets the criteria and standards of scientific investigation—science not in some narrow and parochial sense, but in the sense that particular topics or subjects require different forms of scientific inquiry."[99]

The defect of traditional American political science had always been that it was culture-bound, concentrating its attention on American government and politics and treating the United States as *sui generis*. One of the claims of scientific empiricism was that American political scientists could transcend the limitations of American government and examine all systems comparatively, this being the hallmark of a science. For Eulau to conclude that the main success of scientific empiricism was in American politics would seem to indicate that American scholars were being thrown back on the traditional single-case approach.

By stressing the success of scientific empiricism in American politics, Eulau avoided an assessment of the full implications of its failure in comparative politics. He did not feel compelled to question the method of study of scientific empiricists or to consider the possibility that it might be culture-bound after all. In affirming that the great bulk of the work in American politics met "the criteria and standards of scientific investigation," he assumed that the American approach to political science reflected a universal, or at least dominant, civilization based on modern science and technology. That approach was not considered to be the product of a particular American culture.

In sum, it would seem that the attempt to reach out for a genuine science of politics that would encompass the whole world has not yet been successful. Many scholars find themselves resorting instead to some form of Marxism or contenting themselves with the examination of particular countries (usually their own) and their peculiar characteristics. It may be that instead of stressing similarities and searching for empirically verifiable laws, as an earlier generation of sociologists tried to do, political scientists comparing political systems may need to bear in mind the approach of anthropologists like Clifford Geertz whose concern was less with verifiable laws of society than with an exploration of the meaning and interpretation of cultures, cultures very different from that of the United States, the dominant civilization.[100]

Because it reflects the problems faced by many other countries in adopting the methods of American political science, Canada's response to the challenge of scientific empiricism is of more than parochial interest. It also illustrates the perennial problems facing scholars who are peripheral to a dominant civilization. These scholars accept their role as part of the larger civilization, but at the same time they feel they must resist the impact of that civilization when it appears to threaten their culture. It is interesting to see how not only philosophers but social scientists in Canada reacted to Americanization.

2   The Canadian Response to Scientific Empiricism

Macpherson versus Lipset

The Canadian response to the challenge of scientific empiricism seems to have been mixed. In 1954 Lipset wrote a two-part review of *Democracy in Alberta* for the *Canadian Forum*.[101] In the first part he suggested that the book's author, C. B. Macpherson, would have profited more from comparing Canada's experience of one-party democracy with that of a number of other countries than from endorsing socialist values in his analysis and taking Canada's British political tradition for granted. "It is unfortunate that Professor Macpherson, in looking for the explanation for the Canadian political pattern, did not go south of the border for comparison. Had he done so, he might have noted that American politics, unlike Canadian, has a mechanism to contain protest in 'homogeneous' communities within single parties through the primary system." Later on, Lipset went on to say, "Rather he seems to have approached his investigation under the influence of a theory which posited that European and North American democracy developed as the political system most adequate to the needs of an expanding bourgeois class, and that as the capitalist system began to decline that democracy, in the form of alternative governments competing for office, also declined." He challenged Macpherson's class analysis: "The assumption that class is the sole 'real' basis for partisan cleavage is a vulgar Marxist hypothesis that has been refuted time and time again by history."

In the second part of his review, Lipset criticized the book's concluding remarks, in which Macpherson indicated that the "quasi-party" system might one day spread beyond Alberta and become a federal phenomenon with the Liberals playing the dominant role of Alberta's Social Credit Party. Lipset questioned Canada's adherence to British parliamentary government: "As against Professor Macpherson's concept of the quasi-party system as an outgrowth of a declining capitalism or an economically or attitudinally homogeneous society exploited by an outside power force, I would suggest that contemporary Canadian politics should be seen as the product of the failure of British parliamentary institutions to work in a complex North American federal union."

In responding to this critique, Macpherson rejected the attribute of "vulgar Marxist" and pointed out that he had referred to "maturing or mature" capitalism, not the "decaying" capitalism attributed to him. He agreed that the British system of disciplined parties and Cabinet control, maintained by single-member constituencies, created greater problems in Canada. But this did not explain the long predominance of one party. Lipset's own explanation, according to Macpherson, did not explain why Canada had stuck to the single-member, plurality-vote electoral system. He doubted whether the solution lay in the comparative method. "To explain this," he wrote, "requires more than a comparative analysis; it would need an analysis in depth such as I tried to provide for the provincial scene."

In other words, Macpherson insisted on the single-case approach to Canada, much as American scholars did for the United States. In general, his response to what Lipset assumed to be a more scientific and less ideological approach to Canada's problems conforms to the pattern we have earlier described as "philosophical federalism." That is, Macpherson shared the willingness of many Canadian intellectuals to tolerate differing and often conflicting views. Macpherson courteously thanked Lipset for his "stimulating and instructive views" and his "excellent comments on the differences between the Canadian and the U.S. party system." Instead of either accepting or rejecting Lipset's alternative approach he wrote that Lipset's "comparative examination is instructive, but I think that it provides at most a supplement, rather than an alternative, to my tentative explanation of the Canadian party pattern." Lipset's analysis was "a welcome addition" to his own. In those days it would seem a Canadian thought he could combine the European class analysis with the comparative method of American political sociology: scientific empiricism and socialism were not incompatible. In the early 1950s scientific empiricism did not seem to pose much of a threat to Canadian social science.

In the 1960s, the American approach to comparative politics received a warm welcome from a new generation of Canadian scholars. For many political scientists the ideas of Talcott Parsons were mediated by a fellow Canadian, David Easton, and it was easy to assume that the theory being espoused was scientific and universal and not necessarily American. Many students of Canadian government and politics welcomed the publication of a new textbook that based its analysis on Easton's input-output analysis of the political process instead of treating Canadian government as an offshoot of the British parliamentary tradition.[102] Some younger scholars tended to start from the assumption that since British civilization had given way to American civilization, Canada would have to come to terms with this as a fact of life. And since American political institutions were so different from the Canadian parliamentary system it made sense to shift one's focus from government itself to those elements of the political process and political culture—voting behavior, interest groups, elite behavior and the like—where the two countries had something in common.

In making this assumption, Canadian political scientists, like their American counterparts, came to regard (European) political philosophy as less relevant than contemporary (American) political sociology, and to consider the study of political institutions to be the study of "formal" institutions of government rather than the reality of the political process that underpinned the governmental system. Political sociology, comparative politics, and empirical theory were all, it seemed, creatures of a new universal civilization of which the United States was the center. In the 1960s, a time of prosperity, optimism, and university expansion, Canadians were for the most part eager to adopt the newer approaches to their discipline. Just as there was no threat to Canada's identity if Canadian satellites were launched from American rockets, so there seemed no threat to Canadian scholarship if political scientists used the research methods, the computer technology, and the data archives of American survey research.

Yet within a few years there was much less complacency about the impact of American political and social science on Canada. The Vietnam War, the Watergate crisis, and Canada's own problems of national unity caused scholars to see national differences where previously they were concerned with common problems.

Meisel versus Presthus

Twenty years after the Lipset-Macpherson exchange, the *Canadian Forum* published an exchange between two other social scientists, Robert Presthus and John Meisel.[103] Both were political sociologists and both were committed to the methods of scientific empiricism. Presthus taught at York University, Meisel at Queen's. Presthus, an American, had settled in Canada and written a book describing the role of elites in the Canadian political process. Meisel, a Canadian, was, like both Lipset and Presthus, a student of the political process, having produced books and articles on Canadian elections. Like them he was an advocate of opinion research to ascertain popular (and elite) perceptions of the political system.

Presthus's undertaking was difficult and ambitious, involving more than 1100 extended interviews with members of the political elite across Canada. It was the first piece of survey research to examine the widely held view that Canadian politics depended on a form of elite accommodation. But if Presthus expected his reviewer, as a fellow empiricist, to be sympathetic to his study, he was due for a disappointment. Meisel took issue with *Elite Accommodation in Canadian Politics* for what he considered to be serious scientific and scholarly deficiencies.

While paying tribute to the "first major survey-based study of Canadian interest group characteristics and strategies" and its "very rich source of information," Meisel suggested at the outset that the book's conclusions "are not directly supported by the many fascinating data gathered by the author but constitute a philosophical set of speculations closing the book." However, he did not pursue this line of criticism, a line that would have led him into the exploration of the relationship between the scientific method and the researcher's world view. He explained, "It is tempting to dwell here exclusively on the exploration of this ambiguity in Presthus' work . . . but the importance of this work . . . demands that a more nitty-gritty approach be taken and that we focus on its flaws, which are massive." He went on to say: "There are strong grounds for criticizing (1) the theoretical context and research design, (2) the author's analysis, and (3) the way in which the findings are presented."

Meisel dealt with each of these points in turn. He suggested that there was an inadequate linkage between the research findings and the three theoretical perspectives (structural-functionalism, interaction theory, and elite accommodation) offered at the beginning; that there was an unwarranted assumption that large corporations operated through the intermediary of trade associations rather than directly; and that it was unrealistic to treat all groups as if they were equal.

In querying the author's analysis, Meisel said, ". . . I found myself frequently startled by judgments of the author which seemed naive or otherwise unacceptable."

Meisel went on to note further that the book showed little use of the available literature. He also criticized the presentation of the findings, the "indiscriminate piling up of data," the use of two sets of data the results of which were frequently incompatible, the apparent unawareness of certain nuances in French, the use of jargon, and sloppy editing.

In a later issue of *Canadian Forum,* Presthus took issue with the review in an article entitled "Mr. Meisel Stands on Guard: Nationalism and the Academic Elite." He criticized Meisel's

> . . . failure to really engage the basic substantive proposition of the book. As the title, *Elite Accommodation in Canadian Politics,* suggests, interviews with 1,123 political activitists (parliamentarians, high bureaucrats, and interest group leaders) provide considerable support for the thesis that public policy is largely, and with many exceptions, the product of conflict, co-operation, and compromise among this elite, with little participation by backbenchers, by citizens, and indeed by most interest groups, among whom participation is limited to only some one-quarter of the hundreds of groups drawn in a random sample. . . . This interpretation of the Canadian political process was surely known before my research, but I am unable to find any systematic attempt to document it using survey data.
>
> Mr. Meisel leaves the validity of this conclusion and the original, hard-won data that support it virtually untouched.

In his book, Presthus had concluded that democracy in Canada suffered from governmental secrecy, Cabinet hegemony, the weakness of backbenchers and the monopoly of access to government by established groups. Canada was still heavily dependent on immigration for its supply of highly skilled and professional manpower because its elites, reinforced by the parliamentary system, limited access to higher education. "Equally important is the lack of political sophistication and interest on the part of large proportions of Canadians, again reinforced by residues of elitist values, the assumptions of the parliamentary system, and limitations on the opportunity for higher education which is critical in distributing larger shares of political resources among more citizens."[104] In his article, Presthus reiterated his critique of Canadian society, and extended it to the social sciences in Canada: "Very briefly, the reviews can be understood only in the context of certain structural aspects of Canadian society and the social sciences. The primary ingredients include cultural nationalism, anti-Americanism, educational elitism, a bureaucratic ethos which emphasizes conformity, hierarchy, and deferential authority patterns, and the considerable extent to which social science has been a servant of power in Canadian society." Indeed, Presthus went so far as to suggest that the review raised "questions about the extent to which going Canadian values provide an appropriate milieu for the development of an analytical political science."

He contrasted the Canadian response to his work with that of reviewers elsewhere and suggested that educational elitism and deferential authority patterns had made social science in Canada a servant of power in Canadian society. In particular, he cited the limitation that ". . . the criteria of recruitment and mobility have often been ascriptive rather than achievement-oriented."

Presthus went on to ask whether "nationalism may become an easy surrogate for the grinding work required to advance a discipline? Canadian social science today seems dangerously near a position where facts, originality and productivity are not always relevant. Some of its practitioners appear increasingly ideological and provincial, constrained to demonstrate their loyalty to a negative and self-defeating nationalism. . . ."

As a scientific empiricist Presthus did not suggest (except by implication) that Canadians might profit from copying the United States. He assumed his values to be those of a universal social science. In the appendix to his book he wrote: "On the other hand, changes are obviously underway. A nucleus of young Canadian scholars, trained in the most advanced behavioral methods, is beginning to turn its skill to *Canadian* social and political institutions . . . we can expect within the next decade a *risorgimento* in Canadian social and political science, in which the 'new men' will push the field beyond its ideological focus to one of cool analysis."[105]

Presthus himself had arrived at York in 1967, initially as chairman of the political science department. Within the space of six years he had not only raised the money for, and conducted, his interviews across the country but had actually seen the book through the press. One suspects that there were times when he found the obstacles to social science presented by what remained of British civilization in Canada somewhat tiresome: "I suspect that Mr. Meisel's disenchantment also reflects an ambivalence he shares with many Canadian scholars who are torn between the innaposite appeals of the British literary tradition and the language of modern social science. One cannot however discuss the tactics and findings of factor analysis and multiple regression in evocative literary style."

In 1954 Lipset and Macpherson had been able to agree to disagree. Each accepted the scholarship of the other, but recognized that there were fundamental differences of world view: the scientific versus the socialist.

Twenty years later such "philosophical federalism" was no longer possible. It is true that Presthus started with a number of basic assumptions: a preference for the comparative method; an interest in comparisons with the United States and to a lesser extent with other countries, notably France; a desire to emancipate the study of Canadian politics from dependence on the British model; and doubts about the suitability of the Westminster parliamentary tradition for Canada. In fact, Presthus and Lipset had started from similar assumptions.

Meisel, unlike Macpherson, had no recourse to Marxist doctrine as an alternative framework of analysis. He shared Presthus's commitment to scientific empiricism. But he had not employed this method to ask whether Canadian society was undemocratic. He was in no position to produce contrary scientific evidence to challenge Presthus's findings, on which the latter had based his conclusions about the elitist nature of Canadian society. He attacked Presthus by questioning his methods. Presthus, as a committed social scientist, deeply resented the challenge to his methodology, and concluded that Meisel had abandoned the canons of scientific empiricism to defend Canada's elitist society, of which he was undoubtedly a member.

The real issue between Meisel and Presthus was never debated, or at least not directly. Neither disputed the basic facts: both were scientific empiricists. Their disagreement was over values. Meisel, like the Canadian philosophers of an earlier era, was resisting the American challenge to the more elitist Canadian world view. But on this occasion the challenge was never made explicit because of Presthus's own claim to "cool analysis" rooted in the methodology of scientific empiricism, which Canadian and American social scientists had come to accept. The debate never focused on the philosophical assumptions underlying the scientific methods adopted, in particular the view that one's own country could bear comparison with any other, elitist or not. Unable to challenge the conclusion that the Canadian political system depended on elite accommodation, Meisel declared Presthus's judgments "unacceptable" on issues that empirical investigation had not been able to resolve. He questioned these judgments by asking a number of rhetorical questions, for example: "is the Canadian process of elite accommodation shaped mainly by the nation's dual political culture as is asserted, or by the value system and the structure of the economy?" and, how valid is it to speak of "organic societies such as Canada where government has usually been looked upon as a benign presence, contrasted with the anti-government drift of individualistic societies such as France and the United States?"

Meisel and Macpherson were both part of the Anglo-Canadian scholarly tradition, graduates of the University of Toronto and the London School of Economics and Political Science. Presthus and Lipset were products of the American sociological tradition of scientific empiricism; they tended to assume that those who differed from them in method were, in effect, prescientific. Although both Lipset and Presthus were sympathetic to the Anglo-American tradition in its broadest aspects, they touched a sensitive nerve when they criticized Canada's uncritical adoption of the Westminster parliamentary tradition.

Neither Lipset nor Presthus considered the possibility that American society could be examined more critically as a result of his Canadian experience. Yet it was arguable that the abandonment of the Westminster model by the Americans had not enabled them to escape serious social problems, problems that the separation of powers and the primary system had been unable to resolve. And presumably American politics should be examined comparatively by Canadians, much as American scholars have examined Canada. While there were numerous American studies of Canada there were almost no comparable works by Canadians on the United States. In the 1950s Macpherson was able to deflect Lipset's criticism by considering the comparative method to be "supplementary" to his. In the tradition of Canadian "philosophical federalism" he was able to tolerate assumptions different from his own. In the 1970s, what appeared to be a simple disagreement about methodology was really a clash of world views, with Presthus offering Canadians an alternative vision of their country. When the two scientific empiricists challenged each other's scientific credentials they were at the same time defending the world view within which each pursued his own scientific method.

Some years later, Meisel was to reflect on his fascination with election studies and the use of survey research. He explained,

> I was, in short, moving into the orbit of political science as it was developed most massively, although certainly not exclusively, by scholars in the United States.
>
> Drifting towards behavioral political science did not, however, obliterate my belief that the most important phenomenon in politics was the value system of a society and hence its dominant and contending political ideas.

It was this underlying concern with values which explains the passion of the exchange between the two social scientists.[106]

It was of course arguable that in the 1970s Canadian scholars, like the Americans in the nineteenth century, were still at heart colonials, preferring to be ideological and provincial in their approach to scholarship and research. But to some extent, Canadian social scientists were confirming Braudel's thesis that every great civilization knows what to accept and what to reject from outside. Attempts were being made to develop a distinctively Canadian approach to the social sciences.

Certainly in the 1970s Canadian political scientists, like political scientists elsewhere, were moving into new areas. Fears of becoming a scholarly "branch plant" of the United States led some Canadians to turn from political sociology to political economy in which Canadians since Harold Innis had long been pioneers. Some became interested in a European scholarship that was more philosophical than scientific in its approach, for example, phenomenology or critical theory. The increased concern about the future of Canada led to greater interest in the structure that was being challenged. And of course the "territorial imperative" reasserted itself as specialists in Canadian government and politics resisted the notion that their field was best interpreted by students of comparative politics and empirical theory. Donald Smiley suggested a number of possible approaches to Canadian politics, including political economy, neoinstitutionalism and Marxism. He noted that "none of the major explanatory hypotheses recently used in the analysis of Canadian politics—Marxism, the Hartzian formulation, and consociationalism—has emerged from the behavioral movement."[107] His notion that Canadians were at liberty to choose one of several possibilities, but should resist being a miniature replica of the United States, is reminiscent of the "philosophical federalism" of Canadian philosophers.

3 Conclusion

The scientific empiricists envisioned a new world of scholarship, a world in which the scientific method developed for the study of American politics would make a distinctive contribution to the study of all political systems. In their book *Comparative Politics: A Developmental Approach,* published in 1966, Gabriel Almond and his collaborator, G. Bingham Powell, acknowledged the debt of comparative politics to students of American politics: "During the last decade an intellectual revolution has been taking place in the study of comparative government. . . . The study of foreign political systems has been greatly influenced by an earlier revolution in the study of American politics."[108] They went on to express the view that there had been an unfortunate divorce between political theory ("an essentially historical subject matter") and comparative and foreign government ("a formal and descriptive study of the great powers of western Europe"). It was their hope that the new scientific approach to comparative politics would reunite these two fields.

However, as they proceeded to link their theorizing with the empirical world outside the United States they discovered that many of the problems they faced in this enterprise were as intractable as ever. In the process they seem to have developed a new respect for traditional political science with its study of the history of other countries, and for political philosophy with its concern for universal values. By the time they reached their last chapter, "Towards a Theory of Political Development," they had become quite cautious. They regarded "the confusing and often threatening events of the past twenty years" as "part of a challenge to all the social sciences to help men describe, explain and predict the events of social life in order that they may grapple with their problems in a rational manner. . . . We believe that the ultimate test of the strength of a scientific theory is its ability to generalize and predict."[109]

Having asked themselves what might be an appropriate theory for the "tens of thousands of young men of Asia, Africa, and Latin America . . . in attendance at Western seats of learning," they proceeded to recommend neither the study of the revolution in comparative politics, which they had proclaimed in their first chapter, nor even a theory of political development, since "much of such a theory of political development is still to be worked out."[110] Instead, they suggested a "political theory and history which stressed the long and costly struggle in Europe over the development of the state and of the nation."[111]

Almond and Powell did not abandon their commitment to what they considered to be the scientific approach to comparative politics. In their compilation *Comparative Politics: A World View* (2d ed., 1980), of which they were general editors, they encouraged students to take three steps in their analysis of political systems: simple description; then classification of systems; and finally the search for regularities in relations among variables. They still expressed the hope that "with the rise of imagination and logic we can develop theories about social and political relationships."[112] But they did not develop a theory themselves. They noted that the rise of communism and the failure of democracy in the Third World "has shaken Western faith in the inevitability of democracy in history" and "shaken its confidence in the superiority and exportability of its values and institutions."[113]

Instead of producing a theory of their own, Almond and Powell appear to have adopted the stance we earlier attributed to Canadians, that of "philosophical federalism." "Without accepting any particular theory about basic human needs and values, we can say that each of these goods, and others not listed here, have been valued by many people in many societies."[114]

In their concluding chapter they noted the limitations of the seven country studies included in their volume. Each had been written by a different author, and each author had adopted a framework of analysis he found suitable for his system. Almond and Powell contented themselves with a typology of industrial and "preindustrial" nations. They did not explain how they came by this typology, a classification that was further subdivided into nine different categories. Curiously enough, the seven states in the volume were illustrative of only four of these nine categories. Five of the categories were allotted to the "preindustrial" nations—but the three preindustrial states in the book all fell within the same category. Almond and Powell provided four pages of questions to be asked (and presumably answered) by students, and a further nine pages that consisted of a classification index. But they did not proceed further. They gave no instances of regularities in relations among variables (what we earlier called Step 3). The gap between political theory and the study of actual political systems remained as wide as ever.

It would seem that in the last analysis the scientific empiricists who were proponents of comparative politics owed less to the natural scientists than to the eighteenth-century rationalists with their belief in progress, their faith in science and their confidence in the triumph of reason over revealed religion. In the 1970s that faith was shaken. Ideology, particularly Marxism, and to a lesser extent nationalism, had taken the place of rationalism and both Marxism and nationalism (and also religious enthusiasm) were proving to be much stronger forces than many social scientists had expected. Not surprisingly, many of the scientific empiricists now preferred to concentrate their energies on the study of their own political system.

But the study of one's own system, whether American or Canadian, appears to be qualitatively different from the study of other systems. Those who study their own political system (the domestic approach), tend to know their own system better than any outsider who has not grown up within it (and who practices the comparative approach). They also have a sympathetic audience in their own country, one that can easily identify with their implicit philosophical assumptions.

On the other hand, the outsider can draw attention to the limitations of the domestic approach. Foreign scholars have contributed a great deal to the understanding of Canada. Social scientists like Lipset, as Macpherson agreed, supplemented the single-case approach with a comparative perspective. And as Presthus insisted, it is easy for domestic scholars to become complacent, too often accepting a value system that merits dispassionate analysis.

Useful comparisons between foreign political systems are difficult to make in the absence of comparable data, similar world views, and accepted standards of comparison. There is always a tendency for researchers to fall back on their own experience, to the political system they know best, and to use that system (or more often its ideals) as the model, often unconsciously. It has proved easier to make comparisons within a single political system such as the American or Canadian, for which an abundance of comparable data exists at all levels of government, and where, for the most part, there are agreed-on values.

The usefulness of the methodology of scientific empiricism for comparisons between systems has therefore been more limited than was once expected. And, in the United States, despite attempts to be value-free, the basic assumptions about the virtues of the American system as expressed by the pragmatists have often crept back in. In the study of Canada, the differing basic assumptions were for a while obscured by basing discussion on an ideal type that included Canada in a category called "Anglo-American." Here, however, the referent turned out to be not the Anglo-American societies themselves but the United States. Canada was not subjected to strictly scientific canons of judgment, yet it was made to seem somewhat deviant from the norm.

Some Canadians were to respond to the challenge of scientific empiricism by concluding that there was an element of "cultural imperialism" in the effort to incorporate their country into a comparative framework. They were tempted to reject the American example *in toto,* without any serious examination of what the United States stood for. George Grant was one of a number of Canadians who perhaps underestimated the capacity and determination of Canadians to resist the blandishments of "the American Empire." He noted, "of all the peoples on the earth Canadians are least able to understand the process of Americanization: it envelops us as a mist, penetrating every sphere of our cultural, political, social, and economic environment. For that very reason we seem to feel powerless."[115] The sense that American penetration was all-pervasive encouraged many scholars to resist American influence on a broad front, making little distinction between what might be acceptable to Canadians as part of a common civilization and what had to be modified and even rejected because it represented a different culture. As two critics put it, "non-Americans have been concerned about something called American civilization or culture for quite some time."[116]

From an American perspective, Canada itself envelops those who try to understand it in its own, often barely visible, mist. Mackenzie King's much-criticized politics of obfuscation seems in this context to appear not so much an expression of Canadian inadequacy as the expression of the Canadian genius. For King was having to deal with three delicate issues later to be called the three axes of Canadian federalism: the emancipation of Canada from the British Empire; the preservation of Canada amid increasing Americanization; and the retention of Quebec support for Confederation. In dealing with those issues he succeeded in not alienating the British, the Americans or the Quebecois.

The good, gray, bland Canadian, typified by Prime Minister King himself, has been the despair of lively intellectuals. Much of this is camouflage so that he does not present a clear colorful target for well-armed opponents to shoot at. Canadians are perhaps in a way as difficult to understand as the Chinese: they are "inscrutable occidentals" who through quiet but effective diplomacy have met the American challenge in all its manifestations. In the realm of ideas, neither philosophical pragmatism nor scientific empiricism was to prove successful in incorporating Canada into the American mold.

Despite its weaknesses, behavioral science was, and is, an attempt to be truly scientific in the study of political phenomena. But "science" in this context often leads social scientists to those elements that peoples have in common (e.g., voting behavior) rather than to the differences between them (e.g., Canada's two cultures).

It was tempting for Canadians to assume, after the replacement of French and British civilization, that the science and technology that distinguished American civilization would be nothing but advantageous to them. But as we have seen in this chapter, the social sciences were part of culture as well as of civilization. However, just as English-speaking and French-speaking Canadians had come to realize that culturally they were different from the people in France and England, so in due course they concluded that despite their affinity with the neighbors to the south they were culturally differentiated from Americans too.

To American social scientists the behavioral approach made it possible to compare the United States and other societies, using a common frame of reference. To Canadians, the method had its limitations because of its bias toward the universal and against anomalies. They tended, instead, to put an emphasis on the historical, for it was through the experience of a very different history—indeed, in Canada, social histories—that Canadians came to be aware of their cultural identity.

4
Taking Tradition for Granted: English Canada's Attachment to Westminster

Canada's history has often been interpreted in terms of two cultural solitudes: "English Canada" and Quebec. But what has made Canada interesting, and different, has been the interaction of diverse traditions. For example, the majoritarian viewpoint, which seems so natural to English-speaking Canadians committed to the doctrine of parliamentary supremacy, is different from the dualism of most francophones, with their preference for a truly federal system with a constitution designed to protect the rights of the minority community.

So long as Canada was part of British civilization, English Canadians remained attached to the Westminster tradition. This they tended to take for granted.

1   Taking Tradition for Granted

Canadians believed that the peaceful Confederation of the British North American provinces in 1867 stood in marked contrast to the violence that had disfigured the politics of the United States. But with the end of the War Between the States, Americans came to realize that their most intractable problem since Independence, the reconciling of sectional differences, had been overcome—at least in terms of ending slavery, and more, in terms of protecting the Union from secession. In Canada by contrast, successive crises were to make it all too plain that the country's fundamental problem of national unity was no nearer to resolution than it had ever been. At the same time, Canadians did not sufficiently recognize that Canada's capacity to survive as a "peaceable kingdom" owed as much to the imperial connection as to the skill and determination of successive Canadian leaders to make Confederation work. A century later it became apparent that Canada was as far from resolving the relations between English- and French-speaking Canadians as the United States had been in reconciling the interests of Yankees and Southerners in the decades before the Civil War.

The ongoing debate about its identity that continued to pervade Canada not only resulted in a profound unwillingness among its intellectuals to pursue arguments to their logical conclusions (the "philosophical federalism" we have already noted), but also affected the policies of its leaders as they struggled to avoid confrontation and to establish what Lijphart and Presthus have called elite accommodation.[1] The more successful of these, notably Sir John A. Macdonald in the period from 1867 to his death in 1891, and Mackenzie King from 1921 until his retirement in 1948, were masters of procrastination.[2] Despite their assertion of Canada's autonomy, they never forced the pace of decolonization and retained an admiration for British political institutions. Until 1918, Canada was "the eldest daughter of the Empire." Then she became "the senior Dominion." After 1945, Canada played a leading role as a senior member of the Commonwealth. It was customary for English Canadians, and especially those resident in Ontario, to take the British connection for granted. They assumed that their outlook on the world, and not that of French Canadians, represented the Canadian political tradition. After all, it was the British Parliament's British North America (BNA) Act that provided legitimacy for the Canadian political system. This increasingly archaic document was to be strenuously defended by the more conservative English Canadians against those who would replace it by a more modern Constitution. The consensus was that "it has served us well."[3]

In speaking of an English-Canadian political tradition we are of course distinguishing the majority of English Canadians from those French Canadians who did not take the Westminster system of government for granted. We must also be careful not to assume that the four Atlantic and four Western provinces, each of which had its own history, shared all of Ontario's assumptions about the nature of Canada and Confederation. Other Canadians often felt that as the largest of the ten provinces—with a population equal to the rest of English Canada—Ontario exercised hegemony over them.

Even so, French Canadians believed that in politics there was an English-Canadian world view, one that was based primarily on the connection with the United Kingdom. In fact there were different English-Canadian interpretations of this connection; proponents of the various interpretations ranged from continentalists like Frank Underhill (who, as we saw earlier, looked forward to a Canada which accepted its role as an American nation) to imperialists like Arthur Meighen, who as Conservative leader of the Opposition in the Canadian House of Commons in the mid-1920s defended imperial unity and the emblems of this unity that Canada had preserved: ". . . I believe that it has—on ourselves and on the world without—a wholesome effect to see these visible signs of our unity remain, to see our appeal to the Privy Council preserved, to see our power of amendment exercised through the old British Parliament; to see in a word that the British Empire is the British Empire still."[4]

Insofar as there were differences of a territorial nature, these were thought of in terms of federal-provincial conflicts. (Hence, in the famous explanation of how citizens of different nations would write an essay on the elephant, Canadians were said to entitle their contribution: "The Elephant and Federal-Provincial Relations.")

Because the Anglo-American political tradition was taken for granted there was not much interest on the part of most Canadians in exploring the fundamental bases of the political system. There was little political analysis of the very real problems created by the attempt to fuse the Westminster parliamentary tradition with an American-inspired federalism. Instead, Canadians came to pride themselves on their "parliamentary federalism." This, they assumed, had enabled them to reconcile the British and the American political systems.

The Widespread Acceptance of the English-Canadian Political Tradition, 1867-1960

Of the thirteen Prime Ministers who led Canada between 1867 and 1960, eleven represented the English-Canadian political tradition. Only two of the thirteen were French Canadians, and both of them, Sir Wilfrid Laurier (1896–1911) and Louis St. Laurent (1948–57), accepted that tradition's assumptions.

Among these assumptions was the belief that the British Constitution, with its conventions and flexibility, was preferable to the American. Another assumption, not unconnected with the first, was that parliamentary supremacy was and should remain the linchpin of the Constitution of Canada. This meant, to give one example, that the Parliament of Canada and the provincial legislatures, not the courts, should be responsible for civil liberties.

A third assumption was that all change should be gradual. Canada in 1867 was a new nation comprising two cultures: it could not be expected to settle all its problems at once. Given time and good will, Canadians would slowly develop a sense of a common political nationality. Inevitably, they would be drawn away from Britain's orbit, and in due course the imperial tie would give way to Canadian institutions of government and be replaced by the "logic of federalism." This would be made possible by the development of new conventions of the Constitution and by reinterpretation and amendment of the BNA Act. Incremental change would be achieved through consensus, not only in Parliament itself, but in Canadian society.

A fourth assumption was that the Canadian people could elect a Liberal government in Ottawa and Conservative, Cooperative Commonwealth Federation or Social Credit governments in the provinces. While such a situation might stimulate confrontation, it would also help to protect provincial autonomy. It was assumed, of course, that all parties were committed to the preservation of Confederation and that ultimately general consensus would be achieved. After 1936 a more nationalistic party replaced the Conservatives in Quebec, but as a conservative party the *Union Nationale* was primarily concerned with preserving the status quo in Quebec, not challenging Confederation.

After the defeat of the second Liberal French-Canadian Prime Minister, St. Laurent, in 1957, the Conservative Party took power once again, as it had between 1930 and 1935 and from 1911 to 1921. It was during the ministry of John Diefenbaker (1957–63), one of the more pro-British of twentieth-century Prime Ministers, that English Canada's assumptions were first seriously challenged in Quebec, where what came to be called the Quiet Revolution (discussed in Chapter 6), got underway after the provincial election of 1960. Within a few years, English Canadians were to be treated to the spectacle of Quebecois voting overwhelmingly for a Prime Minister, Pierre Elliott Trudeau, committed to a strong, united Canada, and a provincial premier, René Lévesque, equally committed to taking Quebec out of Confederation.

A Divided Majority: Different Assumptions about the Nature of the Tradition

English Canadians have not voted solidly Conservative. Much of the success of Liberal prime ministers in Canada (and after the 1896 election Liberal prime ministers governed the country for most of the time), lay in the willingness of both French and English Canadians, especially in Ontario, to support their policies. We need to remind ourselves, when talking about an "English Canadian" tradition, that English Canadians were politically always a divided majority. Traditionally they were divided into Liberals and Conservatives. While the Conservatives gradually lost the support of French Canadians because of their commitment to the British connection, the less committed Liberals were able to continue drawing support from both language groups.

The attitudes of English Canadians toward the British political tradition therefore varied considerably. Naturally there was much greater support for the British connection in 1867 than a century later. At one extreme were those who were emotionally committed to the connection. One may recall the loyalists who refused to accept the American Revolution and instead emigrated to Canada; the English-speaking pre-loyalists who had settled in Nova Scotia and Quebec before 1775; all those who resisted the American invasion of 1812; Tories like Bishop Strachan who had actively opposed the Rebellion of 1837; and the conservative opponents of responsible government in the 1840s and Confederation in the 1860s. After Confederation there were conservative imperialists who supported British proposals for imperial federation; who persuaded a reluctant Sir Wilfrid Laurier to permit Canadian participation in the Boer War; and who backed Laurier's cry in 1914: "Ready, aye, ready."

The loyalists and imperialists gave way to others who, even after the granting of Dominion status, still remained committed to the support of Britain, especially in times of crisis. These "committed loyalists," as we may call them, such as Arthur Meighen (who supported the governor-general against the Liberal prime minister in the Byng-King controversy of 1926) were just as eager as their forefathers to go to war on behalf of the British Empire in 1939; and their descendants supported Britain in the Suez Crisis of 1956.

Not all members of the Conservative Party were loyal supporters of the British connection. Nevertheless, those Canadians who were emotionally committed to the connection were usually Conservatives and set the tone. These committed loyalists were angered by the apparent indifference of many of their opponents, especially French Canadians, to the need to promote the interests of the Empire. Not surprisingly, as the Conservative Party came increasingly to be seen by French Canadians as the party of *"les anglais"* (a nicely ambiguous expression), it made less and less headway in Quebec.

A second "moderate" English-Canadian perspective, however, predominated in English Canada after the 1830s, except in times of crisis when emotions ran high. This moderate perspective accepted the Westminster model of parliamentary government and took it for granted. Although opposed to the Rebellion, these English Canadians were supporters of responsible government under Robert Baldwin in the 1840s, and Confederation in the 1860s under the leadership of Sir John A. Macdonald and George Brown. They were skeptical about the value of imperial federation for Canada, bent as they were on achieving autonomy within the Empire, and they were unsure about the merits of the British case in the Boer War. But they never doubted that Canada should go to war alongside Britain in 1914 and 1939. As British power declined, those who accepted the Westminster model were not unhappy to see interference by the British government in Canadian affairs diminish. The value of the connection now lay in the continuation of the Monarchy and the continual adaptation of the Westminster system of parliamentary government. The main concern of most English Canadians after the Second World War was an independent Canada, but a Canada that nevertheless took for granted the parliamentary institutions it had inherited from Britain.

A third perspective was that of Canadians who acquiesced in the system. These "acquiescent" Canadians were not at all committed loyalists, and unlike those moderates who positively accepted the Westminster model they did not take it for granted. Among those who acquiesced were those who, for example, were less eager to volunteer for service overseas with the armed forces in the two world wars. Insofar as those who acquiesced in the system saw merit in the Westminster model it was because they identified it with Canada's traditional form of government, not because of its British heritage.

There were in addition some English Canadians whose perspective was more like that of many French Canadians, sharing a certain skepticism about the long-term value of the BNA Act and even of the Westminster model. Their concern was for a Canada that devoted its energies to the creation of a distinctive Canadian society, and not one tied to the experience Canada had shared with the United Kingdom. A few

English Canadians went even further and strongly opposed the British connection. They rejected the BNA Act and the whole Westminster tradition as harmful to national unity.

A United Majority: Taking the Westminster Parliamentary System for Granted

Too much emphasis should not, however, be placed on the divisions before 1960 within English Canada over the British connection. As the saying went, the Conservatives favored the unity of the Empire and the autonomy of Canada, while the Liberals favored the autonomy of Canada and the unity of the Empire. Both accepted a pragmatic approach to problems as they emerged, and both believed in the slow evolution towards self-government: "The preservation of continuities, the respect for tradition and the slow building of precedents moulded Canada's political culture and the country's national character. A progressive political tradition that ensured stability was described as a 'British' inheritance and carried social implications."[5]

In general, in the period before 1960, English Canadians did not question the assumptions underlying the Westminster parliamentary system. Admittedly some were skeptical of its long-run viability, and some simply acquiesced in the system so long as it seemed able to hold Canada together. At the other end of the spectrum, a vocal minority of loyalists remained emotionally committed to the British connection in all its aspects. It was the "Westminster" tradition (whatever that might mean) upon which most seem to have agreed, especially in Ontario. It was in Canada's largest province that the tradition was most clearly articulated—and Ontario's viewpoint was widely assumed to represent the Canadian world view. Canadian historians and political scientists tended to reflect Ontario's perceptions in the same way as their British counterparts reflected those of England.

One of the assumptions that moderate Ontarians made—and others tended to accept—was that all Canadians were committed to the same goal of a self-governing, united Canada modeled on the British political system. The country's gradual emancipation from imperial rule and its transformation from colony into nation was "one of the most venerable themes in Canadian historical literature."[6] By the 1920s the writings of Canadian historians "which treated the Canadian experience as the enlargement of freedom, assumed a teleological cast."[7] It is not surprising that when the political scientist R. MacGregor Dawson published his *The Government of Canada* in 1947, he magisterially introduced the subject under the following chapter headings:

1. Representative and Responsible Government
2. Confederation
3. Dominion Status

Typical of Dawson's approach were statements such as, "The first half of the nineteenth century witnessed the steady economic and political development of British North America, and as the colonies increased in importance and virility, so their dissatisfaction with their government increased also."[8] "Their" government was, of course, the imperial government in London.

By 1949 the Canadian government was able to transform the old imperial relationship into one of equals, partly by statute and partly by convention. The Statute of Westminster, for example, appeared neatly to combine both. It gave authority for full Canadian independence, should it be desired. It left legal authority over the Canadian Constitution, at Canada's request, with the Parliament at Westminster. In practice it gave the Canadian Parliament control over the destiny of Canada, since it made (or was thought to make) the role of the British Parliament in the amendment process a mere formality.

In accepting the Ontario view that all Canadians shared the same goal, Canadians were able to explain any differences that manifested themselves as growing pains in an eminently peaceable kingdom. The various crises of Confederation were glossed over as aberrations, or were ignored altogether. It seemed important not to make too much of the disagreements in Canada's past (to which we shall return), for example, the Rebellion, Nova Scotia's resistance to Confederation, the hanging of Louis Riel and its aftermath, the conscription crises in both world wars, or even the emergence in the 1920s and 1930s of third parties of protest in the West and of nationalist parties in Quebec. It was more useful to see Canada as a whole developing towards political nationhood.

From this perspective, Canada's differences were interpreted as a sign of vitality, of healthy growth. All were minor in relation to the dominant motif: Canada's gradual but inexorable emergence as an independent and great North American power.

Within that framework Canada's development was perceived as having proceeded relatively smoothly. The apparent zigzags in its course could be explained by the metaphor of the swing of the pendulum (which, unless we are to mix metaphors, we should perhaps refer to in the present context as the swing of the compass). In the Parliament of Canada the two main parties alternated in power as the compass swung from Liberals to Conservatives and then back again. The minority in opposition would one day be transformed into a governing majority.

The swing of the compass was also evident in federal–provincial relations. There were periods—for example, after Confederation and after the Second World War—when for a time power flowed naturally to Ottawa, and for good reason. But there were other periods, notably after 1896 and after 1960, when power once more gravitated towards the provinces.

It was the great merit of the BNA Act that it enabled these swings to take place, and yet was able to contain them. It confirmed Canadians in their view that it was the flexibility of the British Constitution, based on conventions, which made Canada's political system so adaptable to change. In the last resort it was Parliament, not the provinces or the regions or ethnic groups, that possessed residual power. As the preferred term, the "swing of the pendulum," implied, however much there might be a swing in one direction the pendulum would swing back again.[9]

In sum, until the 1960s the English-Canadian political tradition was largely taken for granted. However English Canadians might differ over the degree of their commitment to the British connection, they accepted the fact that Canada was formally a monarchy and that its political system was modeled on that of Westminster. They assumed that change would occur gradually and that Canada would continue to evolve, and would do so within the framework of the BNA Act. The doctrine of the swing of the pendulum allowed the political parties to alternate in control of government and permitted periods of centralization to be followed by years of decentralization to the provinces. The belief in the Constitution's flexibility was encouraged by the fact that it was always possible for the BNA Act to be amended by Parliament or reinterpreted by the courts.

English Canadians might be divided on certain issues, notably the nature of the British connection, but they were agreed on others, particularly the desirability of retaining Westminster parliamentary government. They saw no contradiction between parliamentarism and federalism. Yet both the British and Americans believed the federal principle to be incompatible with the doctrine of parliamentary supremacy. One is therefore compelled to ask how Canadians convinced themselves that they had managed to reconcile the two doctrines.[10]

They succeeded because they interpreted what they called "the Westminster tradition" in a variety of ways, some of which were more compatible with federalism than others. And true to their notion of "philosophical federalism," the Canadian equivalent of England's ability to "muddle through," they cheerfully assumed that so long as things worked in practice the principles themselves must have been reconciled. This was expressed in a nutshell as follows: "The Canadian political personality has always been one to grapple with the real issues and avoid unnecessary theoretical decisions."[11] In other words, Canadians were not unaware that in principle there was a contradiction between Westminster's parliamentary supremacy and such federal principles as checks and balances and judicial review. An older generation understood that the contradiction was resolved by the imperial connection: the imperial government preserved Canada's federal system by serving as umpire. Whether this umpire was the British government itself or the imperial Parliament or the Judicial Committee of the Privy Council, it was an umpire *ab extra,* that is to say, it was outside Canada itself.

A later generation of Canadians preferred to ignore the contradictions in principle between parliamentary supremacy and federalism. Instead they came to assume that if the imperial ties were removed Canada would survive because of the inherent logic of federalism. They felt free to concentrate their energies on securing Canada's political autonomy without worrying about the consequences.

So long as Canada remained part of the British Empire, the contradictions were obscured. However, were the imperial connection to be finally abandoned, it was likely that the contradictions would be exposed. One solution to this problem was to preserve the British connection, but to assume that it was merely "formal" and had no imperial connotations. Canadians came to believe that in any given situation it was the right of Canada, and not the United Kingdom, to determine the applicability of the connection. Canadians would therefore always be able to "avoid unnecessary theoretical decisions" (i.e., the reconciliation of two incompatible principles) by continuing "to grapple with the real issues" (i.e., become absorbed with the details of federal-provincial relations).

2   The Westminster Model of Parliamentary Supremacy

The Westminster doctrine of parliamentary supremacy, so widely held in English Canada, distinguished government in the Commonwealth from the political system of the United States. In 1981, when the Attorney General of Prince Edward Island wished to express his opposition to the Federal Government's move to give the courts rather than Parliament the power to interpret its proposed Charter of Rights and Freedoms, he declared (like many Canadian statesmen before him), "The supremacy of Parliament is something this country is built on."[12]

"Parliamentary supremacy" is not as easy a concept to explain in modern Canada as it was for A. V. Dicey when he described the British Constitution of the nineteenth century:

> First, there is no law which Parliament cannot change. . . .
> Secondly, there is under the English Constitution no . . . distinction between laws which are not fundamental or constitutional and those laws which are fundamental or constitutional.
> Thirdly, there does not exist . . . any person or body of persons . . . which can pronounce void any enactment.[13]

In English law parliamentary supremacy meant the Queen-in-Parliament and thus comprised the executive, the legislative, and even the judicial branches of government. It included the House of Lords, which in turn contained the nine Law Lords who formed Britain's highest court of appeal, also known as the House of Lords. The Law Lords also acted as members of the Judicial Committee of the Privy Council, the highest imperial tribunal. In other words, it exemplified the fusion of institutions at Westminster, even if the executive, legislative, and judicial powers remained distinct.

Of course even in Dicey's day there was a sense that what was exercised by Parliament was best described as legal sovereignty. The growth of political parties and the extension of the franchise increasingly made Parliament dependent on the popular will. If Parliament were legally sovereign, then the people were politically sovereign. More recently it has also been argued that in Britain it is not really Parliament as a whole which is supreme but the Cabinet. This may be true—but only up to a point, as any prime minister faced by a revolt within the party or by a determined and unrelenting Opposition soon discovers. During a period of minority government, the power of Parliament becomes obvious even to the general public. We may therefore assume, with the qualification that Parliament is not politically independent of the electorate and the Cabinet, that "parliamentary supremacy" or "parliamentary sovereignty" has long been the most important feature of the Westminster political system.[14]

But why should English Canadians, whose system was also dependent on the federal principle, have been so committed to the British doctrine of parliamentary supremacy? Why did they not realize that the two principles were incompatible? Federalism, after all, involved the distribution of powers between national and regional (i.e., provincial and state) governments in such a way that the regional legislatures in their own spheres were *coordinate* with the national legislature. Each order of government, each legislature, had its powers allocated to it by the Constitution. Parliamentary supremacy, as understood in the United Kingdom, meant the *subordination* of regional legislatures to the national Parliament. For this reason, Parliament at Westminster never allowed federalism to be adopted for the United Kingdom: Ireland, Scotland, and Wales stood in a subordinate relationship to Westminster. For this reason, too, parliamentary supremacy was rejected in the United States as unsuited to a federal polity.

How, then, did Canadians come to regard their "parliamentary federalism" as Canada's distinctive and innovative contribution to political thought? This is the fundamental question to be asked of the English-Canadian world view. It does not appear ever to have been fully answered. One reason for the reluctance even to pose the question has been the fact that the doctrine is not an easy one to explain in the Canadian context. It has many facets, some more compatible with federalism than others. Moreover, it is deeply ingrained in the English-Canadian mind. To challenge it is to question certain fundamental assumptions about the nature of government in Canada.

However, if we are to understand why the contradictions between parliamentary supremacy and federalism have become increasingly acute we need first to understand just what parliamentary supremacy in all its various manifestations meant to Canadians and why it exercised such a profound influence on English-Canadian thought.

Historic Meaning: Emancipation from the Crown

One important reason for examining the doctrine of the supremacy of Parliament is that in Canada, as in England, the doctrine had great historic significance. Parliamentary supremacy was associated with freedom, i.e., with the emancipation of British subjects from the domination of the Crown, a Crown whose center was the Court of St. James—or in Canada's case the Colonial Office—located in Whitehall. As Canadians obtained their freedom from their master in Whitehall, it was Westminster which became their model.

Historically, the term "parliamentary supremacy" was associated with the efforts in both Britain and Canada to curb the authority of the Monarch or her/his representative, preferably without violence and without the need to change the form of the system. It is not surprising that in English Canada especially there should have been opposition to any violent or revolutionary solution. There was no republican experience as there had been in seventeenth-century England soon after the first American colonies were founded. Moreover, when the Tories left the American colonies for British North America they were of course colonists loyal to the Crown.

Even so, there was disappointment on the part of those American loyalists who moved to Canada and discovered that there was no Legislative Assembly of the type to which as Americans they were long accustomed. In 1791 the British government divided Canada into two provinces and established two legislatures, one for the English-speaking settlers in the new province of Upper Canada (after 1867 to be called Ontario) and one for the French Canadians and English minority in Lower Canada (after 1867 once more known as Quebec).

A later generation of historians was to call the era after 1791 the era of "representative government," in other words, the first step in Canada towards parliamentary supremacy. It was a nice touch, because in fact all the term really meant was that the colonies, including the colony conquered from the French, now possessed assemblies that could air their grievances and exercise limited powers of finance and legislation. It was no better than the system against which the American colonies had rebelled in 1775. (Nova Scotia had possessed such an assembly since 1758.)

"Representative government" was a particular misnomer for the two Canadas. Here the British authorities were under the impression that the lesson to be learned from the American War of Independence was that more, not less, Crown authority was essential for colonial rule. In both Canadas executive power lay with an imperial governor assisted by an executive council of men he appointed to administer the province. To offset the Legislative Assembly there was a Legislative Council consisting of men appointed by the governor for life. It took a rebellion in Upper Canada in 1837 and a series of serious uprisings in Lower Canada in 1837 and 1838 (collectively known to posterity in English Canada as the Rebellion of 1837) to convince the British government that their attempt to impose tight imperial rule, supported by a local oligarchy, was unworkable.

The British proceeded to follow the suggestions made by the Governor-General, Lord Durham, who had been sent out both to administer the colonies and to report on their condition. In 1840 the two Canadas were reunited as a single Province of Canada in the hope that the expanding English-speaking population of Upper Canada would soon outweigh, and perhaps assimilate, the predominantly French-speaking population of Lower Canada.

Durham's Report made it clear that the British government still regarded Canada as having cost "a vast expense of blood and treasure" and the British North American colonies as being able to provide compensation. The colonies, he wrote, ". . . are the rightful patrimony of the English people, the ample appanage which God and Nature have set aside in the New World for those whose lot has assigned them but insufficient portions in the Old."[15]

Durham's hope that Canada would become an English-speaking country was never realized: Within a few years another governor general was reading the Speech from the Throne in both English and French. But the Durham Report did outline a strategy for an evolutionary approach to self-government very different from the American experience. Reformers in both English and French Canada were able to seize on this proposal and to cooperate in demanding that "responsible government," as it was quaintly termed, be granted.

The British did not at first follow up on Durham's proposal to give the Province of Canada (which he assumed would be firmly under British control) responsible self-government. Nevertheless the so-called "Family Compact" of appointed officials who had helped the Governor of Upper Canada to rule the province, and the "Chateau Clique" in Lower Canada, lost their political power. The new governors turned to more moderate and representative leaders in both sections of the Province of Canada, known officially between 1841 and 1867 as Canada East and Canada West. Yet while the Act of Union of 1840 might replace the Constitutional Act of 1791, only historians of the Union period were to refer to Canada East and Canada West. The old terms retained their favor until Confederation and beyond. (There are still an Upper Canada Law Society and two private schools named Upper Canada College and Lower Canada College.)

Memories of the Rebellion were much shorter. When twentieth-century historians and political scientists came to eulogize the transformation of "representative" into "responsible" government, they said little about the Rebellion. Chester Martin, professor of history at the University of Toronto, ignored the rebellions in his *Empire and Commonwealth* (1929). They appeared to him "as unfortunate aberrations in an otherwise steady evolutionary pattern."[16] The sole reference to the Rebellion in the index of R. McG. Dawson's textbook *The Government of Canada* is to a page where one may read: "The story of the fight for responsible government in all its aspects, the rebellions in Upper and Lower Canada, the more restrained yet equally effective tactics in Nova Scotia . . . cannot be discussed in these few pages."[17]

Like Martin, Dawson preferred to dwell on the transformation from representative to responsible government. He devoted three pages to the Durham Report, which recommended this form of government. The rebellions were simply not part of the mainstream of the English-Canadian tradition.

Once memories of the rebellions began to recede in the 1840s, the British government took the next and most crucial step. Having granted representative institutions in 1791, and having abandoned the local oligarchies that effectively ran the provinces for nearly half a century, the British agreed to meet the Canadian demand for "responsible government" throughout British North America in 1848. This meant that the ministry henceforth would be responsible to the legislature and not to the Crown. Parliament and not the Crown was to be supreme.

English Canadians were for the most part satisfied that domestically they now enjoyed the blessings of the Westminster system of parliamentary government rather than colonial rule by a governor and his appointed executive council, aided by the appointed legislative council. The Canadian legislature styled itself the Parliament of Canada even before 1867. In some ways 1848 was to Canadian reformers the equivalent of 1688 for their English predecessors. Robert Baldwin, the staid Anglican lawyer who led the Reform forces in Upper Canada, was the Canadian equivalent of an English Whig. He believed that power now lay with a Parliament representing the people, not with the Crown.

There was not much evidence in the Canada of 1848 of the turmoil that made the year one of revolutions in Europe. Indeed, the transfer of power, already announced the year before, appeared to vindicate the Reformers in their decision a decade earlier to oppose the Crown but not to engage in armed rebellion. The Canadian expression "responsible government" was a wonderful euphemism for the same kind of self-government that the Irish less felicitously called "Home Rule." For the British to reject the Canadian proposal could after all be interpreted to mean that they favored irresponsible government.

Even so, 1848 proved to be a milestone in both Canadian and Imperial history. Much of Britain's First Empire had dissolved in violent revolution. The Second Empire was to be peacefully transformed into a Commonwealth by evolution. Loyal Canadians were henceforth to believe that they could continue indefinitely to obtain by negotiation what it had taken the Americans a War of Independence to achieve.

After 1848 the next important event in the constitutional development of Canada was, of course, Confederation. Not surprisingly, during the negotiations and debates of 1864-66 that led up to the British North America Act of 1867, the suitability of the Westminster system of parliamentary supremacy was taken for granted. It was unnecessary, it seemed, for Canadians to look forward to the day when they would declare their independence—or to involve themselves in the search for a better political system that might, like the American, proclaim itself "a government of laws, not men."

Indeed, one of the underlying reasons for Confederation was that Canadians wished to avoid being absorbed into the United States. The French-Canadian leader, Sir E. P. Taché, is reported to have said in the debates on Confederation, "If we desired to remain British and monarchical, and we desired to pass to our children these advantages, this measure . . . was a necessity."[18] In other words, Canadians not only rejoiced in the principle of parliamentary supremacy but also did so within the context of an unbroken link with the British Empire. The British North America Act stated in its Preamble that "the Provinces of Canada, Nova Scotia, and New Brunswick have expressed their Desire to be federally united into One Dominion under the Crown of the

United Kingdom of Great Britain and Ireland, with a Constitution similar in Principle to that of the United Kingdom." This made clear the monarchical character of the new Dominion (which some would have preferred to call the Kingdom of Canada), its parliamentary system of government, and its federal basis. The second paragraph, which implied a limit to the extent of Canadian parliamentary supremacy in the direction on the one hand of the provinces and the other of Britain's own interests, was glossed over and less often quoted: "And whereas such a Union would conduce to the Welfare of the Provinces and promote the Interests of the British Empire."

The preference for the Westminster model of Crown and Parliament over the American republican system of a President and Congress dependent on the will of the people is comprehensible in the context of the 1860s. The British Empire was at its height under Queen Victoria: the American Republic, emerging from a terrible civil war, was at its nadir. The very notion of a republic offended those who cherished Canada's loyalist tradition; Jacksonian democracy appalled the Canadian elites engaged in bringing about Confederation; and the exercise of States' Rights by the Confederacy until the Civil War restored the Union and its central government suggested a fundamental flaw in the American federal system. English Canadians were therefore willing to accept the view that there should be a strong central government in Ottawa based on the principle of parliamentary supremacy. Curiously enough, parliamentary supremacy in the form of responsible government had not been a great success in the old Province of Canada, where there had been constant deadlocks among the various parties. It seems to have been assumed that it would work better in the new federal Parliament because with the addition of the Maritime provinces and the grant of extra seats to Ontario, French Canadians would definitely be in a minority. Moreover, it was hoped that issues that had caused such irritation in the old legislature would henceforth be local issues to be handled at the provincial level in the new provinces of Quebec and Ontario where each "race" enjoyed a majority.

The Supremacy of the House of Commons

In both England and Canada, the Westminster tradition came to involve more than parliamentary supremacy over the Crown. By the end of the nineteenth century it was becoming clear in England that the House of

Commons was going to establish its firm ascendancy over the House of Lords: in Gladstone's words, the Lords were to be "ended or mended." After the Parliament Act of 1911, the term "parliamentary supremacy" would mean for most practical purposes the supremacy of the House of Commons. But in 1867 the House of Lords was still a powerful body. The Colonial Secretary, Lord Carnarvon, was himself a member of the upper house.

Although something analogous to the House of Lords had been proposed for the Canadas in 1791, the proposal was never implemented. Instead the upper houses were called legislative councils and consisted not of hereditary peers but of members appointed for life. After the Act of Union a legislative council was appointed for the Province of Canada, but it lacked the power of its predecessors. From 1856 its members were elected, not appointed.

From the beginning, the proponents of responsible government argued for ministerial responsibility to the lower house alone. Not surprisingly, then, when the various colonies of British North America obtained responsible government in 1848 they took it for granted that the ministry was responsible solely to the Legislative Assembly, not to the Legislative Council as well. The upper chamber was associated in their minds with colonial rule and as such should play no part in the making and unmaking of governments.

After 1867, the same principle of lower house parliamentarianism was applied when the House of Commons replaced the old Legislative Assembly and the Senate took the place of the Legislative Council. Consequently, the Senate did not acquire the status and power of the American Senate, or even of the House of Lords in those days. The Senate was soon recognized to be a fairly innocuous body. While in Europe debate continued over the composition and role of upper houses, Canada seemed to have resolved the problem of a second chamber by simply assuming that a powerful upper house was incompatible with responsible government.

Why then should there have been an upper house at all? For one thing, there was concern in the Canadian legislature about the spread of democratic ideas. By the 1860s the franchise for the lower house in many Western countries was having to be widened. Other countries that were establishing new legislatures at that time created second chambers whose members had to meet certain property qualifications. Canada was no exception. In Sir John A. Macdonald's inimitable phrase, "the rights of the minority must be protected, and the rich are always fewer in number than the poor."[19]

"There must be," said George-Etienne Cartier, speaking on behalf of the conservative French-Canadian majority in the Legislative Assembly, "a power of resistance to oppose the democratic element."[20]

For another thing, the alternative to the upper house was a single house representing Canadians solely by population. While many Upper Canadians favored such "Rep. by Pop.," the Lower Canadians (and Maritimers) were opposed. Hence the decision to establish a Confederation. As George Brown, the Upper Canadian Liberal leader put it to the Legislative Assembly of Canada; "Our Lower Canadian friends have agreed to give us representation by population on the express condition that they could have equality in the Upper House. On no other condition could we have advanced a step."[21]

It was agreed that each of the regions or divisions of Canada should be equally represented. The Maritimes, Quebec, Ontario, and later the West, were each allotted 24 seats. Sir John Macdonald, who had favored a legislative union, and who often referred to the provinces as "local governments," admitted that there was a need for an upper house to represent provincial and sectional interests.[22]

Yet there seems to have been an understanding that the Senate, representing the federal principle, should never be allowed to undermine the principle of parliamentary sovereignty in the sense of the supremacy of the House of Commons, the house to which the ministry was alone responsible. Moreover, the American experience, where a powerful Senate had contributed to the disintegration of the Union, had a powerful effect on the minds of Canadians as they created their own union.

It has been suggested that creation of the Senate may have been merely a ploy by Upper Canada to lure the other provinces into a federation that it would dominate.[23] But it is doubtful whether the politicians of the future Ontario were quite so unscrupulous, or those of the other provinces so naive, as to justify such an interpretation.

The most plausible explanation for the creation of a Senate that proved to be relatively impotent is probably the most obvious one. The British North American politicians wanted provincial as well as popular representation in Parliament. But they had resented the veto power of the pre-1837 Legislative Councils, and had grown used to responsible government being interpreted to mean responsibility to the lower house alone. It was not worth sacrificing this principle, won only in 1848, and especially not if it meant the possibility of the deadlock that had plagued the Canadian legislature since 1840 or the disaster that had overtaken the United States. The Senate, after all, was conceived by English Canadians primarily as a bulwark of provincial conservatives against the radical democratic tendencies of the time, and this function it performed satisfactorily.

Moreover, as F. A. Kunz has pointed out, Canadians were able to find alternatives to a US-style Senate to ensure the protection of provincial interests.[24] There was no single president, but a Cabinet. From the beginning the Cabinet represented in its various members all the regions of the country. This proved to be an important Canadian gloss on the principle of Westminster parliamentarianism. Secondly, provincial rights were written into the BNA Act, and the interpretation of these provisions remained with the Judicial Committee of the Privy Council which could, it was hoped, protect the provinces' interests.

Twenty years after Confederation, when the hanging of Louis Riel suggested to the French Canadians that Confederation had not sufficiently protected their interests, two other alternatives to a powerful US-style Senate began to emerge. The first was the embryonic Federal-Provincial Conference. Here the prime minister and the provincial premiers met as partners (and as adversaries), each defending his constitutional rights. The second was the use of provincial governments to further provincial interests. The ability of French Canadians, and indeed of all Canadians, to vote into power, at the provincial level, a party opposed to the party in power in Ottawa was to cause tensions that became a part of Canadian life. In 1887 Quebec elected a Liberal provincial government opposed to Macdonald's federal Conservatives, and a new Quebec premier, Honoré Mercier, who was largely responsible for the first Federal-Provincial Conference.

The Senate could never have become a powerful body. Senators, after all, were appointed, and appointed for life, by the Prime Minister of the day. They therefore lacked the electoral base of American senators. Unlike members of the House of Lords, they lacked the charisma that attached to inherited titles (although after the Life Peerages Act of 1958 the appointment for life of politically active members caused the Lords to be more akin to Canadian senators).

It is true, as we shall see, that in the 1970s a concern developed in Canada for a more powerful upper house representing provincial interests, and perhaps replacing Federal-Provincial Conferences. English Canadians did not recognize the need for such a Senate in the 1860s. In establishing Confederation, despite the adoption of the American term "Senate" neither the Canadians nor the British were emulating American federalism. Canada retained a constitution similar in principle to that of the United Kingdom—one where government was responsible primarily to the House of Commons. There were concessions to the federal principle, but this principle was to be upheld not by a Canadian body such as the Senate but by the imperial authorities themselves. Insofar as Canada was to be federal, it was to be as an imperial federation under imperial auspices.

Legislative Supremacy, Federal and Provincial

One can readily understand how important historically the doctrine of parliamentary supremacy over the Crown must have been in Canada as part of the colony's attempt to secure self-government. One can even understand the emphasis on lower house supremacy and the reluctance in 1867 to grant the Senate more powers, even if this reduced regional representation in the legislature. But how was parliamentary supremacy to be reconciled with the existence of autonomous provincial legislatures in a federal system, a system where the likelihood of conflict between the two orders of government was very considerable?

Once again we need to remind ourselves of the impact of the Westminster tradition on English-Canadian perspectives. The victory of Parliament in the seventeenth century was won not only over the Crown but over the courts. Parliamentary supremacy therefore also meant the supremacy of the legislative branch over the judiciary. In the early years of that century, before the battle was fully joined between Parliament and the King, the English Courts, led by the redoubtable Chief Justice Coke, had fought against the extension of the Royal Prerogative, including the use of Prerogative Courts, for example, the notorious Star Chamber, as rivals to the common law courts.

Coke had also defended the common law against Parliament, arguing in Dr. Bonham's case (1610), "And it appears in our books, that in many cases, the common law will controul Acts of Parliament, and sometimes adjudge them to be utterly void. . . ."[25] Once Parliament had defeated the Crown, the courts in turn succumbed to Parliament's overriding authority. The notion of parliamentary (or legislative) supremacy meant that the courts were never to pass judgment on the validity of parliamentary statutes as being repugnant to the common law. Parliament could not be declared to be acting unconstitutionally or *ultra vires,* to use the English term. As supreme body, Parliament, which in law was called the King-in-Parliament to preserve the notion of the fusion of powers, was entitled to pass whatever legislation it wished. It was the courts' responsibility to clarify and interpret legislation, but to do so as narrowly as possible. There was to be no attempt to construe the Constitution broadly after the manner of the American Supreme Court (although in practice some interpretations proved broader than others).

The doctrine of legislative supremacy over the courts was taken for granted in Canada from the time courts were established. The BNA Act did not change this principle. All that happened in 1867 was the division of the legislative power between two orders of government, which between them retained the full power of legislative supremacy. Because of what was called "the exhaustive distribution of power" among the various legislatures, the courts had no greater field for independent action than before. This Canadian "legislative supremacy," while different from Britain's "parliamentary supremacy" was nevertheless considered to exemplify the same principle of parliamentary sovereignty. "Federalism, whether Canadian or otherwise, is inconsistent with the existence of one omnicompetent legislature like the United Kingdom Parliament. Nevertheless, the notion of parliamentary sovereignty is a pervasive element of Canadian constitutional law."[26] In this context it meant legislative supremacy over the courts.

Indeed, it has often been argued in Canada that the doctrine of parliamentary supremacy over the courts has been upheld by the courts themselves. During the case that led the Judicial Committee to declare that Canada's abolition of criminal appeals to the Privy Council in 1933 was proper, Lord Sankey observed, according to Cheffins and Tucker, that "the Dominion Legislature was supreme and endowed with the same authority as the Imperial Parliament, within the assigned limits of subject and area, just as it was said in *Hodge v. The Queen* that Section 92 of the Act had in regard to the provincial legislatures."[27] Cheffins and Tucker later summarized the situation in the United Kingdom and Canada as follows: ". . . in the United Kingdom the Courts and the Executive are all, in legal theory, totally subordinate to the will of the United Kingdom Parliament, or, in Canada, to either the Federal or Provincial Legislatures if acting within their proper spheres."[28] It is interesting that they did not pursue the full implications of the expressions "within the assigned limits of subject and area" and "if acting within their proper spheres." These terms clearly indicated that both Canadian orders of government were in a subordinate position to some external authority, namely the BNA Act.

One might perhaps have expected the doctrine of legislative supremacy within Canada, and within the limits set by the BNA Act, to be treated as of lesser significance than the overriding parliamentary supremacy of the British Parliament, which alone possessed the general power to amend the BNA Act itself. But the role of the British Parliament as umpire *ab extra* came to be treated simply as an exception to the rule that the legislative power was exhaustively distributed between the Parliament of Canada and the provincial legislatures. For example,

> There are some exceptions to the general rule that legislative power is exhaustively distributed. A few powers are withheld from both the federal Parliament and the provincial Legislatures. The most obvious withheld power is a general power to amend the B.N.A. Act itself. That power continues to reside with the United Kingdom Parliament . . . most of the B.N.A. Act is in fact amendable by ordinary legislative action; the sections distributing legislative power are the principle provisions which remain protected.[29]

Nor was this legislative supremacy of the federal and provincial legislatures thought to be unduly modified by the need for another umpire *ab extra* to adjudicate between the federal and provincial governments— the Judicial Committee of the Privy Council. So firmly was the doctrine of parliamentary supremacy held that the role of judicial review could also be treated as of lesser significance.

> The gaps in Canadian legislative powers are not, individually or cumulatively, very significant. For most purposes, the Canadian Parliament and Legislatures, acting within the bounds of the B.N.A. Act, enjoy powers of the same order as the United Kingdom Parliament at Westminster. Whatever can be done at Westminster can be done in Canada, either by the Canadian Parliament or the provincial Legislatures. This means that the scope of judicial review in Canada is almost exclusively confined to enforcing the federal distribution of powers.[30]

Parliamentary supremacy, then, was reconciled with federalism in Canada by emphasizing the analogy with Westminster, by stressing the exhaustive distribution of powers between the two levels of government, and by limiting "judicial review" to the narrow area of interpretation of legislation concerned with the distribution of powers. Furthermore, the function of "judicial review" was itself carried out in Whitehall by the Privy Council.

Majority Rule

Another assumption made by proponents of parliamentary supremacy was majority rule. Parliament and provincial legislatures could not only legislate untrammeled by the courts, but could make their will felt so long as a majority of legislators were prepared to vote for a policy (even if a majority of voters had shown a preference for the opposition parties, as happened in Britain when a strong Labor government took office after the election of 1945).

Majority rule was based on the belief that the minority could always come into power through the natural swing of the political pendulum. In practice, of course, the "minority" meant the Opposition in the legislature, not those numerous minorities that did not identify with either party and that could never themselves hope to become the majority voice. Nevertheless it was assumed that in time such minorities would learn to associate their interests with one party or another. When the party it supported was in power each minority was assumed to have sufficient influence to make its voice heard.

Majority rule could work to the disadvantage of permanent minorities in Canada. It could also limit the freedom of the individual since, as we have seen, before 1960 no area of individual activity was protected by a Bill of Rights against invasion from one or another level of government. Consequently, despite the protection of the common law, the courts might not always be able to support the rights of the individual.

There was more to the doctrine of majority rule than the belief that a swing of the political pendulum would bring the Opposition to power and would right past wrongs. There was also an assumption that the legislature had moral sensibilities that would prevent the majority from misusing its power.[31] It was assumed that at "Question Time" private issues could be raised by individuals through their members and that the Minister responsible would take action so that the whole machinery of government could be made to work in an individual's favor, thanks to the intervention of the Member of Parliament (MP) or the Member of the Legislature Assembly.

Majority rule meant a government of men (and later a few women) as well as a government of laws. It assumed that there could be speedy and cheap political redress of wrongs that could be righted elsewhere only by a slow and expensive legal process. Supporters of majority rule were convinced that the legal redress provided by a Bill of Rights entrenched in the Constitution and upheld by the courts was no substitute for action on behalf of an elector by an MP.

Supremacy of the Parliament of Canada over the Provincial Legislatures in Times of Crisis

To suggest that the Parliament of Canada was supreme over the provinces was objectionable to most English Canadians. It was, after all, a constitutional tenet stated in the BNA Act, and ingrained in the minds of Canadians, that the provinces were part of a federal system. This meant that certain powers, notably those enumerated in Section 92, belonged exclusively to the provinces. At no time did the Parliament of Canada expressly attempt to take these powers to itself by requesting an amendment to the Constitution.

It is true that the Parliament of Canada, unlike the American Congress, possessed residual power. This meant that it could legislate in all areas not expressly assigned to the provinces. The beginning of Section 91 empowered Parliament to "make laws for the Peace, Order and good Government of Canada." However, Parliament was limited in its activity by decisions of the Judicial Committee of the Privy Council, which restricted the scope of this clause. For example, in the *Aeronautics* case (1932) the Judicial Committee ruled that while the powers of Parliament enumerated in Section 91 were of paramount authority, the general power to make laws for peace, order, and good government must not touch on the subjects enumerated as provincial in Section 92. In his judgment, Lord Sankey described the BNA Act as a great constitutional charter and insisted that the Judicial Committee should not allow "general phrases to obscure the underlying object of the Act, which was to establish a system of government upon essentially federal principles."[32] The Judicial Committee feared that a blanket endorsement of this residual power would enable the federal Parliament to legislate in areas of provincial jurisdiction, thus in effect destroying the federal system.

Moreover, unlike the American Supreme Court, which allowed Congress broad powers of regulation over interstate commerce, the Judicial Committee gave a narrow interpretation to the Canadian Parliament's power in respect of the "Trade and Commerce" clause of the BNA Act. Conversely, it gave a broad interpretation of the provinces' powers over property and civil rights.[33]

An exception was made in times of crisis. Many English Canadians—and the courts—were prepared on occasion to allow Parliament sweeping powers of legislation in what seemed to be the national interest in moments of crisis. (Indeed, by the end of the 1970s, at least one authority had concluded that the use of the emergency power had assumed such significance that it could even be termed "Canada's other constitution.")[34] In other words, Parliament was ultimately paramount over the provinces, but only in situations where the integrity of Canada was threatened.

The residual power was to be used if any group or province attempted to undermine the integrity or unity of Canada by resorting to force. Parliament could invoke the emergency power "in time of real or apprehended war, invasion, or insurrection," thus ensuring the "peace, order, and good government" of the country. Such a power was taken for granted in Britain where of course the doctrine of parliamentary supremacy (exercised, for example, in Ireland) was not limited by the rules governing a federal system. If frequently used in Canada, however, it could significantly limit the federal character of the state.

3 Limitations of the Westminster Model: The Power to Amend the British North America Act

The general power to amend the BNA Act was legally the prerogative of the Parliament of the United Kingdom. However, in practice this general power of amendment was never exercised by the British authorities except on the initiative of Canada. Moreover, specific parts of the Act could be changed without any consultation of Westminster at all. From the beginning, the legislature of each province was given the exclusive power to amend its own provincial constitution "notwithstanding anything in this Act" by Section 92.1. An example of the provinces' right to change their constitutions was the decision of the Ontario legislature in 1960 to extend the maximum duration of the Legislative Assembly from the four years laid down in Section 85 to five years.

One of the most controversial issues in Canada was the nature of Canada's role in the general amending process. Despite its doctrine of parliamentary supremacy, until 1949 the Parliament of Canada enjoyed no right comparable to that of the provinces over their constitutions, generally to amend the Constitution of Canada. It could merely request that an amendment be made. One of the first controversies was over the right of Parliament to be consulted at all. For a number of years after 1867, the government of Canada sometimes approached the British authorities on its own initiative. To demonstrate its displeasure, the Canadian House of Commons in 1875 voted on the motion, "And this House is of opinion that no changes in the provisions of the British North America Act should be sought for by the Executive Government without the previous assent of the Parliament of this Dominion."[35] The Liberal Prime Minister, Alexander Mackenzie, seconded the motion and it was passed 136–0. Yet it was to be another twenty years before the last instance occurred when the principle of obtaining parliamentary sanction was violated. Even after 1895, all that the Parliament of Canada was entitled to do was to present a joint address of both houses to the Parliament of the United Kingdom requesting that an amendment be passed.

It is not certain that the British government itself had by then come to recognize its limitations in dealing with Canada. Writing to Charles Stewart Parnell in 1889 about the role of the Westminster Parliament should Irish home rule be granted, Mr. Gladstone asked, "Shall there be a clause explicitly reserving the supremacy of Parliament over Ireland in common with the rest of the Empire?"[36]

Interestingly enough, no such explicit clause was put into the BNA Act, nor was one necessary. In practice the British Parliament always acted on a request from Canada. Moreover, it never acted unless requested to do so by the Parliament of Canada. It never acted on the request of a province. These seem to have become accepted British conventions by the turn of the century. The Government of Canada came to assume that its Parliament alone had the power, in practice, to amend the Constitution of Canada.

Less clear was the Canadian convention whereby the Parliament of Canada consulted the provinces before requesting an amendment. On at least ten of sixteen occasions between 1867 and 1949 when the BNA Act was amended by the Parliament of the United Kingdom, the provinces were not consulted at all. Parliament in Ottawa considered that on these occasions the amendments proposed were of exclusive federal concern. It was not until 1907 that consultations with the provinces took place. On that and subsequent occasions the provinces were consulted because the proposed amendment was considered to be of direct concern to them all. On one occasion, the transfer of control of natural resources in the West to the provinces, only the provinces affected were consulted.

If any tendency at all could be found, it was in the direction of more consultation with the provinces rather than less. Six of the ten occasions when none took place occurred before 1916 (apparently without provincial objection). Not until the 1940s did the federal government act unilaterally again: in 1943, 1946, and twice in 1949. On each of these occasions one or two provinces protested that federal–provincial consultations should have taken place.[37]

Consultation would appear also to have meant consent. Consequently it was argued by some provincialists that amendments that directly concerned all the provinces could be proposed only after the Parliament of Canada had consulted all the provinces and obtained their unanimous consent.

At the other extreme it seemed to the federal government that just as the provinces could amend their own constitutions, whether or not these were part of the BNA Act (as they were in the case of Ontario and Quebec), so the Parliament of Canada should be able to amend the Constitution of Canada—at least in those areas not exclusively assigned to the provinces. This view was supported by the 1949 amendment to Section 91 of the BNA Act, which stated in part,

> . . . the exclusive Legislative Authority of the Parliament of Canada extends to all Matters coming within the Classes of Subjects next herein-after enumerated; that is to say,—
>
> 1. The amendment from time to time of the Constitution of Canada, except as regards matters . . . assigned exclusively to the Legislatures of the provinces, or . . .

The section went on to indicate a small number of areas, notably schools and language, in which the Canadian Parliament was still prohibited from acting.

The 1949 amendment was of course a very significant one. Passed without provincial consultation by a government headed by a French-Canadian prime minister, Louis St. Laurent, the BNA (No. 2) Act,

1949, reflected the enormous growth in federal power that was a consequence of the Depression and the Second World War.

It remained to be seen whether the position reached by the Federal Government in 1949 could be maintained. The doctrine of parliamentary supremacy was now assumed by Ottawa to mean that the Parliament of Canada had for all practical purposes the power to secure amendments to the BNA Act, with or without provincial consultation. The British government, for its part, seemed willing to reiterate its belief that the role of the British Parliament when acting on "a proper request from Canada" was purely a formality, and did not involve "looking behind the request" to see if it had provincial support.

A broader issue than amendments themselves was the nature of the amending procedure. This became an issue after Canada, along with other Dominions, had obtained the concurrence of the British government to a proposal to pass a bill to be known as the Statute of Westminster (1931). This bill ratified the agreements reached at imperial conferences. The most noteworthy agreement, reached in 1926, defined the equality of status of the Dominions and the United Kingdom: "Their position and mutual relation may be readily defined. They are autonomous Communities within the British Empire, equal in status, in no way subordinate one to another in any aspect of their domestic or external affairs, though united by a common allegiance to the Crown, and freely associated as members of the British Commonwealth of Nations."

To implement this agreement it was necessary to pass a bill stating that the Colonial Laws Validity Act of the United Kingdom was no longer applicable to the Dominions. Under that act, Dominion statutes were void if they were in conflict with statutes of the imperial Parliament. However, repeal of this act would mean in Canada's case that unless Canada introduced a special amendment procedure, the British North America Act could be changed by an ordinary act of the Canadian Parliament: it would no longer be superior to all Canadian legislation. There would be no appeals to the Privy Council for judicial interpretation and no Addresses to the British Parliament requesting changes in the BNA Act.

The question now arose, Who was to represent Canada and to wield the power to change the Constitution previously lodged with the British Parliament? According to the doctrine of parliamentary supremacy, the power should have passed to the Canadian Parliament. On the other hand, if Canada were a federal state, then the Parliament in Ottawa could not alone exercise the power to amend the Constitution. The federal government consulted the provinces to see if agreement could be reached on an amendment formula that would involve the provinces but not require unanimous consent. In the United States amendments required the concurrence of three-quarters of the state legislatures or conventions. However, no similar formula was agreed upon in Canada.

The alternative was to transfer the power of amending the Canadian Constitution to the Parliament of Canada, which would then be as supreme as the British Parliament. The provinces naturally objected to this arrangement. In 1930 the premier of Ontario, Howard Ferguson, vigorously protested to the prime minister against some of the proposals to be embodied in the Statute of Westminster, on the grounds that the provinces had not been consulted on this matter so vital to their interests. He even went so far as to refer to the BNA Act as "the Provincial Treaty," saying, "that this agreement should not be altered without the consent of the parties to it."[38] He clearly implied that the BNA Act was a document that could not be entrusted to the Parliament of Canada alone, and thereby made subject to the doctrine of parliamentary supremacy in the British sense of the term. It was largely because of the determined opposition of the province of Ontario that, at the request of the Parliament of Canada, the provisions of the Statute of Westminster which made the Colonial Laws Validity Act a dead letter expressly excluded the BNA Act.

We noted earlier W. L. Morton's observation that Canada's original Constitution was the result of actions by "obscure provincial politicians." It was thanks to such provincial politicians as Howard Ferguson of Ontario that after 1931 Canada remained in law subject to the provisions of the Colonial Laws Validity Act and thus to the British Parliament.

The controversy of 1930–31 suggested that a distinction was to be drawn between actual amendments to the BNA Act, which were proposed by the Parliament of Canada, with or without provincial consultation, and a new amendment procedure, which would bypass the Parliament of the United Kingdom. By insisting, as they did, that the powers of the British Parliament could not be transferred to the Parliament of Canada, the provinces were in effect drawing public attention, perhaps for the first time, to the contradiction between the doctrine of parliamentary supremacy and the principle of federalism. On an issue which the imperial government itself was in no position to resolve, the result was a deadlock.

The very fact that the federal government consulted the provinces on this important issue, and took no action because of lack of provincial support, helped to create the impression that there might be a new convention in the making: namely that no new amendment procedure would be adopted until federal-provincial agreement was obtained. But what if, after say fifty years, no such agreement had yet been reached? Could the federal Parliament, under the doctrine of parliamentary supremacy, take advantage of the 1949 amendment to propose a procedure to end the deadlock and thus finally transfer full sovereignty to Canada?

Further, how should the British Parliament respond if the Parliament of Canada unilaterally proposed "patriation" of the BNA Act? It had always acted automatically on "a proper request from Canada," but would such a request, for which it was arguable there was no precedent, be a "proper request"? And who represented Canada in such a situation?

It was to be some while before such questions again became the subject of widespread debate in Canada—and the United Kingdom. For a long time, it seemed to many English Canadians that the power to amend the BNA Act lay for all practical purposes with the Parliament of Canada. As Carl Berger paraphrased the words of George Wrong, professor of history at the University of Toronto until 1927, "The Parliament of Canada had over Canada the same authority that the Parliament of Great Britain had over the people of Great Britain, and this included, of course, the power to amend its own constitution."[39]

Professor Wrong, like many English Canadians in the 1920s, was preoccupied with the assertion of Canada's equality with the United Kingdom. By equality he meant, of course, the equality of Canada as a nation, and its right to be treated in international law as an independent country. Yet the events preceding the passage of the Statute of Westminster demonstrated that while the provinces might approve those actions of the federal government that led to Canada's *international* independence, they were very sensitive to the *constitutional* implications of breaking the bond with Britain. No one questioned the right of the Parliament of Canada to speak for Canada on international questions. But the right of the Canadian Parliament to be the sole representative of Canada on constitutional issues was a very different matter.

Yet even after 1931 there were many who did not appreciate the distinction between international and constitutional law. Canada had made not one but two decisions regarding its independence, the one international and the other constitutional. Over the years, Canada had elected to become an independent state in international law, with power passing from London to Ottawa. But it had chosen, in 1931, *not* to become independent in constitutional law. Howard Ferguson had insisted in 1930 that the BNA Act was not to be treated by Canadians as an imperial statute that could be transferred from Westminster, at the request of the Canadian Parliament, to Parliament Hill, Ottawa. To him it was a treaty between the provinces and therefore any transfer to Canada required provincial consent.

Some Canadians assumed that, despite the contretemps of 1931, Canada was nevertheless evolving slowly toward constitutional independence, just as previously it had evolved into an internationally accepted independent state. Those who were to govern Canada from Ottawa were able all too easily to overlook Howard Ferguson's constitutional roadblock. The role of the British Parliament was assumed to be merely a formality. The right of the Parliament of Canada to speak for Canada on both international and constitutional questions appeared to have been established.

It was to be only a matter of time before the Canadian Parliament, in 1949, persuaded the Parliament of the United Kingdom to declare the BNA Act to be the Constitution of Canada—to be amended by the Parliament of Canada. Admittedly there were certain exceptions, notably those matters "assigned exclusively to the Legislatures of the provinces." But this proviso did not protect matters not assigned exclusively to the provinces. It did not cover the BNA Act. Also in 1949, a year that was to be the high point of federal power, Canada without provincial consent joined the North Atlantic Treaty Organization and sent troops to Europe; admitted Newfoundland as the tenth province without altering its disputed boundary with Quebec; and abolished all appeals to the Judicial Committee of the Privy Council, including appeals from the provinces.

4 The Adaptability of Parliamentary Government

So long as liberal-minded English Canadians occupied themselves with emancipating Canada from imperial rule, they found it politic to state that their aim was the laudable goal of transplanting the Westminster model of parliamentary government to Canada. After all, at Westminster the British Parliament itself had once shared Canada's aspirations of freeing itself from the control long exercised by the Crown.

The British Parliament had succeeded in becoming supreme by leaving the Monarch's prerogative power as part of the unwritten part of the British Constitution. As a result the Monarch was in a weak legal position when defending his or her powers, with nothing to fall back on but tradition. Sometimes Parliament replaced Crown prerogatives by statutes. An example of statutory change was the Army Act, which required annual renewal by Parliament and which was the instrument whereby Parliament ensured its control over the army. Often, however, the form of the prerogative remained. For example, many of the prerogatives of the Crown came to be wielded by ministers responsible to Parliament (who styled themselves nevertheless as "Ministers of the Crown") instead of secretaries of state appointed by the Monarch. The notion of ministerial responsibility, central to parliamentary government, was simply a convention of the Constitution. It was only by convention that the Cabinet required the confidence of the House of Commons.

So long as it was part of the British Empire, Canada depended very much on the Crown and on the use of the prerogative power. But Canadians, too, had discovered that it was possible to whittle away the prerogative over time, from the winning of responsible government onward. Thus after 1873 no British government exercised its legal power to disallow (i.e., to veto) Canadian legislation under Section 56 of the BNA Act. After 1878 no governor-general used his legal right under Section 55 to reserve (i.e., refuse to sign) a bill pending the Monarch's pleasure.

Their experience helped to convince Canadians that the British Constitution was a more flexible instrument than one, like the American, based on a written document with a rigid separation of powers and amendable only after a long and difficult procedure. It confirmed them in their belief that the doctrine of parliamentary supremacy, whether in Britain or in Canada, made peaceful evolution possible.

Parliamentary supremacy came to mean the replacement of the authority of Whitehall by Westminster, which served, so it was believed, as the model not the master. The Statute of Westminster symbolized this transfer. It gave legal authority for full Canadian independence whenever that was desired. It left formal authority over the Constitution, at Canada's request, with the Parliament at Westminster. And in practice it gave Canada control over her own destiny since it appeared to reduce the role of the British Parliament to a formality.

5 Summary and Conclusion: Importance of Agreed Conventions

It is not surprising that the Attorney General of Prince Edward Island should have stated that the supremacy of Parliament was one of the foundations on which Canada was built. He was certainly speaking the truth as far as most English Canadians were concerned. Parliamentary supremacy, as Peter Hogg indicated, was a pervasive element of Canadian constitutional law. In one sense it symbolized Canada's gradual attainment of independence from the Crown. In another sense it meant that responsibility of the government of the day went to the popularly elected House of Commons or Legislative Assembly. In yet a third sense it meant legislative supremacy over the courts, whether in Ottawa or the provinces.

Parliamentary supremacy was also interpreted to mean majority rule. Should English-speaking Canadians ever be united, this could mean rule by the English-Canadian majority at the federal level. Indeed, many English Canadians interpreted the federal system to mean something different from the checks and balances *within* the federal government as practiced in the United States. They assumed that English-Canadian majority rule at Ottawa and in nine provinces was counterbalanced by the majority rule of French Canadians in Quebec.

Parliamentary supremacy was at times taken even further. It was used to justify Parliament's encroachment on provincial matters through the use of the residual, emergency, and other powers given to the federal government in 1867. (Among these was the "declaratory" power whereby the federal government could declare works wholly within a province to be for the general advantage of Canada, and thus bring them under its jurisdiction.) It was also taken to mean that in amending the Constitution of Canada the Parliament of the United Kingdom merely confirmed what the Parliament of Canada proposed. It was even taken to mean that the Government and Parliament of Canada could, if necessary, alter the constitution significantly without the agreement of the provinces.

In Canada, as in Great Britain, the doctrine of parliamentary supremacy was very much dependent, for its broad acceptance, on adherence to certain long-established conventions. Among the familiar conventions of both constitutions was the assumption that the prime minister and Cabinet would resign once they no longer had the confidence of Parliament or the electoral support of the people. Other conventions were that the upper house, though subordinate to the lower, was more than a rubber stamp for decisions reached in the House of Commons; that legislative supremacy over the courts did not mean unfairness toward the minority. In Canada, however, parliamentary supremacy rested on an additional practice. It also meant that the Parliament of Canada would exercise restraint in the use of its various powers to interfere in provincial affairs—and that the United Kingdom Parliament would not be asked to adjudicate disputes between the federal government and the provinces when formally amending the Constitution.

Until 1981 this last convention appeared for the most part to have been observed. It was not clear, however, whether it was being followed by the government of Canada out of respect for Canada's own political tradition or whether its continued observance was due to restraints initially imposed on Canada during the imperial era when federal disputes were adjudicated by the Judicial Committee.

Canadian federalism had its origins in an "imperial federalism" that encouraged Canadians to believe that the doctrine of parliamentary supremacy on the Westminster model was the best alternative to colonial rule. So preoccupied were Canadian liberals with securing autonomy that they perhaps overestimated the ability of the Westminster model to preserve Canada's federal system. In any event, it is important not to underestimate the significance for the preservation of the federal structure of another aspect of the British connection: the role played by Whitehall as umpire in Canadian affairs.

In this chapter we have asked how Canada succeeded in reconciling two contradictory principles: the parliamentary supremacy associated with the Westminster tradition and the judicial review that had become an integral part of American federalism.

We now have part of the answer. Confederation did not see the establishment of the Westminster system in all its aspects. A basic assumption of that tradition was the supremacy of Parliament. In Canada Parliament was limited in two vital ways. First, the British North America Act specifically exempted certain fields from the Canadian Parliament's jurisdiction by entrusting them to the provinces. Secondly, the general power to amend the BNA Act remained in the hands of the British Parliament. In law, at least, Confederation established what we shall call imperial federalism, not parliamentary supremacy.

Over the years, imperial federalism was modified by the Canadian Parliament. On the one hand, Parliament used its numerous powers to establish its primacy over the provinces. On the other, it persuaded the Parliament of the United Kingdom that the latter's role in the amendment process was largely formal. For all practical purposes it was the Parliament of Canada, and not the Parliament at Westminster, which was "supreme."

Even so, the Canadian Parliament never claimed to be legally supreme in the omnicompetent sense associated with the British Parliament. In Britain there was no BNA Act restraining Parliament; and, of course, nothing like a Section 92 had even been contemplated for, say, Scotland, Ireland, and Wales. Nor was there any other legislative body claiming to exercise even the most formal control over Parliament itself. Parliament, and Parliament alone, was sovereign and could never be charged by the courts with acting *ultra vires,* i.e., beyond its competence.

Canada's parliamentary federalism did not, then, mean parliamentary supremacy in the British sense of complete parliamentary sovereignty. It simply meant that Westminster was the model, a model to be adapted to Canadian conditions. Among those conditions was the country's federal structure.

In law, the United Kingdom Parliament was supreme. Yet much depended on the nature of the conventions surrounding the exercise of this power, particularly in the light of the Statute of Westminster and the negotiations preceding its passage. After the 1949 amendment to the BNA Act, however, the government and Parliament of Canada assumed that for all practical purposes the Parliament of Canada, and even the House of Commons alone, was supreme.

But the Westminster doctrine of parliamentary supremacy, as Dicey noted, was quite clear: it meant not only supremacy for all practical purposes but supremacy in law. The Parliament of Canada was not supreme in law.

In Canada, the notion of parliamentary supremacy depended to a great extent on convention, since as far as the law went it was the British Parliament that was supreme. Federalism, on the other hand, depended on the legal distribution of powers specified in the Constitution. It was to be the federal principle, dependent on law, that was to challenge the parliamentary principle, dependent on conventions. These conventions were assumed to be the same, whether in Westminster, Ottawa, or the provincial capitals. In practice there came to be much disagreement over their precise nature. This was to raise the question of whether a practice could be treated as a convention unless there was widespread agreement as to its nature.

5
The "Reconciliation" of Parliamentary Supremacy and Federalism

We go to the Imperial Government, the common arbiter of us all, in our true Federal metropolis—we go there to ask for our fundamental Charter.—D'Arcy McGee

1   The "Reconciliation" of Parliamentary Supremacy and Federalism

If, then, the Canadian Parliament was not supreme, just what institution was? One possibility is that the question was wrongly put: that no single institution exercised supremacy. Perhaps power was divided between the Parliament of Canada and the Westminster Parliament.

In a sense this was true. Power *was* divided. Although the British Parliament was supreme in law, by convention the power was exercised by the Canadian Parliament. This Parliament alone requested amendments to the Constitution, requests always granted by Westminster. And although by convention the Canadian Parliament enjoyed sole power to make recommendations for changes in the BNA Act, after 1907 it became increasingly common for Ottawa to consult the provinces on matters that directly affected their interests.

But if power was divided between the Canadian Parliament and the provincial legislatures, then there was an obvious alternative to the principle of parliamentary supremacy: the Constitution. In a federal system the principle of constitutional supremacy ensured that each government remained within its assigned limits. Certainly, in the United States, whose Supreme Court gradually became the Canadian model, the Constitution was regarded as supreme. The American Supreme Court interpreted the Constitution and exercised authority as an umpire through what Americans called the principle of "judicial review."

When the Canadian Supreme Court replaced the Judicial Committee of the Privy Council as the final court of appeal, it came to be assumed that the principle of judicial review, a term rarely used in earlier times, had a place in the Canadian political system. Analogies were even drawn with the United States Supreme Court's celebrated case of *Marbury v. Madison* in which Chief Justice Marshall, with masterful logic-chopping, had first established the principle of judicial review. Canadian courts, it was argued, had always practiced judicial review.

Before 1949, however, the Judicial Committee could not properly be described as having exercised the principle of judicial review on the American model. It was, after all, an imperial tribunal: it acted on behalf of the Crown: and it was subject to the ultimate authority of the British Parliament—in conformity with the doctrine of parliamentary supremacy. It practiced the same judicial interpretation that ordinary English courts adopted in dealing with the question of whether local governments were acting *ultra vires*. In its judgments, the Judicial Committee did not declare acts of Canadian legislatures to be unconstitutional: it merely said that they were *ultra vires*, that is, outside the limits set by the British Parliament. The Judicial Committee might appear to Canada to be an umpire *ab extra*, but looked at from within the British political system it was very much an umpire *ab intra*, without independent legal authority.

After 1949, when the Judicial Committee ceased to be final court of appeal, it was often suggested in Canada that the Supreme Court should now model itself not on the Judicial Committee, with its often narrow interpretation, but on the American Supreme Court with its broad powers of judicial review.[1] But nothing in Canada corresponded to the American Constitution, the authority for Marshall's claim that the Supreme Court should exercise the power of judicial review. Moreover, in the United States the Constitution was revered as the creation of the American people through their representatives gathered in a Constitutional Convention in Philadelphia. Hence the opening words of the Preamble: "We, the people of the United States . . ."

Chief Justice Marshall was able to argue his case supported by two doctrines: the supremacy of the Constitution and the sovereignty of the American people. He lived in a new country that had vigorously opposed British parliamentary supremacy and the prerogatives of the Crown. It was therefore doubly difficult for his opponents to challenge the logic of his argument.

By British standards, the American Constitution was a remarkably novel document. It separated the executive, legislative, and judicial powers through separate institutions (although it blended their powers). Through the first ten amendments (the Bill of Rights), it prohibited the government from encroaching on certain rights, which the Constitution declared henceforth belonged to individual citizens. Most important for our purposes, the Constitution distributed power between the federal government and the states. Neither the separation of powers within government, nor the passage of the Bill of Rights, was essential to the federal structure of the United States. What was essential was the distribution of power between the federal government and the states. It was this federal distribution of power that the British government could never accept for Ireland within the United Kingdom itself, for the simple reason that it would end the supremacy of Parliament. Yet this same distribution of power was granted to Canada. However, Canada was different from Ireland. Federalism was possible in Canada because the British Parliament remained supreme in Canada over both orders of government. Canada's federalism, as established in 1867, can perhaps be described as a form of "imperial federalism."

With the passage of time and the emancipation of Canada from imperial control, in both the United Kingdom and Canada, it was increasingly regarded as anachronistic for Canada's federation to be considered fundamentally one of imperial federalism.[2] Yet little attention seems to have been given to the need to replace imperial federalism by another form, for example, by what we may call "constitutional federalism." Instead, as we have seen, the British Parliament retained its crucial role in the amendment process. Yet this was regarded even by British ministers, as simply a formality.[3] The Judicial Committee came to be thought of as a useful institution of Canadian federalism and not as an instrument of British imperialism.[4] Its successor, the Supreme Court of Canada, was encouraged to transform its role from that of judicial interpretation of the BNA Act into judicial review of the Constitution.

But if the principle of judicial review, with its connotation of a broad interpretation of the Constitution, came to be generally accepted, what would happen to the old principle of parliamentary supremacy? Canadian jurists were able to convince themselves that the two principles could be reconciled—and indeed that they had been reconciled from the outset. They did so by stating that whereas in the United States there were areas of individual rights into which no legislature could trespass, in Canada there were no such areas. Just as Parliament in the United Kingdom was supreme, so in Canada the legislatures, Parliament and the provincial assemblies together, were supreme.

In other words, they took one of the features of the Canadian political system that distinguished it from the American (the absence of a constitutional Bill of Rights), and contrasted it with one aspect of parliamentary supremacy—legislative supremacy over the courts. But we have already seen that the feature they chose, the absence in Canada of a Bill of Rights entrenched in the Constitution, had nothing to do with the federal principle. And of course they virtually ignored the "formal" role of the U.K. Parliament.

In sum, Canadians were asked to believe that the very distribution of legislative power which was fundamental to federalism in both Canada and the United States, and which created the contradiction between federalism and parliamentary supremacy, had actually resolved the problem. For example, in September 1981, when the Supreme Court reviewed—and reviewed broadly—the proposed Constitution Act, it reiterated what had come to be the conventional wisdom, stating, "There is also an internal contradiction in speaking of federalism in the light of the invariable principle of British parliamentary supremacy. Of course [sic], the resolution of this contradiction lies in the scheme of distribution of legislative power."[5]

The Court did not address itself to the fundamental problem facing Canada, once the British Parliament ceased to be supreme, of reconciling the doctrine of parliamentary supremacy with a federal system. The adjudication of disputes between the two orders of government in a federation required an umpire generally regarded to be *ab extra,* and the amendment of the Constitution, either by the people themselves, or by both orders of government.

So long as the term "parliamentary supremacy" referred to the British Parliament, and so long as the Judicial Committee served as umpire *ab extra,* the contradiction between the two principles created no problem. Admittedly, the British Parliament rarely had to act. But the fact that it dealt with few issues was irrelevant. What mattered was that the fundamental issues *were* legally the responsibility of that Parliament alone.

When Canada became virtually independent in 1949, there was little awareness that here was a theoretical decision that ought not to be avoided. Instead, Canadians assumed that the system had operated satisfactorily throughout Canada's long period of gradual emancipation and that it surely would continue to operate as before.

Thus, the reconciliation of the two principles was not thought to present an insuperable problem. The Fathers of Confederation were, after all, pragmatists: "Pragmatic in their approach to politics, they were not impressed by lofty statements of principles and goals."[6] Nor did later generations of Canadians go in for grand theory: for all practical purposes the system worked well. Canada had succeeded in evolving from the colonial (or imperial) federalism of 1867 (in which the imperial authorities retained ultimate supremacy through the governor general, the Westminster Parliament, and the Judicial Committee of the Privy Council), to a system of federalism that after 1949 took on a strong resemblance to the constitutional federalism practiced in the United States.

2 The Evolution of "the Logic of Federalism"

Although Canada evolved from the imperial structure established at Confederation to the modern "parliamentary federalism" that English Canadians were to take for granted, it did so slowly because Canadians took some time to grasp the implications of Confederation and the nature of the federalism on which it was presumably based. Peter Russell began his book *Leading Constitutional Decisions* with a section entitled "Judicial Review and the British North America Act." In it he wrote, ". . . the judicial interpretation of the British North America Act was accepted at the outset with little awareness of its full significance. The Fathers of Confederation were remarkably insensitive to the problems connected with judicial review under a federal constitution."[7]

Whether the Fathers were quite as insensitive as Russell claims is an issue to which we shall return. The interesting thing about these two sentences at this point is the way they illustrate the metamorphosis in historical perspective of contemporary Canadian scholarship. The first sentence conveys the flavor of 1867 when "judicial interpretation" of the "British North America Act" was the responsibility of the Judicial Committee of the Privy Council. The second sentence implies a transition to a more American approach, one adopted after the abolition of appeals to the Privy Council. The BNA Act is referred to interchangeably as the "federal constitution" and it is subject to "a process of judicial review" (by a Canadian Supreme Court). Even the politicians of 1867 are now called "Fathers of Confederation" analogous to the "Founding Fathers" of the United States. Russell concludes his opening paragraph by arguing that, while Canadian history had no counterpart to Chief Justice Marshall and the famous case *Marbury v. Madison* which in 1803 enabled the American Supreme Court to establish the principle of judicial review, nevertheless in practice Canadian courts assumed "precisely that power" with regard to the BNA Act.

> Nor were Canadians ever to witness a case like *Marbury v. Madison,* in which Chief Justice Marshall successfully claimed for the United States' Supreme Court the role of arbiter of the Constitution with the power of striking down any act of government, national or local, which in the Court's view violated the terms of the Constitution. *Yet it was precisely that power which, from the outset, the Canadian judiciary, without explicit acknowledgment and despite the incompatibility of judicial review with the traditional British practice of parliamentary sovereignty, assumed with respect to the B.N.A. Act.* (Emphasis added.)

Russell went on to suggest that while Canadians nowadays "are apt to look upon judicial review as a necessary ingredient of a federal state," this was not so after Confederation, especially to the jurists who comprised the Judicial Committee. Then, he admits, "the courts' power to pass on the constitutional validity of legislation might have been as much a corollary of imperialism as of federalism." Yet he elliptically adds, "No doubt in time . . . the theoretical underpinning of judicial review has come to turn exclusively on the *logic of federalism*" (emphasis added). At the same time there has developed "a much keener awareness of the role of the judiciary as the indispensable umpire of the federal system."[8]

We have quoted Russell at some length to show how Canadian scholars shifted their interest from the Privy Council to the subordinate Canadian courts, and then viewed the Canadian courts in the context of the American federal system with its judicial review. Their students now have to be reminded that it was not always thus, and that the system "might" have owed much to the imperial structure in which it was established. This historical background, however, is not thought to be of crucial importance. "The theoretical underpinning of judicial review has come to turn exclusively on the logic of federalism."

Russell is not alone in assuming that "the logic of federalism" has come to be the basis of judicial review in Canada. Earlier, Edward McWhinney commented, "In respect to federal states like Canada, Australia, India, and Pakistan, there is no doubt a certain logic in the courts' assuming the power of judicial review, as umpires, as it were, of the federal system."[9]

How does the "logic of federalism" provide the theoretical underpinning of judicial review? The question is, of course, easily answered in the case of the United States. As we have seen, the American system is based on constitutional, not parliamentary, supremacy, as well as on the federal distribution of powers, which Canada copied in 1867. Above all, the Constitution provides for an independent Supreme Court, a Court which under Marshall's leadership successfully argued the case for being the constitutional arbiter. In Canada, however, judicial review evolved out of the old imperial structure and was exercised with such prudence that it did not in practice challenge the doctrine of parliamentary supremacy. Our next task, therefore, is to ask whether in fact the logic of federalism could also evolve out of imperialism. To do this we need to compare the imperial federalism of 1867 with the American constitutional federalism with which analogies would later be drawn.

3 The "Logic" of Imperial Federalism Contrasted with the "Logic" of Constitutional Federalism

Any argument based on "the logic of federalism" makes the assumption that there is only one type of federalism, or at least there is the assumption that all federations are built on the same principles and therefore have the same logic.

Of course, all federal structures do have certain features in common. Both Canada and the United States have a distribution of powers between two orders (or levels) of government, a distinction that distinguishes federal states from unitary states like the United Kingdom. It was this feature that K. C. Wheare noted when he stressed the coordinate relationship between the orders of government in a truly federal structure.[10] He distinguished this from the subordinate relationship between, for example, local governments and Whitehall in Britain. Moreover, this distribution of powers characteristic of all federal systems requires, as McWhinney observed, an umpire to ensure that each order of government remains within its assigned sphere.

Beyond this, however, systems differ. Canada was established as a product of colonial, or what we have called *imperial federalism*. That is, although from a Canadian perspective it was a colonial form of federalism, from the British viewpoint it was imperial federalism. We shall use the term imperial federalism advisedly, in order that we shall not too readily conclude that once Canada ceased to be a colony the principles (or the "logic") of its federal structure automatically ceased to be those of imperial federalism.

This imperial federalism should not be confused with the federalism of the United States. We shall call the American type of federalism *constitutional federalism* because it owed its legitimacy to the American Constitution, not to the imperial authority exercised by the British government over Canada. What is called the logic of federalism is in fact the logic of constitutional federalism. American constitutional federalism was indeed based on a certain logic, but this was the logic of Chief Justice Marshall in his masterly argument in *Marbury v. Madison*.

Marshall argued that it was the people who had established the principles of American government. These principles were fundamental to the Constitution. One of them implicitly rejected the notion of legislative supremacy by defining and limiting the powers of the legislature:

> It is a proposition too plain to be contested, that the constitution controls any legislative act repugnant to it; either that or the legislature may alter the constitution by an ordinary act. . . . If then, the courts are to regard the constitution, and the constitution is superior to any ordinary act of the legislature, the constitution, and not such ordinary act, must govern the case to which they both apply . . . a law repugnant to the constitution is void.[11]

It may well be, as Russell has argued, that Canadian courts have exercised precisely the same power as their American counterparts. Peter Hogg, having recognized the imperial origins of Confederation, has also drawn an analogy between the Privy Council and the American Supreme Court: "The Privy Council . . . used an argument similar to the one which had been accepted in *Marbury v. Madison*. If a statute was inconsistent with the B.N.A. Act, then the B.N.A. Act had to prevail, because it was an imperial statute. . . . After the Supreme Court of Canada was established in 1875 it naturally assumed the same power."[12]

The crucial question, however, is whether the logic employed by Marshall to give the American court the legitimate right to practice judicial

The "Reconciliation" of Parliamentary Supremacy and Federalism 157

review is applicable to Canadian courts. If not, then it is not the logic of federalism which has given the Canadian courts legitimacy but something else. Indeed, it is arguable that their legitimacy stems from imperial federalism and that they have no legitimacy outside the federal or provincial jurisdiction that established them.

If the "logic of federalism" means the logic of Chief Justice Marshall, then that "logic" should not be applied to the very different imperial federalism of 1867. Instead of having a constitution that expressed the will of the Canadian people, Canada remained in law a colony, with ultimate power wielded by Britain. That power was exercised by the same kind of authority any imperial power exercises until the colony successfully claims autonomy or independence. To describe the relationship between Canada and the United Kingdom solely in terms of colonialism and legality is, of course, to do an injustice to the spirit of Confederation. The BNA Act was a joint affair; if Canada remained a colony, this was in large measure at its own request. As Canada matured, so the imperial bond weakened. In practice, then, Confederation may be better described as an example of *quasi-imperial federalism.* In law, everything was still stated as if the relationship were purely colonial: in practice Canada was treated as autonomous in its domestic affairs, up to a point at least. But the constitutional relationship between Canada and the Mother Country was never a federal one. The Canadian Parliament remained legally subordinate to Westminster. Canada was never constitutionally coordinate with the United Kingdom.

Since the notion of "the logic of federalism" is widely thought to have superseded the prerogative of imperialism, we need to remind ourselves just what Canada's imperial federalism was like. First, Confederation was created within the context not only of the British Empire but of the British Constitution. This was a political system not based on any single document called a "constitution" and in which no statute was regarded as "constitutional" and therefore superior to ordinary statutes. In British law, all statutes were the same. The BNA Act, in British eyes, was a statute like all the others. Second, it was, of course, Parliament that was supreme, not any constitutional document.

In the third place, the role of the English courts was that of interpreter of acts of Parliament and adjudicator of the actions of local governments. Such subordinate bodies could be found to be acting within the limits set by Parliament (*intra vires*) or to have exceeded those powers and to be acting *ultra vires.* The colonies were treated as local governments, and as such were subordinate to Parliament. Colonial laws were therefore interpreted in the same fashion as local government edicts and were treated as either *intra* or *ultra vires*. No special and different "imperial" law had been devised to meet the demands of colonies like Canada en route to self-government. The BNA Act might eventually be thought of as the "Constitution of Canada" in Canadian eyes, but in British law it remained the BNA Act. In the absence of a special imperial constitutional law or of a single British document called a Constitution, there was no way for British courts to declare legislation "unconstitutional." There could be no "judicial review" in the American sense.

The courts, after all, whether Canadian or British, were subordinate to Parliament, and therefore it was incumbent upon them not to challenge the authority of Parliament. Under no circumstances could acts of Parliament be declared unconstitutional. It was the duty of the courts to interpret statutes as narrowly as possible in order not to seem to be usurping the role of Parliament. If there was any "logic" to imperial federalism it was the logic flowing from the doctrine of parliamentary supremacy.

The logic of American constitutional federalism as enunciated by Marshall was very different. The American Constitution *was* a single document. This document *was* admitted to be superior to any act of Congress as well as to any act of the President or of the States. This being the case, the Constitution required a guardian to protect it against encroachment by one or other of the institutions of government. This guardian, argued Marshall, could only be the Supreme Court, in whom the judicial power was vested by the Constitution itself. The Supreme Court could therefore declare acts of Congress void if they were repugnant to the Constitution. The legitimacy of the Court lay in the fact that it owed its origin to the Constitution (implemented by Congress in the Federal Judiciary Act, 1789). Moreover, the Constitution expressed the will of the American people, so that the Court could claim to be acting on their behalf. This being so, it behooved the Court to interpret the Constitution broadly and not to be inhibited by actions of the other branches of government.

This is not to suggest that the United States Supreme Court established its ultimate supremacy over the Constitution, a supremacy analogous to Parliament at Westminister. It could interpret the Constitution, but could not amend it. Were the Court's decisions deemed inadequate or unsatisfactory, Congress could propose an amendment that could then be ratified by the States. When it came to amendment, no institution was supreme.

The "logic of federalism" therefore meant in effect the logic of American constitutional federalism, a logic expounded by John Marshall when he established the right of the Supreme Court of the United States, through the exercise of judicial review of the Constitution, to declare acts of Congress void. It was clearly a very different "logic" from that introduced by the BNA Act in which the Parliament of the United Kingdom remained supreme and the Judicial Committee of the Privy Council confined itself to judicial interpretation. It is difficult to grasp how, given such differing circumstances, Canadian courts could "from the outset" have exercised "precisely the same power of judicial review" as the American courts.

4 The Decline of Imperial Federalism

A product of imperial federalism, the BNA Act made no reference to either a Supreme Court of Canada or to judicial review. Section 101 merely stated: "The Parliament of Canada may, notwithstanding anything in this Act, from Time to Time provide for the Constitution, Maintenance, and Organization of a General Court of Appeal." This was very different from the language of Article III of the U.S. Constitution, which said, "the judicial power of the United States, shall be vested in one Supreme Court." It was not clear from the BNA Act whether a "General Court of Appeal" meant a Supreme Court with final jurisdiction in the American sense, or a court of appeal within the imperial system with the Privy Council at the head. The imperial authorities seem to have assumed the latter, while the Canadian government seems to have had in mind a court more like the American.

Matters came to a head in 1875 when the Parliament of Canada passed a bill to establish a Supreme Court of Canada and to make it Canada's final court of appeal. This proposal was rejected out of hand by the imperial authorities.

> Section 47 provided that "[t]he judgment of the Supreme Court shall in all cases be final and conclusive. . . . Saving any right which Her Majesty may be graciously pleased to exercise by virtue of Her Royal Prerogative." The Imperial authorities threatened

disallowance of the whole Act on the ground that it purported to bar appeals from the Supreme Court to the Privy Council. It was only after the Canadian government conceded that the Act did not extend to appeals by leave—the "prerogative" appeals—that London agreed to allow the Act to take effect.[13]

The British government's refusal to allow the abolition of appeals to London meant that the Privy Council retained the all-important right to grant leave to appeal. While the British refusal could be, and was, interpreted as motivated in part by imperialism, it was not without significance in protecting the federal structure of Canada. The distribution of power between the federal and provincial governments remained in the hands of an umpire *ab extra,* with the Judicial Committee attempting to interpret the will of the British Parliament and to meet the needs of Canada's evolving federalism. The continuation of appeals by leave had one very important consequence: like other litigants, provincial governments retained direct right of access to the Judicial Committee. Indeed, 77 of 159 cases on the Canadian Constitution brought to the Judicial Committee bypassed the Supreme Court of Canada altogether.

The Judicial Committee therefore performed a "quasifederal" as well as an imperial role. It acted in what it considered were the best interests of Canada, and did not simply further the interests of empire. Indeed, what we may call its "quasifederal" role came to predominate, and this probably caused observers to assume that the imperialism characteristic of the earlier period had given way before the logic of federalism. What had happened, of course, was a much less significant shift: from quasiimperialism to quasifederalism.

What about the Supreme Court of Canada itself? In its early days it did attempt to interpret its role as analogous to that of the American Supreme Court. In *Severn v. The Queen* (1878) and *City of Fredericton v. The Queen* (1880), the court displayed a willingness to make a broad interpretation of the so-called "trade and commerce" power. However, this period was short-lived: "Within a decade the Court had succumbed to the reality of its subordinate position in the judicial hierarchy and remained, with few exceptions, a 'captive court' until its emancipation in 1949. In the words of Professor Laskin, 'the task of the Supreme Court was not to interpret the Constitution but rather to interpret what the Privy Council said the Constitution meant.' "[14] The restrictions on the role of the Supreme Court, the creature of the Parliament of Canada, are not surprising. Under imperial federalism one of the responsibilities of the Judicial Committee as external umpire was to ensure uniformity of treatment throughout the Empire. The British were proud of the part played by the Judicial Committee in ensuring that British justice prevailed throughout their far-flung dominions. They insisted on the preservation of appeals to the Privy Council even when the Irish established the Irish Free State in 1922.[15]

During the period when Canada's dominant ethos was the development of political nationhood, English-Canadian critics frequently criticized the Privy Council for its narrow interpretation of the BNA Act and for its concessions to provincial autonomy. These concessions were often interpreted as examples of imperial policy of "divide and rule," and it was only later that the Privy Council's commitment to the preservation of Canadian federalism was fully recognized.

That the Judicial Committee lasted as long as it did was due in some measure to support in Canada itself for an external umpire. We have already seen how in the 1920s English-Canadian imperialists like Arthur Meighen, the Conservative leader of the Opposition, supported appeals to the Privy Council as expressions of imperial unity. Another source of support was the French-Canadian community. Though committed to Canadian autonomy, the French were ambivalent about the substitution of Ottawa for London as the federal umpire. Traditionally, the French Canadians from time to time looked to the Crown for impartial justice.

During the debate in the old Parliament of Canada in 1865 on the proposal for a General Court of Appeal, French-speaking members expressed their opposition to any proposal to establish as Canada's final court of appeal a *Canadian* court. They assumed that such a court would be dominated by lawyers drawn from the English-speaking Protestant majority. Henri Taschereau remarked that they "would be less satisfied with the decisions of a Federal Court of Appeal than with those of Her Majesty's Privy Council."[16] The French-Canadian leader, George-Etienne Cartier, had reassured the House, ". . . but I do hold, and the spirit of the Conference at Quebec indicated, that the appeal to the judicial committee of Her Majesty's Privy Council must always exist, even if the Court in question is established."[17] It was, we are told, on this basis that "the Lower Canadians permitted Section 101 of the BNA Act to become law."[18]

Yet only a decade later, the English-Canadian majority in the new House of Commons seems to have lost the sensitivity displayed in 1865, and to have ignored Cartier's promise that appeals to the Privy Council must always exist. By then, Cartier was dead and the influence of the French Canadians was less conspicuous. After failing to make the Supreme Court Canada's final court of appeal in 1875, English Canadians were to express dismay over many of the judgments of the Privy Council, not the least of which was its failure to interpret broadly the clause that gave residual power to the Federal Government. But it was the Judicial Committee's reasoning, often misinterpreted by supporters of a strong Dominion government, that a broad interpretation of the residual power was inconsistent with Canada's federal structure.

5 The Emergence of Judicial Review

Before 1949 it seems to have been general Canadian practice to consider the recommendations of the Judicial Committee to be matters of "judicial interpretation," following British usage. This was, of course, correct nomenclature since the Privy Council was in fact interpreting such imperial statutes as the BNA Act, and doing so in accordance with English law.

After 1949 the term "judicial review" became increasingly popular, just as the preferred term for the BNA Act became "the Constitution of Canada." Barry Strayer entitled his book *Judicial Review of Legislation in Canada;* Edward McWhinney's book *Judicial Review* went through several editions; and, as we have seen, the term was freely employed by such authorities as Peter Hogg, Peter Russell, and Donald Smiley.

While the use of the term "judicial review" to describe the more recent decisions of the Supreme Court of Canada is comprehensible in modern terms, it is surprising to find the term "judicial review of the Constitution" used to describe the Privy Council's judicial interpretation of the BNA Act. McWhinney wrote, "The role that the Privy Council actually played in exercising ultimate judicial review of the Canadian Constitution is perhaps the most controversial aspect of Canadian constitutional history after the passage of the B.N.A. Act in 1867."[19]

Once the notion of "judicial interpretation of the BNA Act as an imperial statute" gave way to the belief that there was "judicial review of the Constitution," it became easier to criticize the Judicial Committee for its narrow interpretation of statutes, and to contrast this with the broader (and livelier?) review practiced by the American Supreme Court. "It has meant a tart refusal to allow counsel to refer to legal

The "Reconciliation" of Parliamentary Supremacy and Federalism 163

periodicals as authorities in their argument of cases; a refusal also to consider these social and economic materials with which the United States Supreme Court has become familiar since the Brandeis Brief was first employed."[20] Or again: "The courts simply treated the Canadian Constitution as an 'ordinary' statute (as distinct from a constitution), and therefore as subject to the normal common-law rules of statutory construction, and so arrived inevitably at a cramped, fettering ruling as to the ambit of national legislative powers."[21]

Clearly it was easy for English-Canadian observers who believed in the unfettered national legislative powers of the Parliament of Canada to forget that the Privy Council labored under severe constraints. It had no alternative, as an imperial tribunal, but to treat the BNA Act as an ordinary statute of the British Parliament. So long as it accepted both the supremacy of the British Parliament and the federal character of Canada, it could hardly contribute to making the Parliament of Canada supreme. In treating both orders of government in Canada as comparable to English local governments, and therefore as capable of acting *ultra vires* but not unconstitutionally, the Judicial Committee was conforming to the rules of imperial federalism whereby both orders of government in Canada were subordinate to the imperial Parliament.

The point is not to defend the imperial role of the Privy Council, but to recognize that in criticizing the Judicial Committee for its narrow construction, leading Canadian scholars were themselves abandoning the "logic" of Canada's parliamentary federalism, namely the doctrine of parliamentary supremacy. Under the new "logic," the BNA Act was treated as if it were a constitution in British as well as Canadian law. A corollary of this was the effort made to redefine British judicial interpretation of the BNA Act as judicial review of the Constitution. Having made this transition it was easy to make the "logical" assumption that the Judicial Committee was really to be treated as part of the Canadian Constitution; that it acted as a court; and that this being so it could therefore be compared to the American Supreme Court.

In fact, the Judicial Committee was not a court in the usual sense at all. It certainly was different from ordinary English common law courts, having been established long ago by royal prerogative. When the English Parliament abolished other prerogative courts such as the Star Chamber in 1641, it left the Privy Council's role as a tribunal untouched, presumably because at that time it was not certain that Parliament's jurisdiction extended to the colonies. It is true that in 1833, when the

Judicial Committee was established to handle appeals to the Privy Council in a more judicial fashion, it was given statutory authority by Parliament for its composition. It comprised judges, some of whom in their capacity as domestic judges served as Law Lords in the House of Lords. But in law the Privy Council remained an integral part of the Executive branch of government, associated with Whitehall, not Westminster—or the Inns of Court.

The Judicial Committee displayed its Executive character in its day-to-day deliberations. It did not meet as a court, the judges wearing robes, but as a committee, its members meeting informally as committees do. Business was conducted informally. As an advisory body to the Sovereign, the Committee itself published no reports and revealed no dissenting opinions. Its advice was tendered to the Crown and was then published, like other executive orders, by Order-in-Council in the Sovereign's name. It is not surprising that the Irish resented having to appeal to this Committee as their highest tribunal.

Once the Statute of Westminster was passed, it was clearly only a matter of time before the Dominions replaced the Judicial Committee with courts of their own. The Committee nevertheless continued to act for Canada until 1949 as a useful umpire *ab extra*. This helps to explain why it was sometimes forgotten that its legitimacy emanated from the imperial prerogative. No substitute, such as the Supreme Court of Canada, could expect to survive as a prerogative court. In other words, if the Judicial Committee were to be replaced, it would be necessary to ensure that its replacement had a legitimacy of its own different from that provided by imperial federalism. Such a legitimacy could not be automatically provided by "the logic of federalism."

In sum, we need to remind ourselves that the Judicial Committee of the Privy Council did not play a role comparable to that of the American Supreme Court. It did not engage in judicial review of the Constitution. It did not enjoy the legitimacy of a written Constitution emanating from the people, but depended on the prerogative power. Its status was not even that of ordinary English courts: it was part of the executive branch. Its function was not that of broad review but of careful interpretation in conformity with the doctrine of parliamentary supremacy, the supremacy of the British Parliament. Finally, the Judicial Committee did not really interpret a Constitution but an Act of the British Parliament which by English law had to be treated as an ordinary statute.

By adopting the American language of discourse, Canadians may have hoped that they could convince themselves that Canada could evolve from British imperial to American constitutional federalism—replacing one civilization by another—by simply adopting American practices as they seemed convenient, and dropping British traditions that were no longer appropriate. This would, of course, have been in conformity with the notion of the Canadian political personality as one with a preference for "real issues" and "avoidance of unnecessary theoretical decisions." Canadian intellectuals could continue to enjoy the luxury of "philosophical federalism." After all, it was a cardinal English-Canadian assumption that the American principle of constitutional federalism had been successfully grafted onto the British principle of parliamentary democracy. Whatever might be their theoretical incompatibility, the two principles worked together in practice as "parliamentary federalism." But when questions of theory, and in particular of the legitimacy of the Supreme Court, began to emerge after 1960, the limitations of parliamentary federalism became apparent. Difficult constitutional problems could no longer be avoided.

If judicial interpretation of the BNA Act were to give way at a theoretical level to judicial review of the Constitution, some new theoretical underpinning was required. We saw in Section 2 how the natural evolution of changing parliamentary conventions had enabled parliamentary supremacy to replace the Crown's prerogative. But it was not possible to change the federal system, dependent on a legal distribution of powers, through convention.

As Smiley pointed out after acquiescing in the conventional view, parliamentary sovereignty and federalism had been "reconciled" in Canada by an "exhaustive" distribution of legislative powers between Parliament and the provinces: "The continuing adherence of Canadians to the traditions and practices of the Westminster model has both shaped the federal system, and precluded certain kinds of changes in that system."[22] Among the changes he indicated as precluded were:

1. a broad interpretation of the Constitution;
2. a Legislature in which both chambers were (roughly) equal; and consequently
3. a Parliament which served as an effective outlet for sentiments and interests specific to particular provinces and regions.

All three of these characteristics were to be found in the American system of constitutional federalism and were in fact basic to it. If changes in this direction were precluded for Canada, then the transformation of the Canadian parliamentary system into one of constitutional federalism was impossible. Clearly, in Smiley's view, the "logic of federalism" had not been able to cause Canada to evolve beyond very strict limits. The Westminster doctrine of parliamentary supremacy made further evolution impossible.

Chief Justice Marshall's logic directly challenged the Westminster model. It was a logic that required a constitutional document that could be broadly interpreted by the courts and not left subject to narrow interpretation; it required a Constitution expressing the will of the people of Canada, not the will of the Queen-in-Parliament; and it meant the end of imperial federalism and parliamentary federalism. In Kuhn's terminology, there had to be a new paradigm. Or, in the language of discourse used by French Canadians (and copied by them from France), what was required was a new regime.

The Americans and the British had always believed that their systems were mutually incompatible. It is not surprising that many English Canadians, brought up under parliamentary supremacy, were reluctant to take a step towards an American federal system that ran counter to all their loyalist traditions. It is even less surprising that, for them, "memorable history" had ended when the Canadian political system finally achieved autonomy. R. MacGregor Dawson remarked in 1937, "The few constitutional issues which have occurred since the passage of the Statute of Westminster have been of secondary importance in the development of Dominion status, which reached its natural culmination in 1931."[23] Yet Dawson had been well aware in his book on constitutional issues (published in 1933) that Canada had not obtained complete constitutional independence, and that a serious issue remained unresolved.[24] At the time he published his book on Dominion status in 1937, the Judicial Committee was declaring Canada's "New Deal" legislation to be *ultra vires*.

Dawson may, of course, have meant that there were no "constitutional issues" of the sort that had bedeviled relations with the United Kingdom in the 1920s, a time when Britain still acted as the imperial power. Since 1931, imperial federalism was assumed to be dead and the Judicial Committee to be acting as part of Canada's Constitution. As Smiley was to put it in the 1970s, ". . . judicial review of the British North America Act did not evolve as an instrument for securing Imperial influence in

The "Reconciliation" of Parliamentary Supremacy and Federalism   167

Canadian affairs, but rather as a practical device for delineating the respective legislative powers of Parliament and the provinces."[25]

If, then, truly memorable history, that is, the struggle for nationhood, was over, it was now important for the government of Canada to retain what was left of the British connection to avoid the two other dangers of irreconcilable conflict with the provinces and the Americanization of the Canadian political system.

If, following the "logic of federalism," the Supreme Court evolved in the direction of the American Supreme Court and interpreted the Constitution broadly, it could, like the American court in the Dred Scott decision of 1857 (a decision less often quoted than *Marbury v. Madison* by Canadian scholars) contribute to an irreconcilable deadlock between the federal government and one or more provincial governments. By extending its role the Court might also appear to indicate that further Americanization of the Canadian political system (for example, replacement of the appointed Senate by a body truly representing the provinces) was necessary.

Moreover, if the Supreme Court was caught in the middle, whether between the British and Canadian governments or the federal and provincial governments, delicate questions concerning its legitimacy as an impartial umpire might well be raised.

6   Legitimacy of the Supreme Court

The abolition of appeals to the Privy Council seemed long overdue by the time it was finally achieved in 1949. It symbolized Canada's independence in not only international law but in constitutional law. We have already noted that the Privy Council drew its legitimacy from the authority inherent in the imperial prerogative: in law the Judicial Committee was, after all, simply a committee to advise the Crown. We have also noted that the "logic" of imperialism, based ultimately on the supremacy of the British Parliament to whom the Crown was itself subject, was never really replaced by "the logic of federalism." That logic was the logic of American constitutional federalism as expounded by Chief Justice Marshall. Marshall, as we have seen, declared that the Constitution was supreme over acts of Congress and that the Supreme Court, established in accordance with the Constitution, could alone interpret the Constitution on behalf of the American people.

No such transformation occurred in Canada, nor could it occur so long as Canada remained a monarchy, with the legitimacy of many of its institutions dependent not on the will of the Canadian people but upon the Crown. Moveover, the 1949 decision meant not only the abolition of appeals from the Supreme Court of Canada, but the abolition of the traditional right of the provinces to appeal directly to Whitehall. Yet that was a decision taken solely by the Parliament of Canada, not by the provinces themselves. Indeed, the provinces and the people of Canada were never consulted. The only other body involved was the Judicial Committee itself, which was consulted as to the appropriateness of the transfer in a reference in 1947. In affirming the legality of what the Canadian Parliament proposed to do, the Judicial Committee no doubt believed that with the passage of the Statute of Westminster the British government had no reason to be advised to react negatively as it had in 1875.[26] Nor, of course, did it pay any attention at all to the promise made by Cartier to his French-Canadian colleagues in the old Parliament of Canada in 1865 that appeals to the Privy Council would never be abolished. And little attention appears to have been given in Canada generally to the theoretical implications for Canadian federalism of the 1949 decision to abolish appeals to an umpire *ab extra*.

At that time, the main concern was Canada's international position, rather than the effect of "patriation" of judicial appeals on federal-provincial relations. It was, after all, a period in Canadian history when the power and prestige of the federal government was at its height. Louis St. Laurent, the Prime Minister, was a lawyer who had appeared on many occasions before the Judicial Committee. He thought of the move in terms of Canada's rise to international importance as a middle power, a country that no longer required an external umpire.

In any case, English Canadians were not accustomed to asking fundamental theoretical questions about the Constitution and the nature of their political system. It was assumed that the logic of federalism meant that there had to be an umpire. If so, the natural heir of the Privy Council was the Supreme Court. And of course the Supreme Court, following British tradition, would act impartially and with a closer understanding of Canada's conditions. As a result of its actions over the years, the Supreme Court would come to have the legitimacy long enjoyed by the Judicial Committee. Presumably, since Canada remained a monarchy, the source of that legitimacy (appointment of judges by the Crown) would remain much the same.

The "Reconciliation" of Parliamentary Supremacy and Federalism 169

"Philosophical federalism," as we have seen, assumed that there was no need to press an argument to its conclusion. The view of English Canadians was always that if a system worked, that was enough. Insofar as they thought about the matter, their view could be summarized in the form of a number of loosely related propositions:

1. The Judicial Committee had interpreted the BNA Act and had done so as an instrument of empire.
2. In the course of time the imperial BNA Act came to be thought of as the Constitution of Canada, an independent country. (Indeed the BNA Act [no. 2] of 1949 expressly declared the Act to be the Constitution of Canada.)
3. To conform to this change, the Judicial Committee transformed its role, becoming an instrument of Canadian federalism. It now exercised judicial review of the Canadian Constitution.
4. Just as there was never any need to explain or defend the imperial prerogative which had given the Judicial Committee its initial legitimacy, so there was no need to explain or defend the new role of the Judicial Committee: it acted according to the logic of federalism.
5. The transfer of power in 1949 meant no change in principle. It merely determined that the role formerly played by the Judicial Committee could now be played by the Supreme Court. Judicial review of the Constitution was now as much an accepted element of Canadian federalism as the doctrine of parliamentary supremacy.
6. Insofar as the Supreme Court lacked the legitimacy of the Privy Council provided by the imperial prerogative, this would be remedied in time as the Supreme Court by its decisions established its own legitimacy in the eyes of the Canadian people.
7. One way of earning legitimacy was for the Supreme Court to behave according to the same rules as the Judicial Committee, interpreting the Constitution in conformity with the doctrine of parliamentary supremacy, and appearing to be impartial in its adjudication.

All of this depended on the basic assumption that the Supreme Court could, like the Judicial Committee, operate within the framework of parliamentary supremacy. For the Judicial Committee this was easy; the British Parliament *was* supreme. For the Supreme Court, on the other hand, the notion of parliamentary supremacy could present serious problems. All that could be hoped for was that the provinces would not begin to challenge the jurisdiction of the federal authorities, including the Supreme Court, before its legitimacy was established beyond doubt.

Until about 1960 things seemed to be working as hoped. If the Supreme Court was criticized at all, it was criticized for acting just like the Judicial Committee, especially by scholars who thought that the era of constitutional federalism inspired by *Marbury v. Madison* had at last arrived in Canada.

Canada had not yet faced a crisis of legitimacy. "Parliamentary federalism" had apparently been successful, and it was conveniently overlooked that in law it was the Parliament of the United Kingdom that was supreme. "Federalism" appeared to be compatible after all with parliamentary supremacy; it was forgotten that Canada's federalism had been imperial, not constitutional, and that it was the Judicial Committee that adjudicated.

Once the Parliament of Canada assumed the sovereign legislative role of the British Parliament, as it seemed intent on doing by the 1949 amendment of the BNA Act, and once the Supreme Court modeled itself on the American Supreme Court and began to undertake genuine judicial review of the Constitution, then the contradictions between the British tradition of parliamentary supremacy and the logic of constitutional federalism stood exposed.

In making the analogy between Canadian and American federalism and assuming that the Courts in each country played a similar role, Canadians were encouraged to forget that any further development in the direction of constitutional federalism by Canada would be fraught with difficulty. In the first place, whereas the American Constitution was established *de novo* by the States, any new constitution would have to take into account an already existing federal government in Canada. Furthermore, a new constitution was more than likely to be introduced by the federal government itself, not by the provinces. It was therefore unlikely to have the same popular backing (in myth at least) as the American Constitution, since it would be the creature of the federal government and not of a constitutional convention.

Only if the federal government's initiative in drafting a new constitution completely failed and a constitutional convention were then called, would Canada be in a state at all similar to that of the United States. Such a convention was conceivable even in Canada, and might have to be called to find out just what type of constitution a majority of the people of Quebec really wanted. For a constitution proposed solely by the federal government could always be said by the *Parti Québecois* to

The "Reconciliation" of Parliamentary Supremacy and Federalism 171

represent only the federalists in Canada. On the other hand, the federal government could argue that the people of Quebec elected not only the *Parti Québecois* but also the governing political party in Canada, and by an overwhelming majority in 1980 and 1984. Were the Quebec electors compelled to elect delegates to a constitutional convention they would have to choose between federalism and separatism: they would no longer be able to have it both ways, electing separatists to Quebec City and federalists to Ottawa.

6
From Conquest via Rebellion to Dualism: French-Canadian Perceptions before 1867

Of the two main transcendental categories of understanding, space and time, Anglophones lay the greatest emphasis upon space, and Francophones upon time.—Léon Dion, *Quebec, the Unfinished Revolution*

1   A Different Language of Discourse

The sense of time in French Canada has always been different. For French Canadians, history has deeper roots than it has for English-speaking Canadians outside Newfoundland. "Memorable history" has never been identified with the period of Confederation from 1867 onward. When the license plates of Quebec motorists remind the world *"Je me souviens,"* the memory is of an old regime. Before the great changes of the 1960s, truly significant history for many French Canadians stopped with the Conquest of 1760.

French Canada's sense of space has also been different. With the Dominion of Canada established from the Atlantic to the Pacific, English Canadians who had been confined to the eastern fringes of North America were able to extend their vision across the continent. French Canada's sense of space, by contrast, was to contract. Long accustomed to regarding the American interior from Detroit to New Orleans as their preserve, the *Canadiens,* as the French were called, had already found their vision limited by the Conquest: The English-speaking Americans claimed the continent up to, and beyond, the forty-ninth parallel. Later, the English-speaking Canadians began to assume that the land west of the Ottawa River was in fact theirs. For the *Canadiens,* Confederation brought with it a new dream, the dream of dualism in the Canadian West, of a partnership between English and French to open up the new frontier. But this dream was to fade, owing to the inability of the French to firmly establish their presence in the prairie provinces.

French Canadians, then, had a deeper sense of history than the English, a history that after 1760 was cultural rather than political. They also had a more confined sense of space, reduced from a vision encompassing most of North America to those parts where the French presence still made itself felt. So different was the historical experience of the French-speaking Canadians from the English, an experience in which first conquest and later rebellion played an important part, that their interpretation of Canada's history had little in common with the "Rise of Liberty" school of liberal English-Canadian historians, that is, with the evolution from colony to nation within the British Empire and Commonwealth.[1] Political history for the French did not evolve slowly, from precedent to precedent. Rather it seemed to proceed in stages, each stage being a turning point marked, as far as the French as a community were concerned, by the establishment of a new regime to which they were expected to adjust.

Even the terms used to describe the French-Canadian political tradition were different. Instead of a heritage of settlement designed to give each colonist his individual freedom, there was the folk memory of the Conquest and of a Church-oriented society; the French were to regard themselves primarily as a community. Later, instead of acquiescing in the British colonial system, they rebelled against imperialism. This was followed not by the belief in majority rule and representation by population that became popular in Upper Canada, but by an adherence to "dualism," an assumed social compact between English and French. Finally, instead of treating Confederation as the birth of Canada, many French Canadians regarded the whole enterprise with cool detachment, as yet another compact.

French Canada's relations with the British Empire were necessarily different from those of English Canada. Britain was not the mother country. However hard French Canadians tried, Britain for them could never be more than an admired mother-in-law in an arranged marriage. As Bergeron put it, *"Nos bras sont à l'Angleterre, mais nos coeurs sont à la France."*[2] ("Our arms are England's, but our hearts are France's.") French Canada might reconcile itself to becoming part of British and later North American civilization, but culturally (before the Quiet Revolution at least), French Canadians identified themselves with France.

Even so, the relations between French Canada and France were not at all like those between English Canada and Britain. The Conquest had broken the umbilical cord: French Canadians had been left to fend for themselves in an alien empire on a distant and inhospitable continent. Unlike the English Canadians, the French Canadians did not think of themselves as a branch of the French nation. French Canada was more to be compared with a tree that had been cut down and left to die. But it had not died. Instead it had developed its own roots, and in due course had grown into a new tree.[3]

In other words, if we are to interpret the French-Canadian political tradition with any sensitivity, we have to remember that French Canada's memories as a colony were very different from the perceptions of English Canada. We therefore have to become accustomed to a different language of discourse, a discourse that has used such terms as Conquest, Rebellion, dualism, and changes of regime as key words.

2   Regime Change

Because the crucial date in Canadian history from the perspective of English Canada is 1867, English-Canadian university textbooks on Canadian government have traditionally placed just one document in their appendix: the British North America Act. But because for French Canadians there are other turning points, French-Canadian texts include as appendixes extracts from earlier documents.[4] These include the Royal Proclamation (1763), the Quebec Act (1774), the Constitutional Act (1791), and the Act of Union (1840). The difference in attitudes toward constitutional documents symbolizes the two different approaches to Canadian history.[5] To many English Canadians, 1867 is the year when Canada, as they understand it, really began; the rest is prologue. To French Canadians, Confederation is one of a number of turning points to which they have learned to adjust. What happened was a recognition, at last, of French Canada's autonomy in Quebec; if anything it was an epilogue.

If Confederation was to English Canadians the birth of a new nation, the Dominion of Canada, then to French Canadians the Conquest of Quebec by the British had been the death of the old Canada, of New France as a political entity. Inevitably, the English-Canadian perspective had been in large part that of the conqueror. Just as inevitably, the French perspective had been that of a conquered people. To the French, the earlier British documents were important because they delineated the role that French Canadians were expected to play within the British Empire, first as a subordinate culture and later as a political subsystem.

"Colonialism" is an ambiguous term. To English Canadians it has meant the settlement in Canada of British colonists who in the course of time demanded autonomy from the mother country. To French Canadians it has meant the conquest by another country whose settlers, as well as the official imperial representatives, then played a leading role in the governance of the colony. For many of the French, therefore, the limited goal of the English colonists in the nineteenth century, autonomy within the Empire, was never enough.

To view Canada as a colony divided between free British settlers and oppressed French *habitants* is, however, to ignore the willingness of the imperial authorities from an early stage to establish a regime that would allow the French a degree of participation in the governing of the province. Even in the Royal Proclamation of 1763 defining British policy towards Quebec, the British government promised to "summon and call General Assemblies" and:

> . . . until such Assemblies can be called as aforesaid, all Persons Inhabiting in or resorting to our Said Colonies may confide in our Royal Protection for the Enjoyment of the Benefit of the Laws of our Realm of England;
> . . . with Liberty to all Persons who may think themselves aggrieved by the Sentences of such Courts, in all Civil Cases, to appeal, under the usual Limitations and Restrictions, to Us in our Privy Council.

The promise of an assembly was not fulfilled for some decades. Moreover, the Proclamation imposed the Test Act, whereby Roman Catholics wishing to obtain public office had to renounce their faith; it also established the Royal supremacy over the Church. Even so, though a conquered colony, Quebec emerged from the *ancien régime* and began to share in the liberties free Englishmen enjoyed throughout the Empire, at least as far as the criminal law was concerned. Like the British settlers, French Canadians were entitled to appeal, if necessary, to the Privy Council in London for redress.

The old French civil law, which governed property and "civil rights," remained intact. Here was another area in which the British forbore from exercising the right of conquest. They did not replace the French civil law with the English common law. Only the English criminal law was introduced.

The Quebec Act of 1774 recognized the distinctive culture of Quebec and confirmed the right of French Canadians to enjoy "the free Exercise of the Religion of the Church of Rome, subject to the King's Supremacy," and to continue to enjoy, "their Property and Possessions, together with all Customs and Usages relative thereto, and all other Civil Rights." The term "civil rights," it should be noted, referred to the rights of the French as a community. It meant something quite different from the terms "civil rights" and "civil liberties" in the Anglo-American tradition: English Canadians thought of these in terms of the individual, not the community.[6]

The regimes established by the Royal Proclamation, 1763, and the Quebec Act, 1774, were replaced in 1791 by the Canada (or Constitutional) Act. Thirty years after the Conquest, French culture remained intact, but as a result of the loyalist migration from the former American colonies there were now many English-speaking settlers in the western part of the province. Under a vigorous Lieutenant Governor, John Graves Simcoe, British civilization was becoming firmly established in what was later to be Ontario.[7] The Constitutional Act divided Canada into *two separate Provinces,* to be called the Province of Upper Canada and the Province of Lower Canada. Each was provided with an appointed Legislative Council as upper house, and an elected Legislative Assembly, which together with the Crown would ". . . make laws for the peace, welfare and good Government thereof." It was these three eighteenth-century documents of 1763, 1774, and 1791 that were to form the basis for Quebec's claim always to be treated differently from the rest of Canada.

The fourth document, the 1840 Act of Union, was different. It reflected the growing pride of the British in the imperial role of their civilization. In India, in 1835, the English language had replaced Persian as the official language. In Canada, the Act of Union (1840) not only replaced the separation of Upper and Lower Canada by the "reunion of the said two Provinces" but declared that in the new Province of Canada the proceedings of the legislature "shall be in the English language only."[8]

The Royal Proclamation and the Quebec Act were important to French Canadians because these two documents enabled them, the original Canadians, to preserve their culture. The other two constitutional documents, the Constitutional Act and the Act of Union, were significant because they established new political regimes, dividing and then reintegrating the old Province of Canada that was centered on the St.

Lawrence River. The Act of Union, which followed the Rebellion, was clearly intended to absorb the French Canadians into an expanding British civilization.

The political history of French Canada is not, of course, adequately described by a study of constitutional pronouncements. Whereas to English Canadians the various documents—particularly the British North America Act—were symbols of Canada's evolution toward dominion status, to the French these four enactments merely represented changes in the formal structure of government instigated by the British. They certainly did not transform *Quebec* from a colony into a nation: they merely signaled the advent of yet another regime. Daniel Johnson, shortly before he became premier of Quebec in 1966, described the Fathers of Confederation as men *"qui nous amène à notre cinquième constitution: celle de 1867."*[9] In other words, the document that was revered by English Canadians as their one and only constitution was to French Canadians their fifth. Nor was it expected to be the last.

The French interpreted Canada's history from a perspective that stressed their own specific role in the emergence of North American civilization. Their historians wrote extensively about the French regime before 1760: they had comparatively little to say about Confederation itself. The preoccupation of French Canadians was not with the political development of Canada as a whole, but with French Canadian culture and Quebec society.[10]

The end of New France as a political system in 1763 did not mean the end of French society and culture or the end of the *ancien régime* as a social institution. When the British took over political control of Quebec they did not attempt to destroy what was left of the existing society, a society which for most Canadians revolved around the family, the seigneury and the parish.[11] The British did, however, intend to create a different Canada. The loyalists who came to Canada were British Americans who, although they might have rejected the American Revolution politically, nevertheless reflected the aggressive, acquisitive, Protestant, individualist society of the American colonies. Like the Americans, they were interested in new techniques in agriculture and in developing new markets for their products. The French Canadians, however, remained untouched by the revolutions of the eighteenth century, whether American or French—or even what passed for a revolution within the industrialization of England.[12] Because of the important position in Quebec society of a Church supported by a politically apathetic peasantry, the term "French Canada" became, for the English Canadians, synonymous with backwardness and passivity.

French-Canadian scholars have also had to admit that the French Canadians formed what today would be called a "less developed" society. They have been divided in their explanations of why this was so. Clerical writers defended the French Canadians as having spiritual rather than material goals. Rationalist critics, like Pierre Trudeau, accused their countrymen of being largely the cause of their own misfortunes. A third viewpoint, that of radical critics, sought to distinguish between the Church and seigneurs (the collaborators) on the one hand and the peasants on the other. The "passivity" of the peasants, the radicals insisted, was really a passive resistance that often became insubordination.[13]

Not surprisingly, liberal political scientists like Dawson tended to regard the French-Canadian tradition as *sui generis,* as a deviant case that in the context of the Dominion as a whole was best ignored. In their works there were usually no separate chapters devoted to the institutions peculiar to Quebec. The middle classes were assumed to have accepted the English-Canadian political tradition, except for a minority of rebels, *Rouges* and radicals. The idea that the French experience of changing regimes offered an alternative interpretation of Canadian history was rarely if ever considered. Indeed, English Canadians often rationalized the Conquest itself, insisting that it brought to French Canada the blessings of liberty.[14] For example, to English Canadians, the cases before the Canadian Supreme Court prior to 1959 involving Jehovah's Witnesses, and particularly their right to proselytize in Quebec, involved civil liberties. By contrast, the two French-speaking judges from Quebec formed a consistent minority resisting what English Canadians called "the imposition of national values on local values." The French-Canadian judges did not see the situation as one primarily involving civil liberties but ". . . presumably as simple situations involving the community protection of public safety or public morals."[15] According to McWhinney, in English Canada these cases were thought to be analogous to the desegregation cases in the United States, where national values were also imposed on the deviant South. As recently as the mid-1960s, Ramsay Cook could conclude that "the fact is that the English Canadians have not yet come to accept the view that French Canadians are different from other minority groups and therefore have a right to special treatment."[16] This failure to recognize the distinctive world view of the French Canadians in nineteenth- and twentieth-century Canadian history was to have serious consequences after the Quiet Revolution.

Only recently, and in large measure because of the sympathetic inquiries of historians like Professor Cook, did there develop a greater willingness to come to terms with the French-Canadian perspective of regime change. Because its interpretation took into account not only Confederation but the Conquest, the Rebellion, and Canada's first experiment with English-French "dualism" between 1841 and 1867, the francophone tradition was based on a world view that stressed the role of the two "charter races" in Canada. Indeed it tended to regard Confederation from a dualist perspective, as a compact or treaty between the two "races," to use the French term.[17] It also treated with appropriate seriousness the various crises after Confederation that strained this relationship.

In sum, whereas the English-Canadian political tradition was to concentrate on modern Canada after 1867, the French-Canadian tradition was much more conscious of Canada's long history. Confederation to the French was the fifth in a series of regime changes, to be compared with those of 1763, 1774, 1791, and 1840–41. The French-Canadian political tradition retained vivid memories of the Conquest, the Rebellion, the sectional dualism of the old province of Canada, the view of Confederation as a "pact between the races," and the various occasions when the supposed "pact" was broken by the English-speaking majority. These events, as we have seen, tended to be little more than footnotes in the dominant English-Canadian tradition.

3   A United Society: the Trauma of the Conquest
    and the Role of the Church

We have described the history of Canada after 1791, including the history of Quebec, as one of increasing participation in the government of the country. And just as English Canadians were to be divided in their attitude toward the British connection, so also were the French. Certainly, in explaining the divisions within French Canada it makes sense to treat them historically. At any one time a particular world view tended to predominate, with the majority of French Canadians subscribing to its assumptions. And no world view, whether of conquest, rebellion, or dualism, replaced its predecessors. Each became an integral part of French Canada's history, an accretion to the special culture that came to be associated with Quebec.

Turning, then, to the historical experience of French Canada, we need to be aware that what has traditionally united the French Canadians has been the trauma of defeat. Judging by the number of references in French-Canadian writings to the year 1759–60, it would seem that French-Canadian intellectuals never forgot the Conquest and all it stood for.[18]

The British themselves did not grasp the full significance of the Conquest for the French, and tended to believe that the constitutional documents from 1791 to 1867 effectively replaced the Royal Proclamation of 1763. They thought of the conquest of Quebec by British land and sea forces as a thrilling episode in their island's long dispute with the mightiest of European empires, a dispute in which they were ultimately to be victorious. By 1760 the British had for a number of years been methodically attacking the various French colonies of North America in turn. With their superior sea power they had first taken possession of the Maritime provinces. The fortress of Louisburg had been captured in 1745. Ten years later they had deported from what was to become New Brunswick those Acadians who refused to swear allegiance to the British Crown. Generations of British schoolchildren were to be told how British troops scaled the heights above Quebec City in 1759 and went on to win the Battle of the Plains of Abraham, a battle in which both commanders, Wolfe and Montcalm, lost their lives.

For the French Canadians, the battle fought above Quebec City in 1759 was part of a larger tragedy, the loss of New France. Indeed, for the French Canadians it was the capture of Montreal in 1760, and with it the permanent loss of New France, which was the more significant event. For the capitulation of Montreal made the Conquest complete and led to the Treaty of Paris in 1763. By that treaty, France renounced all claims to Acadia (Nova Scotia) and ceded Cape Breton. The future of Canada as a political entity was sealed. At that point, British civilization replaced French as the dominant civilization in North America.[19]

English Canadians, in due course, were to share in the excitement and the glory of the Conquest. It was not always made clear that it had been a battle between the British and French armies (with supporting Indians), and not between the inhabitants of what was subsequently to be known as English Canada and French Canada. The gulf between

British civilization and French culture was not made narrower by the assumption that the British victory symbolized the superiority of British civilization. After the Rebellion Lord Durham stressed the gulf when he referred to Canada as two warring nations. A century later, when passions had cooled, Hugh MacLennan (in 1944) detected two solitudes.

From the start, the culture of French Canada suffered from the absence of the political leadership it had enjoyed for over a century under the *ancien régime*. The new British civilization initially made itself most felt in the fields of government and administration, that is, in Quebec City. Later it was most felt in commerce, particularly in Montreal. Following the capitulation the French political authorities—the Governor, the Intendant, and their officials—embarked for France. They were replaced by a British governor who later served as Commander-in-Chief of all British North America. Under the French regime, the more adventurous colonists had explored the continent, traveling as far south as New Orleans, which remained in French hands. Now, the 60,000 French settlers who were left behind in Quebec were mostly *habitants,* independent peasants whose families were still steeped in the traditions of rural France.

Indeed, eighty years later, Lord Durham observed that the French Canadians still practiced old-fashioned farming, and that few were engaged in manufacturing and commerce. "Whatever energy existed among the population was employed in the fur trade, and the occupations of hunting, which they and their descendants have carried beyond the Rocky Mountains, and still, in great measure, monopolize in the whole valley of the Mississippi."[20] Only a few "seigneurs," as the larger landowners and land agents were politely called, remained.[21] Thanks to the Conquest, the *Canadiens* remained, for a generation or so, a people without an indigenous political or commercial ruling class. That class, largely French, had abandoned them to the British, who now formed the commercial bourgeoisie.

In the 1950s, Pierre Trudeau was to offer a vivid self-portrait, which some modern historians consider a caricature, of the French Canadians after the Conquest:

> A people vanquished, occupied, leaderless, kept aside from business life and away from the cities, gradually reduced to a minority role and deprived of influence in a country which, after all, it had discovered, explored and settled, could have but a limited choice

of attitudes that might help it to preserve its own identity. A system of self-defense was thus developed; but as it grew out of bounds, it invested French Canadians' every distinguishing characteristic with inordinate value and made them hostile to all ideas for change, or even for possible improvement, that came from the outside.

That is why, pitted against an English, Protestant, democratic, materialistic, business-minded, and later industrial environment, our nationalism's system of self-preservation glorified every contrary tendency; and made a cult of the French language, Catholicism, authoritarianism, idealism, the rural way of life, including later, the myth of a "return to the land."[22]

The departure of French administrators, and the withdrawal of the French-Canadian people into themselves, provided an opportunity for a new leadership to emerge, one that was not political but spiritual and social. The Roman Catholic Church became the dominant force, as it was for people elsewhere in similar situations, notably the Irish and the Poles. By "social" leadership is meant not only the religious and moral outlook of the French Canadians, which remained strongly Catholic until the 1960s, but the cultural milieu as expressed in language, literature, and philosophy. The education of the young people was the responsibility of the Church.

In other words, while the Treaty of Paris signaled the end of the dominance of French civilization in Canada, the Conquest did not bring with it an end to French Catholic culture. In confirming the right of the *Canadiens* to their separate cultural life, the imperial government's Quebec Act succeeded in its main object: ensuring that under the leadership of the Church (and in contrast to metropolitan France), the *Canadiens* remained aloof from the conflict that was about to break out between Britain and her American colonies. (Decades later, in the War of 1812, French and English Canadians were to join in resisting the American invader.) The Church, for its part, preferred to accommodate itself to the Conquest, and to support the British Crown with its conservative but tolerant regime, rather than to side with the aggressively Protestant republicans to the south. The Church learned to acquiesce in, if not to accept, the Conquest.

But was there only one Conquest? Is it perhaps arguable that the British North American colonies owed their character to two conquests?

Twenty years after the Treaty of Paris sealed the victory of Britain over France, another Treaty of Paris recognized the emancipation of the United States from colonial rule. Settlements of defeated American Tories (or loyalists) were established not only in the Maritimes but along the northern shores of Lake Ontario across from New York State and in various other parts of Quebec, particularly Montreal and the new "Eastern Townships" not far from the New England border.

It is true that Canada was founded by two nations, both of which were losers. But other analogies between French and English Canada are misleading. The majority of twentieth-century French Canadians were to be the descendants of the small community that experienced the Conquest. The majority of English Canadians, however, were not descended from the loyalists. Most were the offspring of nineteenth- and twentieth-century immigrants who did not bear the scars of military defeat. On the contrary, many of them prided themselves on belonging to something much greater than Canada alone: the British Empire. Some were fiercely Protestant. The Protestant Orange Order, and later the imperial ethos, became powerful forces during the reign of Queen Victoria. They contributed to the broadening and deepening of the British political tradition, which was confused with loyalism in those parts of Ontario and the Maritimes where the loyalists actually settled. (Thus, when Mrs. Pauline McGibbon retired as Lieutenant-Governor of Ontario in 1980, a dozen or so loyalist societies arranged a formal dinner in her honor in Toronto). In any case, there was a vast difference between the status of the middle-class loyalists who had been able to leave the American colonies and to establish themselves in Canada with the active support of the British government, and the Quebec *habitants,* often illiterate, deserted by the government of France.

The immigration of the loyalists was to be in some ways to the political advantage of the *Canadiens:* Lower Canada also obtained a Legislative Assembly in 1791. This meant that, having already been granted cultural autonomy before the American War of Independence, the French Canadians, after the French Revolution, were able to start on the long road to political autonomy. But progress was slow. In Europe, Belgium was to secure its independence from the Netherlands in 1830 and Hungary was to obtain autonomy from Austria in domestic affairs in 1867. Latin America had long ago broken away from Spain and Portugal. By contrast, the French Canadians, apart from the small professional middle class, remained relatively docile, their nationalism dormant. They might obtain limited autonomy in 1867, but apart from the sporadic outbreaks of 1837 and 1838 they did not rise up as a people against the British Crown. The *habitants,* for the most part accepted the leadership of the Church. And the Church in Quebec always opposed any rebellious tendencies. Whereas the English Canadians could be viewed in political terms, as a people supportive of the British connection, the French Canadians could not. They were a community, not a polity, and such support as they gave was to the Church.

Why did the French Canadians accept the Church's leadership for so long? The obvious explanation is the one we have given: that with the departure of the French civil authorities the Church was the only French national institution left.[23] Moreover, so long as political autonomy was not feasible, the Church offered an alternative to the goal of political independence: spiritual salvation. By not directly challenging the English notion of royal supremacy, the Church was able to continue its sacred mission. Its prime concern was religion, not nationalism. In providing spiritual leadership it coincidentally preserved and maintained the cultural identity and autonomy of the *Canadiens.*

Radical writers have drawn a distinction between the role of the Church after the Conquest and after the Rebellion. They have pointed out that the eighteenth-century *habitants* were not particularly religious and that whatever clerical historians may have suggested, the Church was too weak to exercise much control over the peasantry.[24] Certainly in the late eighteenth century, people in North America were generally far less religious than later generations. It is not surprising, therefore, that a radical, secular alternative to the Church emerged in Canada in the 1830s before the religious revival. But Lower Canada being the conquered colony it was, it is equally unsurprising that the radicals' challenge to the predominance of both the imperial authorities and the Church proved unsuccessful.

In view of the failure of the Rebellion, and the absence of any other powerful movement, it is reasonable to regard the Church as a significant intellectual and spiritual force in French Canada until the 1950s. And once the radicals had been defeated in 1837–38, there was no other defense against English hegemony. Writing in 1906, André Siegfried concluded, "Little wonder, then, if the Church is doubly dear to the French of Canada, who see in it not merely the exponent of their faith but also the accredited defense of their race."[25] As a conquered "race" the *Canadiens* learned to depend on the Church rather than on the state. In the absence of political autonomy "the state" meant the British Empire and the successive governors sent out to deal with the recalcitrant, and largely French, Legislative Assembly of Lower Canada. It is true that after this Assembly was merged with that of Upper Canada in 1841, and especially after the establishment of responsible government a few years later, the *Canadiens* were brought into the government as well as into the administration of their section of the united province. But there was still no sense that "the state" represented French Canada. Canada was part of the dominant civilization of the century, the British Empire, and that empire represented to French Canadians state power. "French Canada" meant a culture, guarded by the Church, a culture largely spiritual in its outlook. Even after Confederation it was to be a long time before the Church lost its influence over the social and political orientation of French Canadians. The Church, for its part, had a vested interest in acquiescing in the political status quo.

Acquiescence did not mean positive acceptance of British rule. The Church did not meekly give in to the demands of the imperial authorities or their successors in the Government of Canada. It fought tenaciously for its own spiritual autonomy and for the cultural autonomy of the French Canadians, for both the faith and the language. They were considered inseparable.

The Church acquiesced in the sense that it preferred British, and later Dominion, rule to the available alternatives. It saw no comfort in the example of the United States. The clergy did not want French Canadians to lose their separate spiritual identity in the secular American republic. After 1789 they could no longer look to France. The Church recoiled with distaste against the bloody, anticlerical and radical French revolution. It was disturbed by Napoleon's excesses. As Henri Bourassa, the early-twentieth-century nationalist, was to observe, "Assuming that we would have escaped the bloody Reign of Terror, it is more than probable that Napoleon would have sold us to the Americans without even consulting us, as he did with Louisiana."[26] Nor did the Church offer any encouragement to those radicals in Quebec who wanted to secede from the British Empire and to set up an independent State of Quebec, for these radicals, too, wanted a secular republic.

Protestants, though religious, tried to separate Church and state. While the world outside was therefore becoming increasingly secular in the nineteenth and twentieth centuries, the Catholic Church in Quebec continued under British and Dominion rule to enjoy a power and prestige denied to the Church in either France or the United States—or for that matter in Britain or in English Canada. Elsewhere in due course taxes were the responsibility of the state; education was in the hands of secular authorities; and health and welfare were, in varying degrees, a public responsibility. Not so in Quebec. Here the Church continued to levy tithes (or their equivalent) on the faithful to pay for its expenses. Moreover, it could impose special taxes for capital projects such as the magnificent churches, schools, and colleges that came to dot the Quebec landscape.

The British did attempt to introduce secular education, but failed. The first attempt, the Education Act of 1801, created a Royal Institution for the Advancement of Learning supervised by the governor, the lieutenant-governor, the Anglican bishop, the chief justice, and the Speaker of the Assembly.[27] It was intended to establish free primary education throughout Lower Canada and to provide two royal grammar schools, in Quebec and Montreal. Despite its English and Protestant orientation, the Act was passed by the Legislative Assembly: for once the Church was asleep.[28] However, the Act was not implemented. In 1824 the Assembly passed the Parish Schools Act which gave control of teaching to the curés and the local parish wardens. This Act was passed at the instigation of the clergy during a period of reconciliation between the Church and the Assembly. But little was done to implement this Act either. Only thirty-five schools were built.

A second attempt to introduce secular education—this time under French-Canadian auspices—was made by the Legislative Assembly through the Assembly Schools Act of 1829. By 1830, 981 such schools were in existence, and by 1836, 1530.[29] They were suspected, however, of being more concerned with turning out turbulent *patriotes* than loyal Catholics. In 1836 the Legislative Council refused to renew the Act.

Instead, education in Quebec came to be organized on denominational lines, with Protestant school boards for the English-speaking Protestants and Roman Catholic boards for the French-speaking Catholics. The education of Catholics at all levels, from primary school to University, was the responsibility of the Church. The *habitants,* for the most part, remained poorly educated. The middle classes sent their children to seminaries or classical colleges originally established to provide priests from local sources (rather than from France). Faced by a radical alternative, and impressed by the Church's loyalty to the Crown, the imperial authorities acquiesced in the Church's dominant role.

Even the various Orders of the Church, such as the Sulpicians, Jesuits, and Recollets, came to be treated with great tolerance by the British authorities. So congenial was the clerical atmosphere of nineteenth-century Quebec in comparison to France that thousands of French monks and nuns are reported to have crossed the Atlantic. The Church was able to take responsibility not only for education but for hospitals and charitable work as well. Although the principle of Royal Supremacy over the Church was never directly challenged, in practice Rome appointed the bishops from a list of three candidates nominated by the Church of Quebec.

The dominant role of the Church from the Conquest onward, in secular as well as in sacred matters, was to be challenged by a radical movement. While the mass of the peasants might be docile, by the early nineteenth century there was a growing professional middle class which resented the Conquest and dreamed of an autonomous Quebec. Its representatives were vocal in the Legislative Assembly in the early decades of the nineteenth century and by the 1830s were passing resolutions and organizing petitions in the hope of bringing about drastic changes in the imperial system that would open up opportunities for the *Canadiens*. The *Patriote* party included many who believed that the winds of change blowing elsewhere would lead to reform in Canada itself. Frustrated by the imperial government's lack of response to their demands some of them decided that the only way of dealing with the British was to follow the American example and to rebel.

To the trauma of the Conquest and to the sense of being a closely knit spiritual community loyal to the Church (and through the Church to the Crown), there was now added another expression of the French Canadian world view: rebellion. This manifestly meant rebellion against the Crown as symbol of political authority, and by implication against the Church as spiritual authority.

4 A Divided Society: Rebellion

If change of regime and memory of the Conquest (sustained by loyalty to the Church) comprise the first two themes of the French-Canadian tradition, recollection of the rebellion forms the third. The rebellion was a long time in erupting; unlike those of its counterpart in Upper Canada, its ultimate consequences were to be profound.

Early in the nineteenth century, the elected members of the House of Assembly of Lower Canada began to demand more powers for the Assembly. The small French middle class, impotent in the face of the Governor and his nominated Executive and Legislative Councils, was radicalized by the colonial regime, a regime little different from the one experienced by the American colonies before 1776. The focus of French discontent was the Assembly, as it had been for the Americans. After his election as Speaker in 1815, the young seigneur, Louis-Joseph Papineau, began to emerge as the leader of the *Parti Canadien*. Under Papineau, the *Patriote* Party, formed in 1827 as successor to the *Parti Canadien,* fought for self-government and attracted a number of influential members of the political elite. They at first prudently proclaimed themselves "friends of the king, of the Constitution, and of the country." According to two French-Canadian scholars, the party's ethos was, "liberal with a view to integrating the Canadian tradition into a fully worked-out framework of British parliamentary institutions." Papineau they described as, "a great parliamentary liberal, a great patriot forced by the circumstances to be a nationalist."[30]

Others have described Papineau differently. Fernand Ouellet has quoted from his maiden speech in the Legislative Assembly, in which he said, "I have found the good political doctrines of modern times explained and revealed for the love and regeneration of the peoples in a few lines of the Declaration of Independence of 1776 and the Declaration of the Rights of Men and Citizens of 1789."[31] Monière has noted that in 1827 Papineau was a republican influenced by American ideas of government. He was also primarily concerned with old Quebec. "His view was centered on Lower Canada: the *Patriote* leader never imagined a Canada embracing all the British North American colonies, and he opposed the inclusive vision of the commercial middle class."[32] If the Church's conservatism was antistatist, Papineau's radicalism was anticommercial and antiindustrial. "Economic development was to be anchored to the sole resource that was accessible to French Canadians—agriculture."[33]

The Rebellion took about a decade to ignite. In 1827 there was presented to the Crown a monster petition containing 87,000 "signatures" (most of them were "marks"). However, the Legislative Assembly was unable to obtain redress of its grievances because of the opposition of the governor, supported by the largely English executive and legislative councils. The imperial reaction to Canada's pleas for reform in the early 1830s was very different from the response of the great metropolitan powers to their own unrest. In France, the Bourbon regime finally came to an end with the July Revolution of 1830. In England, Parliament agreed to the passage of the Great Reform Bill of 1832, after widespread agitation that nearly led to the emasculation of the recalcitrant House of Lords. The United States gave expression to a new radicalism by the election of the frontier Democrat Andrew Jackson as President. But Canada remained unchanged. Violence accompanied the elections in 1834 in Lower Canada. The English speaking oligarchy of merchants, officials, and hangers-on at the Château St. Louis, the governor's mansion (hence the term "the Château Clique"), retained its veto power in the appointed Legislative and Executive Councils.

In the elected Legislative Assembly, however, the *Patriotes* were the dominant group, and it was frustration over their continuing impotence that led many of them to become more radical. Their party already possessed its own emblem, a flag with green, white, and red stripes not too dissimilar from the French revolutionary tricolor. (When Quebec finally obtained its distinctive flag in 1948, the conservative *Union Nationale* government selected the fleur de lys, emblem of the Bourbons). The *Patriotes'* slogans of social progress, democracy, reform, and liberty, reflected the radical thought common in continental Europe at the time.

Led by the *Patriotes,* the Legislative Assembly in 1834 presented to the Crown the Ninety-Two Resolutions, as they came to be commonly called. They contained a demand for structural change and suggested, among other things, that the Westminster parliamentary system might not be suitable for Canada. They also proposed that the Legislative Assembly of Lower Canada be treated as analogous to the House of Commons in Britain. There was a barely veiled threat in some of the Resolutions that failure to meet these demands might lead to secession:

> 43. Resolved, that the constitution and form of government which would best suit this colony are not to be sought solely in the analogies offered by the institutions of Great Britain, where the state of society is altogether different from our own . . .
>
> 79. Resolved, that this House, as representing the people of this province, possesses of right, and has exercised within this province when occasion has required it, all the powers, privileges and immunities claimed and possessed by the Commons House of Parliament in the Kingdom of Great Britain and Ireland.
>
> 86. Resolved, that this House hopes and believes . . . that the

people of this province may not be forced by oppression to regret their dependence on the British Empire and to seek elsewhere a remedy for their afflictions.[34]

It was difficult for the government in London to reconcile a demand for parliamentary (or responsible) government with imperial rule, particularly since, unlike the English settlements in North America, Quebec had been acquired through conquest. Despite the loss of the American colonies, the British had never developed an ideology of empire.[35] They had no means of overcoming the resentment of colonists towards the imperial power. It was not surprising, therefore, that in 1837 Lord John Russell, in his so-called Ten Resolutions, rejected the demands of the *Canadiens*. Unfortunately, at this time the whole of North America was experiencing a serious depression. By 1837 the *habitants* had experienced several years of rural distress owing to population pressures on the limited arable land available and the exhaustion of its fertility by primitive agricultural methods. The year of the Rebellion saw the culmination of a series of poor harvests in Canada, and a run on the banks in the United States. The stage was set for a confrontation.

The rebellion in Lower Canada was far more than the footnote in history it became elsewhere.[36] The unrest in the province was much more widespread. In addition to economic unrest, there was the long and bitter conflict between the impotent French-speaking majority and the powerful English oligarchy. Popular sympathy, therefore, tended to be with the rebels.

Opinions differ on the extent of the Rebellion. Some observers have remarked on the ease with which the various uprisings were put down by the British troops, and the unwillingness of many people, including Papineau himself, actually to take up arms. While some priests were sympathetic to the *Patriotes,* the hierarchy was implacably opposed to the insurrection. Even those most sympathetic to the rebel cause have stressed the incapacity of its leaders. Like Mackenzie in Upper Canada, Papineau proved to be in no way capable of providing military direction, and no one remotely comparable to George Washington emerged to lead the *Patriote* forces. In Lower Canada, "not only Papineau but also the revolutionary elite in general failed to provide leadership."[37]

Revolutionary fervor was highest in the Richelieu Valley to the east of Montreal. It was in the villages of St. Denis and St. Charles that the *Patriotes* made their first stand. There, in November 1837, the British commander, Sir John Colborne, determined to take the initiative: ". . . Colborne launched his troops in the first phase of what he planned as a full-scale military campaign. The veteran of Waterloo had 6,000 men under his command. Opposing them were an unprepared, ill-armed *Patriote* militia; their leaders having forsworn the offensive, they waited, defensively, for the enemy onslaught."[38] Poorly organized, poorly armed, and poorly led, the rebels were no match for the British regulars. The insurrection here was easily crushed, as it later was elsewhere. Even so, there were further risings or raids from across the American border throughout much of 1838.

The Governor, Lord Durham, dealt leniently with the rebels, but, overruled by London, he resigned and returned to England late in 1838. He was replaced by Colborne, who dealt sternly with those rebels his troops captured. Twelve *Patriotes* were hanged and another fifty-eight were transported to Australia. (In Upper Canada, where 30,000 persons are estimated to have signed petitions for clemency, twenty-one rebels were executed and sixteen transported). The French Canadians were to retain vivid memories of the Rebellion, of the executions, transportation, and above all of the villages burned by the marauding troops.

Many sympathizers with the rebels' cause fled the country, including Papineau. He lived in Paris for several years, and was enabled to remain there by LaFontaine, who was able "to authorize Parisian friends to extend credit to Papineau."[39] The other *Patriotes* were tempted to denounce Papineau for failing to provide leadership in their hour of greatest need. They refrained from doing so when it was argued that "for all his faults, he could be a Franklin without being a Washington."[40]

Why was the Rebellion, despite much popular sympathy, such a disaster? One reason, as we have seen, was lack of leadership, organization, and arms. Another reason may well have been the memory of the Conquest, and a sense of the futility of revolt. In the third place, many French Canadians remained conservative, and were still under the influence of the Church. The *Patriotes,* after all, chose as their models the French and especially the American republics, even to the extent of establishing a body called the Sons of Liberty (*Fils de la Liberté*) and publishing a declaration of independence. These models aroused the hostility of the Church and of the faithful, for it was under the British monarchy that the Church had found itself able to pursue its sacred mission in North America without secular distractions. Jean-Jacques Lartigue, the first Bishop of Montreal (and Papineau's cousin) refused to provide absolution for unrepentant rebels and offered a *Te Deum* to celebrate Queen Victoria's coronation in 1838.

The rebels themselves were divided. Papineau did not attack the ancient régime with its seigneuries and Church tithes. He himself was a seigneur who owned 178,000 arpents (acres) of land at a time when half the *habitants* owned fewer than fifty.[41] At the time of the second rebellion in 1838, with Papineau out of the way, the leaders became more radical in their demands. They read a proclamation declaring Lower Canada independent, providing exemption from all seigneurial dues, and abolishing tithes. As Ouellet has noted, "the rupture between Papineau's conservatives and the radicals gave the latter the upper hand in the second rebellion. Nelson's declarations of independence in February and November of 1838 proclaimed abolition of the old social regime and also universal suffrage, appealing directly to the urban and rural proletariat."[42]

It was an appeal before its time. The failure of the radical members of the middle class to organize a successful revolution put an end not only to the threat of secession and of a republic, but also to talk of a secular state in Lower Canada. (Indeed, seventy years later, the Rebellion was not even indexed by André Siegfried in his book *The Race Question in Canada*). If there was to be change in French Canada, it would have to be change within the British Empire, and within the Westminster tradition of parliamentary supremacy. And it would have to avoid directly challenging the preeminent role of the Church.

Nevertheless, despite its failure, the Rebellion had important consequences for the French-Canadian political tradition. In the first place, it ended the direct political power of the old colonial oligarchy. As a political entity, the Chateau Clique, like Upper Canada's Family Compact, ceased to matter. Instead, the British government began to search for a middle way between the disgraced oligarchies and the rusticated radical republicans.

As it happened, the *Patriote* forces had been divided even before the rebellions. Many of those who had shared the radical criticism of the colonial regime in the 1830s, among them Hippolyte LaFontaine and George-Etienne Cartier, drew the line at armed insurrection and separated themselves from their more violent colleagues. Even so, the imperial authorities issued warrants for the arrest of several of them in 1838. This enabled LaFontaine and Cartier in later years to claim that they had suffered exile for their beliefs. The failure of the Rebellion and the exile of those who had taken an active part in its promotion, left the field open to the moderates once the emergency was over and constitutional government reestablished.

These French-Canadian liberals, scenting the possibility of reform, came to play an important role in the Assembly. A decade after Lord John Russell had rejected the proposals, "responsible government" was introduced by Lord Elgin. With government in the hands of both English-Canadian and French-Canadian "Reformers," the defeat of the old colonial oligarchies was complete.

A second consequence of the Rebellion was that the radical cause, although it suffered defeat on the battlefield, and afterwards was usually represented by only a minority of French-Canadian members in the Assembly, came to symbolize feelings that were to be expressed by (and echoed by later generations of) nationalist sympathizers. Both Hippolyte LaFontaine, who led the French-Canadian Reformers in their demand for responsible government in the 1840s, and George-Etienne Cartier, who became the leading French-Canadian Conservative politician from the 1850s until his death in 1873, remained proud of their nationalist and radical roots as *Patriotes* in their youth.[43]

Both the French-Canadian Reformers and the formidable bloc of Conservatives or *Bleus* who succeeded them in the 1850s were quite willing to cooperate with English Canadians in Upper Canada to make responsible government work. The real successors to the defeated radicals were not the liberals, who (like Cartier) became increasingly conservative, but the *Rouges*. These men belonged to the anticlerical party of Lower Canada which formed a minority group during the Union period.

The radical *Rouges* of the 1850s and 1860s were of a different generation from the older radicals. When Papineau returned from exile in 1845 and once again took his seat in the Assembly, he found himself embittered and unable to resume his previous leadership role.[44] Attacked by the Reformers for taking part in the insurrection, in which he had behaved so ignominiously, he was for a long time denied the credit for inspiring the first genuine resistance to imperial rule.

The radical tradition after the Rebellion had no real counterpart in Upper Canada. For one thing, William Lyon Mackenzie and his followers were discredited as traitors to the loyalist tradition.[45] For another, Upper Canadian liberals were now inclined to be nonconformists concerned less with fighting colonialism than with challenging the hegemony of the Church of England over Protestant education, a challenge which was to give rise to the religious pluralism of Upper Canada. It was this religious division between Catholic and Protestant, and among Anglicans, Presbyterians, and Methodists of the Protestants, which preceded (and helped to foster) philosophical federalism. Upper Canadians were also able to find release for their abundant energies in dreams of Western expansion.

In Lower Canada the conflict resembled that between conservative Catholics and radical freethinkers in France in the days before the victory of the secular Third Republic. The radicals remained, for the most part, a minority, eager to criticize the Church but unable to curb its enormous power. It was to be a long time before they could once again seriously challenge the dominant position of the Roman Catholic hierarchy. In 1844 an attempt was made when a literary and scientific society, the *Institut Canadien,* was founded by a group of young men, mostly of liberal persuasion and supported by Papineau. By 1854 there were numerous such "freethinking" societies.

Members of the Institute hoped that "For a population hitherto without a library, the Institute would function as a popular university and meeting place for young French Canada."[46] But, after 1847, the Institute abandoned its political neutrality, under Papineau's influence. Later, it came out in support of annexation by the United States, and in 1850 a majority of members voted to drop the clause in the Institute's constitution that restricted membership to French Canadians. The Institute found itself opposed by the ultramontanes of the Church. The more zealous ultramontanes wanted to censor books in its library and to proscribe some of the materials that were circulated.

As French Canada became more conservative, once responsible government was achieved, the Church took advantage of this change in mood by setting up rival *Instituts Nationaux*. Gradually, the social base of the radical movement was eroded: "Three paradoxes further explain the *Rouge* decline: their ideology was the expression of an increasingly limited element of the petty bourgeoisie; it was anticlerical while conceding that the clergy played an essential role in society; and *Rouge* ideology, working in the institutional environment of a union where French Canadians formed a minority, never managed to reconcile nationalism with democracy."[47]

The aims of the radical *Rouges* were different from those of the radical "Grits" of Upper Canada with whom they had, of necessity, to form a political alliance. The Upper Canadian Grits were not republicans, they disliked "French power" and they were opposed to the claims of the Catholic Church. In their opposition to the Church of England the Grits were not being anticlerical: they merely wanted to make room for other denominations. The *Rouges,* on the other hand, were heirs of the French enlightenment who hoped to replace revelation with reason. Theirs was a philosophy that could appeal to young, educated French-Canadian professionals denied access to positions of responsibility held by English Canadians. But it was hardly likely to inspire a province-wide movement among the *habitants.* The Church, with its emphasis on the role of the French-Canadian community, was able to appeal to nationalist sentiments alien to the *Rouges,* with their stress on the brotherhood of man and their American sympathies. One by one the *Instituts Canadiens* closed their doors. The last to close was the Montreal *Institut* in 1869, banned by Bishop Bourget for having propagated pernicious doctrines.

The radical tradition was to be as important in its immediate consequences as in the long run. In the short run, the Rebellion provided a sharp antithesis to the Church. Out of this polarization there emerged a secular, but not anticlerical, liberalism as a compromise middle way which was to accept collaboration with *les Anglais.* In the long run, of course, the Rebellion was to provide inspiration to generations of separatist-inclined young French Canadians.

5 Dualism as French Canada's Leitmotiv

From one perspective, the Conquest and the Rebellion can be said to be the "formative events" of the French-Canadian political tradition. But neither the conservatism of the Church after 1760 nor the radicalism of the rebels in the 1830s would have as broad an impact on Canada's political system as a whole after Confederation as the innovations that characterized the Union of Lower and Upper Canada between 1841 and 1867. The success of the Union owed much to a number of French-Canadian leaders who started their political careers as radicals, but who ultimately came to terms with Canada's status as a colony, with French Canada's inherent conservatism, and with English Canada's attachment to the Westminster tradition. It was these French-Canadian politicians who practiced the art of accommodation with the Church and *les anglais.* Sometimes suspected by English Canadians of not being committed to the Westminster system, and often dubbed by the radicals as *vendus,* compatriots who had sold out, these French-Canadian reformers were nevertheless to make an important contribution both to the development of Canada and to the preservation of Quebec's autonomy. Their particular legacy was the establishment of what has been called "Canadian dualism."[48]

Sectional Dualism

In time, the term "dualism," like "parliamentary supremacy," came to have various interpretations, which caused some confusion among English Canadians as they tried to grasp what the French Canadians really wanted. In its earliest manifestation, the word simply meant "sectional dualism," the transfer of the two provinces of Upper and Lower Canada into sections of a single Province of Canada in which English-speaking Upper Canada, despite its smaller population and its canal debts, would have equal representation with the Lower Canada of the *Canadiens.*

In his *Report on the Affairs of British North America,* published in 1839, Lord Durham had proposed the Union as one means of ensuring the assimilation of the backward *Canadiens* into an expanding British civilization. It was this policy of assimilation that made many French Canadians from that time onwards suspicious of British (and later English-Canadian) motives in any proposal that might affect their cultural autonomy.

In fact, of course, the recognition of the dual nature of the country, and the decision to have representation from two distinct sections, each with a half-century of history as a separate colony, meant that the separate identity of Upper and Lower Canada remained. From the start, therefore, although there was legislative union, it was based on the principle of "sectional dualism."

The Failure of Assimilation

In this respect, the Province of Canada turned out to be not at all what the British Government had intended. Lord Durham had assumed that the French Canadians would be gradually absorbed into a growing English-speaking community. By erecting barriers against the use of French and by encouraging British immigration (the British American Land Company alone was granted 850,000 acres in the unoccupied Eastern

Townships of Lower Canada), it was hoped that what the British considered to be the world's most advanced civilization (then at the very beginning of the Victorian era) would inevitably triumph over what appeared to be a backward culture. The Church, however, continued to predominate in rural Quebec; and many of the *habitants* remained virtually illiterate, unimpressed by the advances in civilization that had occurred elsewhere in North America.

The imperial government's first miscalculation was its assumption that through Union it would be able to control the new legislature. It is true that within Canada East there seemed to be a formidable minority, English and Tory, that could, with a little manipulation by the imperial authorities, win up to half the seats in that section. Assuming that the English majority in Canada West (later Ontario) and the English minority in Canada East (later Quebec) cooperated, they could outnumber the French in the Assembly by two or even three to one. Unfortunately for the British, this assumption proved to be unsound. In Upper Canada the English-speaking members were rarely united on any issue, being divided by religion, regionalism, attitude to the Crown, and perspective on the Far West. In Lower Canada too it soon became apparent that quantitatively the English minority was anything but formidable.[49] The proportion of constituencies returning English Tories declined from half to a little over a quarter of the section's seats.[50] The first Speaker of the Assembly to be elected was French-speaking.

The British appear to have made other miscalculations. One was fiscal. They did not foresee that the different economic interests of Toronto and Montreal would make them rivals and would inhibit cooperation between the English-speaking commercial interests of the two cities. Moreover, in consolidating the debts of the two former provinces to the advantage of Upper Canada with its more extensive canal system, they ensured that all Lower Canadians, whether English or French, would have to bear an increased burden of public debt. Naturally, the Montreal English-speaking businessmen found it difficult always to identify with their English-speaking rivals to the west. Ethnic identity proved less powerful than economic rivalry.

A third miscalculation was the assumption that the majority of English Canadians, while perhaps not loyalists, would nevertheless support the Crown in the struggle to assimilate the French. Lord Durham, whose remarks on Canada's "race relations" are still widely quoted, had created the impression that the English and French were implacably opposed to each other as races. But a large proportion of English-speaking Canadians were not communicants of the Church of England or loyalists. They included Scottish Presbyterians and Irish Catholics as well as many English Nonconformists. It was not long before differences of interest and principle were found to take precedence over racial antagonism.

The Rebellion succeeded in discrediting the old Tories—the Family Compact and the Chateau Clique. A vacuum of colonial leadership occurred, which was soon filled by others. By declining to implement Durham's proposal for responsible government, which had had much support in the Canadas long before the Rebellion, the British government disappointed moderate opinion. Proponents of parliamentary reform soon emerged in both sections. And so, instead of the English Canadians joining forces in defense of the Crown against the French, they were divided into loyal Tories versus Reformers who wanted responsible government. The leader of the Reform party in Upper Canada was Robert Baldwin, a respected Anglican lawyer from Toronto. He joined forces with Hippolyte LaFontaine, a French Catholic lawyer from Montreal. LaFontaine had exchanged the radicalism of his *Patriote* youth for a moderate parliamentary liberalism. The British government thus found itself opposed by two growing reform movements that were willing to combine forces in their common endeavor to end colonial rule.[51] Baldwin and LaFontaine succeeded in resisting the blandishments of successive governors who attempted to divide the two leaders and to buy off their supporters with promises of office.[52]

In other words, when offered the choice of obedience to the imperial authorities or cooperation with the French Canadians, the Upper Canadian reformers chose the French. The foundations of Canada as a dualist state were therefore laid in the early 1840s. The English Reformers agreed to the use of French by their Canada East colleagues in the Assembly. Cooperation was taken so far that on one occasion LaFontaine, defeated in his Quebec constituency of Terrebonne by a Tory opponent who was strongly supported by the Governor, was elected by the Reformers in the Fourth York riding (electoral district) of Ontario. In the same year, after Baldwin had been defeated in his riding of Hastings in Canada West, he was elected to the Assembly by the French-Canadian voters in the riding of Rimouski, deep in Lower Canada. (The voters were not at all comparable in numbers to the electorate of the 1970s, which comprised about 60 percent of the total population. In those days men alone could vote, and only if they were property owners. It has been estimated that in 1872 only 15 percent of the total population constituted the electorate in central Canada.)[53]

Canadian history books are replete with references to Lord Durham's dictum of "two nations warring in the bosom of a single state." It is only fair to add that Durham made this observation at the time of the Rebellion and that he died in 1840 before he could revise his judgment. In the 1840s there was an extraordinary degree of cooperation between reformers of both sections. Indeed, by 1848 the governor-general, Lord Elgin, felt obliged to read the Speech from the Throne in both languages. When Durham's proposal to grant responsible government was at last put into effect, and British control over the patronage and political economy of Canada East as well as Canada West finally abandoned, the policy of assimilation was seen to have failed.

The British made a fourth miscalculation. They seem to have assumed that it would be possible to assimilate French Canada without undertaking a thorough reorganization of its public administration. That administration had always been conducted in French throughout much of Lower Canada, and had operated within the constraints of French civil law and Church supervision of education.

To have reorganized French Canada's administrative system would no doubt have been an enormous undertaking. It would also have involved the repeal of the guarantees of the Quebec Act and subsequent pieces of legislation that had enabled Lower Canada to preserve its cultural identity virtually intact. This, the British were unwilling—and perhaps unable—to do. Admittedly, when the Legislature met in 1841, members were expected to speak in English. But so long as the bulk of the people in Lower Canada spoke only French, much of the administration of the section still had to be conducted in that language. It would have been difficult, if not impossible, for the English superintendent of the largely secular educational system of Upper Canada to function adequately in Catholic and French Lower Canada. Nor could the Attorney General of Upper Canada, trained in the common law, deal with the civil law tradition of the other section. And so, in addition to the dual representation in the Assembly, there was a dual system of government and administration.

This all meant that, despite all the talk of assimilation—talk that was to be remembered in alarm by successive generations of French Canadians as they saw their position in Canada gradually being eroded— nothing happened. Existing administrative practices were not modified to meet the demands of the policy of assimilation. Instead, government was adapted to administrative needs and a new principle of government allowed to emerge, that of sectional dualism. This served both as an alternative to the imperial policy of assimilation and as the forerunner of Canadian federalism.

In sum, the British made at least four miscalculations. They did not expect that (1) the proportion of Assembly seats held by English-speaking Tories would rapidly decline; (2) sectional self-interest, common to Montrealers of both races, would prove to be stronger than racial antagonism; (3) the Rebellion would be followed by a joint English-French Reform programme designed to limit imperial rule; or (4) the administration of Lower Canada would have to continue to be carried on largely in French and subject to the constraints of the civil law and (in education) of the Roman Catholic church.

Other Dualist Features of the Union Period

There were three other remarkable features of the dualism of the Union period. One was the early assumption that there should be *dual leadership*. According to the Westminster parliamentary system, only one minister could be appointed First Minister (the term "Prime Minister" came into use in 1867). In Canada each section had its own leader, and he usually held the portfolio of Attorney General West or Attorney General East. Thus there were, in practice, two First Ministers. Since by law the Governor could only appoint one of them, the leaders from each section had to agree on which of them should be appointed (or whether, as happened later, the honorific title should go to a third member of the government, possibly in the Legislative Council). When this dual leadership was first introduced, in 1842, Baldwin gave precedence to LaFontaine. It was thus LaFontaine, a French Canadian and a Roman Catholic, who five years after the Rebellion had the distinction of becoming First Minister.

Dual leadership in government meant more than two First Ministers as Attorneys General. It also meant the appointment of two Superintendents of Instruction and two Ministers of Public Works. The division of the civil service into an English-speaking service for Upper Canada and a largely French-speaking one for Lower Canada required separate representation for each section in Cabinet. (Fortunately, at that time the role of government was limited and so the Ministry could still be of reasonable size.)

A second feature of Canada's duality was the inability to agree on a common capital. Long before the "philosophical federalism" of live and let live that came to characterize the mood of Canada's intellectuals, dualism had reflected, and perhaps caused, an approach to political problems which discouraged pressing arguments to a logical conclusion about which there would be no consensus. This was particularly manifest in the long arguments over the appropriate capital for the united Province of Canada. Despite the British government's hopes for assimilation of the French Canadians, English Canadians were reluctant to have their desires imposed on the French. Instead, government was carried on from successive temporary capitals: Kingston, Montreal, Toronto, and Quebec City. Once Kingston was eliminated as a possible permanent capital, and once Montreal had taken itself out of the running with the burning down of the legislative buildings by a mob in 1849, only Toronto and Quebec were left. Government then alternated between the two cities, with no agreement that either should become the permanent capital. So, long before the British Raj introduced the idea of a summer government in Simla, English- and French-Canadians had grown used to seeing their politicians and civil servants (one-third of whom were French Canadians) sailing up and down the St. Lawrence every four years.[54] Only in 1860 (the anniversary of the Conquest) did construction begin on a new permanent capital. The legislature still having failed to reach agreement on the site, Ottawa, Ontario, across the river from Quebec, was selected by Queen Victoria.

A third dualist feature of the Union period was the widespread assumption that matters in the legislature should be determined by a "double majority." Had this principle been fully implemented, it would have meant that legislation affecting a section could not be implemented unless a majority of members from that section expressed approval. This did not prove practicable because a ministry supported by a majority in one section could often rely only on a minority of supporters in the other. The "double majority" meant in reality simply that each government depended on two blocs of supporters, one from each section, and not upon a single homogeneous party. (This was a forecast of political parties after Confederation, which occasionally met in Ontario or Quebec caucuses.)

Unlike sectional dualism, none of these three dualist features was directly to affect Canadian politics in Ottawa after Confederation. The two first ministers were then replaced by a single prime minister; Ottawa became the permanent capital of Canada; and the double majority principle disappeared from view, to be given barely a line in English-Canadian history textbooks until the 1960s.[55] But as Canada developed as a Confederation, these features of the Union period reappeared in a modified form. English-Canadian prime ministers like Mackenzie King often depended on a "Quebec lieutenant," even if he was given no title like first minister. Each province proudly had its own capital, with Quebec remaining *the* capital for French Canadians. Even the double majority may have reappeared in a different guise after 1907 when certain sections of the BNA Act were deemed to require provincial as well as federal consent.[56]

The Failure of Dualism: Deadlock in the Legislature

The more innovative aspects of dualism were introduced in the 1840s before the French became a minority. English Canadians tend to remember the failure of dualism and the successive deadlocks in the legislature in the late 1850s and early 1860s when the French were a minority on the defensive. It was deadlock which led to the adoption of Confederation as an alternative.[57]

In assessing the Union period it is useful to divide it into two parts, distinguishing the innovative years before 1848 from the more difficult period that followed the grant of responsible government. In the 1840s there was a common desire to reduce the powers of the Crown. At that time the French Canadians formed the majority of Canadians; their parliamentary leaders were reformist in spirit and willing to adopt the Westminster model.

All was changed by the publication of the results of the 1851 census. This showed that Upper Canada had overtaken Lower Canada in population, and made it clear that *la revanche des berceaux* was no match for massive British immigration.[58] The French might not be capable of being assimilated, but they could be reduced to minority status by a people who firmly believed in the principle of majority rule. As Canada West became more radical and aggressive, so Canada East became more conservative and obstructive. The days of LaFontaine and Baldwin were over. The two leaders, still relatively young men in their forties, recognized that times had changed and that they no longer commanded the support of their sections. Not long after they secured responsible government, both handed over the reins of government to others.

Each is reported to have been worn out by the struggle to obtain responsible government, and upset by the new radicalism that rejected their constitutional liberalism and social conservatism. In Upper Canada, the erstwhile reformers responded instead to the call of "an aging and highly belligerent William Lyon Mackenzie" on his return from exile in 1851, after which he "stamped back into active politics."[59] In both Upper and Lower Canada there emerged a new polarization, which had little room for the outplayed constitutional reformism of the reform leaders. In Upper Canada the Clear Grits were often able to obtain a majority of seats, and among their distinguished liberal leaders were Egerton Ryerson, the Methodist superintendent of education, and George Brown, the Presbyterian editor of the Toronto *Globe*. Brown promoted both western expansion and representation by population. In Lower Canada the radical *Rouges* were always a minority, characterized by their enemies as "mouthpieces of socialism, enemies of order and all moral restraint . . . foes of God and country."[60]

The Grit majority in Upper Canada was often divided, whereas the Conservative majority in Lower Canada united in defense of French Canada's interests. It proved easier for the Conservatives to form a government than for the radicals, whether Grit or *Rouges,* although John A. Macdonald frequently had the support of only a minority of Upper Canada members. When the divisive issue of Catholic (called "separate") schools arose in Upper Canada in 1855 it fell to Macdonald to introduce the bill. It passed with the support of the Lower Canada Catholic majority, but against the wishes of the Protestant majority of Upper Canada.

It was now to be the French Canadians' turn to see the great advantage of dualism. Sectional equality became the bulwark that sustained French Canada's position in the face of an expanding English-Canadian population demanding representation by population. As the French became defensive, the conservatives among them adopted the title *Bleus* and protected their interests by exercising what seemed to the English to be a bloc vote. Some of the French would have preferred the adoption of the double majority principle, thus ensuring that no bill could be passed without the concurrence of the Conservative majority in Canada East.

In retrospect, the Union period sometimes was regarded as a golden age when the double majority was not only preached but practiced. Sir John A. Macdonald gave the principle a novel twist when he observed in the Confederation Debates, "although we have nominally a Legislative Union in Canada . . . yet we know, as a matter of fact, that since the Union in 1841, we have had a Federal Union; that in matters affecting Upper Canada solely, members from that section claimed and generally exercised the right of exclusive legislation, while members from Lower Canada legislated in matters affecting only their own section."[61] This observation would have been more convincing had governments in fact been able to rely on majorities in each section. This was not often the case. Usually after 1848 a majority of conservative *Bleus* was able to join forces with a minority of Upper Canada Conservatives. Only occasionally was the Grit (or Liberal) majority in Canada West able to form a government supported by the radical *Rouges* in Canada East.

Of course there were no parties in the modern sense. But there were groupings of like-minded members, and in the 1850s they began to acquire party labels. But while collaboration between the English Liberals and French radicals proved difficult, the Conservatives in the two sections found cooperation easier. Certainly, the system of "separate" or Catholic schools would not have come into existence in Canada West had not pressure been exerted by the Catholic legislators from Canada East. It is arguable that the last straw for the Protestant Upper Canadians was the Separate Schools Act of 1863, and that this made possible the decision of the Grits to form a coalition with Macdonald's Conservatives a year later. The French conservatives also felt pressure, over the permanent capital and over the Militia Bill that was finally passed in 1862. It is not surprising that both sides found the pressures and the deadlock between evenly matched groupings increasingly hard to sustain. The frequent changes of government suggested a lack of leadership, and just at the time when the American Civil War made firm leadership more than ever desirable.

The Union Period Under Review

The Union period gave French Canadians their first experience in participating in the government of Canada. Their leaders learned the art of accommodation, and at the same time were able to retain their distinctive identity as representatives of a different culture with its own language and religion. Yet political parties were not, for the most part, based on confessional (i.e., religious) or racial (i.e., language) differences. There was relatively easy communication between English and French. Partly this was the fortuitous result of the Act of Union and the consequent need for the parties in each section to find partners in the other. And partly it was the consequence of the determined policy of leaders like LaFontaine never to allow the French Canadians to be tempted to organize themselves as a separate (minority) party. Had Lord Durham lived beyond 1840 he would have revised his assessment of the politics of Canada.

If the period before 1848 enabled the French to learn the art of co-operation, the period after 1848 taught them how to exploit to the fullest the political system the British had imposed upon them.[62] All in all, the French Canadians behaved very differently from the Irish with their separate, and separatist, Irish Party. In the end the French did quite well out of the Union regime. Instead of being assimilated they became partners in the government of Canada.

The French-Canadian perspective was nonetheless very different from the English, for whom parliamentary government simply meant a representative system that permitted individual freedom of expression and bargaining between different interests. In Upper Canada the shifting alliances reflected the various divisions in the section: between Protestants and Catholics; between Anglicans, Presbyterians, and Methodists; between town and country; and between various regions of Upper Canada. To English Canadians, with their liberal assumptions about the freedom of the individual, sectionalism merely meant yet another interest, symbolized by the geographic division between Upper and Lower Canada.

But for French Canadians with their Catholic tradition of corporate behavior, "sectionalism" meant something more. It implied a compact between them and the English Canadians, without which the system would never have worked. Lower Canada was more than a geographical entity: it was the home of a distinctive culture. The French members of the legislature were not sent there to vote as individual representatives but to act as vigilant defenders of their compatriots. Not surprisingly the French were reluctant to give up the power that they had acquired through the Act of Union. Yet they realized that the equality of the two sections could not be preserved indefinitely. The dependence of governments in the 1860s on a handful of independent members ("loose fish"), the frequent changes of ministry, the inability of governments to implement policy and the increasing sense of outrage on the part of the English Canadians, all these caused many of the French to join with the English in seeking ways and means of ending the deadlock.

In the end it was a "Great Coalition" of both groups, the *Rouges* excepted, which in 1864 enabled the first steps to be taken towards yet another regime, Confederation. The French were divided over the benefits from a federal system, but a majority of members concluded that it was at least preferable to the alternative, the replacement of the Union by a system like the British, based on representation by population.

In retrospect, the Union period appears as a brief but crucial middle period in the two centuries of the French-Canadian political tradition. In the first period, from the Conquest to the Rebellion, the *Canadiens* formed an overwhelming majority of the population of Lower Canada. Even so, their representatives in the Legislative Assembly were impotent in their dealings with the governor and the Chateau Clique, the largely English-speaking oligarchy that dominated the Executive and Legislative Councils. In the third period, after 1867, the French Canadians were a minority with diminishing influence in an expanding confederation, although they formed a majority in Quebec itself.

But during the middle period, that of the Union from 1841 to 1867, they were for awhile about equal in numbers to the English, and about equal in political power. In 1860, for example, with 45 percent of the population they controlled 42 percent of the seats in the Assembly. Because of the Act of Union, Canada East and Canada West became partners in a system that the French at least were never to forget. Sectional dualism became an integral part of the French-Canadian political tradition.

By the 1860s, then, a majority of French-Canadian leaders had come to terms with the parliamentary tradition with its assumptions of Cabinet government and parliamentary supremacy. But the nature of parliamentary government in Canada was unique. Instead of the principle of majority rule that was so pervasive at Westminster, where Ireland, Scotland, and Wales were overshadowed by England, there was the equal representation of Canada East and Canada West. Instead of a single Prime Minister, there were two First Ministers. And instead of a single system of public administration there were two systems, the one English, Protestant-inspired yet secular, and the other French, and under the influence of the Catholic Church.

The deadlock over such matters as a permanent capital for Canada symbolized the deep divisions in the country. To the English Canadians the solution lay in "representation by population" and majority rule; to the French, destined to be a permanent minority, the principle of dualism established in the Union period, together with the folk memory of the Conquest and the radicals' rejection of imperialism, was destined to be carried over into Confederation. In 1867 it was still not clear how the Westminster parliamentary system would accommodate this very different tradition. Much would depend on whether the Upper Canadian Grits and the Lower Canadian *Rouges* would come together as Macdonald's Tories and Cartier's *Bleus* were able to do, and whether united under a single Liberal banner they could create a combination that could be made attractive to the voters in both English and French Canada.

6 Conclusion

The memory of the Conquest served French Canadians well for two centuries. But the Conquest depended for its perpetuation on a nationalism that was cultural rather than political, a nationalism that was above all defensive. This long period has been characterized by Léon Dion as "conservative nationalism."

> [It was a period during which the] will to survive was nourished both by the claim to superiority of French-Canadian culture and by the fact that this culture was the people's one and only true possession. . . . Language and faith were the most sacred of such traditions. And neither stood alone, as attested to by the often quoted saying "our language is the guardian of our faith." . . . French Canadians were perceived as having a spiritual role to play in North America, which they might only fulfil by resisting any seepage into their culture of "Anglo-Saxon materialism" and of pervasive Protestantism.[63]

As long as the predominant unifying force was cultural (or conservative) nationalism, the Church had a vital role to play as defender of both the faith and the language, that is of the culture. The Church, of course, was for the most part a conservative influence. So pervasive was the conservative spirit that as late as 1955 a Quebec sociologist could complain in the magazine *Cité Libre,* "The tragedy is not that there is a 'right,' but that it takes up the whole place."[64]

The Conquest was accepted by French Canadians as the turning point long after Confederation appeared to indicate acquiescence in a political system based on the Westminster tradition. The French could plausibly maintain that acquiescence by their leaders did not involve acceptance of a pact that at best was the most that a conquered people could expect. The memory of the Conquest could only dim if and when the French Canadians were specifically asked to choose between the status quo of cultural autonomy, and an alternative that offered a new political system with something like independence. Not until 1980 was such a direct choice offered to them.

The events of 1837–38 passed into history, to be temporarily submerged by the advances obtained through Union and Confederation. But they remained part of French Canada's experience, providing as an alternative to the passivity under Conquest and acquiescence in dualism, the rousing remembrance of Rebellion and resistance. By the 1930s there were again *indépendantiste* candidates in Quebec elections.[65] French Canadians remembered that they had once before proposed an alternative independent regime for Canada, one devised not by the British, nor by the Upper Canadian majority, but by the *Canadiens* themselves.

The Rebellion was vividly recalled in the 1960s by those latter-day "rebels" who became committed to the violent separation of Quebec from the rest of Canada. Once the violence was over and a separatist party, the *Parti Québecois,* became an increasingly important force in Quebec, the full significance of the Rebellion in Quebec's collective memory became apparent. It provided a reference point for all those whose nationalism prevented them from reaching an accommodation with the rest of Canada.[66]

Yet the dominant motif for French-Canadian participation in Canadian politics was not the Conquest or the Rebellion but dualism. The assumption that Canada was basically a dualist society was as fundamental for French Canadians as parliamentary supremacy was for the English. Dualism was the dominant element in the French-Canadian perspective. And unfortunately, like parliamentary supremacy itself, it was open to a variety of interpretations from separatism to cultural autonomy. Moreover, it changed its meaning over the years, and this led to considerable confusion among those conservative English Canadians who preferred to believe that it simply meant the recognition that there was a French culture in Canada and a French language spoken by a majority of the people of Quebec—a recognition first granted in 1763.

One aspect of dualism that was to reappear in the 1960s was the notion of equality. Sectional representation under the Union meant the equal representation of Canada East and Canada West. Quebecois longed for the days when their province as Canada East was the equivalent of Ontario as Canada West. Some of them never accepted the cardinal fact of Confederation: that it transformed French Canada and Quebec as a province into a permanent minority. The search for equality, the revival of some form of double majority, and the recognition of Canada as a dual society, were all notions that antedated 1867 and that were revived when Daniel Johnson proposed his either/or solution for Quebec—equality or independence. In fact, the French Canadians had lost their demographic superiority, and with it the rationale for full political equality, by 1851.

The importance of dualism lay in the fact that together with the Conquest and the Rebellion it provided French Canadians with a much longer political memory than the English. For a century after Confederation it provided a counterpoint to the English Canadian doctrine of parliamentary supremacy and majority rule.[67] After 1960, when the long period of unquestioned English-Canadian hegemony came to an end, it was the principle of dualism that seemed to offer an alternative relationship between English and French, whether in the form of a restructured federalism or of sovereignty-association.

7
Dualism versus Majority Rule

By its very nature federalism is anti-majoritarian. Does this prove that federalism is undemocratic? Certainly it does, if democracy be defined in terms of majority rule.—William S. Livingston

1   The Emergence of French Canada

Before Confederation, as we saw in Chapter 6, there were three main motifs in the political history of Quebec (Lower Canada). The first was a conservative, cultural, clerical nationalism. This was the regime that succeeded the Conquest of 1760 when the Church became the guardian of the cultural heritage of a leaderless people. The second motif was a radical political nationalism that reached a climax in the rebellions of 1837–38 with their forlorn hope of an independent republic. The third motif was the moderate or liberal nationalism of the Union of the Canadas from 1840 to 1867, a period during which the foundations of Canadian dualism appeared to have been firmly established under constitutional reformers willing to collaborate with their opposite numbers in Upper Canada. LaFontaine was perhaps most representative of constitutional liberalism, while Cartier was identified primarily with economic liberalism (and political conservatism).

But to see French Canada as simply evolving from one form of nationalism to the next, from the cultural nationalism of the Church via the radical nationalism of the *Patriotes* to the collaborative nationalism of LaFontaine and Cartier, each phase succeeding and replacing its predecessor, is to misinterpret the significance of events in French Canada. Such a developmental perspective is more suitable for an understanding of Canada's evolution from representative to responsible government and then parliamentary federalism than for explaining the impact of conservative, liberal and radical nationalism on Quebec.

In Quebec, all three forms of nationalism survived Confederation and continued to be a source of conflict and competition. Shortly after Confederation, conservative cultural nationalism came to predominate. Radical nationalism, though buoyed for a time in the 1860s by the victories of republicanism and secularism in Europe, was confined to a small number of activists as they struggled to sustain the fight against the dominance of the Catholic Church. After Confederation, and especially after the death of Cartier in 1873, collaborative liberal nationalism lost some of its momentum for a while. Conservative nationalism won the day. The most important feature of Quebec's life after 1867 was a cultural nationalism in which a revived Church was the dominant influence.

Nevertheless, the three motifs of pre-Confederation nationalism in Quebec did not simply succeed one another. Each of the three themes of Conquest, Rebellion, and Dualism, expressed through cultural nationalism, separatism, and collaboration respectively, continued to resurface. Any attempt to describe French Canada from a developmental perspective is therefore fraught with difficulty.[1]

After 1867 there was still another facet of francophone nationalism. With the incorporation of the various provinces in Confederation, there emerged an entity that can be called "French Canada." Originally, Canada consisted of the St. Lawrence River region east from Montreal, where the bulk of the settlers of French origin (the *Canadiens*) lived. After 1791, the term "Lower Canada" was used for the original Canada. Confederation transformed Lower Canada into the province of Quebec and added to the Canadas the provinces of Nova Scotia and New Brunswick. Situated east of Quebec, New Brunswick had its own French-speaking inhabitants, a people traditionally known as *Acadiens* or Acadians.[2] The *Acadiens* were not the only francophones to join the *Canadiens* in Confederation. In 1870, when Manitoba, the sparsely populated settlement west of the Great Lakes, joined Canada as the fifth province, over half its inhabitants were French-speaking. Many of these were the descendants of French Canadians who had married Indian women, and were called *Métis* to distinguish them from the "half-breeds" who spoke English. The Dominion therefore included three distinct groups of French-speaking people: the *Canadiens,* the *Acadiens* and the *Métis*. Each of them inhabited different provinces. (It was the *Canadiens* who established the Franco-Ontarian settlements west of the Ottawa River.)

Before 1867 the three groups had been largely cut off from one another, the *Canadiens* being barely aware of the problems of the *Aca-*

diens and the *Métis*. After Confederation, thanks to the extension of the railways, telegraphs and newspapers, communications between the various communities improved. It became customary for anglophones to refer to all French-speaking people as "French Canadians." These in turn called those who spoke English, whether native-born Canadians, British or Americans, simply *les anglais*. It was not until the 1960s that the more restrictive term *Québecois* achieved Canada-wide prominence, the term "French Canadian" being replaced by "francophone," the French word for French-speaking.

In 1867 the population of British North America was somewhat less than that of the thirteen American colonies at Independence—about 3.5 million. Of these, about a million, or 30 percent were of French origin. About 85 percent of those who spoke French lived in Quebec.[3] A century later, the number of French-speaking people outside Quebec was itself about a million, a not inconsiderable total. French-speaking Canadians still numbered nearly 26 percent of the population in 1981, according to mother tongue: slightly under 25 percent, or 5.4 million, spoke French at home. In other words, after a rapid decline from majority status before the 1851 census, the French Canadians held their own for the remainder of the century, and then very slowly declined. This was a remarkable feat in a country rapidly expanding through immigration, an immigration almost entirely into the English-Canadian community.

2 The New Dualism: English-Canadian and French-Canadian Perspectives

The English-Canadian Perspective: British Civilization versus French Culture

Both English and French Canadians after 1867 recognized "dualism" as a fact of life in Canada in that clearly there were two peoples or races who had somehow to live together. Beyond this basic recognition, however, the interpretation of the term differed considerably. English Canadians did not ascribe to dualism the preeminence it was given by the French Canadians, who were concerned to preserve French culture. To the English, it was simply one of several important characteristics that made the Dominion of Canada distinctive: there were others equally important.

Perhaps the most significant feature of the country to English Canadians was its great size and sparse population. The admission of the West into Confederation transformed Canada into a vast continental state with strong regional loyalties; and the regions themselves were larger than most countries. At least five regions became prominent in English-Canadian thinking: the Maritimes, Quebec, Ontario, the Prairies, and British Columbia. In other words, English Canadians recognized the importance of dualism, but viewed it as part of a wider problem facing Canada, that of regionalism.[4]

The creation of Canada as a continental polity stretching from the Atlantic to the Pacific—and from the forty-ninth parallel to the Arctic—preoccupied English Canadians after 1867. East of Quebec there were four "Atlantic" provinces, comprising the three Maritime provinces of Nova Scotia, New Brunswick, and Prince Edward Island (which joined Confederation in 1873) and the fourth, Newfoundland and Labrador (which did not join until 1949). West of Ontario there were four more "Western" provinces, consisting of the three Prairie provinces of Manitoba, Saskatchewan, and Alberta, together with British Columbia on the Pacific Ocean. Much of the West became part of Canada when the Hudson's Bay Company transferred its lands to the Dominion in 1869. Manitoba, the province nearest to Ontario and Quebec, became a province in 1870. British Columbia, a separate colony since 1858, joined Canada the following year. The inland territory became the provinces of Saskatchewan and Alberta only in 1905. In 1912 the boundaries of Quebec, Ontario, and Manitoba were extended north to their present limits. Beyond the provinces, the Yukon and the Northwest Territories remained under federal jurisdiction. Canada's claims extended to the North Pole.[5]

The preoccupation of English Canada was, therefore, with the opening up and linking together of a vast continent divided into enormous regions, of which Quebec was but one. They accomplished this in the first instance by completing the railway from Montreal to Halifax (the Intercolonial) in 1876, and then building the Canadian Pacific from Montreal to Vancouver, with the last spike driven in 1885. This incredible enterprise caught the imagination of Canadians, and has been vividly described in a book appropriately entitled *The National Dream*.[6] Yet there was also apprehension. Both western and eastern Canada struggled against the overwhelming power and population of Ontario and Quebec, the two provinces known as "central Canada." Whichever political party was in power depended on the support of one, or preferably both, of these provinces. The Ontario–Quebec axis was vital to Confederation.

Within central Canada, Ontario was the more populous, the more prosperous, and the more dynamic province. It was Canada's industrial heartland, and the intellectual and ideological center of English Canada. The Protestant, imperialist, and pro-British sentiments that swept across English Canada in the decades after 1867 owed their inspiration to feelings generated in Ontario, and particularly Toronto. The province had favored legislative union, but agreed reluctantly to accede to the demands of Quebec and the Maritimes for a federal structure. Even so, Protestant Ontarians continued to view the West as their patrimony. They had joined Confederation on the assumption that the West was theirs to exploit, to settle, and to assimilate into British civilization.[7]

The final element in the regional equation was the resentment often felt by inhabitants of the other provinces to Ontario. An early incident is revealing of the difference between Ontario's viewpoint and that of the eastern provinces. In 1869 Sir John A. Macdonald chose as the first Lieutenant Governor of Manitoba William McDougall, a former colleague of George Brown, the fiercely Protestant Ontario Grit or Liberal. McDougall was opposed by the *Métis,* who rebelled under Louis Riel when he tried to enter the territory before the agreed date, and in due course McDougall resigned. By this time Cartier was acting Prime Minister. He selected a Maritimer, Adams Archibald, one of the Nova Scotia Fathers of Confederation, to replace the Ontarian. Unlike McDougall, Archibald was bilingual. However, it was from Protestant Ontario that the settlers came who swamped the French-speaking population already there.

English Canadians expected both dualism and regionalism to manifest themselves through the federal structure set up in accordance with the BNA Act. The Act gave the provincial governments their own sovereign authority, particularly in Sections 92 and 93. It was a carefully worded document, drafted to give English Canadians the power they wanted to develop the Dominion; to offer French Canadians in Quebec the assurances they deemed necessary to protect their culture; and to provide the English-Canadian minority in Quebec the safeguards necessary if they were to survive in a province where the French formed the majority. Majority rule was expected to prevail at both the federal and provincial levels of government.

A majority of Canadians favored a strong Dominion government led by Macdonald and Cartier, one that would successfully defend Canada's interests in its dealings with the United Kingdom and the United States. They saw no reason to establish a central government that would be too weak to represent the country in what they tactfully referred to as "external affairs."

In sum, English Canadians accepted dualism as a fact of life, but they viewed Canada as a continental polity divided into regions. They did not ascribe preeminence to French–English cultural dualism. In the West and the East there was some resentment toward central Canada, and particularly toward Ontario with its imperialist ambitions for the West. The Dominion government was expected to be strong enough to bind the country together and to defend its integrity.

Above all, dualism was expected to have political expression through the federal and provincial governments and to be based on the legal definition of powers granted to each order of government in the BNA Act. The Act allocated power to one level of government or the other. Unlike the American Constitution, it did not include a bill of rights protecting citizens from the intrusion of both levels of government. The main question asked of government action in Canada was whether it fell within federal or provincial (or imperial) jurisdiction. In every case, the majority prevailed.

For English Canadians, dualism was confined to the legal recognition of the rights of French Canadians. Since these had been granted with some reluctance during the negotiations leading to the passage of the BNA Act, their extent was restricted. The BNA Act acknowledged the existence of language and religious rights in three main areas: the use of French in the Parliament of Canada (Section 133); the preservation (by implication) of the civil law tradition in Quebec (Section 92:13); and the protection of Roman Catholic (not French) education in Ontario (Section 93).

Language had been a cause of controversy in the Province of Canada from the beginning. The 1840 Act of Union had forbidden French; the 1848 amendment to that Act had made French an official language in the Legislature; 1867 confirmed this decision. Section 133 stated that French as well as English was to be used in the Parliament of Canada and the Legislature of Quebec; in the records of both Legislatures; and in "any Court of Canada established under this Act and in or from all or any of the Courts of Quebec." But the right to use French in Ottawa did not make *Canada* bilingual. Ontario and the other provinces were not required to recognize the French language at all.

The civil law presented few problems, having been maintained in Quebec since the Conquest. Section 92 listed sixteen items in which provincial legislatures "may exclusively make Laws." Among these was a provision referring to "Property and Civil Rights," which in effect protected the French civil law. (It is not to be confused with the American term "civil rights.")

Education, the third item of importance to French Canadians, caused much controversy in the years after 1867. Section 93 declared education to be exclusively provincial. Paragraphs 1 and 2 confirmed the rights established *by law* for Catholics in Ontario and Protestants in Quebec in the Separate Schools Act of 1863. The insertion of the phrase "by law" meant that the provision did not extend to other provinces where there was as yet no law.

There was some concern among the English-Canadian minority in Quebec lest the provincial legislature pass a law taking away or limiting their educational rights. Paragraph 3 of Section 93 provided for recourse to the Federal Cabinet in such an eventuality: "an Appeal shall lie to the Governor General in Council." The federal government could then disallow the provincial legislation. If the governor general in council (i.e., the federal Cabinet) concluded that the provisions of paragraphs 1 and 2 were being violated, it could ask Parliament to override the provincial legislature by passing remedial legislation: "the Parliament of Canada may make remedial laws for the due Execution of the Provisions of this Section . . ." (93.4). In other words, while Quebec was assured that education would be within provincial jurisdiction, the French-Canadian majority was not allowed complete freedom to deprive the English-speaking minority of its constitutional rights. As it happened, Quebec was anxious to prevent federal intervention in its affairs and the rights of the Protestant minority were never in any danger.

As the law stood, an appeal against provincial legislation could be taken directly to the federal government. Such an appeal was political, not judicial. However, aggrieved persons might wish to establish the fact that provincial legislation violated the BNA Act and was *ultra vires*. In such a case, they could take the matter to court for a ruling.

Section 93 needs to be fully grasped if the various crises of Confederation over education are to be understood. First, these crises erupted after other provinces introduced legislation establishing nondenominational public school systems. The BNA Act referred only to protection for Catholic schools established *by law* at the time of the Union: such schools existed only in Ontario and Quebec. In Quebec there were two school systems, one Catholic and the other Protestant. Ontario was different. There were also two systems, but one was Catholic (separate) and the other nondenominational (public). Pupils in nondenominational schools were taught the Bible, a book common to all Protestant denominations. Second, Section 93 dealt with tax-supported schools. There was no legislation prohibiting voluntary or private religious schools. Third, protection was afforded only to religious schools: nothing in the legislation protected English in Quebec or French in Ontario. The remedies provided were designed to protect the Protestant minority in Quebec: federal action would presumably have the support of Canada's Protestant majority. Finally, Section 93 was not designed to assist other provinces to establish school systems like Quebec or Ontario, since elsewhere the Protestants were expected to be in the majority and perhaps unwilling to finance Catholic schools out of taxes.

In sum, except where the Catholics formed a majority, or a powerful voting bloc, as they did in the Province of Canada in 1863, it was highly unlikely that Catholic schools would be financed out of public funds. The BNA Act did nothing to protect the Catholic education of *Acadiens* and *Métis,* privately financed in 1867. It said nothing about the language of instruction and so did not protect the language of French minorities outside Quebec. It merely recognized, in a clear and precise fashion, certain limited rights of French Canadians to their culture (92) and in Quebec to their religion (93). The French language could be used in Parliament (133).

The new dualism of the BNA Act, such as it was, was a trade-off between English and French, and between Protestants and Catholics, in "Central Canada." Catholic schools were protected in Ontario, just as Protestant schools were in Quebec. The civil law was recognized in Quebec: elsewhere the common law prevailed. When French was recognized in Ottawa to match the recognition of English in Quebec, it was the result of hard bargaining. The mandatory "shall" for recording parliamentary debates in French was not inserted until the third stage of the drafting of the Act. Provision for bilingual statutes was not added until the fourth stage. In practice, English proved to be the working language in the capital. Section 133 did not reflect the later notion that Canada was to be a bilingual and bicultural society.[8]

There seems to have been a basic English-Canadian assumption that "French Canada" meant Quebec and that the other provinces would be largely English-speaking and Protestant, like Britain itself. The Dominion as a whole was to be an expression of British civilization, making allowances for the preservation of a French and Catholic culture in Quebec. No concessions were made in 1867 to *French-speaking* Catholics outside Quebec, and no legal provision made to protect *Catholics* outside Quebec and Ontario whose schools were not established by law. In the provinces of eastern and western Canada, majority rule, British and Protestant, was expected to prevail.

The French-Canadian Perspective: The Compact Theory of Two Cultures

The new dualism, seen from a French-Canadian perspective, appeared very different. Especially to those who lived in Quebec, dualism was not simply one of several important Canadian features: it was the country's most distinctive attribute and the very basis on which French Canadians had consented to Confederation.

Dualism was regarded by French-speaking Canadians as cultural rather than political. Basically, Canada was an association of two cultures, the one English and Protestant, individualist and materialist, and the other French and Catholic, corporate and spiritual. In creating Confederation, Canadians were laying the foundations for a new type of country whose national identity was based on its two cultures.

The French Canadians' emphasis on culture influenced their view of the nationality Canadians should take. From the beginning, leading French Canadians appear to have given some thought to the creation of a distinctive Canadian nationality. Their starting point was not the Empire or the Dominion but Canada as an association of two cultures. Their emphasis was on the duality of Canada, as a country of two "races" or cultures, or as they often said, of *"deux nations."* They distinguished between the *state* as a political entity and the *nation* as the expression of cultural differences within the state. Political nationality (being a British subject or a Canadian citizen) was quite different from cultural nationality (being a French Canadian).

In the 1865 debate on Confederation, Cartier faced head-on this conflict over political and cultural nationality. He actually advanced the novel idea that Canada should offer its people two different modes of nationality. There would be a single *political* nationality, which everyone shared, and also a *cultural* nationality, which they shared with their language group.[9] In Cartier's view, according to one historian, "confederation was indeed to be a new nationality, but it was to be a 'political nationality,' not an absolute one that would absorb the old cultural and linguistic nationality of the French into that of the English."[10] Put another way, there would be a new unhyphenated Canadian political nationality. At the same time, the two cultural and linguistic groups would preserve their own separate cultural nationalities. Political nationality would not, therefore, replace the older cultural nationality: it would simply be added to it.

Such a concept was difficult for English Canadians to accept. They still thought of themselves as British subjects. The term "Canadian" suggested a certain independence analogous to the use of the term "American" which the loyalists had rejected.[11] In the heyday of Victoria's Empire, Canadians were proud to call themselves British. Sir John A. Macdonald's statement on the matter was simple: "A British subject I was born; a British subject I will die."

Gradually, as Canada obtained greater autonomy, the mood changed somewhat. English Canadians, both Liberals and Conservatives, came to regard themselves as citizens of Canada as well as British subjects. As we have seen, it used to be said that one difference between the Conservative and Liberal parties was that the Conservatives believed in the unity of the Empire and the autonomy of Canada, whereas the Liberals upheld the autonomy of Canada and the unity of the Empire. As we shall see in Chapter 8, there was a subtle, but significant difference between the parties. Even so, all English-speaking Canadians believed in an unhyphenated political nationality and stressed Canada's fundamental unity as a nation.

English Canadians found the concept of two nations difficult to accept, since it appeared to question their basic assumptions about national unity and majority rule. Dualism challenged their vision of the Dominion as a symbol of British civilization. Confederation for many English Canadians in Ontario, especially the Grits, had meant final victory in the long struggle against the French, bringing to an end the dualism of two equal sections.

Both "races" agreed that the Dominion government transcended the provinces and enjoyed full responsibility for the incorporation of the Western Territories. But they differed in their conception of that government. English Canadians regarded it as a political system based on a Protestant English-speaking majority: French Canadians seem to have thought of the Dominion Government led by Macdonald and Cartier as the guardian of a dualism with which they were familiar. At the time of Confederation plans were already under way to begin the incorporation of the Territories by the construction of the Pacific railway. Who would actually settle in the prairies was still an open question.

There was some difference of perspective on the role of Quebec. English Canadians knew that as a province the French would use their majority to preserve their French culture, but at the same time they assumed that as part of Canada and the Empire the province would continue to be dominated by British civilization. Montreal was regarded less as a Quebec city than as Canada's entrepôt. At one time it was twice as large as Toronto and Quebec combined. Its English-speaking university, McGill, acquired an international reputation.

The English Canadians had one great advantage over their French-Canadian counterparts. They did not have to choose between defending French culture and helping to promote the dominant British civilization. Life for them was relatively straightforward: for the French, their ambivalence over French culture and British civilization made life much more complicated.

Fundamental to the French-Canadian concept of dualism was what has been called the "compact theory of Confederation." This theory had no agreed definition. For centralist English Canadians it was a threat to the polity, associated with the American Confederacy and the notion of states' rights, which Canada had tried to avoid. For English Canadians who were opposed to a strong central government, it was often confused with the notion of provincial rights, and so was used to challenge federal incursion into the provincial sphere. Among Quebec nationalists, too, many eagerly used it to defend the provincial rights of Quebec.

But to French Canadians the compact theory involved much more than this. It was not just a political doctrine that could be expressed through federal-provincial conflicts over jurisdiction. More than anything else it expressed the French-Canadian sense that Canada represented the coming together of two distinctive cultures, each of which deserved appropriate recognition. It was a theory that drew attention to the very different philosophical assumptions of English and French Canada. Implicitly included in it was a distinction between the Protestant, secular, materialist, and above all individualist assumptions about the nature of men taken for granted by most English Canadians, and the Catholic, sacred, spiritual and above all corporate philosophy that was taught by the Church in French Canada. The compact theory made plausible the French-Canadian argument that they formed a special community, were a corporate entity, and had community rights.[12]

By describing the compact in philosophical and cultural terms rather than in legal and political language, the French Canadians managed to confuse their literal-minded opponents in English Canada. At the same time they were able to avoid a head-on political collision with the English-Canadian majority, a conflict in which they would presumably be the losers. The compact theory enabled the French to draw a parallel between Quebec and the other provinces. They could argue that whereas in Quebec the rights of the English were protected by law, elsewhere the rights of the French were protected by convention—the convention of a compact between two cultures.

Naturally, proponents of the notion of Canada as an English-speaking Dominion who knew their BNA Act, like R. MacGregor Dawson, could dismiss the compact theory as sheer invention. A more detached observer, Ramsay Cook, could wryly note, "Perhaps the greatest value of the compact theory was its imprecision."[13] In a sense, the theory was used by French Canada to flesh out the Constitution, moderating some of its harshness. The English Canadians, after all, were able to modify by convention those parts of the Constitution that displeased them, notably the powers of the Monarch and the governor general. It had been through the conventions of the Constitution rather than through formal amendments that such a transformation as the introduction of responsible government in 1848 had been possible.

In their dealings with the French-Canadian minority, on the other hand, English Canadians stuck to the letter of the BNA Act, with its restrictions on the use of French and on denominational schools. They regarded the compact theory used by the French Canadians as an attempt to soften the impact of the law. The French were often unable to have the law itself changed in their favor, but usually a compromise was reached regarding actual practice.

Why were English Canadians unwilling to concede the dualist demands based on the compact theory? One reason was their firm commitment to the doctrine of majority rule. A second was the English-Canadian inability (or unwillingness) to concede that individual rights were not enough, and that a minority had corporate rights, which must be respected. Yet perhaps the most important reason had to do with French Canada's claim to be a nation. English Canada's insistence on the overarching political aspect of nationality made it unsympathetic to the notion of a second, French-Canadian cultural nationality. There was the suspicion that the acceptance of such a claim would inevitably lead to the assertion of a separate political nationality.

The emphasis in English liberal theory on majority rule and individual rights meant the rejection of any corporate claim to rights and of a corporate nationality other than that expressed by the State.[14] The "National Dream" of a transcontinental railway was assumed to be the dream of all Canadians, of a single Canadian nation.

Indeed, the English term "nation" was often used interchangeably with the term "state" or in conjunction with it, as in "nation-state." A. R. M. Lower entitled his history of Canada *Colony to Nation*.[15] Not surprisingly, therefore, the French Canadians' description of themselves as *"une nation dans une nation"* was translated into something quite different, "a state within the state."[16] No country could be expected to tolerate a state within the state.

Indeed, the British themselves, like the French, long preferred the old-fashioned term "race" to describe a group that had its own culture but was without corporate political power. The 1919 version of *God Save the King,* second verse, began:

> One realm of races four
> Blest more and ever more
>   God save our land. . . .

The third verse, referring to the Empire, began

> Of many a race and birth
> From utmost ends of earth
>   God save us all. . . .

There was another important reason for the reluctance to recognize the compact theory. Confederation created a new Canadian nation (or state) that one day might become autonomous (or even independent). English Canadians had no wish to encourage a rival French-Canadian nation (or state) that might one day be autonomous (or even independent) within North America. The limited cultural autonomy granted in the BNA Act was something quite different from the "nationhood" of the compact theory. It was no accident that the Act avoided any reference to anything approximating two cultural nationalities, or to an alliance between two founding peoples, or to a compact between the races.

It should also be remembered that many French Canadians (including Cartier) shared much of the conventional English-Canadian view of Confederation in Queen Victoria's day. They took for granted Canada's role in the Empire and had no wish to declare their independence of Great Britain. Canada, after all, was part of British civilization. If Canadians had a mission in those days it was to extend British rule, the British flag, and British justice across North America. They also supported Britain's imperial aims, and were proud that the boatmen supplied for the Nile expedition to attempt the rescue of General Gordon in 1884 included French Canadians, English Canadians, and Indians. It is difficult to grasp the different picture that Canadians had of themselves a hundred years ago. Most Canadians accepted the fact that they were British subjects. Neither English nor French Canadians were yet fully conscious as a group of their political nationality as Canadians. The English were proud to be part of a worldwide empire governed from London; the French were equally proud of their mission in North America as members of a universal Church directed from Rome.

Many French Canadians in Victorian days managed to combine political loyalty to the Empire with spiritual zeal on behalf of the Church. They saw no conflict between their cultural and political loyalties. Yet it was just this missionary zeal which upset the Protestants. There was some fear that Quebec might overwhelm Canada with its militant Catholicism, given its high birthrate, and the decline in net immigration. Such fears discouraged the recognition of dualism beyond what was laid down in the BNA Act. English Canada wanted to regard the political assimilation of Quebec as final. There was no point in reopening the debate on Canada's future: debate had ended in 1867.

One final difference between English and French Canada needs to be noted. The English-Canadian identification of the state with the nation and of both state and nation with the Empire made it easy for English Canada to have a sense of both imperial unity and Canadian identity. The French Canadians, supreme only in their province, tried to find a different role for their small "nation" in the imperial system. A model to which some of them turned was the empire of Austria-Hungary, the so-called "Dual Monarchy," established like Canada in 1867. In the Austro-Hungarian Empire the Austrians, a part of the German nation, shared power with the Hungarians, a quite distinct nation. Each retained its own language and culture, being united (as were Norway and Sweden) by the Crown. If Germany as a nation was similar to England, then Canada was comparable to Austria-Hungary, with the French Canadians, like the Hungarians, sharing a common political nationality of their own.

In the long run, the centralist fear that there could be challenges to the legitimacy of the government of Canada, like those to the actions of the United States government in 1861, seems to have had some justification. A compact, like a treaty, is by definition an agreement entered into by two or more parties on the assumption that the bargain will be kept. For the compact theorists, Confederation could easily be viewed as a conditional rather than a final agreement, much as the Austro-Hungarian Empire or the Kingdom of Norway-Sweden were to the Hungarians and the Norwegians. The French Canadians had accepted a single political nationality as British subjects and Canadian citizens on the assumption that their distinctive culture would be respected and given autonomy: that culturally they did indeed comprise a nation. They assumed that they had joined Confederation as a community, not as individuals. Theirs was a nation that had come to terms with another nation, *les anglais*.

The notion that Confederation was a compact, and was therefore conditional on the terms of the agreement being kept, became widespread among Quebec nationalists. Not surprisingly, the idea that the terms of Confederation could be renegotiated by one of the parties was anathema to most English Canadians. They rejected the compact theory out of hand.

The French-Canadian interpretation of the new dualism, in the sense of a Canada composed of English and French Canadians by means of a compact, survived all the efforts of the Imperial and Dominion governments to create Canada as primarily an English-speaking nation. At the height of the second world war, Canada could still be described by a Canadian novelist as "two solitudes."[17] He could just as easily have written the French "deux nations," for the country remained an association of two communities who spoke not only different languages but used different "languages of discourse." As Léon Dion has noted, the English thought of Canada primarily in terms of space (geography), the French in terms of time (history).[18] This is clear from the Canadian

Dualism versus Majority Rule

National Anthem; the French version (a translation) appears to refer to a different Canada:

English
O Canada! our home and native land!
True patriot love in all thy sons command.
With glowing hearts we see thee rise
The True North strong and free:
And stand on guard, O Canada, we stand on guard for thee.
O Canada! glorious and free!
We stand on guard, we stand on guard for thee,
O Canada! we stand on guard for thee.

French
O Canada! land of our forefathers,
Your brow is crowned with glorious garlands!
The arm that knows how to wield the sword, knows how to carry the cross!
Your history is a saga of brilliant exploits.
May your valor, tempered by faith,
Protect our hearths and rights,
Protect our hearths and rights.

In sum, dualism to French Canadians meant four things:

1. The dualism of French and English was the most significant factor in Canadian politics, and was far more important than regionalism and federal-provincial relations.
2. While a single *political* nationality for all Canadians was acceptable, French Canadians in addition would continue to enjoy a distinctive *cultural* identity.
3. Dualism did *not* mean what English Canadians thought it meant, namely, that Canada as a whole (Quebec included) was British in civilization, and that Quebec alone was entitled to preserve French culture. French Canadians also had interests in Canada as a whole, and in the development of its civilization. Moreover, they were entitled to preserve their culture wherever there were significant numbers of French Canadians.
4. The compact theory, with its stress on two races or cultures, was an essential feature of dualism. It enabled French Canadians to chal-

principle of majority rule by English Canadians not only
vernment of Canada but in the provinces.

nadian Dualism and Quebec Nationalism

Introduction

The introduction of a federal system meant the establishment of two orders of government, between which French-Canadian politicians had to choose. Those who chose to serve Canada had to leave their comfortable Quebec milieu for the new capital where the English Canadians formed a majority.[19] Equally unsettling as they tried to adjust to their minority role in Canadian affairs, they were often accused by people in Quebec of being *vendus* who had really sold out to the English.

In fact, all French-Canadian politicians instinctively subscribed to the principles of dualism, whether they decided to serve in Quebec City or Ottawa. All were determined to defend the vital interests of their race or culture within the limits of the political system in which they operated. It is therefore useful to distinguish between two types of French-Canadian dualist: those who may be called "Pan-Canadians," willing to serve in the federal Parliament, government and public service, and those who are better described as "Quebec nationalists," preferring to devote their political energies to Quebec, where they were at home among their own people.

While the two perspectives were different, the politicians themselves could not always be differentiated from one another. For one thing, a politician might serve at one time in the Quebec legislature and at another be a member of Parliament. For another, *Quebec* nationalism took some time to develop. Until the first world war, to be a "nationalist" in the commonsense meaning of the term, usually meant being a *Canadian* nationalist, that is, one opposed to the imperial connection. Not until the 1930s was it possible to distinguish clearly between the Pan-Canadian outlook of those who served Canada, and the Quebec nationalism of those who promoted the interests of Quebec.

The Church, moreover, did not fit into this dichotomy, which was essentially political in character. As noted earlier, the Catholic clergy were traditionally associated with a conservative, clerical nationalism. After Confederation, the Church's "nationalism," if that was any longer the proper term, was not confined to the province of Quebec. The hierarchy exercised pastoral care throughout Canada wherever there were French-speaking communities. In addition, there were numerous English-speaking Catholics, particularly the Irish, for whom the Church had responsibility, and the bishop might be Irish or French Canadian. Some of the conflicts that occurred originated in clashes between English- and French-speaking Catholics. The Roman Catholic Church itself, it must be remembered, was a universal church. Quebec nationalism might be one of its vehicles, but its main concern was the preservation and promotion of Catholicism, and the spiritual welfare of its communicants, not their political aspirations. Many of the clergy were former Royalists from France.[20] Indeed, the Church retained its antistatist outlook; that is, it remained anxious to preserve its traditional responsibility for education and welfare in a society where (outside Quebec) pressures arose for province-wide, nondenominational systems. The Church was opposed to the transfer of these functions, especially education, to a secular state.

In short, the dichotomy between Pan-Canadianism and Quebec nationalism, which became increasingly clear after the 1930s, took some time to develop. Politicians moved between Quebec and Ottawa. So long as the British Empire had a claim on the loyalty of Canadians, French-speaking "nationalists" tended to be Canadian nationalists. The Church continued to play a role that did not fit into either the Pan-Canadian or the Quebec category. As a French-Canadian institution, the Church's primary concern was with both the Quebecois and French Canadians elsewhere. However, English-speaking Catholic bishops played an important role outside Quebec among the Irish and other English-speaking Catholics. The Church as a pressure group was involved in politics, but it was not a political institution. It was antistatist and opposed to the transfer of responsibility for education and social policy to the State.

The important role played by the churches in Canada generally, and in Quebec in particular, after Confederation complicated the relationship between English and French Canadians. For much of the century the primary concern of many Canadians was not politics *per se* but religion, and it was the conflict between Protestantism and Catholicism that aroused the greatest passion. Protestants often assumed that the Roman Church was committed to the promotion of the French language as much as the Catholic faith, but this was not always so. On secular issues the Church had long ago reached an accommodation with the British

Crown, whose conservatism it found preferable to the radical republicanism that seemed to be the alternative in both Europe and North America.

Confederation did not end the tension between English and French Canadians in their very different concepts of Canada. It also exacerbated tensions within French Canada itself. Before 1867 Ontario had been disunited. Settled by Loyalist Americans; by Scottish, Irish, and Welsh immigrants; by English Dissenters; and by people from elsewhere in Europe, it had been divided between Tories and Grits, and between Protestants and Catholics. The Protestants themselves were deeply divided, particularly between Anglicans, Presbyterians, and Methodists. By comparison, Quebec appeared to be monolithic. There were some radical *Rouges,* but the majority were Catholic and conservative.

After 1867 it was in Quebec that the divisions appeared to be more pronounced. It is true that many French Canadians subscribed to the doctrine of dualism, with its assumption that French Canadians everywhere had the right to preserve their distinctive culture; but they differed over the best means of achieving their goals. Now two sets of political institutions were available: the government of Canada and the government of Quebec. Many French Canadians became attached to the government of Quebec as *their* government, but others found Quebec nationalism too restrictive and preferred the broader vision of Canada as seen from Ottawa. These persons we have called "Pan-Canadians" rather than "federalists," the more common term in recent years. To use the term "federalist" to describe francophones loyal to Canada may give the impression that they shared the federal perspective of English Canadians. This was often not the case. The dualist views of Pan-Canadians were different from the views of most English Canadians, whose federal concerns extended equally to all regions of Canada. (The term "federalist" most properly applies to those political parties in Quebec that after the emergence of the separatist movement were willing to remain part of Canada as a federal system.) "Pan-Canadian" implies a larger vision encompassing Canada and French Canada.

Internal divisions in Quebec were complicated by the fact that after Confederation both Pan-Canadians and nationalists were frequently embroiled in disputes with a revived Catholic Church over the proper boundary between secular and sacred concerns, particularly in the upbringing of the young. The Church's missionary zeal, sustained by a hierarchical organization committed to the propagation of the faith and governed ultimately from Rome, often clashed with the pragmatic realism of politicians like Laurier who had to deal directly with the anglophone Protestant majority in Canada's secular political system.[21]

Like Cartier, Wilfrid Laurier (1841–1919) was of French-Canadian ancestry and yet familiar with the English-Canadian milieu. He graduated in law from McGill where he was valedictorian. A noted orator, he was elected to the Quebec Legislative Assembly in 1871 and to the federal Parliament in 1874 when the Liberals won. He became leader of the Liberal Party in 1887 and was Prime Minister from 1896 to 1911. The rational Pan-Canadian outlook of Laurier (knighted by Queen Victoria on the morning of her Diamond Jubilee) and his Pan-Canadian successors in Ottawa, St. Laurent (1948–57) and Trudeau (1968–84) was often in striking contrast to the appeal to sentiment favored by the Quebec nationalists.[22]

Pan-Canadian Dualism: The Pan-Canadians' Dilemma

The Pan-Canadians' vision, from Cartier to Trudeau, encompassed all of French Canada, not just Quebec. Pan-Canadians were concerned about the French-speaking minorities who had no provincial government to support them. Since to the Pan-Canadians, dualism was not a political division between the federal government and Quebec, but an association of two cultures, of English and French Canada, it was on these communities that the future of Canada as a dualist society depended.

For the Pan-Canadian politicians located in Ottawa, the main focus of interest was Canada. This meant that in the event of a conflict between the interests of Canada and Quebec, they might have to take the side of Canada. These leaders assumed that despite their minority role in the federal government they were a necessary bulwark for all of French Canada against majority anglophone rule. Yet in times of crisis they were faced by a difficult choice. They might decide to argue against federal policy, but in the knowledge that they could be outvoted in Cabinet. They could thereupon choose to resign as individuals, which occasionally happened, but then government was carried on without them. They could resign as a bloc, but the absence of French-Canadian representation in the Cabinet would play into the hands of the nationalists, and so no group of Cabinet ministers ever did this.[23] Adolphe Caron defended his colleagues' decision not to resign from the government that condemned Louis Riel to death, on the grounds that they had a duty to the Crown to keep the peace in Canada as a whole: ". . . I have said that I considered it was my bounden duty to my country, to my Province, to act as I have acted as an adviser of the Crown. Mr. Speaker, as Ministers of the Crown, occupying, as we do, the Treasury benches, we are here representing, not one individual Province but the whole Dominion of Canada. I deemed it was an obligation for us, occupying those positions to maintain the peace and order in the Dominion."[24]

In England the parliamentary system had proved an admirable device for channeling dissent. The so-called "aristocratic embrace" enabled the Crown, the House of Lords, and the Cabinet to charm or cajole rebellious members into acquiescence. In Canada, the Westminster tradition also exercised an influence on those who participated in government. In the privacy of the party caucus or the Cabinet, minority representatives could be seduced into silence. Sir John A. Macdonald once hoped that Louis Riel could somehow be brought to Ottawa and made a Senator, if not a Cabinet minister. "If we once get him here . . . he is a gone coon."[25]

For some time, Pan-Canadians had little difficulty in accepting a double political nationality that involved being both Canadian citizens and British subjects, as members of one of the many races in the multi-racial Empire. But, at the turn of the century, Britain's war against the Boers, a subject nationality with whom the French Canadians could identify, strained their loyalty to the Empire. After the death of Queen Victoria there began a reappraisal of the acceptance of a double political nationality that involved allegiance not only to Canada but to Britain and the Empire.

Pan-Canadianism also meant acceptance of the British Constitution, i.e., the Westminster parliamentary system of majority rule and the Crown as the executive. Here again, some modification occurred in the twentieth century. A distinction was drawn between the Court of St. James in Whitehall and the Parliament at Westminster. From Laurier onward, Pan-Canadian leaders demonstrated little of the emotional commitment to the Monarchy displayed by Cartier. Indeed, some later Pan-Canadian leaders seemed to regard the Westminster parliamentary system itself more as a convenient tool than as a tradition to be revered. To them the British Parliament was not the Mother of Parliaments: at best, it was their mother-in-law.

Nevertheless, from Cartier on, a number of Pan-Canadian leaders were willing to live in Ottawa and to dedicate their primary loyalty to Canada and its federal system. Yet even this presented them with a dilemma. Though they claimed to be a bulwark for the defense of French-Canadian interests and Canadian dualism, they could not persuade Quebec nationalists, or even at times the Quebec voters, that the federal authorities were sensitive to their concerns. The Pan-Canadians were always in a minority in Dominion politics.

The Dominion government was a very different institution from the old government of the united Canadas. If one thing was clear after Confederation it was that the old sectional dualism of the Union period had come to an end. No longer were there rotating capitals between Toronto and Quebec City: after 1866 there was a permanent capital, originally selected for the Province of Canada. And although Ottawa overlooked the province of Quebec, it was situated on the Ontario side of the Ottawa River. Nor were there henceforth two first ministers who by convention were of equal stature: instead, the governor general appointed the first person to enjoy the title Prime Minister of Canada, when he called upon John A. Macdonald. The old convention, having been set aside, was not mentioned again. His implication was clear: the influence of French Canadians in Dominion affairs was to be limited. Smiley has noted that when the governor general, Lord Monck, wrote to Macdonald from London on May 14, 1867, offering him the position, part of his letter stated:

> In authorizing you to undertake the duty of forming an administration for the Dominion of Canada, I desire to express my strong opinion that in future, it shall be distinctly understood that the position of First Minister shall be held by *one* person, who shall be responsible to the Governor General for the appointment of other ministers and that the system of dual First Ministers which has hitherto prevailed, shall be put an end to. I think this is of importance, not only with reference to the maintenance of satisfactory relations between the Governor General and his Cabinet, but also with a view to the complete consolidation of the Union which we have brought about.[26]

Smiley went on to suggest that the French-speaking Fathers of Confederation had regarded the French-Canadian ministers in the federal Cabinet as the most important line of defense of French-Canadian interests. In the Cabinet it had been agreed that Ontario should have five places, the Maritimes two each, and Quebec four. However, one of Quebec's ministers was to be English-speaking, thus reducing the French-Canadian component to three of thirteen members. The governor general's letter made it clear, in addition, that Cartier, one of the three, was not to be a first minister. Not surprisingly, Smiley has described the governor general's letter as "one of the most significant documents of Canadian constitutional history."[27] Moreover, at first it was Macdonald alone who was knighted by the Queen. Only after Cartier refused a lower award was he granted a similar honor. Lower Canada, or Canada East, had become the province of Quebec, one of several lesser partners in Confederation.

Even more significant than Queen Victoria's decision to select Ottawa as the permanent capital of Canada and the governor general's determination to appoint only one first minister, was the end of equal sectional representation in the legislature. This was the price Quebec paid for provincial autonomy. The first Dominion Parliament clearly reflected Quebec's minority status. The new province retained the 65 seats held by Canada East, but these were now part of a House of Commons numbering 181.[28] Such were the consequences of the campaign for representation by population.

In the Senate, Quebec succeeded in retaining parity with Ontario: each had 24 senators appointed by the Governor General-in-Council. But the Maritimes also had 24, as in due course had the Western provinces. In due course, Quebec's Senators numbered 24 of 104, or less than a quarter of the total. In any case, the appointed senators, whether from English or French Canada, proved to be relatively impotent, since under responsible government the Cabinet was responsible to the House of Commons alone. Most important, as we have seen, was the fact that the French-Canadian presence in the federal Cabinet was very much that of a minority, outnumbered even by the ministers from the Maritimes.

Quebec Nationalism: Its Slow Development

Rebellion against the Conquest had manifested itself in the earliest form of Quebec nationalism, the demand of the *Patriotes* in the 1830s for an independent republic modeled more on American lines than on the British Constitution. With the advent of responsible government no comparable independence movement occurred in Quebec until the late 1960s when the *Parti Québecois* was formed. By then, Canada was independent of Great Britain and the issue was the relationship between Quebec and the rest of Canada.

Between the *Patriotes* of the 1830s and the *Parti Québecois* of the 1960s there were three notable nationalist movements in Quebec: the *Parti National* (1886); the *Ligue Nationaliste* (1903); and the *Union Nationale* (1935).

The *Parti National,* formed by Honoré Mercier in 1886, was a popular movement intended to bring all French Canadians together under one banner. In practice it was exploited by the Liberals as a means of loosening the Conservative hold on the French Canadians and the clergy.[29] The *Parti National* won the Quebec provincial elections held in 1886 and 1890, and during its six-year term of office it called the first interprovincial conference. The party declined after the involvement of Mercier in scandal, but its brief success made it clear that nationalist sentiment was not dead in Quebec.

The *Ligue Nationaliste* arose out of opposition to the first French Canadian Prime Minister. The execution of Riel was followed not only by the emergence of the *Parti National* as a force in Quebec politics from 1886 to 1892, but by the selection of Wilfrid Laurier, a rising Quebec politician who had been sympathetic to Riel's cause since the 1870s, as leader of the (Liberal) opposition in Ottawa in 1887. Laurier became the first such leader since Cartier and went on to become the first French-speaking prime minister of Canada. As we shall see in the next chapter, as a Pan-Canadian leader he was constrained by the need to mollify English Canada at a time when imperialist sentiment on behalf of Britain's activities abroad was at its height. He had to balance strong English-Canadian feeling for participation in the South African War, which broke out in 1899, against equally adamant French-Canadian opposition, and sympathy for the Boers. Some years later, when all the powers engaged in naval rearmament, Laurier wanted to insure that Canada's naval defenses were adequate without letting Canada's vessels become part of the imperial fleet.

For the first, but by no means the last time, the appointment of a French Canadian as Prime Minister of Canada failed to prevent the emergence of a new nationalist movement. The *Ligue Nationaliste* was the creation of Henri Bourassa, a former Liberal M.P. who had criticized Laurier for agreeing to cooperate with Britain during the South

African War. Later his party was opposed to the creation of a Canadian navy and in 1911 put up candidates against Laurier's Liberals on the issue. Ironically, the seats won by the *Ligue Nationaliste* had little impact on the outcome of the 1911 elections, which the Conservative party easily won. The Conservatives were the party most closely associated with British imperialism, and preferred that Canada provide ships as part of the Royal Navy. They stayed in power through the war until 1921. Bourassa (1868–1952) himself also saw service in the Quebec Legislative Assembly. But he was more interested in ideas (he founded *Le Devoir* in 1910) and in opposing the Liberal government of Laurier than in providing an alternative nationalist government in Quebec.

The third movement in Quebec before the Quiet Revolution changed the character of Quebec nationalism was the *Union Nationale,* originally a coalition of conservative and progressive forces which defeated the ruling Quebec Liberal Party after nearly four decades of power in the 1936 provincial election. Once installed as premier, the Conservative leader, Maurice Duplessis, abandoned his radical allies and gave Quebec a long period of the traditional cultural and conservative nationalism associated with the province so long as the Church was powerful. Duplessis stayed in power until his death in 1959 (apart from the war years from 1939 to 1944). It was during his corrupt regime that Quebec appeared as a "deviant case" more comparable to Huey Long's Louisiana than to other Canadian provinces.

The importance of the *Parti National* lay in its ability to raise the French-speaking Canadians' nationalist consciousness, dormant since the 1830s. The significance of the *Union Nationale* lay in its capacity to establish Quebec as a powerful province, controlling its own affairs and able to withstand federal pressure. The transformation of the economy which occurred during Duplessis' rule made possible the large government expenditures of the succeeding Liberal governments in the 1960s.[30] In retrospect, the radical *Patriotes,* the liberal *Parti National* and the conservative *Union Nationale* provided the nationalist foundations on which the socialist-inclined *Parti Québecois* was able to build.

Bourassa's *Ligue Nationaliste* was different. His vision extended beyond Quebec and encompassed the French-Canadian minorities elsewhere. He saw Canada as a society in which two cultures cooperated on a basis of equality. Bourassa's main concern was the removal of British influence and the creation of a Canadian identity based on dualism. His notion of a single political nationality and a dual cultural nationality was similar to that sketched by Cartier forty years earlier. "To the continuing English Canadian demand for a single unhyphenated Canadianism, people like Bourassa responded with a dualist theory. Confederation, they said, was the result of an agreement between two races to live together on a basis of equality and cooperation."[31]

Bourassa's main legacy was an ideological underpinning for a twentieth-century Pan-Canadianism that eliminated Britain from the Canadian system. Instead of a British Canada he promoted the notion of a bilingual and bicultural society, which was to influence a later generation of Pan-Canadians and which led to the establishment of the Royal Commission on Bilingualism and Biculturalism in 1963. The genealogy of Canadian nationalism is interesting. Bourassa was the grandson of Papineau, just as Laurier's successor as Prime Minister, Mr. King, was the grandson of the other rebel leader, William Lyon Mackenzie. Each contributed to the independence of Canada. One of Bourassa's successors as editor of *Le Devoir,* André Laurendeau, was the co-chairman and the inspiration of the Commission on Bilingualism and Biculturalism, which became known as the "B & B Commission." An important consequence of the work of Bourassa and Laurendeau was the establishment of Pan-Canadianism as the official ideology of the government of Canada with the passage of the Official Languages Act in 1969.

In sum, Quebec nationalism before the 1960s was designed to raise the consciousness of the French Canadians. The *Parti National* challenged the long hegemony of the *Bleus,* closely associated with the Conservative Party; the *Ligue Nationaliste* caused the Liberals to query Canada's association with the Empire; and the *Union Nationale* established the right of governments in Quebec to make their own policy and to resist federal intervention in provincial affairs.

Yet just as striking as the persistence and transformation of Quebec nationalism was the continued support for Pan-Canadianism. The dualist theory of a Quebec nationalist like Bourassa was hardly separatist. Indeed, in many ways Bourassa was Pan-Canadian in his sympathies. Conversely, the Quebec Liberal Party, though federalist in its fundamental orientation, was distinctly nationalist in its defense of Quebec's interests vis-à-vis Ottawa long before the victory of the *Union Nationale* in 1936. Until the 1960s, all parties in Quebec took continued participation in Confederation for granted. The voters continued to return Pan-Canadians to Parliament and to support Pan-Canadian leaders such as St. Laurent and Trudeau. Laurier's victory in 1896 was hardly a flash in the pan: for almost half (thirty-nine) of the eighty-eight years from 1896 to 1984, French Canadians held the office of prime minister.

Indeed, what requires explanation is the slowness of the development of Quebec nationalism after Confederation. One might have expected the nationalist movement, so prominent before the Rebellion, to have been given a new lease of life by the determination of the *Rouge* leaders to oppose Confederation. This did not happen.

4 The Resistance to Nationalism

Clericalism

The period after Confederation was not conducive to the development of nationalist sentiment for a number of reasons. For one thing, it coincided with the zenith of Victorian imperialism, a mood very different from Britain's indifference towards the colonies in the 1830s. For another, it was a period when Dominion politicians still controlled provincial affairs. In Quebec, the government had not yet become predominantly French. Until nearly the end of the century, up to half the Cabinet was drawn from the English-speaking business community. The Canadian Pacific Railway might be located in Montreal, but the Government with which it was most involved was in Ottawa. Most of its directors were English-speaking. The Confederation agreement, for all practical purposes was "a distribution of governmental powers which assigned economic matters to the Dominion and matters regarded as having a direct cultural incidence to the provinces."[32] And in those days "culture" was within the competence of the Church.

Within Quebec there was rivalry between Quebec City, no longer the capital of Canada and increasingly French-speaking, and Montreal, where the anglophone business community was concentrated. The province was further divided between town and country, with the Church anxious to preserve and extend the rural orientation of the Quebecois. The clergy's role was much greater in the country parishes.

The *Rouges* were in no position to extend their following, becoming a wing of the Liberal Party. They still looked across the Atlantic for inspiration, and backwards to the eighteenth-century Enlightenment for reinforcement of their belief in the power of reason over revelation, their emphasis on the secular rather than the sacred, and their concern for the brotherhood of man in general, rather than the nation in a narrow sense. Such a philosophy had limited appeal for the traditionalist Quebecois, with their deep involvement with the family and the parish and their acceptance of the Church as defender of their culture and their nation.[33] The liberalism of the *Rouges* was very different from the liberalism of English Canada, which was influenced by the Gladstonian liberalism in England with its appeal to Nonconformist Christians rather than to anticlericals. Moreover, whereas the modern type of liberal nationalism that had spread across continental Europe after the French Revolution was very much a political nationalism, in Quebec the traditional nationalism propagated by the clergy was apolitical and conservative.

In sum, at least half-a-dozen factors inhibited the advance of nationalism in Quebec. These were: the heyday of imperialism, the predominance of Dominion politicians, the important role played by the anglophone minority, the divisions within Quebec society, the inability of the *Rouges* to strike a nationalist chord, and the greater degree of interest in religion than in politics. The Church took full advantage of this situation. It continued to identify itself with the Crown as symbol of authority, cooperated with Dominion politicians, and promoted accommodation with the business community. Yet the Church itself was no more united than Quebec, and reflected the divisions within the province's francophone community.

Many of the conflicts within the Church originated in clashes between the moderate Gallicans who accepted the dependence of the Church on the secular authorities, and the zealous ultramontanes who looked to Rome and were determined to advance the cause of Catholicism through an independent Church. The Gallican Sulpician Order had supported the dualist society of pre-Confederation Canada; the ultramontane Jesuits rejected the separation of Church and state and stressed the missionary role of the Church, not only in Quebec but across Canada, even if this meant friction with English-Canadian Protestants.

French-Canadian *habitants* were encouraged by the Church to have large families and by the ultramontanes in particular to colonize the empty spaces of Quebec (and to some extent other provinces). This they did not as individuals in the Protestant English manner, but as organized groups of families who would clear the land and extend the boundaries of French Canada and its culture. In this way, much of North America, it was hoped, might still be won for the Roman Church. The settlers were accompanied by a priest for spiritual guidance. In addition to his regular pastoral duties, he would be responsible for ensuring that the children were educated in the Catholic faith and French language, thus preserving the community's distinctive identity. The organization traditionally adopted to further this end was the parish, a Church-oriented local unity. This was a very different structure from the secular municipality favored in Protestant areas. When the French Canadians migrated to new territory they took the parish with them: English Canadians set up municipalities. As late as 1907, André Siegfried was moved to remark that the *Canadiens* had not abandoned hope that the "revenge of the cradle" would succeed in making Canada French and Catholic once again. "The French Canadians will have to give up the idea that they will prevail by force of numbers. . . . Canada will not become French again."[34]

The ultramontanes were concerned about the role of the Church not only in Canada but in its relations with the universal Church. Just as English Canada at that time cannot be understood without reference to the Empire, so the role of French Canada cannot be seen in perspective without reference to Rome.

For example, in 1870 the Vatican gave up control of the Papal States to a unified Kingdom of Italy. At the same time, Napoleon III's Second Empire was swept away by Protestant Prussia, leaving France in the hands of radical republicans. By contrast, in Canada the Church was riding high. The Bishop of Montreal, Ignace Bourget, typified the aggressiveness of the ultramontanes. He was a prelate who had sympathized with the *Patriotes* in his youth; in the 1840s had joined the *Rouges* in pressing for the colonization of the lands left empty in the Eastern Townships. Later he raised a contingent of Canadian Zouaves to defend the Papacy against Garibaldi and brought new religious Orders over from France. His great new cathedral of Notre Dame in Montreal was modeled on St. Peter's in Rome.

The division between Gallicans and ultramontanes was compounded by the fact that Bishop Bourget represented Montreal, while the more moderate Gallican Archbishop Taschereau spoke from Quebec City, the headquarters of the Church. Frequently the bishops took their quarrels to Rome itself, "but each time that Rome was consulted, the decision went against the ultramontanes, whose obstinate conviction of the justice of their cause finally led them to the brink of rupture with that Holy See whose defenders and supporters they claimed themselves to be."[35]

The zealots within the Church had little use for the liberal nationalism of the Union period, which was identified with Orders like the Sulpicians (with whom Cartier was associated). They had even less use for the radical (and often anticlerical) nationalism of the *Rouges*. The failure of the *Rouges* to capitalize on nationalist sentiment at Confederation and to establish themselves as a governing party was due in part to the success of the Church in maintaining its dominant ideological position in Quebec society.

For a vignette of the currents of thought at work in Quebec after Confederation we may turn to the so-called "Guibord affair." The affair began when Bishop Bourget refused to allow a member of the *Institut Canadien* named Guibord to be buried in consecrated ground. The *Institut Canadien,* as we have seen, was established by liberal intellectuals, some of them *Rouges,* to stimulate free discussion in Quebec. It provided library facilities for people to read secular materials. The Church, opposed to the organization's criticism of religious orders and of the ultramontanes, and to its support for secular education, retaliated by establishing the rival *Instituts Nationaux*. In 1869 the Yearbook of the *Institut Canadien* was condemned by Rome and placed on the *Index* (the list of books specifically restricted) by the Holy Office. Gradually the pressure mounted until all branches of the *Institut Canadien* closed their doors.

Guibord, a Catholic, had been a vice president of the *Institut Canadien*. A suit brought by the *Institut* against the curé who had refused Catholic burial turned into a spectacular trial in Montreal, pitting Gallicans against ultramontanes, supporters of free speech against the Church authorities, and Church against state. The judge, a Gallican and a liberal, ordered the parish to provide a Catholic burial. His verdict was overturned by higher courts in Canada and was finally appealed to the Privy Council in London. The Judicial Committee sustained the lower court. Finally, in 1875, Guibord's body was buried in a Catholic cemetery in accordance with the dictates of British justice (at, it may be added, the insistence of the governor general). To one English-Canadian historian it appeared that "in its larger consequences the Guibord affair was a triumph for civil rights in Quebec."[36] To many devout Catholics, however, it was the Church that had the last word. Bishop Bourget proceeded to deconsecrate the grave.

Bishop Bourget and the ultramontanes were not entirely successful in their promotion of a zealous Catholic Quebec. They were prevented from establishing a University of Montreal as a rival to Laval University in Quebec when Archbishop Taschereau, a former Rector of Laval, successfully appealed to Rome against the project. Nor were the ultramontanes able to capture the Quebec wing of the Conservative Party. Their proposal to transform the party by the adoption of a Catholic program in 1871 backfired when Cartier, Taschereau and others objected on the grounds that it would only encourage the emergence of a strong Protestant party in English Canada, a party that could polarize the country and enable English Canada to bring to bear the full force of its majority.

The electors proved indifferent to the proposal to thrust organized religion into the political arena. Only one of the candidates supported by the ultramontanes was successful in the 1871 provincial election. Within the Conservative Party, however, the feud between ultras (or Castors) and moderates continued. Over the long term, religious differences contributed to the weakening of the party that had dominated Quebec since the Union period.

Limited Modernization

Quebec politicians after 1867 therefore faced a number of difficulties in establishing a truly autonomous political system. In the first few years, Federal leaders like Cartier were entitled to retain seats in the provincial legislature, a provision that established federal predominance. Economically, Quebec was dependent on the cooperation of the English-speaking business community: The provincial treasurer was the representative of the Bank of Montreal, the government's recognized creditor.[37] Culturally, the politicians in Quebec were influenced by the Catholic Church: Mercier, leader of a *Parti National* government, enraged Protestant Canada by asking the Pope to be arbiter in disputes over estates formerly belonging to the Jesuit Order. If between elections, therefore, the government of Quebec had to negotiate with various elites—the federal government, the business community of Montreal and the Church of Rome—at election time it had to win the support of the masses (as the voters were often called in Quebec), and this it achieved by the widespread use of patronage. Politics in Quebec became notorious for corruption, which led to the charge that the political culture of the province was fundamentally undemocratic.[38]

If Quebec's politics were in flux, so was Quebec society. The old seigneurial system of landlord and tenant gave way to a social structure in which independent small-scale commodity producers played a large part. Indeed, it was the changes in the economy and society of the province that ultimately made the victory of the Liberals possible, despite the opposition of the Church. While there was not much movement from Quebec to western Canada after Confederation, there was considerable migration to towns and cities in New England as well as in Quebec, where the new industries were located. The Church fought hard to prevent the urbanization and industrialization it feared would change the character of the province, but its efforts at colonization failed to stop the migration to the cities. Nor could its antistatist outlook prevent the politicization of the Quebec voter.

There have been two very different interpretations of Quebec's process of modernization. The economic approach has drawn attention to the continuous development that took place throughout the nineteenth and twentieth centuries and has pointed out that, despite the widespread view of Quebec as a rural society until the Quiet Revolution, it had already become largely urban by the time of the 1931 census. The other interpretation, more sociopolitical, has emphasized the conservative nature of Quebec society until after the second world war, and the ability of the Church to prevent radical ideas from spreading to the mass of the people.

In fact, both interpretations have merit.[39] For decades, Quebec was a province with an economy characterized by many of the usual features summed up by the term "modernization." But despite its economic transformation it did remain a conservative society, much like the American South until the 1960s. The failure of the society to change as rapidly as the economy may have been due in part to the dualist nature of French Canada: the tension between British civilization and French culture. There remained a wide gulf between the modern sector of the Quebec economy, largely controlled by *"les anglais,"* and Quebec's French-speaking society, which until the mid-twentieth century was influenced by European Catholic thought, especially French. In retrospect it is extraordinary that the Church was so successful in maintaining the Catholic tradition for so long. One observer has gone so far as to sum up the intellectual life of Quebec in the twentieth century as follows:

> . . . after World War I the ideas which were most influential among the French-Canadian *élite* were those of the modern repre-

sentatives of the Catholic tradition in France, such as Péguy, Mauriac, Mounier, and Maritain. It is only since the Second World War that those writers who are in the secular and anti-clerical tradition, such as Gide, Malraux, Camus, and Sartre, have found a receptive audience in some intellectual circles.[40]

French Canada remained a "traditional" society long after the rest of Canada (and Quebec itself) had been "modernized," to use the language of the social sciences. It was in Quebec that French-Canadian culture was best preserved, and it was in Quebec that in due course emerged a nationalist movement to challenge the Pan-Canadianism of the Federal government, even under French-Canadian leadership. The Church in its heyday had been aggressive in its missionary activities; by contrast, Pan-Canadian politicians in Ottawa were compelled by their dependence on the anglophone majority to be more circumspect in their policies. Indeed, they were usually on the defensive.

Support for Pan-Canadianism

Despite the influence of the Church and growing interest in a Quebec nationalism that had an emotional appeal, the French Canadians continued to support their more cerebral Pan-Canadian leaders in Ottawa, even though these leaders sustained setbacks at the hands of the anglophone majority. No doubt many of the French feared that without a presence in Ottawa they would find themselves in an even weaker position, losing more than they would gain were they to cut themselves adrift from English Canada.

There is another reason for the persistence of Pan-Canadian sentiment. French Canadians were reluctant to abandon their historic dream of a continental French Canada.[41] Their vision of North America might be different from the English but it, too, encompassed Canada, not just Quebec. Even if the country was never again to be French and Catholic, Canada remained the land they had discovered and explored, and in the development of which they were entitled to play a role. This helps to explain why the French never supported a French-Canadian or a Catholic party in Federal elections, preferring instead to vote for one or the other of the two main parties. Quebec nationalism, while always an attractive option, had its limitations.

At a party in Quebec City to celebrate his seventy-fifth birthday in

1957, Louis St. Laurent, then still Prime Minister of Canada, addressed himself to the theme of Canadian unity. In this speech to the assembled gathering he repeated the words of the first French-speaking Prime Minister, Wilfrid Laurier: "As for me, gentlemen, I do not want any small republic such as San Marino or Monaco. . . . My ambition is to be the citizen of a great country."[42] Geographically, of course, the huge province of Quebec bore no comparison with the tiny principalities of Europe. But spiritually Quebec conjured up the small community founded on the shores of the St. Lawrence and destined to be forever surrounded by "a sea of Anglo-Saxons." For many French Canadians like St. Laurent, accustomed to being part of a larger Canada, Quebec did not offer a large enough stage. To withdraw behind its borders was, paradoxically enough, to admit final defeat for French Canada at the very same time as, from the Quebec nationalist viewpoint, final victory.

French Canada, like English Canada, learned to live with its contradictions. English Canadians managed to put into practice the incompatible doctrines of parliamentary supremacy and federalism. French Canadians combined Pan-Canadianism (and the notion that French should be recognized throughout Canada) with Quebec nationalism. ". . . [B]ilingualism and special status for Quebec were not alternatives to each other; they went necessarily together."[43]

"Je me souviens," the motto of Quebec, could well have been the motto for both races. The English Canadians retained their own memories, of the British Empire under Queen Victoria, of British civilization straddling the world, and of the Westminster parliamentary system they treasured as the finest symbol of that civilization. The French Canadians retained memories of the French Empire, the days when France's glorious culture and language were given precedence everywhere. They were rightly proud of the contribution that their ancestors had made to the opening up of the North American continent, and recalled the exploits of their explorers and missionaries, as well as their *voyageurs* and *coureurs de bois* engaged in the fur trade throughout the West.

For English Canadians, the sense of their British heritage was tempered by a determination to escape colonial rule and to create an autonomous Canadian society. For French Canadians, the nationalists' concern for Quebec's French heritage was in constant tension with the Pan-Canadians' insistence on Quebec's participation in the creation of a new Canada. For Cartier and his Pan-Canadian successors in Ottawa, memory of Quebec's past greatness was a spur to new endeavors on a continental scale.

In retrospect, Cartier appears as a singular figure in Canadian politics. His career spanned the Union period of dualism and the early years of Confederation. His self-confidence enabled him to believe that the French were primarily Canadians. Together with *les anglais* they would create a country which combined two great civilizations which, working in cooperation, were destined to prevent Canada from falling into American hands. He could promote the notion of a single Canadian nationality because Confederation assured the French that they would preserve their distinctive cultural identity. After all, the French in North America were the original *Canadiens:* how could they be made to give up their country?

5 The Attempt to Combine Pan-Canadianism and Nationalism: Sir George-Etienne Cartier

George-Etienne Cartier was the first Pan-Canadian francophone. He also continued to strive to be a nationalist as leader of his party in the Quebec Legislative Assembly. His career, which spanned the Union and post-Confederation periods, showed how difficult it was to combine the two roles. After Cartier, it was taken for granted that the roles should be separated, a Pan-Canadian leader like Laurier, St. Laurent, or Trudeau in Ottawa being matched by a nationalist such as Mercier, Duplessis, or Lévesque in Quebec City.

If we are to understand the complexities created by the emergence of French Canada, to glimpse the different perspectives held by English and French Canadians, and above all to become aware of the pressures applied to a Quebec politician who decided to be a Pan-Canadian, we can do no better than glance at the political career of Sir George Etienne Cartier. It was a career that began when he was first elected to the Legislative Assembly in 1848 and ended with his death at the age of fifty-nine in 1873.

With the resignation of LaFontaine in 1851, Cartier soon became the leading French-Canadian member of the Cabinet. On a number of occasions, notably the ministry of 1858-62, he served as the first minister. In 1851 he was appointed chairman of the legislature's standing committee on railways, and retained this position not only until Confederation but afterwards when the Parliament of Canada established a similar committee. (He remained chairman until his death, and thus was the leading political figure involved in Canada's railway development.)

Pan-Canadians like Cartier who saw the foundation-stone of the Union Parliament Buildings laid in 1860 and the buildings opened in 1866, could see the continuity of the Canadian political system: Confederation was old Canada with additions. Nationalists noticed instead the break with tradition: Quebec City was transformed within a year from being an alternate capital of Canada into the capital of a province.

Cartier was able not only to combine being a minister with the chairmanship of Parliament's most important parliamentary committee, in 1853 he was chosen by the British financial and political backers of the Grand Trunk Railway, the biggest business in the Canada of its day, to be their agent and solicitor. Like Macdonald, he retained his law practice throughout his political career. It was an age when the Canadian State (such as it was) gave credence to Marx's famous dictum that "the executive of the modern state is but a committee for managing the common affairs of the whole bourgeoisie." Canadian ministers saw no conflict of interest in accepting paid positions with the business interests they were supposed to regulate, and Cartier was not an exception. One biographer has given examples of Cartier's "relaxed political morality,"[44] but other biographers have said that he was personally honest and did not accept bribes, a view confirmed by his critic, General Wolseley.[45] (Wolseley commanded the expedition to the Red River in 1870 when Cartier was Minister of Militia.) Cartier's law firm, in which LaFontaine became a partner, often acted as intermediary for English-speaking entrepreneurs in Montreal. One of Cartier's most valuable legacies to Quebec as Attorney General for Canada East, the modernization and codification of the province's civil law (1859–66), also benefited English-speaking business firms and, indirectly, Cartier's law firm as well. In other words, Cartier's legal, political, and business interests neatly coincided. As a sympathetic biographer put it, he was the embodiment of three continuing desires: "that of the French Canadians for cultural sovereignty, that of Montreal for economic ascendancy, and that of British financiers connected with the Colonial Office for Grand Trunk solvency and material expansion. He made their desires his own, and like a nova, an exploding star, he burned himself out in their accomplishment, in ensuring that a steel life-line would be thrown from one ocean to the other."[46]

Cartier's credentials as a representative of French Canada were impressive. At the age of twenty he was the first secretary of the patriotic St. Jean Baptiste Society, when it was founded in 1834. In 1837 he fought in the first rebellion and had to flee into exile. In the 1840s he became legal adviser to the Sulpician Order, the dominant French-Canadian force in Montreal and whose school, the *Collège de Montréal,* he had attended (as had Papineau, LaFontaine, and Riel).

Cartier's concern for the well being of Montreal as an imperial city was in sharp contrast to the willingness of many of its English-speaking businessmen, dismayed by responsible government and the growing power of French Canadians, to sign the 1849 Annexation Manifesto proposing union with the United States. The manifesto alerted the British to possible further unrest on the part of the British colonists unless Canada received some of the money being invested in North American railway expansion. Cartier, who had been pardoned by the governor in 1839 for his part in the first rebellion, had since established his credentials as a loyal servant of the Empire, like his father and grandfather before him. It was he who was chosen as the agent of the British in establishing Montreal as Canada's rail center. By the time the Grand Trunk was completed in 1860, the railway extended across the whole Province of Canada from Sarnia (and Detroit) in the west via Toronto and Montreal, across the river and down the lower St. Lawrence to Rivière du Loup (which led nowhere unless the line were extended to the Maritime Provinces). A southeasterly line from Montreal joined up with the St. Lawrence and Atlantic Railway, which ended at the ice-free port of Portland, Maine. Over 1,100 miles long, the Grand Trunk was the longest railway in the world, and the magnificent Victoria Bridge across the St. Lawrence at Montreal was the world's longest bridge. Cartier was first minister in 1860 when the Prince of Wales opened the bridge.

Cartier defended the interests of Lower Canada, of the Imperial Government (and British financiers), and of Montreal as a business center, in insuring that no serious rival of the Grand Trunk emerged. When an American company constructed a railroad across northern New York State to Ogdensburg, on the St. Lawrence, hoping to tap the Canadian market once a bridge was built across the river, Cartier refused to allow any bridge to be constructed west of Montreal. Similarly, when the Quebec City political leader Joseph Cauchon pleaded for a line to link Quebec with Montreal along the populous north shore of the St. Lawrence, Cartier postponed action on this proposal, giving priority to the Grand Trunk.

At Confederation the "little Napoleon," as he was sometimes called, stood at the peak of his career. In the first federal election, held in 1867, his supporters, the *Bleus,* won forty-seven of Quebec's sixty-five seats. In the provincial election they did even better, gaining fifty-one out of sixty-four. Under the terms of Confederation, Cartier was able to remain a member of both legislatures, and so he led his party in Quebec as well as Ottawa. Yet he still had to choose where to have his official residence. Cartier had been one of the few French Canadians to approve of the shift of the capital to Ottawa, and it was in Ottawa that he decided to live (in 1866).[47]

However, in Ottawa, after 1867, Cartier was no longer first minister. He now represented not a "section" but a minority group. Even within that group his influence began to wane. The Sulpicians, as a Gallican Order, were on the defensive against Bishop Bourget and the aggressive ultramontanes. As their solicitor, Cartier was committed to the protection of the interest of the Sulpicians.

It was railway policy that was most responsible for Cartier's undoing. The company he had always backed, the Grand Trunk, was uninterested in an all-Canadian route across the uninhabited Canadian Shield to open up western Canada, preferring instead a more profitable southern route through Chicago. Cartier therefore lacked the backing of his railway in the pursuit of a Canadian line linking Montreal and Vancouver. He became embroiled, as did Macdonald, in machinations between the Toronto and Montreal business interests that hoped to be chosen to build the Pacific railway. American entrepreneurs were deeply involved with the Montreal railway and shipping magnate, Sir Hugh Allan, and his syndicate. Large sums were provided through Allan for the Conservatives in the 1872 election campaign. The Opposition discovered that Cartier had asked for money in writing, and there was the presumption that the Pacific contract would be awarded to Allan and his associates after the election. Questions were raised in the House of Commons and ultimately the incriminating correspondence in which specific sums were allocated to each minister was obtained and published. This "Pacific Scandal" caused such consternation among Macdonald's supporters in the House that he was compelled to resign, paving the way for the Liberals under Alexander Mackenzie to take office in 1873.

For Cartier, the nadir of his career had already come with the 1872 election. (By the time the Pacific Scandal broke, he was dead.) On this occasion, the second federal election following Confederation, Cartier was specifically asked by his supporters in Quebec to promote the interests of his province. In particular, he was asked to support the construction of the Quebec North Shore Railway from Quebec City, the terminus of which was expected to be in east Montreal—Cartier's own *comté* (electoral district). But Cartier, the Pan-Canadian, was already committed to the construction of the Intercolonial Railway from Rivière du Loup on the *south* shore of the St. Lawrence to Halifax, Nova Scotia, as well as to a Pacific railway. It is true that both lines served Montreal, but the city the Intercolonial served was the entrepôt of Canada, controlled by British and American business interests, not the cultural heart of francophone Quebec. Cartier's fellow French Canadians did not share his enthusiasm for a Canada that stretched from sea to sea, particularly the remote West beyond Ontario. They were more interested in the economic development of Quebec's North Shore and the western part of the province to be served by a proposed Northern Colonial Railway.

As Cartier's support in his own province declined, he attempted to advance the cause of French Canada in the West. He was not only an enthusiastic suitor of the British Columbia delegation that came to Ottawa and agreed to join Confederation in 1871 on the promise of a Pacific railway, but he did much for the *Métis* when Manitoba was admitted as a province in 1870. As acting prime minister at that time he made sure that Manitoba's new constitution was modeled on the bilingual constitution of Quebec, and that its government was supplied with a number of competent Quebecois nominated by Cartier himself. But he was unable to control Louis Riel, the key figure for French-Canadian hopes that the West might be developed as a dual society. There was a period of confusion in late 1869 when power at the Red River was being transferred from the Hudson's Bay Company to the government of Canada, without any consultation of its inhabitants. During this time the young Riel formed a provisional government to negotiate with Canada on behalf of the *Métis* and others. Faced by opposition from the pro-Canadian party at the Red River, Riel's government had authorized the execution of one of the ringleaders, an Orangeman from Ontario named Thomas Scott. Many people in Ontario, already annoyed to discover that Manitoba was not to be an English-speaking Protestant province, were incensed to learn that an "illegal" government had "murdered" Scott.

Cartier had a different reaction. Remembering his own youth and the Rebellion, he was sympathetic to Riel's predicament, and advised him to follow his own example by going into exile and awaiting a pardon from the Crown. As acting prime minister, Cartier thought he was in a position to take action on Riel's behalf. He was unaware that when the governor general forwarded to London his Cabinet memorandum requesting a pardon, he added a note that it was "not to be regarded as a Minute of Council nor as an expression of the United Cabinet."[48] One of Cartier's biographers has described this action as a stab in the back. But it is worth remembering that 1870 was very different from 1839, when a rebel could be pardoned by a governor on behalf of the Crown. Under responsible government, Cartier did not have the power to override the English-Canadian majority in his cabinet, a majority that presumably made its views known. And so, whereas Cartier had been able to return to Canada and to become a prosperous lawyer after the 1837 Rebellion, Riel went into what became virtually permanent exile (although a conditional amnesty was granted in 1875).

Cartier, the proponent of a single political nationality, served the imperial and federal governments (and English Canada) well. But Cartier, the advocate of a separate French cultural nationality, failed fully to satisfy the French Canadians. It was his rejection by Montreal East in 1872 that caused him to obtain reelection from Provencher, a new riding in Manitoba intended for the irrepressible Riel.[49] Whereas Montreal East would have been the terminus of the railway Cartier refused to build, Provencher was on the route to the Pacific that the CPR would one day take. Alastair Sweeny has written, "Until his death in 1873, Cartier was the chief servant of Britain's imperial design in North America, at the same time as he was the personification of the growing desires of his own people. He saw that the forging of a Canadian nation was totally in the interests of the French Canadians, however much they might protest against the fact."[50]

Cartier's limited success on behalf of French Canada makes Sweeny's sympathetic judgment only partly true. Pan-Canadians might agree that Cartier's attempts to further the interests of French Canada in the West were on the whole well conceived, but Quebec nationalists would find it difficult to discover just what he did for the Quebecois. The "Canadian nation" that Cartier helped to create after 1867 was largely English Canadian.

Yet to dismiss Cartier as the ultimate *vendu* is to do him an injustice. In his own way he was a visionary, and one whose Pan-Canadian perspective distinguished him from English Canadians. He likened himself to his namesake, Jacques Cartier, who had discovered the St. Lawrence and Quebec in his search for a northwest passage to China, and who had been stopped by rapids, above Montreal, later appropriately named "Lachine." George-Etienne Cartier believed that it was his destiny to "bring together the China of Asia and the Lachine of Montreal."[51] It may have been awareness of this vision that brought out the immense crowds for his funeral in Montreal. Had Cartier lived, he would have reached seventy-one when the Canadian Pacific Railway was completed, 250 years after his family arrived in Quebec from France, and 450 years after Jacques Cartier sailed up the St. Lawrence: he would have appreciated the anniversary.

Cartier has long been honored in English Canada. In the 1960s, Ontario commemorated a century of Confederation by naming its trunk road across the province the Macdonald-Cartier Expressway. It would have been equally appropriate to have paid tribute to Cartier as the moving force, a century or more earlier, behind the trunk road's predecessor, the Grand Trunk Railway. Although Cartier was the French-Canadian leader whose willingness to participate in the coalition government of 1864 made Confederation possible, Quebec itself did not accord him any similar honor. "Today Cartier is not revered in Quebec as one of the great historic leaders of French Canada. It is considered that Dorion's policy of fighting the Great Coalition and all its works, was a much sounder policy in 1864 than the one pursued by Cartier."[52]

Nevertheless, as we have already noted, French Canadians did not abandon the Pan-Canadian aspirations represented by Cartier in favor of a narrower Quebec nationalism. They remained dualists, and they continued to support both Pan-Canadian and nationalist leaders. But they no longer expected a single leader to fulfill both goals. Quebec voters frequently elected as provincial premiers nationalists such as Honoré Mercier (1886–91), Maurice Duplessis (1936–39 and 1944–50), Daniel Johnson (1966–68), and René Lévesque (1976–85). But they also voted for Pan-Canadian leaders such as Wilfrid Laurier

(1896–1911), Louis St. Laurent (1948–57), and Pierre Trudeau (1968–84) at the Federal level.

After 1867, as Cartier was to discover, it was difficult for a Pan-Canadian leader to represent both the Pan-Canadian and nationalist personalities of Quebec, whether in economic, cultural, or constitutional affairs. In economic policy, the Canadian economy as a whole had to be given precedence over the concerns of Quebec. Thus Cartier himself put the interests of the transcontinental railway over those of the Quebec north shore line. In cultural policy, despite the growing French-Canadian interest in bilingualism and biculturalism, Canada's predominantly British and Protestant civilization inevitably triumphed outside Quebec over French and Catholic culture. Neither Cartier nor Laurier proved successful in their attempts to defend those French-Canadian Catholics who were most strenuously fighting to preserve their culture in New Brunswick and Manitoba in struggles that may be called "crises of Confederation."

8
French Canada and the Triumph of Majority Rule

There is no right, however sacred, of the individual or of a minority, which cannot be infringed or abolished by an Act of Parliament.—Lord Hailsham, *The Dilemma of Democracy*

1   Different Interpretations of the Confederation Agreement on Majority Rule: The Case of New Brunswick

The emergence of separatist sentiment in Quebec in the 1960s encouraged English Canadians to divide francophones into one of two categories. On the one hand there were the *indépendantistes,* as they preferred to be called, Quebec nationalists who were ill-disposed toward Confederation and all it stood for. On the other were the Pan-Canadians, known as federalists, like Pierre Trudeau. These were francophones who were well-disposed to Canada and who were committed to the notion of French Canada, not just Quebec. Their aim was defined by the government of Canada in a proposal to amend the Constitution offered to Parliament in 1978 as, "to ensure throughout Canada equal respect for English and French as the country's spoken languages, and for those Canadians who use each of them." The Government's bill promised "a permanent national commitment to the endurance and self-fulfilment of the Canadian French-speaking society centred in but not limited to Quebec."[1]

The goal of equality might be thought to have become commonplace after the recognition of French as an official language in 1969. After all, were not Canadians—except for the misguided separatists—committed to the goal of a united Canada? What many English did not appreciate was that the nationalist movement in Quebec owed much to unrelenting English hostility over the years to the full recognition of the religious faith and language of the French. There were still some English Canadians who thought of Canada, apart from Quebec, as an English-speaking country, and who believed that bilingualism should be confined to federal institutions. In 1969 the federalist French Canadians under the leadership of Pierre Trudeau were still having to combat the fundamental assumption of countless English Canadians since the days of Sir John A. Macdonald that the whole point of Confederation was what we may call "majoritarian dualism." This gave French-speaking Canadians control over Quebec but left the other provinces, and the federal government, in the hands of the English-speaking majority.

In this chapter we shall see how the Union period's "dualism of equality" was replaced after 1867 by majoritarian dualism and how French-Canadian and Roman-Catholic minorities outside Quebec fought against this assumption. We need to remember that despite the commitment of all parties to bilingualism at the federal level, bitter resistance by conservatives in Manitoba and Ontario to the official recognition of French at the provincial level continued in the 1980s. (It was partly in retaliation that Quebec had withdrawn many of the rights and privileges traditionally enjoyed by its anglophone minority.)

In sum, the conflict between the two "races" noted by Lord Durham has abated but has not entirely disappeared. If we are to understand why it continued to simmer, and why so many French Canadians became disenchanted with the BNA Act, we need to examine the history of Canada since Confederation as it appeared to the French minority. Instead of savoring the satisfaction of seeing Canada evolve from colony to nation, many French-speaking Canadians thought of the political system in terms of continual crises between the majority and the minority.

In the years after Confederation, the idea of linguistic and cultural equality received little sympathy from English Canadians. The British North America Act was written in English, and it did not recognize the equality of the two languages.[2] As a political entity, Canada was an English-speaking federal system that included Quebec. French was given no recognition by any province other than Quebec. Only what was in the BNA Act was part of constitutional law, and that law was subject to majority rule. Majority rule prevailed in Parliament and the provincial legislatures. Only in Quebec were the French a majority.

Such was the legal logic of Confederation. There was no basis in law for the argument that Canada was composed of two cultures; there was no legal entity called "French Canada"; in law there was no implied contract or compact giving French-Canadian minorities the right to remain either Catholic or French-speaking. The concession to the use of French in Parliament and the courts in Section 133 was made in return for the acceptance by Quebec of English in its courts and legislature. The concession of publicly-supported Catholic schools in Ontario in Section 93 was made in return for Quebec's acceptance of publicly-supported Protestant schools.

From the English-Canadian perspective, the crucial sections of the BNA Act were those that prevented the (French-speaking) Catholic majority in Quebec from trampling on the rights of the (English-speaking) Protestant minority there. "Canadian dualism" was to the English Canadians a concept with limited applicability. Canada was British and its political system was based on British principles of government, notably parliamentary supremacy and majority rule.

Cartier understood the nature of the agreement very well. He was able to support bilingualism and Catholic schools in Manitoba in 1870 because its French-speaking population at that time appeared to enjoy a majority. He refused to act on behalf of the Catholics in New Brunswick in 1871 because they were a minority for whom the BNA Act offered no protection against provincial legislation by a Protestant majority. The Pan-Canadians who participated in federal politics after Confederation were faced with a political system that accepted majority rule and parliamentary supremacy at the Dominion level but tempered majority rule by francophones in Quebec to protect the English-speaking minority. They had no grounds for asserting that Catholic (and still less, French-Catholic) families living outside Quebec and Ontario were living in a dualist society and were entitled by the BNA Act to have their schools publicly supported.

Because Pan-Canadians like Cartier were never willing to challenge the principle of majority rule by francophone Catholics in Quebec, they felt they had to accept majority rule by anglophone Protestants elsewhere. Some attempted to temper Protestant or anglophone majority rule by presenting Confederation as a political system based not only on law but also on a social compact between English and French Canadians. While they did not assert that the two languages or cultures were equal under the law, they nevertheless made a number of dualist assumptions about Canada, French Canada, and the BNA Act which, while they fell short of a claim for equality, went beyond the letter of the law. They made several assumptions: Canada was divided not only into English-speaking provinces and Quebec, but into English and French

Canada. It was a country of two cultures, i.e., there was cultural as well as political nationality. French Canada encompassed not only Quebec but also those parts of Canada where there were significant French-speaking minorities. In addition to the legal framework of the BNA Act there was an implicit compact between English and French Canada, whereby the significant minorities outside Quebec enjoyed the right to remain Catholic and French-speaking. These minorities were not to be assimilated.

Although the Pan-Canadians differed from the English Canadians in their dualist view of Canada, they accepted the fact that Canada was a political entity governed by majority rule. They recognized that the constitutional rights of the French-speaking Catholic minorities in provinces outside Quebec were not comparable to those protecting the English-speaking Protestant minority in that province. Confederation had given autonomy to Quebec. It had not given equality to the two unequally-represented cultures.

In theory, therefore, there was a possible solution to the thorny problem of Catholic French-Canadian minorities. While the *laws* governing French-speaking and Catholic minorities were restrictive, the *conventions* of the Constitution might be exploited to mitigate them. But the use of conventions to create an independent Canada was one thing; their use to modify clauses of the BNA Act that restricted Catholic schools and the use of French was quite another. Not only did the legislation governing both religion and language remain unchanged, so did the conventions. The law was strictly interpreted.[3] In Ontario, where Catholics had constitutional rights reaffirmed in the BNA Act, these rights were respected. Elsewhere they were not.

The BNA Act, it bears repeating, had nothing at all to say about the rights of French-speaking provincial minorities. As we saw in Chapter 7, it contained nothing that could later be used on behalf of the *Acadiens* of New Brunswick, the *Métis* and French Canadians in Manitoba, or the *Canadiens* who migrated into northern and eastern Ontario. Section 93 of the act referred only to Protestant minorities in Quebec and Catholic minorities in Ontario who had schools established "by law in the Province at the Union."

Section 93 was drafted so as to have general application in principle. But in practice it applied only to Ontario and Quebec. Paragraph (3) indicated that there was nothing to prevent other provinces from following the example of the Province of Canada and establishing a system of separate schools. But this was unlikely to occur where there was a Protestant majority, meaning in any province other than Quebec.

The case of New Brunswick's treatment of the Roman Catholic minority after Confederation is instructive. In 1867 the Church in New Brunswick had entered into negotiations with the colonial secretary Lord Carnarvon, in the hope of obtaining legal guarantees for denominational schools in the Maritimes; the effort did not succeed. Archbishop Connolly of Halifax realized how inadequate for Maritime Catholics were the proposals (the so-called "Galt amendment") incorporated in Section 93 in the London negotiations to protect Quebec's Protestant minority. According to a historian of the period, Connolly

> refused to be as satisfied with Galt's amendment with respect to the educational rights of minorities as Galt, Langevin, and the other politicians were. What the bishops had wanted were schools recognized by law, as the Protestants had in Lower Canada. What the Galt amendment lacked, for the right of appeal to be used, was what the Roman Catholics of New Brunswick and Nova Scotia did not securely have—separate schools fully recognized by provincial law. Connolly protested strongly and repeatedly but Carnarvon suavely put him off.[4]

At issue was the nature of the province-wide systems of education that were to be established by law after 1867 outside central Canada to replace the one-room schoolhouses of an earlier era. These new systems involved inspection of schools, certification of teachers, compulsory attendance by pupils, and prescribed texts—together with the local taxation and government grants necessary to bear the burden of organized education.

Few leaders in public life seem to have been willing to explain the restricted applications of the BNA Act, and in particular to make it clear that in view of the widespread Protestant hostility to Catholicism, the provisions of the BNA Act governing education in Ontario were not really intended to apply elsewhere. The weakness of Canada's tradition of philosophical federalism was that the elites were prepared to be fuzzy on sensitive issues where accommodation could not be reached.[5] This applied particularly to Catholic-Protestant relations. There were only two Roman Catholic delegates to the London conference that drafted the BNA Act. It was these delegates who had to tackle the problem of education, a problem that had been left unresolved in the negotiations in Canada. Both Catholic delegates, Cartier and Langevin, were French-speaking laymen from Quebec. Cartier was quite clear regarding the limitations of the BNA Act, and he was one of the few leaders willing to explain them when trouble arose. Hector Langevin, however, does not seem to have been fully aware of the importance of majority rule in determining the nature of each province's school system. (Ontario's separate school system, after all, had been imposed by the Legislative Assembly of the Province of Canada in which the Catholics had the upper hand.) Professor Morton has quoted an extraordinary letter that Langevin wrote to his brother in the Catholic hierarchy: "We accord to the Protestants of Lower Canada the protection they ought to have, and in consideration of that we extend our protection to the 700,000 or 800,000 Catholics of Upper Canada to the [Catholics of the] Maritime Province."

Instead of noting how naive politically Langevin must have been to make these often-quoted remarks, Morton (a Manitoban) made the legalistic and misleading observation, "The guarantee of minority rights in education to the English Protestants of Lower Canada had thus spread out into a guarantee of the separate schools of Upper Canada, and so to separate schools, existing or such that might be established, of all the provinces."[6] Nowhere did Morton clearly indicate that a guarantee to separate schools "such as might be established" meant very little, since the principle of majority rule (by Protestants) prevented these schools from being publicly supported. Instead, Morton went on to quote from the speech on the BNA Act made by Lord Carnarvon to the House of Lords in the debate of February 19, 1867, in which the colonial secretary also gave the impression that separate schools elsewhere in Canada would have a right to public funds similar to that existing by law in Ontario. Morton's restrained comment on Carnarvon's speech is worth quoting: "The Protestant minority of Lower Canada and the Roman Catholic minorities of the other provinces, he declared, would under the bill 'stand on a footing of entire equality.' That this statement was not exact did not mean of course that the politicians of the day did not think it practically true."[7]

"That this statement was not exact" was a euphemism for "absurd" because minority rights in 1867 were protected only in Ontario and Quebec. Other Roman Catholic minorities could only "stand on a footing of entire equality" if provincial legislatures elsewhere passed legislation similar to the Province of Canada's Separate Schools Act of 1863.

Given the hostility of Protestant majorities to Catholic minorities, this was highly unlikely.

It is true that Lord Carnarvon had gone on to point out that ". . . in the event of any wrong at the hand of the local majority, the minority have the right of appeal to the Governor General in Council, and may claim the application of any remedial laws that may be necessary from the Central Parliament of the Confederation."[8] But Carnarvon must have known that such an appeal to the Federal Cabinet or Dominion Parliament would be far more likely to result in remedial action if launched by the Protestant minority of Quebec than by the Catholic minorities in the other provinces.

French Canadians, and Catholics generally, discovered that there was often an unbridgeable gap between a statement that was legally precise and one that was, in Morton's quaint phrase, "practically true." It was one thing to establish equal treatment for minorities in Quebec and Ontario as a matter of constitutional law and quite another to make such equality elsewhere dependent on the will, or even whim, of the majority. French Canadians were not being completely unreasonable in later years when they argued that they had been promised equality at Confederation. Morton himself admitted, without comment, "The French Canadians saw Confederation as a compact between Lower and Upper Canada by which the 'national' rights of the French in Canada were guaranteed, and those of the English minorities in Lower Canada equally assured. Any departure from this 'treaty' the *Bleus* would regard as betrayal, and knew it would deliver French Canada to the *Rouges*."[9] To be precise, it was *Roman Catholic,* not French, educational rights in Ontario and Quebec, not in Canada as a whole, that were guaranteed, and the right of French Canadians to use French in *Parliament,* not in Canada generally.

The first crisis of Confederation showed how committed the government of Canada and French-Canadian leaders were to the principle of majority rule, and to the restrictions of the BNA Act. New Brunswick's Common Schools Act (1871) ended the practice of tax support for denominational schools. At that time more than half the Catholics were English-speaking, and it was largely on their behalf that appeals were made to Ottawa, and ultimately to the Privy Council. There were no *Acadien* bishops or politicians. Macdonald stuck by the letter of the BNA Act, telling the House of Commons that no New Brunswick law had ever established a separate school system with a legal right to tax support. Cartier reminded the House that the Fathers of Confederation had never intended to give constitutional protection to Catholics in New Brunswick. Ottawa therefore had no right to disallow the Common Schools Act. The government refused to act on a proposal from a Quebec Member of Parliament to introduce a constitutional amendment extending constitutional protection to all Catholic schools. In 1874 the Judicial Committee upheld the New Brunswick legislation as valid. The following year there was some violence in New Brunswick, but the provincial government stood firm.

Throughout the crisis, the New Brunswick Catholics received little official outside support. Cartier opposed disallowance with the argument that "the fate of the Catholic majority of the province of Quebec would be at the mercy of the federal Parliament."[10] Likewise, Langevin rejected a constitutional amendment because "it would be invoked against Lower Canada any day when there would be a wish to infringe upon our rights."[11] By now, apparently, Langevin grasped the significance of the Confederation agreement. Referring to the role of Catholic MPs from Quebec in Ottawa, he made his commitment to majority rule clear: "Their first responsibility is to see to the general welfare of the Confederation, and the representatives of Quebec must protect above all the interests of Quebec."[12]

The first crisis of Confederation revealed the consequences of the compact made by Quebec at Confederation: in return for majority rule in Quebec, the *Canadien* leaders would not protect Catholic minorities elsewhere. However, one of the longterm effects of the crisis was to stimulate a distinctive national consensus among the *Acadiens*, whose numbers were growing, and who ultimately became a force in New Brunswick politics.

2 The North West Rebellion

The most violent crisis of Confederation in the nineteenth century was not over education. It occurred in 1885 when the *Métis* and Indians staged their final rebellion against the inexorable expansion of British civilization, symbolized by the almost completed Canadian Pacific Railway through the West. The rising took place west of Manitoba in present-day Saskatchewan (then the Northwest Territories). The charismatic bilingual *Métis,* Louis Riel, who had briefly headed the Provisional Government of Manitoba, was invited to return from exile in Montana to assist in the resistance to Canada's expansion westward. The crisis might have been regarded as a last skirmish between the native peoples and the whites, comparable to those in the United States, had not Riel responded to the invitation to come back and lead the rebellion.

Ironically enough, it was the very railway that the Pan-Canadian Cartier had proposed to open up the West for Canadians of both races, that was now used to dispatch troops to put down a revolt which, though it began as a native uprising, was later interpreted as the death-knell of French Canada's hopes to develop the West as a condominium. Riel was captured, charged with high treason, and sentenced to death (although with a recommendation for mercy). But the failure of his appeal to the Queen's Bench of Manitoba and ultimately to the Privy Council led to the decision of the government of Canada that he should be hanged at Regina in November 1885. At this point all the latent tensions between Protestant Ontario and Catholic Quebec once again came into the open.

The North West Rebellion released much pent-up emotion in an Ontario that for over a generation had regarded the West as its preserve. Orangemen had been angry over the execution of the Protestant "agitator" Thomas Scott by the Catholic Riel's provisional government in early 1870. They had been dismayed by the discovery that the Manitoba Act had established a new province on the dualist model of Quebec (followed seven years later by the recognition of French in the Northwest Territories). Feelings ran high when, in 1875, the members of the provisional government held to be ultimately responsible for Scott's "murder" were granted amnesty by the Dominion government.

In 1885, Sir John Macdonald was still Prime Minister of Canada and still depended on the support of both Conservatives in English Canada and *Bleus* in Quebec. He had managed to hold this coalition together by not choosing one group over the other. He had been lucky in previous crises. It had been Cartier who was acting Prime Minister in 1870 when the Manitoba Act was passed. It was the Liberal government of Alexander Mackenzie (1873–78), Prime Minister during the sole interruption of Macdonald's long tenure of office (which ended with his death in 1891), that had offered amnesty to the provisional government of Riel and had extended French to the Territories. But in 1885 it was Macdonald who had to choose between hanging and sparing Riel. Sympathetic to his Quebec colleagues and supporters, Macdonald was also mindful of opinion in Ontario—where he was a member of the Orange

Order. In the end he responded to the strong feelings in his native province, and ordered the execution to proceed.

No one questioned the fact that Riel was guilty of leading a rebellion. The rebellion of 1885 was Riel's second and much more serious act of resistance to the Crown: the British government had executed the leaders of those who in 1837–38 rebelled a second time. Riel had been forgiven, officially at least, for the resistance of 1870, just as Papineau, Mackenzie, and Cartier had been pardoned for their part in the Rebellion of 1837. This helps to explain why the French-speaking members of the Canadian Cabinet protested against the execution but did not resign as a body. It also explains why most of the anguished Quebec MPs did not resign their seats. At the time, though the execution was a serious matter, it did not appear to Pan-Canadians that the compact had been betrayed and that Confederation should be broken up.

However, in Quebec, where the French Canadians had at first shown little sympathy for the rebellion, news of the execution was received with profound shock. Both the political leaders of the 1837 Rebellion had been pardoned, and indeed had returned to their seats in the Legislature. Riel's colleague in the 1870 provisional government, Ambroise Lépine, had had his 1874 death sentence for the execution of Thomas Scott commuted by the governor general to two years' imprisonment and loss of civil rights. And in Riel's case, the jury that had convicted him had recommended mercy.

In Ontario it was widely thought that to commute Riel's sentence would be to respond to undue political pressure from Quebec, and would challenge the belief that all individuals were equal under the law. But in Quebec the execution became a symbol of Ontario's determination to eliminate French influence from the West. It was considered a blow to the concept of Canada as a dualist society. The comments of the anti-French Orangemen in Ontario gave credence to the belief that the main reason for the execution was resentment over the restrictions imposed on Ontario in its western expansion by the federal system. As one newspaper put it, ". . . rather than submit to such a yoke, Ontario would smash Confederation into its original fragments, preferring that the dream of a united Canada should be shattered for ever, than that unity should be purchased at the price of inequality . . . as Britons, we believe that the Conquest will have to be fought over again. Lower Canada may depend on it, there will be no new treaty of 1763. The victors will not capitulate next time."[13]

Far more than any educational crisis, the North West Rebellion came to be viewed as a turning-point in Canadian history. It became a symbol of two deep conflicts: between a traditional native culture and a modern civilization, and between French culture and British civilization. In due course Riel also became a symbol of a third conflict, one between an alienated West and a smug central Canada. In its ultimate consequences, Riel's execution touched a nerve in Quebec. It was the most important factor in the reemergence of a French-Canadian nationalism dormant since 1837: the following year Honoré Mercier and his *Parti National* were swept into office in Quebec. But the Riel Rebellion did not put an end to Pan-Canadian sentiment in Quebec. French Canadians continued to serve in the federal government and Parliament. A succession of Conservative governments continued to govern Canada until 1896. In the federal election of 1887 the Conservatives were still able to win a majority of the Quebec seats in the House of Commons. However, in 1890 another crisis in English-French relations began to develop.

3   The Imposition of Majority Rule in Manitoba, 1890–96, and in Ontario in 1912

In 1890, twenty years after being established as a province, Manitoba passed a Public Schools Act. Like the New Brunswick Act of 1871, this act set up a provincial school system that deprived Roman Catholic schools of the public funds to which they had long been entitled. As in New Brunswick, the Catholic minority was compelled to acquiesce to the will of a Protestant majority that believed in giving public support only to a nondenominational system (Church of England schools also lost support).

However, Manitoba was different from New Brunswick. For one thing it was geographically located at the gateway to Western Canada once the railway was built. Was the West to be treated as an extension of Ontario and to be governed according to the rules laid down by a Protestant majority? Or was it to be considered the joint patrimony of English and French Canada, and therefore a dualist society like Quebec?

The dream of the West as a dualist society may seem today to have been quite unrealistic, but in the mid-nineteenth century it was no more unrealistic than the American southerners' dream of extending the Mason-Dixon line to the Pacific Ocean. For Manitoba was where East and West, English and French, had traditionally met and competed for supremacy. Such settlement as there was in the Manitoba of 1870, a territory beyond the forbidding and uninhabitable Canadian Shield of rock and bog that effectively separated eastern from western Canada, reflected the country's dualist society. There were the descendants of the French adventurers (*or coureurs de bois*) engaged in the fur trade, and of the *voyageurs* whose canoes had transported the precious cargoes across the lakes and down the rivers to Montreal. The *Métis* were the descendants of those French Canadians who had intermarried with the Indians. Over half the population of about 11,000 were French-speaking.[14]

In addition to the French, the *Métis,* and the Indians, there was a growing English-Canadian presence. English explorers from Henry Hudson onward had entered Manitoba from the north. The Hudson's Bay Company, founded by Charles II in 1670, had been given a trading monopoly and practically sovereign rights over the vast region that drained into Hudson Bay, and had taken furs out of the West by this northern route. When Lord Selkirk gained control of the company in the early nineteenth century he brought Irish and Scottish settlers to the Red River settlement, which was to form the heart of Manitoba when it was created as a province. There were also English-speaking "half-breeds" (who eventually adopted the label *Métis*).

Manitoba, then, was a place where Canada's two main cultures met head-on. During the *ancien régime,* the French and English had struggled for control of the fur trade. After the Conquest, Scottish traders in Montreal began to compete for furs in the West with the Hudson's Bay Company. At one time their North West Company was the largest commercial operation in North America.[15] By the 1820s the Hudson's Bay Company had merged with the Nor'westers. The amalgamated company established a true monopoly over the North and West, and enjoyed virtually absolute rule over a territory that now extended from the Atlantic to the Pacific. It was part of this territory (east of the Rocky Mountains) that was transferred to the Dominion of Canada in 1869.

In that small part of the company's former domains that became the province of Manitoba in 1870, there were therefore both English- and French-speaking settlers, both Catholics and Protestants.[16] Many of them were part-Indian. (Although only one of Louis Riel's eight great-grandparents was Indian, he was always called a *Métis* or half-breed.) Nevertheless, the settlements retained their European character. "By

1869 Red River had had a government, courts, churches, and schools for fifty years. It had become a civilized society."[17] It was not allowed to develop in its own way, however. Too many outsiders were interested in the "gateway to the West."

For Ontario, the Red River and the West in general offered scope for British and Protestant settlement. For Quebec, Confederation offered a last chance for the preservation of French and Catholic influence in the West. To the government of Canada, the acquisition of the West meant the construction of a transcontinental railway. Both the British and Dominion governments assumed that the railway meant the extension of the authority and transportation networks of the British Empire around the globe—and the elimination of American influence. When the Hudson's Bay Company transferred its interests in the North West Territories to the government of Canada, the inhabitants of the Red River region, the nucleus of Manitoba, were not consulted.

The legatee of the Hudson's Bay Company, the government of Canada, was a government in which English Canadians composed the majority, and in which Quebecois played an important role. (The Canadian Pacific Railway had its headquarters in Montreal, not Toronto.)[18] The Manitobans were able to convince the Dominion government that it was to be treated more like Quebec than Ontario. As a result of Louis Riel's provisional government, of the encouragement and advice given to that government by members of the Catholic clergy at Red River, including Bishop Taché (nephew of the former First Minister Sir Etienne-Pascal Taché), and of the support offered by Cartier, Manitoba was established in 1870 as a dualist province in which the French language was officially recognized and denominational schools supported from public funds. However, the original province was very small in both area and population (one-twentieth the size of present-day Manitoba) and encompassed little more than the settlements near the Red River where Winnipeg is now located.

In retrospect, the act setting up Manitoba seems an extraordinary document for a post-Confederation Canada in which Protestant English-speaking Ontarians confidently looked forward to colonizing (and exploiting) the new West. Ontario's dynamic capital, Toronto, shared with Liverpool, Glasgow, and Belfast the dubious distinction of being a center for the Orange Order, an organization which attracted the most anti-Catholic members of the various Protestant denominations. Yet, not only did the Manitoba Act recognize the French language and Catholic schools, it also transformed a small but strategically located territory around present-day Winnipeg into a full-fledged province, with its own lieutenant-governor, cabinet, and legislature quite independent of Ontario.

The Manitoba Act proved to be the high-water mark of the compact theory. In many ways its successful passage would seem to have been a fluke. Because of Macdonald's indisposition, it was Cartier who introduced the bill: within eight days it received the Royal Assent.

For a constitutional document proposing that the province officially recognize the French language and support Catholic education, the speed of its passage was remarkable. The bill might not have passed into law so easily had not Cartier been acting prime minister; had the Dominion government not been engaged in delicate negotiations with the Hudson's Bay Company and the British government over the transfer of territory; had there not been concern about American intentions in the Northwest; had there not been a Catholic French-speaking majority in the tiny new province; and had that majority been led by someone less gifted than Louis Riel. Probably the crucial factor was Riel's resistance, which forced the Canadian government to call upon the imperial power for a military expedition (for the last time). According to G. F. S. Stanley, the British refused to accede to the request for an expeditionary force until the Canadian government promised reasonable terms for the inhabitants.[19] If so, then it was the imperial rather than the Dominion government that made the dualist Manitoba Act possible.

In retrospect, Riel and his associates might have been wiser to recognize the limitations imposed on their ambitions by demography. Instead of insisting on provincial status (and a legislature with an upper as well as a lower house!) for their tiny community of a few thousand souls, they could perhaps have settled for an autonomous region within the larger province that was obviously one day going to be carved out of the West, a province in which the *Métis* and Franco-Manitobans would almost certainly be a small minority. However, Riel was not a *Canadien*. He was not fighting on behalf of Quebec's ambitions to have a stake in the West and to preserve Canada's French-English dualism. His concern was his own people and the preservation of an indigenous Western society different from anything in the rest of Canada. He was convinced that in Manitoba he could form a "new nation" that under God (and Riel) would incorporate all its diverse elements. This new nation could avoid the bitterness that had marked relations between the races in central Canada. But although the Manitoba Act survived, Louis Riel's provincial government did not. After its disbandment, Riel was forced into exile for many years.

Because the right to a Catholic education had been acknowledged in Ontario as well as in Quebec, Catholics elsewhere had some reason to hope that purely secular systems would not be established in other provinces. For it was not as though the practice of financing Catholic education had been different elsewhere. For example, in New Brunswick, the government from 1858 on had allowed local school boards to raise taxes for the support of denominational schools.[20] Nor had the Manitoba Act of 1870 broken new ground; it had merely confirmed existing practice. In other words, there had been widespread acceptance of publicly-supported Catholic schools throughout British North America.

Moreover, partly because of the importance of Quebec in pre-Confederation Canada, Catholics in British North America, Irish as well as French, had believed that they enjoyed an acceptance in society and public life greater than that of Catholics in either Britain or the United States. One reason for Archbishop Connolly's willingness to rally Irish Catholics to the cause of Confederation had been the greater social and political tolerance that he believed was accorded to them in British North America. By contrast, in the United States they had "No share in the executive, no seat in the Senate, and but very few members in the House of Representatives." Not even in Catholic Maryland had Catholics full equality in society. Yet in all the Canadian provinces, Connolly continued, there had been "no period since the days of emancipation at which Catholics have not possessed that influence to which their number and position fairly entitled them."[21]

Not surprisingly, this very acceptance of Catholics, together with the willingness to finance their schools out of public funds, increased the resentment over the introduction of a Protestant-style secular system of education, a system to which Catholics had to pay taxes at the same time as their own schools were declared ineligible for public support in the future.

Matters were complicated in Canada by the frequent conjuncture of language and religion. Archbishop Connolly was spokesman mainly for the English-speaking Irish Catholic minorities. Cartier and the other Pan-Canadians spoke for the French-speaking Catholics in the Province of Quebec. The French-speaking Catholic minorities elsewhere were in yet another category. Restrictions on Catholic schools were often interpreted by the French-Canadian minority not only as anti-Catholic but as anti-French.[22] Consequently, the establishment of a public school system in New Brunswick in 1871 had been interpreted in Quebec as another means of assimilating the *Acadiens* in the Maritimes.[23]

The furor in New Brunswick was much less than the Catholic and French resentment over the attitude of many Ontario immigrants into the West after 1870. The settlers from Ontario believed that the new provinces were destined to represent Protestant British civilization, not to reflect Canadian dualism. They saw no reason to provide public support either for Catholic schools or for French as a language of instruction, whether for the new French Canadians or for the *Métis*. With the arrival of immigrants from Eastern Europe, often neither Protestant nor Catholic, the English Canadians came to regard an integrated public school system as essential to help them fulfill their goal of creating a British nation out of the disparate elements that were settling in the prairies.[24] The West was very different from Eastern Canada. In the Manitoba of 1870 the most well-established elite had been the Catholic Church led by Bishop Taché,[25] while many of the English-speaking leaders were relative newcomers. Later, in the 1880s, when Protestant Manitobans began to think of establishing a new education system, religious antagonism was heightened by the fact that two opposed international movements were reaching their zenith: the growth in Canada of British (and Protestant) imperialism and the determination of the ultramontanes to win Canada for the Catholic Church.

But if publicly supported Catholic schools were constitutionally guaranteed in Manitoba in 1870, how did the government manage to deprive them of their public status in 1890? Simply put, the government seized on the fact that at the Union Manitoba did not have a provincial school system like the Canada before 1867. Consequently, such schools as existed were not protected by law. (Indeed there was no provincial government before 1870 to pass such a law.) The Manitoba Act had attempted to remedy this by ending Section 2, paragraph 1 with the words "by Law *or practice* in the province at the Union" (my italics).

The inclusion of the phrase "or practice" had reassured French Canadians, and Catholics generally, that their schools had adequate constitutional protection comparable to that provided by the BNA Act for the Catholic schools in central Canada. (The Manitoba Act was made a constitutional act through an amendment by the British Parliament to the BNA Act known as the BNA Act, 1871.) Catholic schools received their proportionate share of the money contributed for school purposes out of the general taxation of the province. The money raised for this assessment from Catholics was applied to the support of Catholic schools.

Since there was to be so much controversy in the 1890s over Section 93 of the BNA Act and Section 22 of the Manitoba Act, it is worth stating their provisions in full:

BNA Act, 1867	Manitoba Act, 1870
93. In and for each Province the Legislature may exclusively make Laws in relation to Education, subject and according to the following Provisions:	22. In and for the Province, the said Legislature may exclusively make Laws in relation to Education, subject and according to the following provisions:
1. Nothing in any such Law shall prejudicially affect any Right or Privilege with respect to Denominational Schools any Class of Persons have by Law in the Province at the Union:	1. Nothing in any such Law shall prejudically affect any Right or Privilege with respect to Denominational Schools which any class of persons have by law *or practice* in the Province at the Union:
2. All the Powers, Privileges and Duties at the Union by Law conferred and imposed in Upper Canada on the Separate Schools and School Trustees of the Queen's Roman Catholic Subjects shall be and the same are hereby extended to the Dissentient Schools of the Queen's Protestant and Roman Catholic Subjects in Quebec:	
3. Where in any Province a System of Separate or Dissentient Schools exists by Law at the Union or is thereafter established by the Legislature of the Province an Appeal shall	2. An appeal shall lie to the Governor General in Council from any Act or decision of the Legislature of the Province, or of any Provincial Authority affecting any right or privilege

French Canada and the Triumph of Majority Rule

lie to the Governor General in Council from any Act or Decision of any Provincial Authority affecting any Right or Privilege of the Protestant or Roman Catholic Minority of the Queen's subjects in relation to Education.

4. In case any such Provincial Law as from Time to Time seems to the Governor General in Council requisite for the due Execution of the Provisions of this Section is not made, or in case any Decision of the Governor General in Council on any Appeal under this section is not duly executed by the proper Provincial Authority in that Behalf, then and in every such Case, and so far only as the Circumstances of each Case require, the Parliament of Canada may make remedial Laws for the due Execution of the Provisions of this Section and of any Decision of the Governor General in Council under this Section.

of the Protestant or Roman Catholic minority of the Queen's subjects in relation to Education:

3. In case any such Provincial Law, as from Time to Time seems to the Governor General in Council requisite for the due Execution of the Provisions of this Section, is not made, or in case any Decision of the Governor General in Council on any Appeal under this section is not duly executed by the proper Provincial Authority in that Behalf, then and in every such Case, and so far only as the Circumstances of each case require, the Parliament of Canada may make remedial Laws for the due Execution of the Provisions of this Section and of any Decision of the Governor General in Council under this Section.

When the crisis erupted over the schools in Manitoba in 1890 there were two possible interpretations of Section 22. The broad, generous interpretation was that, since the province of Manitoba had in practice provided funds for Catholic schools over the years, it was contrary to Section 22 to deprive them of provincial support. To set up a system of state schools to which all taxpayers had to contribute and to make it necessary for Catholic parents henceforth to pay for their children's Catholic education in addition, could be regarded as *ultra vires*. The narrow interpretation involved ignoring the phrase "in practice" and concentrating on the phrase "at the Union." It could be argued that "at the Union" (Section 22.1) there were only voluntary denominational schools, and that these were not supported by taxation. The establishment of state schools did not, therefore, deprive Catholics of their own voluntary schools, such as they had at the Union.

This narrow interpretation, seized on initially by the courts (in the *Barrett* case), seemed to Catholics and ultimately to the Privy Council preposterous, because all religious denominations, whether in the United Kingdom or in Canada, had the privilege of establishing their own voluntary schools, and there was hardly need of constitutional protection for such an arrangement.

The provisions of Section 22 seemed clear enough to the Catholics in Manitoba (even if they became a minority). If their educational rights or privileges were infringed they could appeal to the Governor General in Council under paragraph 2. The Governor General in Council could disallow the legislation or request Parliament to pass remedial legislation (paragraph 3).

But Section 22 of the Manitoba Act lacked the political clout behind Section 93 of the BNA Act. Section 93 was based on an agreement between Ontario and Quebec over their respective minorities. It also confirmed the permanence of laws already passed by the province of Canada governing denominational schools, e.g., the Separate Schools Act, 1863. These were the laws that had so irritated Ontario's Protestants when the Catholics had used their legislative majority to impose publicly-supported Catholic schools on Upper Canada, where Catholics were a minority.

As in the Canada of 1863, so in the Manitoba of 1870, the Catholics had proved capable of overcoming Protestant objections to their schools by putting together a legislative majority to pass into law an Act protecting publicly-supported denominational schools. But there was no *quid pro quo* behind Section 22, and there was as yet no province-wide system of education.

Consequently, once the Catholics had lost their status as a majority, they became politically vulnerable to a government determined to have its way. The Manitoba legislature cleverly avoided repeal of Section 22. Instead it assumed that in accordance with the principle of parliamentary supremacy and majority rule it had the right to set up a province-wide system, and that, as in the United States, this could be secular. The Schools Act deliberately did not make school attendance compulsory.

It was left to the Manitoba Catholics to go to court and prove that Canada was different from the United States, and that Section 22 had been violated. If successful, they would then have to find means of political redress. The government of Quebec was not likely to support federal intervention in education, and French-Canadian politicians in Ottawa shared Quebec's concerns about the implementations of federal interference in a sensitive provincial sphere. It seemed wisest to regard the matter as one for Catholics rather than French Canadians, and for the Church rather than government.

In establishing a school system, the province did not adopt either of the main Canadian models. For Catholics, of course, the preferred solution would have been a system controlled by the churches, whether Catholic or Protestant. Under such a *Catholic–Protestant system* there would be Roman Catholic and Protestant province-wide school boards. Both would be publicly funded and the Catholic and Protestant superintendents of education would be responsible, under the boards, for all instruction, including religious education, in their respective school districts. This was the system in Quebec, and was the principle underlying traditional practice in Manitoba. It meant an educational structure controlled by religious denominations, and it was not favored by most Protestants.

The second system may be called *Public–Separate* (or *Secular–Catholic*). This was the system adopted before Confederation in Ontario. In addition to the main, secular, school system there was a Catholic system under its own school boards. Each received public funds, with the property taxes of Catholic householders going to the support of "separate," i.e., Catholic, schools instead of the public schools. But this system, imposed on Ontario by Lower Canada in the days of the Union, appears to have found little favor elsewhere. (Had it been adopted in Manitoba, however, there might not have been a crisis over the schools.)[26]

The actual system adopted was one we may call *Secular–Private*. It has often been compared to the American system of secular education supplemented by *private* "parochial" schools. Certainly in organization it was secular. Instead of two religious school boards a single provincial department of education controlled all the publicly-supported schools. Its introduction in Manitoba meant the replacement of publicly supported denominational schools by secular public schools. Henceforth the schools of the various churches could continue, but as voluntary and private schools. As a matter of "equity," all taxpayers were expected to support the public system. They could, if they wished, continue to send their children to denominational schools, but only at their own expense. This secular system owed something to the liberal sentiment in favor of the emancipation of the schools from Church control and much to the divisions between the various non-Catholic denominations: a single Protestant school board was not very practical.[27]

However, public education in Canada was not as secular as in the United States, because in Canada there was no constitutional separation of church and state. At the same time, there was no Canadian Established Church as in Britain. Exactly what Canada's position was with regard to church and state is not easy to say.[28] Certainly the educational system was not unreligious. As in England, it was secular only in the sense of being "nondenominational." The Bible was taught, and religious instruction was given in school time at the end of the day. But because religious knowledge was based on the Protestant Bible, Catholics complained that they were being asked to pay taxes to support what to all intents and purposes were not secular but Protestant schools.[29] In other words, Catholic schools were denied public funds, but Protestant schools disguised as "secular" or "national" schools (in the Catholic view) were to continue to receive government largesse.

The Public Schools Act appeared both unfair and unconstitutional. For if the Manitoba Act were a constitutional act, then presumably it was superior to any ordinary law. One possible loophole for the province was the Westminster tradition in accordance with which there was no law or convention preventing provinces from amending their own constitutions. However, in the case of Manitoba this was not so: the amendment power had been restricted to elections.[30]

In Manitoba, therefore, provincial majority rule should not have prevailed, since there was a body superior to the Manitoba Legislature, namely, the Parliament of Canada, which could decree otherwise. But just as the British Parliament tried to avoid interfering in Canadian affairs, so the Parliament of Canada was reluctant to interfere in provincial matters. This was especially true of education. In 1890, moreover, Manitoba was not repealing any part of the Act. Instead it was creating a public nonsectarian system to replace one operated by the churches under a board of education of which half had been Protestant and half Roman Catholic.[31]

It is doubtful whether the Manitoba Catholics, still less the *Métis* or

French Canada and the Triumph of Majority Rule 273

Franco-Manitobans, appreciated these fine constitutional distinctions. Moreover, much of the pressure to secure the rights of the Catholic minority came from the Quebec hierarchy, whose schools did enjoy constitutional protection. The government of Quebec and federal leaders like Laurier were wary of attacking the convention of majority rule lest it be used against the Catholic majority in Quebec. Perhaps Tocqueville had put the position most succinctly. Examining the conventions of the British Constitution from a legalistic continental perspective, he had observed of that Constitution, "il n'existe point."

Since the Westminster tradition depended on agreed parliamentary conventions, Pan-Canadian dualists in Ottawa had little option but to cooperate with their English-Canadian colleagues by accepting the conventions of legislative supremacy and majority rule. They may have hoped that Carnarvon was right in implying imperial support for all minorities in the event of injustice being done: there was in London, after all, an umpire *ab extra*. It was the imperial Parliament alone that could amend Section 93 of the BNA Act, and it was the Judicial Committee of the Privy Council that would pass judgment on any appeals against unfair treatment. The matter was to reach the Judicial Committee, but it was never brought to the attention of the imperial Parliament.

When the controversy erupted in 1890, the legislature of Manitoba actually passed two laws. One replaced the province's dual system of education under Protestant and Catholic school boards by a nondenominational system under a single board. The other abolished the official use of the French language in the legislative assembly, the civil service, and the courts. In other words, while the conflict was fought over Catholic schools, language was also at issue. In their assault on Manitoba's concept of a dualist society, Protestant extremists were successful in turning public opinion against its Quebec-style educational system. There were a number of reasons for the success of the campaign for a public school system, not least of which was "a deep-set conviction among the British settlers of all kinds, that Manitoba must be made British and that a 'nationalist' school system should be the agent to accomplish this task."[32] In other words, the "nation" into which future generations of Manitobans were to be born or assimilated was not the original Manitoba, the "new nation" envisaged by Riel, or the dualist society of Cartier or Taché, but a province that was to be an outpost of British civilization.

Although language was an issue, the battle was fought on the question of secular education. It was here that the Church could provide leadership on behalf of all those Manitobans who were Roman Catholic. (Cartier and Riel were both dead, but the Church was still under the leadership of Taché, now an Archbishop.) The controversy is interesting because of the way it highlighted the Church's difficulty in dealing with a situation in which a majority had become a minority, but still thought that it retained constitutional rights.

The situation was complex. It opened up the whole question of Section 93 and just what that section was supposed to accomplish. As we have seen, in 1867 practical politicians accepted its limitations as far as Catholics and French Canadians outside Ontario and Quebec were concerned. But in the 1890s the Church was prepared to argue that in principle the section was intended to offer protection to other Catholic minorities. And if Section 93 proved to have its limitations, there was also Section 22 of the Manitoba Act of 1870, with its broader protection of minority rights. To the Church, and especially to its French-speaking hierarchy, if the constitutional provisions of 1867 and 1870 meant anything at all, they meant that religious minorities were not to be at the mercy of provincial legislative majorities. To federal politicians, on the other hand, education was an issue they preferred to leave to the courts and to the provinces. Consequently, once the Manitoba legislature passed the Public Schools Act it was incumbent upon the Catholic and/or French-speaking minority to persuade some external authority to declare the school legislation *ultra vires*.[33]

There were three appeals available to an aggrieved party: (1) to the governor general in Council (i.e., the Cabinet), to disallow Manitoba's legislation; (2) to the courts, to have the legislation declared *ultra vires;* and (3) to the governor general in Council, to intervene on behalf of the minority through remedial legislation.

All three avenues were used. The first failed because the Dominion government, having already tried to discipline Manitoba by disallowing its legislation in other fields, decided that disallowance was inappropriate.[34] Its position was supported by an all-party agreement in the House of Commons that "before provincial legislation affecting education should be disallowed, it should first be submitted to a high judicial tribunal for thorough study and argument."[35] The Dominion government therefore agreed to pay the costs of an appeal against the legislation by reference to the Manitoba Act, Section 22.1, by a Catholic parent, Dr. John Kelly Barrett. Barrett challenged the requirement that as a Catholic he had to pay local taxes toward the new state system (*Barrett v. City of Winnipeg*).³⁶

This second avenue, an appeal to the courts, took several years and was at first unsuccessful. Dr. Barrett's case was dismissed by the Manitoba courts and, though upheld by the Supreme Court of Canada, was ultimately rejected by the Privy Council in 1892. The Judicial Committee, like the Manitoba courts, adopted the unconscionably narrow interpretation referred to earlier. It argued that since there were no publicly-supported Catholic schools *at the Union,* it was not contrary to the Manitoba Act, Section 22.1, for Manitoba to establish state schools that alone would be publicly supported. Such a law did not "prejudicially affect any right or privilege with respect to denominational schools which any class of persons have by law or practice in the province at the Union."

The Dominion government then arranged for another appeal, this time drawing attention to other paragraphs of Section 22. It also took care that it was paid for privately (the new Conservative prime minister being a Catholic himself).³⁷ The case of *Brophy v. The Attorney General of Manitoba* raised wider issues, and the Manitoba Act was given a broader interpretation by the Judicial Committee in a second decision in 1894. The Privy Council ruled that its previous judgment in *Barrett v. Winnipeg* did not dispose of the application for redress; that in regard to the Manitoba Act, Section 22, paragraph 2, the rights and privileges of the Catholic minority were adversely affected by the 1890 legislation; and that under paragraph 3 the Dominion government was empowered to introduce remedial legislation.

Despite this ruling by the Judicial Committee, Manitoba refused to implement it. Only the third avenue was left to the Catholics: remedial legislation by the Dominion Parliament. This was proposed by a reluctant Conservative government at the instigation of the Catholic Church. It was opposed by Wilfrid Laurier and the Liberal Opposition, and not only on the grounds that it would set a precedent for federal intervention in Quebec. Much wrangling took place in Parliament, and before any agreement could be reached on the draft legislation, which favored the Ontario system of a separate school board and the use of Catholic taxes for Catholic schools, Parliament's five-year mandate was completed and an election had to be called.

The 1896 election was won by the Liberals led by Wilfrid Laurier.

The new prime minister proved able to reach a *modus vivendi* with the government of Manitoba whereby the provincial government amended the Schools Act to permit instruction in the Catholic faith (and even in the French language) within the public school system. The English-speaking bishops acquiesced in the compromise: the French bishops, led by the indomitable Taché, refused to yield on a point of principle. Their concern about language seems to have been justified: in 1916 the government eliminated teaching in French.

The Manitoba school crisis had serious implications for French Canada. The government of Manitoba had proved that it could in effect override the provincial Constitution by an ordinary act of the Legislature. The federal government had shown that while it had the power to disallow the legislation or to pass remedial legislation, it was unwilling or unable to do either. The Judicial Committee had indicated that it was capable of the narrowest interpretations when faced with a breach of the Constitution: even after a second appeal it had merely concluded that the Dominion government had the power to introduce remedial legislation. It did not declare the Manitoba government's action to be *ultra vires*.

All these events of 1890–97 confirmed that the Canadian Constitution was modeled on the British: that it operated on the principle of majority rule, not constitutional supremacy. The French were successful in 1870 when they possessed a majority; after they lost their majority the provisions of the Constitution they had fought for were overridden. The Protestant English-Canadian majority in Parliament proved unenthusiastic about coming to the rescue of a small French-speaking Roman Catholic minority deprived of its constitutional rights. Nor were the French Canadians in Quebec willing to endanger their majority position by recommending Federal intervention. And so, in Manitoba, in Ottawa, in Quebec, and in London, the principle of majority rule proved paramount to the Constitution and minority rights. (The one exception was the acceptance by the Supreme Court of Canada of Dr. Barrett's appeal.) The crisis is also significant because of the fundamental constitutional issues it brought to light.

In 1912 yet another education crisis occurred. This one took place in Ontario and involved the third significant French-Canadian minority outside Quebec. In Ontario, of course, publicly supported Catholic schools had long been recognized by law. (One reason for Cartier's willingness to accept Ottawa as capital was that a quarter of its population was Catholic.) The crisis in Ontario involved not religion but the language of education in the increasing number of schools where instruction was being given for the most part in French. In the 1880s, 5 percent of Ontario's population was French-speaking, and the Ontario government of Oliver Mowat "maintained generous concessions to French schools."[39] The educational standards of the French schools in eastern Ontario were often below those of the public English-speaking schools, but the Ontario authorities turned a blind eye to instruction in French by Quebec nuns and priests whose knowledge of English was often below par.[40]

By 1909 the proportion of francophones in the province had doubled to 10 percent, with large concentrations in the eastern section. In 1910 the Franco-Ontarians held a congress in Ottawa to establish *L'Association Canadienne-Française d'Education d'Ontario* (ACFEO) to promote the cause of French. The association demanded the recognition of bilingual schools as French, and even asserted that French was an official language in Ontario. An article published in Quebec described the struggle for survival of the French-speaking community: ". . . we have at present a preponderant voice in some fifteen counties of Ontario, . . . in a century, this province . . . will itself be gallicized by the logic of events."[41]

In response, the government of Ontario decided that a knowledge of English was essential for the children of Franco-Ontarians. In 1912 Regulation 17 was issued, making English the sole langauge of instruction after the third year of public school, and limiting the study of French to one hour a day. French Canadians were outraged and denounced Regulation 17 as a deliberate attempt to assimilate them. It was not until after the First World War, when immigration from Quebec had diminished, that a more conciliatory approach was attempted by the government of Ontario. By then the conflict had died down.

The significance of Ontario's crisis over education was that it appeared to confirm the bias of the BNA Act in favor of the English language. The Act recognized Catholic, but not French, schools in Ontario. While the government of Ontario was prepared in practice to turn a blind eye to publicly-supported Catholic schools that taught their pupils in French, it was not prepared to accept the principle that Canada was a dual society. Nor was it willing to change the law and to recognize bilingualism. It was true, of course, that in Quebec the Protestant schools were also English-language schools, but the analogy was unacceptable to English Canada. English was, after all, the language of the majority of Canadians, as well as being the language of commerce in Quebec itself. English Quebecers, moreover, were relatively affluent, while Franco-Ontarians were relatively poor.

The migration of large numbers of *Canadiens* into Ontario raised the possibility that eastern Ontario would become gallicized like the Eastern Townships of Quebec. Protestant Ontario was aghast. Even greater concern was expressed by the province's English-speaking Roman Catholics (especially the Irish), who saw their English-language institutions (including the University of Ottawa) become French-speaking. The Catholic Bishop of London, Ontario, formerly vice-Rector of the University of Ottawa, created a furor by publicly criticizing the educational standards of the French schools. The Catholic Archbishop of Westminster, visiting Canada for the Eucharistic Congress in Montreal, added to the controversy by suggesting that Catholics should speak English. And so to the English-speaking Protestant fear of Quebec's revenge of the cradle was added the hostility of English-speaking Catholics to the use of French in the schools. The issue was clearly one of language rather than religion.

The Ontario crisis was the more significant because Ontario's fear of becoming bilingual like Quebec coincided with a movement in Quebec in favor of the recognition of Canada as a bilingual society. The 1896 federal election had seen the most important realignment of parties in Canadian history. The Liberals then replaced the Conservatives as Canada's "governing party." It caused the Conservatives, who until 1896 had been able to rely on the ability of the Church to encourage the Quebecois to vote for the *Bleus,* to become in due course an English-Canadian party. English Canadians continued to divide their allegiance between the Liberals and Conservatives. By contrast, French Canadians rejected the call of the Church to support its Canadian-wide spiritual mission and threw their weight behind the Liberals. The French Canadians might be a minority, but they were able to be part of the governing party, whether Conservative (for most of the time between 1854 and 1896) or Liberal (for most of the time after 1896).

The French Canadians were not so monolithic as the seats won by the Liberals might suggest. Many remained devout Catholics and sympathetic toward the *Bleus*. Others were nationalists opposed to the Pan-Canadianism of the Liberal Party. In particular, many of the French were opposed to Canadian support for Britain's imperial adventures.

Cartier, knighted by the Queen, had been able to be both a Pan-Canadian and a loyal subject of the Queen without self-consciousness. Laurier, also knighted, was more diffident in his support of the United Kingdom and the British Empire, notably during the Boer War. Indeed, his former associate, Henri Bourassa, broke with him on the issue of imperialism. No longer could a Pan-Canadian take the imperial connection for granted. Bourassa and his *Ligue Nationaliste* insisted that all who lived in Canada should call themselves Canadians, not British subjects, that they should abandon their colonial ties with Britain, and that they should recognize Canada for what it was—a country of two languages and two cultures. "The chief article in the Nationalist creed was that Canada was everywhere a bilingual country, French being on an equality with English in all the provinces."[42]

The resentment toward the French language that developed in Ontario in the early 1900s must be viewed in the context of the new nationalist movement in Quebec led by Bourassa, for it challenged the whole basis of Confederation as this was understood in English Canada. It was Bourassa's argument that dualism involved more than the Pan-Canadian acceptance of two cultures in Canada: it required recognition that the two were equal. This meant that just as Protestants in Quebec could retain their English language, so Quebec Catholics who migrated to Ontario could continue to speak French.

The Pan-Canadians, as we noted earlier in the chapter, had accepted the position of French Canadians as a minority in Confederation. Nothing in the BNA Act stated that the two languages were equal, except in the federal Parliament and courts, and in the Legislature of Quebec. Now Bourassa was proposing that Canadians generally should accept French as the equal of English. English Canadians and the Ontario government refused to do this. Historically, the status of English in Quebec was superior to French, while elsewhere in the country French had very little standing at all.

In refusing to give French official recognition as a language of instruction, Ontario was conforming to the letter of the BNA Act. However, if there was no constitutional basis for French in Ontario, then there was none for English in Quebec beyond the narrow provisions of Section 133. Anglophones did not see that the provisions making Quebec bilingual might in the future be ignored by the government of Quebec. If Bourassa's compact theory of Canada as a bilingual and bicultural society were rejected, then one day Quebec nationalists could reasonably apply the same arguments for majority rule in the one province where they formed a majority. If it chose, Quebec, too, could adopt a policy of unilingualism.

These various crises of Confederation were later given different interpretations by English and French Canadians. The English tended to look back on them as regrettable incidents that should not be allowed to occur again: they were unfortunate episodes in Canada's evolution as a "peaceable kingdom" and were best forgotten.[43] The French remembered each incident vividly. They became part of the folk-memory and a cause of permanent resentment. A common Quebec view was that the crises revealed an unwillingness to abide by the terms of Confederation. "Je me souviens" expressed a determination to recall not only the original Conquest but the various conquests that followed Confederation.

Essentially, the crises involved conflicts over a relationship that had not been satisfactorily defined at Confederation, and perhaps could not be defined until a "French Canada" involving *Acadiens, Métis,* and Franco-Ontarians, as well as *Canadiens,* emerged.[44] When it did, the principle on which provincial governments other than Quebec operated was that of majority rule, not dualism. The Westerners' need for Canada to assimilate large numbers of immigrants from continental Europe encouraged them in their determination to make Canada an English-speaking country. However, the French Canadians regarded themselves as a minority unlike all the others, and as a distinct culture entitled to resist assimilation wherever francophone communities of any size existed. English Canadians did not accept this principle of linguistic dualism, and they interpreted Section 93 as protecting only Catholic schools. French Canadians found it hard to believe that the BNA Act protected their faith but not their language.

Matters were not made any easier by the extremists on either side. There were English Canadians, some of them British immigrants, who saw Canada as an outpost of the British Empire. These "British imperialists" resisted any concessions to the French language beyond what had been reluctantly granted in Section 133. At the other extreme, there were zealous francophone missionaries, some of them royalists from France, who dreamed of the restoration of Canada as both Catholic and Gallic, whatever the BNA Act might say. In the end, more moderate Canadian voices prevailed and the severity of the law was tempered in practice by political accommodation.

But the Pan-Canadian equality that many French Canadians had come to believe was the hallmark of Canadian dualism proved as elusive as ever. Francophones had not migrated to the West in sufficient numbers to preserve the majority they had in Manitoba in 1870. By the First World War, all the provinces except Quebec were officially unilingual and predominantly Protestant in tone, despite all the efforts of Pan-Canadians to extend both Catholicism and the French language throughout Canada.

4 Canada's Support for the Empire in Three Wars

We have defined a Pan-Canadian as a French Canadian who participated in federal politics and who was willing to accept majority rule. This meant a minority role both for Quebec within Confederation and for French-Canadian minorities in the other provinces. By contrast, nationalists like Bourassa stressed the equality of the two cultures, and resisted Ottawa whenever possible. The Pan-Canadians justified their role as one of resistance to any policy that would have adverse implications for majority rule by francophones inside Quebec. Thus Cartier refused to act at the time of the New Brunswick Common Schools Act, and Laurier opposed the use of the federal government's powers of disallowance and remedial legislation in Manitoba, lest one day the federal government impose its will on Quebec.

Over the years, the character of both Pan-Canadianism and nationalism changed. By the 1960s, Pan-Canadian politicians in Ottawa were less willing to accept a minority position for francophones. Instead they adopted the view of Bourassa's nationalists: that of Canada as a bilingual society of equal cultures. Nationalism also changed, its proponents moving away from Bourassa's emphasis on a Canadian nationalism to one that stressed the role and aspirations of the Quebecois.

A crucial question was: What were the responsibilities of French Canadians to their country if it became involved in hostilities? Were Canada to be directly attacked, as it had been in 1812, there seemed little question: the whole country would resist. However, after 1812 there never was a direct attack on Canadian soil. (The opposition to the Militia Bill in 1862 had not been over the defense of Canada, but over a Canadian plan to defend western Ontario against possible American invasion after the British authorities had declared the peninsula indefensible against the Union forces of the United States.)

Even so, Canada was frequently urged to go to war, as part of the

Empire. Although in the South African War, French Canadians were sympathetic to the Boers (as were many people in England), in the two world wars French-Canadian sympathies were on the side of Britain and France against Germany. There was little opposition to the Dominion government's willingness to send troops abroad—provided they volunteered.

What distinguished the French from the English Canadians was their attitude toward conscription. In the First World War the French Canadians opposed conscription *per se*. In the Second, they opposed conscription for service overseas, because they regarded it as being for the defense of Britain and its Empire, not of Canada itself.

In both world wars, and especially in the first when Canada was still officially a colony, there arose what can be called crises of Empire. These crises involved controversies over the concept of national loyalty. As we have seen, in the nineteenth century Pan-Canadians had little difficulty accepting the double role of Canadian citizen and British subject. That quintessential Pan-Canadian, Sir George-Etienne Cartier, once remarked that "an inhabitant of Lower Canada was an Englishman who spoke French."[45] In effect, this meant the acceptance of a double political nationality, British as well as Canadian, in addition to the "cultural nationality" of being a French Canadian. (In law, of course, all Canadians were treated simply as British subjects and carried British passports.)

In Cartier's day, Canada's Britishness was taken for granted because the Empire provided security against the threat of invasion from the United States. However, the last British troops left Canada in 1871 and in due course the armed forces came under Canadian control. The South African War and subsequent conflicts involved a new relationship between Canada and the Empire. Instead of Britain coming to the defense of Canada, Canada was now asked to go to the aid of the mother country. Those English Canadians whom we have called imperialists were only too eager for Canada to offer its services, but not all English Canadians were willing to fight for what some considered imperial adventures. Even fewer French Canadians felt an obligation in 1914–18 to go to the aid of the country that had conquered them from France, or to support an English Canada that treated them as inferiors. (They felt little obligation to France itself, the country that had deserted them.)

The opposition to "fighting Britain's wars" was articulated by Henri Bourassa, who distinguished between loyalty to Canada and loyalty to the Empire. By contrast, a Pan-Canadian like Laurier was unable to withhold all support for the Empire during the Boer War, or to reject out of hand a Canadian contribution to naval rearmament. Indeed, it was Laurier who, in 1914, as leader of the Opposition, declared that Canada was "Ready, aye, ready."[46]

However, the conscription crisis of 1917 compelled the aging Laurier to guard his Quebec flank by taking sides with Bourassa. The nationalist challenge had the long-run effect of transforming the Liberal Party from one of pro-British Gladstonian liberalism into a North American party willing to promote Canadian autonomy. In the process, the Liberals left the Conservatives with the more difficult task—that of preserving the British connection—once the euphoria of the early days of the First World War was over. In seeking autonomy, the Liberals were sustained by geography: in dealing with Britain, the Conservatives were hampered by history.

From the First World War on, it was difficult for a Pan-Canadian francophone to be a Conservative. An Anglophile like Cartier might take pride in being both Canadian and British; a churchman like Archbishop Taché of Manitoba might avow "my allegiance is, therefore, to the Crown of England"; a Liberal leader like Ernest Lapointe might, as late as 1939, declare his loyalty to the King.[47] But by and large, Conservatism came to mean preservation of the British connection and hostility to French-Canadian dualism and the goal of French autonomy.

The Liberal Party, by contrast, was associated for a long while with continentalism, and was thought to be more interested in the North American economy than in the British political connection. The party also appeared more sensitive to French Canada's concerns. Even so, the Liberals were a heterogeneous party and combined two very different elements. One consisted of English-speaking Canadians, particularly those who did not readily identify with the Empire or the "establishment." It comprised United Church members and Catholics rather than Anglicans, and recent immigrants as well as long-established families. The party attracted those whose business interests inclined them more to the United States than to the United Kingdom. In other words, there were many English Canadians whose primary concern was not the British connection and who looked forward to greater autonomy for Canada within the Commonwealth.

The other element of the Liberal Party consisted of French Canadians. These formed a more homogenous group in terms of religious upbringing and ethnic origin. The French Canadians were attracted to the Liberal Party because of its awareness of Quebec's needs as a distinctive culture and its reservations about imperial ties. Just as an older generation had found Macdonald's Conservative Party broadly based, so a new generation of francophones found the Liberals of Laurier and his successors the more congenial of the two parties, one in which it appeared possible to satisfy their aspirations as Canadians and as French Canadians.

There were, however, strains between English- and French-Canadian Liberals, as there had been between Conservatives from Ontario and Quebec. In time of crisis, especially in wartime, English Canadians tended to become increasingly aware of their British connections, and certainly of the need for all Canadians to pull together to defeat the common enemy. The French-Canadian element found this much more difficult.

There were three crises of Empire, and each strained the capacity of the Liberal Party to hold its English- and French-speaking members together. The first crisis, the South African Boer War, caused the defection of Henri Bourassa and ultimately led to the downfall of the Laurier government in 1911. The second threat to Liberal unity was the conscription crisis of the First World War, and the third was the conscription crisis of 1942–44.

The most serious of the crises was the second, in 1917, when the party was split in two, with most English-speaking Liberals joining with the Conservatives to form Canada's only coalition government to date. French-Canadian Liberals supported Laurier in opposing conscription. Their opposition had some justification, in view of the poor handling of conscription in Quebec and the strong feeling against it that led to riots in Quebec City.

The Liberal Party may have been saved from permanent destruction after the 1917–18 split because of the availability, as successor to Laurier, of a competent English Canadian who was acceptable to both French Canada and the United States. William Lyon Mackenzie King's credentials as an administrator were impressive: he had been appointed in 1900, at the age of twenty-six, the senior permanent official in the new Department of Labor. Nine years later, having won election to the House of Commons, he had become Minister of Labor. His academic gifts were unusual for a politician. He began his graduate work in political economy at Chicago, received his masters degree at Harvard in

1898, and completed his doctorate at Harvard in 1909. Having published articles in leading economic journals he produced *Industry and Humanity* in 1918, shortly before becoming leader of the Liberal Party.

Even more important was King's understanding of Canadian dualism and the political situation in Quebec.[48] Because his maternal grandfather had led the 1837 Rebellion in Upper Canada, he could match honors with Papineau's grandson, Henri Bourassa. Having spent the war years in the United States dealing with industrial relations for the Rockefellers, he had been able to avoid the conscription crisis. Thus, he was in an admirable position to bring English- and French-speaking Liberals together again, as Laurier had done after the death of Riel.

The Liberals underwent their third crisis of Empire under King's leadership as prime minister during the Second World War. In early September 1939 King's "Quebec lieutenant" Ernest Lapointe made a speech in the House of Commons urging Canadians once again to rally to the defense of the Empire of which Canada was a part: "Our King, Mr. Speaker, is at war and this Parliament is sitting to decide whether we shall make his cause our own."[49]

In Quebec in 1939, a nationalist government had been in power for three years under its strong leader, Maurice Duplessis. The *Union Nationale* had little interest in the hostilities in Europe and indeed showed every indication of opposing the war. To strengthen his hand, Maurice Duplessis called a provincial election soon after war broke out. The federal Liberals decided that Duplessis had to be defeated at all costs. Lapointe and the other two Cabinet ministers from Quebec in Ottawa, P. J. A. Cardin and C. G. Power, pledged that there would be no conscription as long as they were members of the government of Canada. They even threatened to resign if the voters did not return the provincial Liberals to power. To ensure victory they employed the argument that without a French-Canadian presence in the Cabinet (which they alone could provide), there would be nothing to prevent English Canada from introducing conscription as in 1917. Their efforts were successful, the *Union Nationale* was defeated, and Duplessis retired to the Opposition bench until 1944. But a pledge had been made not to introduce conscription, a pledge that was to haunt the Quebec Liberal leaders.

By 1942, with the war going badly, it appeared that once again conscription for overseas service might be necessary. Mr. King held a plebiscite on the issue. Seventy percent of Canadians supported the government in its determination to fight the war to the utmost, and a couple of years later, when a shortage of men appeared imminent in western Europe, conscription was adopted to send servicemen overseas. Only a few conscripts were affected, and a few months later the war came to an end. Little damage appeared to have been done.

In Quebec, however, damage *was* done. The French-Canadian vote against conscription was estimated at over 90 percent. Here were most of the 30 percent of Canadians who did not support the federal government's policy. In other words, conscription was imposed once again on a hostile Quebec. Lapointe, who had given his word of honor, was dead, but other leading Liberal ministers from Quebec, English as well as French, refused to break their word: P. J. A. Cardin resigned in 1942 and C. G. Power in 1944 when the first conscripts were sent to Europe. To replace Lapointe, King chose Louis St. Laurent, a corporation lawyer with close ties to the English-speaking business world. St. Laurent had little difficulty in supporting conscription, and had not been in politics when the no-conscription pledge was given. As an old-fashioned Pan-Canadian he was committed to the principle of majority rule, and English Canadians formed the majority.[50]

The second conscription crisis in 1942 did not arouse the animosities of 1917. For one thing, Canada was no longer a colony and there was considerable sympathy for Britain and France in their struggle against Hitler. For another, the issue was handled with more dexterity by King and his Liberal colleagues than by the Conservatives during the First World War. Even so, French Canadians still drew a distinction between the direct defense of Canada at home and the indirect defense of Canada overseas as part of an alliance. There was a deep-rooted fear of heavy losses among young French Canadians, prospective fathers of the large families on whom the *Canadiens* depended. Such casualties would be irreplaceable, whereas their competitors, the English-speaking Canadians, could always make good their losses by immigration. Moreover, as Henri Bourassa had maintained in the First World War, native-born English Canadians had been almost as reluctant as native-born French Canadians to volunteer for active service in Europe.[51]

The Liberals paid a price for introducing conscription. At the provincial level the Quebec Liberal government had already gone down to defeat in the 1944 provincial elections. Duplessis then returned to power until his death in 1959. Many young people were disillusioned with both major parties and turned elsewhere. Pierre Trudeau, destined to be the next Pan-Canadian leader from Quebec after St. Laurent, actively op-

French Canada and the Triumph of Majority Rule 287

posed conscription and refused to serve in the armed forces. At the federal level it was clear that French-Canadian ministers were no more able to prevent conscription in 1942-44 than they had been able to prevent the hanging of Louis Riel in 1885.[52] They might not be *vendus,* but they were certainly impotent.

5   The End of Empire and the External Umpire

Canada's emergence as a powerful and truly independent state after 1945 had two consequences. In the short term, it meant that at last Canada was now really equal with the United Kingdom. By 1960, important ties with the United Kingdom had been broken, and the role of the British government and Parliament as external umpire apparently finally ended (except for *pro forma* amendments to the BNA Act).

In the long run, however, it became apparent that power was transferred from Westminster and Whitehall to Ottawa, i.e., to the federal authorities. Little thought appears to have been given to the need for a new umpire. Canada's search for an identity independent of the United Kingdom resulted in the triumph of a political nationalism expressed through the federal government. Consequently, Quebec's determination to preserve its own autonomy within Confederation led after 1960 to the emergence of a new Quebec nationalism that was political, with its expression being the government of Quebec. No longer could there be a French-English confrontation with the United Kingdom, such as was demonstrated in the 1927 dispute over Quebec's border with Newfoundland (then separate from Canada). Instead there was to be confrontation within Canada itself. This was to take the form not of English versus French Canada nor of the English-speaking provinces versus Quebec, but between a federal government thought to represent Canada's anglophone majority and a Quebec government assumed to represent the francophone majority in that province.

Canada's prowess in war, together with the domestic tension over conscription, accelerated the process whereby the federal government insured that Canada evolved towards independent status. Having established Canada as an arsenal of democracy, having prevented the defection of Quebec, and having transformed the country from a colony into a respected "Middle Power" entering its golden age of diplomacy, the Liberal government gave little sign of appreciating the possibility that with the elimination of the imperial umpire serious structural problems in Canada's political system might require attention. Instead, the dismantling of the British Empire and the end of imperial "interference" in Canadian affairs were looked upon as removing an important irritant in French-English relations, of which conscription was the symbol. Now there would be no need to worry about the loyalty of French Canadians to the imperial cause. In the future, the first loyalty of all Canadians would be to Canada alone. The age of imperialism being over, English Canadians need demand no more than formal allegiance to the Crown. The Crown obliged; and in 1953 Queen Elizabeth was declared to be Queen of Canada.

But to remove Whitehall and Westminster from Canadian affairs was to create complications. There was no longer a superior authority as arbiter between the Dominion and provincial governments. Yet so preoccupied were English-Canadian Liberals with removing the imperial tie that they tended to think the country's most serious political problems were on the way to being resolved: "Memorable history" had come to an end, and historians could concentrate on Canada as a North American society evolving according to its internal economic and social structure.

Yet the absence of attention to the structure of the political system, once the umpire *ab extra* had been removed, meant that it would be the federal government and Parliament, and the supreme court created by Parliament, that would fill the gap. Inevitably this meant that the principle of majority rule would be extended. Indeed, there were many centralist English Canadians who looked forward to the establishment, at last, of a strong central peacetime government that could make firm and, if necessary, unilateral decisions without constantly worrying about provincial sensibilities. In 1948 Mackenzie King retired, and a new era under St. Laurent began. St. Laurent gave little indication that as prime minister he fully understood the nature of the concerns expressed by King over Canada's increasing involvement in worldwide commitments. Mackenzie King knew how fragile Canada's political structure was and how necessary it was to put domestic considerations first at all times. Instead, St. Laurent seems to have believed that French Canadians could rely on the good sense of the English-Canadian majority, rather than on the protection afforded by law.[53]

The failure, or at least the inability, of Canadians to understand the need for structural change once imperial federalism finally came to an end and independence loomed, was the price paid for the absence of any revolution in Canada.[54] Because Canada had evolved from colony to Dominion and then from Dominion to senior member of the Commonwealth, there was no reason for a Declaration of Independence, and consequently no need for a specific date for Canadians to seize on as they tried to assess when the country had finally come of age. Instead, four dates were generally agreed on as landmarks in the progress towards independence: 1848, 1867, 1926, and 1931. Not so well marked, but in retrospect equally significant, was a fifth date, 1949, when a series of events occurred at the high tide of federal power.

The years 1848 and 1867 were not thought of at the time as involving a movement towards independence. When responsible government was granted, it signaled the end of control by the imperial executive only of Canada's domestic affairs. However, a government responsible to a legislature elected by the people could not, except formally, continue to be responsible to the imperial government. As for the second date, 1867, it did more than bring together a number of colonies already enjoying responsible government. One of Britain's intentions behind Confederation involved external affairs: it intended to leave the land defense of Canada to Canadians. The Royal Navy might have Atlantic and Pacific bases, but it was in no position to assist in the defense of Canada along the forty-ninth parallel. Once Canadians were free from British military control they were for all intents and purposes emancipated from colonial rule.

It took time for Canadians to exercise their latent power, but gradually they extended their control over Canadian policy from domestic to foreign affairs. The two most important dates in Canada's twentieth-century history of colonial emancipation were 1926, when the Imperial Conference declared the Dominions to be the equals of the United Kingdom, and 1931, when the Statute of Westminster made their equality statutory. Together, these events clearly established the principle that in international law Canada was an independent country. Canadians interpreted the provisions of the Statute of Westminster to mean that whatever links there might still be with the United Kingdom, they were now independent in fact.[55]

In 1848, 1867, and 1931, the part played by the provinces in constitutional development was crucial. When responsible government came to British North America in 1848, only the provinces were involved. In the negotiations leading to the BNA Act, it was the provinces that determined the nature of the federal government that was established. And in the negotiations leading to the Statute of Westminster, which established Canada's formal independence in international law in 1931, once again the provinces played an important part. They prevented the transfer of the amendment power, unilaterally, from Westminster to Ottawa. Rather than let this happen (and unable to agree on an amendment procedure), the provinces insisted that the amendment of the BNA Act remain a British responsibility. The assumption was that in a federal state the central authorities should not have sole power to amend the constitution. In other words, though Canadians accepted the doctrine of parliamentary supremacy, this had its limits in a federal system.

The events of 1949 followed a different pattern. In that year the government of Canada took four decisions, apparently without much consideration of the long-term implications for Canada's political system of this use of the federal power:

1. Newfoundland was admitted to Confederation as the tenth province. This was accomplished without any adjustment to its Labrador boundary with Quebec, even though Quebec had refused to accept the boundary line drawn by the Judicial Committee between Labrador and Quebec in 1927, when Canada had supported Quebec.
2. The Parliament of Canada assumed the power, with certain noted exceptions, to amend the BNA Act unilaterally. (This new power did not of course permit Parliament to legislate in those fields of jurisdiction exclusively assigned to the provinces in the original act.)
3. All appeals to the Privy Council were abolished. This deprived the government of Quebec (and the other provinces) of the right to take appeals directly from their provincial courts to the Privy Council. Instead, the Canadian Parliament selected as the final court of appeal the Supreme Court of Canada, a court it had itself established in 1875.
4. Canada formally joined the North Atlantic Treaty Organization (NATO). In doing so, Canada was committed to participation in the permanent defense of western Europe. This action raised the possibility that once again Canada's youth would be conscripted for combat overseas.

These four momentous decisions were all taken in the same year (see table 2). In no instance were the provinces consulted, the government of Canada being of the opinion that in amending the Constitution, except in those matters assigned exclusively to the provinces, it did not

Table 2. Canada's Constitutional Development: 1949 in Historical Context

Year	Event	Provincial Role
1848	Responsible government	Requested by the provinces
1867	BNA Act: Parliamentary federalism	Requested by the provinces
1926	Imperial Conference: Equality of the UK and the Dominions	Provinces were not involved in Imperial Conferences
1931	Statute of Westminster: Canada independent in international law	Provinces consulted
1949	1. BNA Act (no. 1): Admission of Newfoundland	Provinces not consulted
	2. BNA Act (no. 2): Parliament assumed the power to amend the Constitution	Provinces not consulted
	3. Judicial Committee replaced by the Supreme Court of Canada	Provinces not consulted
	4. Canada joined NATO	Provinces not consulted

need provincial assent. Interestingly enough, the prime minister, Louis St. Laurent, was a French Canadian, who may have set a precedent for a later French-speaking prime minister, Pierre Trudeau, when the latter tried to amend the Constitution unilaterally.

If any year demonstrated federal hegemony, it was surely 1949. In that year the federal government achieved a dominant position over all the provinces, not only over Quebec. Yet in the long run, the consequences of the transfer of power from Westminster and Whitehall to Ottawa, and the end of the umpire *ab extra,* were far more momentous for Quebec than for the other provinces. It was Quebec that had to acquiesce in the loss of resources that the extended boundary of Newfoundland entailed. It was Quebec's special status that was most likely to be threatened by Parliament's new powers of constitutional amendment. It was Quebec that would suffer most from being unable to take appeals directly to the Judicial Committee. And it was Quebec that would find conscription in support of yet another war in Europe most difficult to accept.

Yet in the immediate postwar years such possibilities seem to have been overshadowed by the satisfaction engendered by Canada's new status in the world: by final independence from the United Kingdom, the extension of Canada's boundaries to encompass all of British North America, and the important part assigned to an independent Canada as part of NATO. In the 1940s and 1950s, Canadians were much more self-confident, and much more outward-looking than they were to become after 1960.

The mood of the crucial year, 1949, appears, then, to have been relatively relaxed. This may explain why it has not been given greater prominence in history books. Indeed, as we have seen, English Canadians expected Canada's independence to remove some of the tensions between English and French Canadians. French Canadians appear to have shared this hope. They had not yet discovered that 1949 meant the replacement of Westminster by a federal government that felt no greater need than the British to conciliate Quebec. In 1949 the main concern of all Canadians was the achievement of genuine independence and the assumption of an important place in the postwar world. Moreover, first the Depression and then the war had enabled the federal government to establish its preeminence. Even the stance of Maurice Duplessis and his *Union Nationale* government was very much that of a defensive nationalism.[56]

6 The St. Laurent Era: Majority Rule Triumphant

It does not seem to have been apparent at the time that the selection of Louis St. Laurent was a break with tradition. Brought to Ottawa in 1941 to fill the Cabinet seat left vacant by Ernest Lapointe, Mackenzie King's Quebec lieutenant who had died in office, he agreed in 1948 to become the Liberal Party leader and prime minister as successor of Mr. King, who retired. Thus was established the Liberal convention of alternate English- and French-Canadian leaders. The Liberals confidently expected that this would enable them to retain their power base in Quebec, and they were right.

Yet St. Laurent broke tradition by being different from previous Liberal leaders, and from French-Canadian leaders in general in his attitude to Quebec nationalism. His mother was not a *Canadienne* but an English-speaking Irishwoman. He himself was from conservative Quebec City, not from Montreal, the center of nationalist feeling. Above all, he lacked the connection with the nationalist tradition of his predecessors. LaFontaine and Cartier could claim to have been *Patriotes* in their youth. Laurier, born too late to be associated with the Rebellion, could claim similar credentials: membership in the *Institut Canadien* and a willingness to defend the cause of Riel. All were politicians through and through.

Louis St. Laurent was not a politician but a corporate lawyer, associated with the largely English-speaking business world of Quebec and Montreal. (Nearly every year he had traveled to London to present cases to the Privy Council, where he was always well received.) When elected to Parliament and appointed to the Cabinet he was a political novice. Admittedly, he soon acquired a reputation for probity and competence, but he remained outside the mainstream of Quebec politics.

The very selection of a legal luminary like Louis St. Laurent was an indication of a potential growing gulf between Pan-Canadianism and Quebec nationalism. Previous leaders from LaFontaine to Lapointe had identified with public opinion in their province. In 1939 all the Cabinet ministers from Quebec had promised to resign if conscription were introduced, and in due course they all did. When St. Laurent was selected by Mackenzie King as Quebec leader in the Cabinet, he accepted the necessity of conscription. Before the plebiscite, St. Laurent said, "The prime minister will not repudiate his promises if you do not agree to cancelling them"—but he did not specify the meaning of "you."[57] He then interpreted the results of the plebiscite, in which English Canadians voted for conscription and French Canadians against it, as freeing the government from its engagement, and argued that for him to leave the Cabinet would be to hand power over to the conscriptionists. When, finally, it was decided in 1944 to send conscripts overseas, he agreed, arguing that "The will of the majority must be respected and must prevail."[58] In other words, he was less of a dualist and more like an anglophone majoritarian than other Quebec politicians. In the 1944 provincial election, the *Union Nationale* was returned to power. Nevertheless, the federal Liberals won the election of 1945, and under St. Laurent's leadership they did very well in 1949 and 1953. There were many people in Quebec who respected the cerebral St. Laurent, even though provincially they preferred Duplessis.

Despite St. Laurent's popularity, his selection as leader suggested that there was something amiss with a political system that could not find its leadership from among Quebec's large number of Liberal MPs, and that had to go outside politics altogether. Even Mr. King had better credentials with respect to Quebec's nationalist tradition: his grandfather, after all, had led the Rebellion in Upper Canada.

With the advantage of hindsight, it is now apparent that the lessons of the second conscription crisis and of the long-term significance of the return of the *Union Nationale* to power in Quebec were not fully grasped by St. Laurent and his colleagues in the federal government. Instead, by giving Parliament extensive power to amend the BNA Act, the federal government established its control over all gray areas of dispute, reducing the provinces to the exercise of those powers exclusively assigned to them by law. In establishing the Supreme Court as the final court of appeal, St. Laurent transferred jurisdiction to a federal court with an English-Canadian majority. By joining NATO, the prime minister made another conscription crisis possible. And in admitting Newfoundland into Confederation without the expected modification of the Labrador boundary, he let a dispute between Canada and Newfoundland become a festering sore between Newfoundland and Quebec. Louis St. Laurent appears to have shown an extraordinary willingness, one comparable to Cartier's, to put Canada's interests (which were often English Canada's) above those of Quebec.[59] And like Cartier, he had spent too much time among the anglophone *haute bourgeoisie*. One begins to understand why the cruel term *"vendus"* was so often used by radical Quebecois to describe French Canadians who had lost touch with their roots in Quebec and had "sold out" to *les anglais*.

However, to accuse St. Laurent of totally ignoring Quebec sentiment is unjustified. In 1949 there was throughout Quebec considerable pride in Canada's achievements during and after the Second World War. Paul Sauvé, Duplessis' second in command, had fought in Normandy, and Duplessis himself had presided over a Victory Bonds drive after returning to power. As far as the two 1949 amendments to the BNA Act were concerned, there was widespread support in Quebec for measures which ended Canada's colonial ties. It is in this historical context of a now independent Canada that we must judge the decision to admit Newfoundland (thus completing Canada as a transcontinental power), to join NATO (as an independent state the equal of the United States), to abolish appeals to the Privy Council, and to take a step towards patriation of the Constitution by giving Parliament the power of amendment. There was no outpouring of opposition to St. Laurent's policies in Quebec. The full implications of this majoritarian perspective for the relationship between Quebec and English Canada were not apparent at the time.

7 The End of Conservative Nationalism: Quebec under Duplessis before 1959

In view of St. Laurent's lack of awareness of the currents at work in the Quebec of the 1940s and 1950s, one might have expected the emergence of a new form of Quebec nationalism comparable to Mercier's in the last years of Macdonald's government, or Bourassa's in the later years of Laurier's. But Maurice Duplessis had preempted this role. His *Union Nationale* party had initially sought power as a progressive and nationalist party. Though Duplessis, a conservative by nature, had sloughed off or absorbed his progressive allies once he became firmly established as premier, he was always able to appeal to Quebec's nationalist sentiment. He remained firmly opposed to federal aggrandizement.

To those liberal intellectuals who opposed him, Duplessis' ability to retain the support of so many Quebecois voters until his death remained puzzling.[60] His leadership was very different from that of the Liberal and *Parti Québecois* premiers who succeeded him. He remained a devout Catholic and a supporter of the Church's leading role in education and the social services (fully aware of how much money this saved the province). He was a gracious host to the British monarchs who visited Quebec in 1939 and 1959, and expressed no republican sentiments. He welcomed investment by multinational corporations whose managers spoke English only. Indeed, he appeared to find the status quo agreeable at a time when the rest of the world, from Viet Nam to Algeria to the American South, was preoccupied with the demand for liberation.

Part of Duplessis' success, no doubt, could be attributed to the failure of the Quebec Liberal Party to offer a credible alternative. The Liberals had been hurt by their collaboration with the federal government during the Second World War. (They had acquiesced in the detention for several years of Camillien Houde, the demagogic mayor of Montreal.) Some of the younger intellectuals who opposed Duplessis as the upholder of an archaic *ancien régime* migrated to the Ottawa of St. Laurent (including Pierre Trudeau, who could also afford to spend time abroad). Even so, many of them had misgivings about the centralizing policies of the federal authorities. Trudeau's writings betray the anguish of the younger liberal generation in the 1950s. Distressed by the behavior of the Quebec government over civil liberties, Trudeau suggested that his native province did not really understand what democracy was all about. Yet even though he preferred the federal government's openness to ideas, there were certain issues of principle on which he sided with the *Union Nationale.* He opposed the St. Laurent government's offer of financial aid to universities on the grounds that it was an encroachment on provincial jurisdiction. Pan-Canadian though he might be, Trudeau thought St. Laurent had gone too far.[61]

The defensive nationalism of Duplessis served Quebec better in its day than was apparent at the time, when its many faults were apparent. But it did not long survive the death of the *Union Nationale*'s paternalistic leader and that of his anointed successor, Paul Sauvé, which occurred shortly thereafter. Like its predecessors, the *Parti National* and the *Ligue Nationaliste,* the *Union Nationale* was very dependent on the quality of its leadership. Duplessis was for many of his followers a charismatic (even tribal) leader to whom they were devoted.[62]

As a nationalist, the conservative Duplessis was less aggressive than Mercier or Bourassa. He was willing to let private entrepreneurs (many of them anglophones) develop, and often exploit, Quebec's natural resources. He was happy to allow the Church to continue exercising its leading role in education, in the social services, and in protecting the culture of the province. His defensive nationalism consisted of resistance to encroachment by Ottawa in fields belonging to Quebec, even when he himself was not prepared to act in those areas. Duplessis governed Quebec in a period when the province seemed little more than a "deviant case" in Canada's "Anglo-American democracy," comparable to the Deep South in the United States. While very much a nationalist, he was a conservative nationalist, and was able to cooperate with the Conservative Party of English Canada in a general election whenever it suited his interests.

However, even under Duplessis, Quebec never really returned to the Conservative fold. The Pan-Canadian Conservatism of the nineteenth century was dead. On the only occasion when the Conservative Party did really well in Quebec, the 1958 election, no Pan-Canadian figure comparable to Cartier emerged. Francophone conservatives in Quebec were first and foremost nationalists, preferring their own *Union Nationale,* and willing to cooperate with the English-speaking Tory Party only to oppose the federal Liberals.

One of the interesting characteristics of Nationalist movements in Quebec was their willingness to associate with other groups to defeat their Liberal opponents. Bourassa and his *Ligue Nationaliste* were willing to ally with the Conservatives in the 1911 election. Duplessis and his *Union Nationale* were prepared to throw their weight behind Diefenbaker in 1958. These were two of the three occasions after 1896 when the Conservatives were able to form a majority government. It is not surprising that in their anxiety to regain power in 1968, presumably with the help of Quebec, the federal Conservatives toyed with the nationalist doctrine of "deux nations."

When René Lévesque came up with the idea of "sovereignty-association" at that time, it was not an entirely new concept. In one form or another it had been around since the 1830s. There had always been a few proponents of separation and political sovereignty. And the *Union Nationale* had practiced something close to association. But Lévesque was the first to put the two together, promoting the idea of political sovereignty for Quebec and economic association for Quebec and Canada. Thus he hoped to have the best of both worlds.

In Quebec, political analysts have often described the changing nature of Quebec nationalism.[63] They have traced *conservative* nationalism from its early nineteenth-century origins, when it was nurtured by the Church, to its last secular gasp under Duplessis. They have noted the *liberal* nationalism that replaced the conservatism of the *Union Nationale* in 1960. And they have suggested that this in turn was challenged by other forms of nationalism, whether *socialist* or, in the case of the *Parti Quebécois,* social-democratic.[64] In the process they have been tempted to subsume the complex history of Quebec before the Quiet Revolution under the general rubric of conservative (or even clerical) nationalism. But, as we have seen, there were periods of radical and liberal nationalism long before Duplessis came to power.

It is tempting for social scientists who focus on Quebec politics to make the implicit assumption that before 1960 French Canada was simply the equivalent of an *ancien régime*. Such an approach, however, is an oversimplification. It ignores Quebec's important role in the federal Liberal Party and pays little attention to the French-Canadian minorities. We must not forget that the people of Quebec did vote as Canadians from 1896 onward for a federal Liberal Party which, initially at least, aroused the hostility of the Church, the chief custodian of the *ancien régime,* such as it was. Once committed to the Liberal Party (except for such an occasion as 1958) the people of Quebec did not waver in their political allegiance. None of the other anglophone parties, whether Conservative, Progressive, Cooperative Commonwealth Federation, or the New Democratic Party formed out of the CCF in 1961, made much of an impact on the province. The sole exception was the Social Credit Party which, as the *Créditistes,* made significant inroads into Liberal strength in a number of elections during the 1960s.

The strength of the Liberal Party in Quebec lay in the fact that it was more sympathetic to Quebec's aspirations (or at least appeared to be) than the other national parties. The Conservatives had firmly supported the imperial connection and conscription. The Liberals had been lukewarm. Quebec's Liberal leaders had been able to argue that they alone stood between Quebec and conscription, that is, between French Canada and Tory English Canada, on this most sensitive of issues, even if, as it happened, they proved impotent.

The Quebec wing of the Liberal Party of Canada had always been able to win support in Quebec by identifying the Conservatives with the imperial government. With the imperial tie removed, it could no longer fall back on this ploy. It therefore portrayed the Conservative Party as the party of English Canada. But then the Liberal Party, too, was a party of English Canadians, especially after the retirement of St. Laurent in 1957 and the election of Lester B. Pearson as his successor. Neither Diefenbaker nor Pearson was bilingual: there was no French-Canadian political leader of the stature of Laurier, St. Laurent, or even Lapointe in Ottawa.

When, in the summer of 1959, the Queen landed at Wolfe's Cove, Quebec, to open the St. Lawrence Seaway with President Eisenhower, it was ten years after the high-water mark of anglophone hegemony, and two hundred years after General Wolfe's victory on the Plains of Abraham. The 1950s, in Canada as well as in the United States of Eisenhower, were a period of relative calm before the stormy 1960s. During this deceptive period the Church in Quebec was losing its hold on the rising generation, and the anglophone managers of Quebec's industries were losing the loyalty of their formerly docile workers. Yet the *Union Nationale,* dependent on its alliance with both Church and business, had retained broad electoral support, thanks to the magic of Duplessis.

It was in 1956 that Pierre Trudeau, politicized by the asbestos strike, had made it clear that fundamental changes in Quebec society were taking place. It was in 1959 that René Lévesque became politically conscious as a result of a strike at the French network of the CBC where he was employed. When Duplessis welcomed the Queen, the era of conservative nationalism was drawing to a close, and never again would a monarch be made welcome in Quebec. But until the death of Duplessis, one could still speak of "French Canada" and assume that Quebec knew its place in an "Anglo-American" society based on majority rule.

9
Quebec and the Rest of Canada: The Limitations of Philosophical Federalism

The transformation of Quebec, which began soon after the death of Maurice Duplessis, led to a reappraisal of the province's role in Confederation and tested the adaptability of the federal system. The relationship between the nationalists and federalists (including Pan-Canadian francophones) in Canada underwent a number of changes. The old cultural nationalism that stressed the role of French Canadians in Confederation was challenged by a political nationalism based on the power wielded by the government of Quebec, which then fought to have its authority extended.

What we have called Pan-Canadianism also underwent a metamorphosis. In 1944, Louis St. Laurent had acquiesced in conscription because he accepted the principle of majority (i.e., anglophone) rule. Twenty-five years later a new generation of Pan-Canadians passed the Official Languages Act to underscore the dual nature of the federal system and the equality of English and French. The rallying cry of earlier nationalists like Henri Bourassa, bilingualism and biculturalism, became the creed of many Pan-Canadian federalists.

Finally, most influential English Canadians responded to the challenge of political nationalism (and the threat of separatism) by abandoning their traditional image of Canada as an "Anglo-American democracy" and replacing it by their own vision of a new dualist society. Individuals who remained committed to the doctrine of majority rule (and anglophone hegemony) found little support for their views among federal politicians. They either resigned from federal politics or were defeated at the polls. The age of imperialism and Protestant extremism appeared to be over. Instead, the Pan-Canadians' goals of cultural and linguistic equality were widely accepted. English Canada, it seemed, was catching up with the dualist philosophy of French Canadians.

Politically, however, the success of the new dualism was still limited.

The proponents of majority rule continued the struggle in provincial politics. In Quebec, even before the federal Parliament adopted the Official Languages Act, for which an older Quebec generation of cultural nationalists had struggled in vain, new vehicles for political nationalism emerged. These new movements were interested in power, not culture: in Quebec, not in French Canada, and in political independence, not in greater cultural autonomy.

For many English Canadians, accustomed to a comfortable life in their "peaceable kingdom," to a widespread acceptance of the political system, and to Canada's role on the world stage as an influential "middle power," the expressions of francophone discontent were puzzling. It was only when the Royal Commission on Bilingualism and Biculturalism published its startling preliminary report in 1965 that the full extent of Quebec's dissatisfaction was brought home.

In some respects, the independence movement that began in the 1960s bears comparison with the unrest of the 1830s. In the earlier controversy the British government had rejected the radicals' demand for a new regime. In the 1960s, the government of Canada refused to admit that the federal political system required structural change. What English Canadians called "Confederation" was not negotiable. But the argument was not simply, as English Canadians assumed, over reform of the British North America Act. It was over the perception in Quebec that Canada had been moving toward a quasi-unitary system as a result of the transfer of London's residual authority to Ottawa after the Second World War.

1   The End of Empire: Toward a Quasi-unitary
    Canada before 1957

Canada, without being fully conscious of the fact, is passing through the greatest crisis in its history. . . . It would appear from what is happening that the state of affairs established in 1867, and never seriously challenged, is now for the first time being rejected by the French Canadians of Quebec.—
Royal Commission on Bilingualism and Biculturalism, 1965

When the Commission drew the attention of Canadians to the seriousness of events in Quebec, the Quiet Revolution was coming to an end. But Canada was still "passing through the greatest crisis in its history" and would remain in a state of crisis through the 1970s and well into the 1980s. This was, above all, political in nature and a test of the capacity of the country's governments, both federal and provincial, to adapt to a Quebec that appeared determined to obtain a much greater degree of political autonomy.

In going on to assert that "the state of affairs established in 1867" had "never been seriously challenged," the Royal Commission was overlooking two previous challenges (one internal and the other external or colonial). While it was true that there had been no serious suggestion before 1960 that the BNA Act should be rejected and replaced by a new constitution, there had certainly been challenges to the Confederation settlement. One had failed, but the other had been crowned with success.

The unsuccessful challenge had been the series of attempts by French Canadians to change the majoritarian interpretation of the BNA Act in favor of Catholic and French minorities. As we saw in Chapters 7 and 8, much of this struggle centered on education. It did not succeed because English Canadians stubbornly adhered to the letter of the law.

The successful challenge had been a sustained effort by successive governments of Canada to have the parts of the BNA Act pertaining to Canada's relationship with the United Kingdom reinterpreted to give Canada autonomy. There was a marked difference between the government of Canada's unwillingness to meet the demands of the French-Canadian minority for equal treatment, and its determination to secure from the British an interpretation of the BNA Act that recognized Canada's equality.

"The state of affairs in 1867" involved more than the internal relationship of the federal government and the provinces. It also meant a colonial relationship with the mother country in which the imperial authorities acted as arbiters between the two orders of government. This we have described earlier as "imperial federalism." Canada's successful challenge to imperialism would eventually have an impact on the internal conflict, and especially on relations with Quebec.

When almost the last of the imperial ties were cut in 1949, barely a decade before the Quiet Revolution, it was assumed that this break had implications only for Canada–United Kingdom relations. The demise of imperialism was thought simply to mean that Canada was now a truly sovereign and independent country. The federal system was considered a separate issue. After all, it was governed by Sections 91, 92, and 93 of the BNA Act, sections which remained untouched. Hence the Royal Commission's conclusion that "the state of affairs established in 1867" had not been challenged.

However, in successfully rejecting imperialism, Canada had also done away with imperial federalism over the years by circumscribing the role of the British governors general, the Judicial Committee of the Privy Council, and the British Parliament as external umpires of its federal system. These external umpires were not replaced.

Because Canadians thought they were abolishing imperialism and not imperial federalism, they saw no reason to examine the relationship of imperialism and federalism. There was no uproar when the federal government acted unilaterally to lessen imperial dependence in 1949.[1] There was little awareness that some form of constitutional federalism would have to replace imperial federalism, and that until this was done the country's federal structure would be defective, with Canada operating as a quasi-unitary form of government.[2]

When, therefore, in the 1960s, "the French Canadians of Quebec" attacked the federal government's hegemony they were not so much challenging the 1867 Act as rejecting the quasi-unitary parliamentary system that had replaced imperial federalism. They were demanding instead a new federal structure. The struggle that ensued was to test Canada's capacity to meet the requirements of what we have called "constitutional federalism." By this we mean a federalism that depended not on the imperial prerogative but on powers and responsibilities specifically assigned in a new Constitution to the executive, judicial and legislative branches of government. We shall examine the implications of the failure to replace the external umpire in each of these institutions.

As far as the executive was concerned, the British governors general had seen their powers whittled away long before 1949. When in 1952 a Canadian governor general took their place, the new Canadian head of state, like his imperial predecessors, was intended to be little more than a figurehead as far as day-to-day politics were concerned, and to represent the Monarch, another figurehead.[3] The governor general was not expected to use his position to curb an errant head of government, still less to exercise his authority as head of state and umpire in a federal system.

Originally the governor general had a dual role. He not only represented the Monarch as head of state, but exercised considerable federal powers on behalf of the imperial government over affairs in Canada inasmuch as he could limit the power of the Dominion Parliament. Despite the acceptance of the principle of responsible government, the governor general retained the power of veto no longer exercised by the Monarch in the United Kingdom. Under Section 55 of the BNA Act the governor general could declare "that he withholds the Queen's Assent, or that he reserves the Bill for the Signification of the Queen's Pleasure." Even if he assented to a measure, the British government could disallow legislation within two years of its passage in Canada, under Section 56. Bills reserved for the Queen's pleasure did not have any force unless royal assent was given within two years (Section 57). By 1878 no fewer than twenty-one bills had been reserved by the governor general.

In 1878 the British government decided to issue new instructions giving the governor general still further powers, such as the right to preside at council meetings, to act without consulting the Cabinet, and even on occasion to overrule the Cabinet.[4] The Canadian government responded vigorously to this assertion of imperial power, and was so successful that the governor general ceased to exercise even his original statutory powers as a federal arbiter except on rare occasions.[5] "Nevertheless, the quasi-imperial relationship was a long time dying."[6] At last, in 1926 the Imperial Conference declared that both disallowance and reservation (of federal legislation) were obsolete.[7] The governor general therefore lost one of his two functions when he ceased to be an agent of the imperial government. Henceforth he was simply the representative of the Monarch as formal executive.

It was to be some time before the practice of imperial federalism by the executive came to an end within Canada itself. The Dominion government still acted like the imperial government in its relations with the provinces. Lieutenant governors continued to disallow legislation on behalf of the federal government until 1943. The last occasion when a lieutenant governor exercised his prerogative of reserving legislation until the federal government had examined it occurred in 1961. This "imperial" relationship between the federal and provincial governments left lasting resentment, especially in the West where the lieutenant governors' powers had been widely used.[8]

To return to the governor general. When he lost his powers as an agent of the imperial government, little thought was given to providing him with a role as head of state in a federal system, i.e., to the value of an impartial head of state like the governor general acting as arbiter between the federal government and the provinces. Instead, the governor general was assumed to exercise his responsibilities on behalf of the Dominion government alone, according to the theory of responsible government devised in Britain. "For just as the constitution of Britain consists largely in the gradual bringing of the royal prerogative under the control of ministers answerable to the House of Commons, the constitutional history of Canada has involved a similar operation with the office of governor general."[9] The British Constitution, of course, was devised for a unitary system in which the executive was responsible not only to Parliament but to the lower house, elected on the basis of population alone.

The role of the governor general is usually treated within the context of parliamentary government. He appoints the prime minister, grants (or refuses to grant) the dissolution of Parliament, and has the power (exercised in Australia in 1975) to dismiss a government. "The most important of these powers is the appointment of the prime minister."[10] In practice, since 1926 the office has created no problems. For one thing, no prime minister has been unable to complete his term, and so the governor general has not had to handle the delicate problem of succession. In such an event, James Mallory has indicated that the governor general would act after consultation with the parliamentary party.

The governor general is not usually considered in the context of Canada as a *federal* system. Party leaders are chosen not by the parliamentary party alone but by national conventions. These conventions give representation to provinces that have elected few if any MPs belonging to the party. Thus Quebec is well represented at Conservative Party conventions and the West at Liberal meetings. Were a prime minister to die or become incapacitated, and were the governor general to consult only the parliamentary party before appointing a new prime minister, a problem could arise. Unless he made an interim appointment, the governor general would be acting within the country's parliamentary tradition but not in accordance with the demands of constitutional federalism. Canada may have avoided the problems that have bedeviled succession elsewhere simply because no prime minister in recent years has died in office or been incapacitated.[11]

With regard to the second power, the *judicial,* here also imperial federalism in the form of the Judicial Committee of the Privy Council was not replaced. We have noted how the Judicial Committee acted as arbiter between the federal and provincial governments until its power passed to the Supreme Court of Canada in 1949. Under the old imperialism, the provinces could take their grievances from their own courts directly to London, bypassing the Supreme Court of Canada. After 1949 that avenue was closed. Instead they had to take their arguments to the

Supreme Court, a body created by an act of the Canadian Parliament and appointed by the federal government. In other words it, too, was not a federal institution—that is, entrenched in the Constitution. Superior court judges throughout Canada were all appointed by the federal government, not by the provinces which administered the courts.

English-speaking scholars have taken pains to defend the Supreme Court against the charge of bias,[12] for even though Quebec judges were federal appointees, they sometimes reflected a different perspective. The civil liberties cases of the 1950s "were handled very differently in the Quebec courts than they were in the Supreme Court of Canada," and the Supreme Court's rebuffs "caused exasperation to many French Canadians."[13] It has nevertheless been admitted that the power of appointment is a political act and that the federal authorities at the very least might be unwilling to appoint judges with a known and pronounced bias in favor of provincial rights.[14] Although he was prepared to defend the "Anglo-American legal tradition" as one "based on acceptance of the impartiality of the judicial process," Mallory noted that the Supreme Court of Canada, like its American counterpart in its handling of race relations, was capable of being a "nationalizing" institution. Writing at the time when the separatist movement was not yet powerful, he concluded, "It is possible that this example has not been lost on those French Canadians who fear that the sheer weight of English Canadian society is inevitably crushing all that is distinctively French in Quebec."[15] In the constitutional crisis that developed after the victory of the *Parti Québecois* in 1976, the Supreme Court and the Quebec courts became increasingly involved in the disputes between the federal government and the government of Quebec, and usually they acted as "nationalizing" institutions.

Until the Supreme Court is entrenched in the Constitution it will remain vulnerable. A situation could arise in which the people of Quebec (or of any province) refused to accept the judgment of the Supreme Court. They could do so not by alleging bias but by questioning the Court's historic legitimacy. The authority of the Judicial Committee had emanated from the imperial authority and the acquiescence of Canadians. The Supreme Court could not inherit the imperial prerogative; it had to depend on Canadian acquiescence in its right to make decisions. It was that right which could be questioned.

In unilaterally transferring the judicial power to interpret the Constitution from the Judicial Committee to the Supreme Court in 1949, the Parliament of Canada relied on a 1947 advisory opinion of the Judicial Committee open to different interpretations. The committee stated that there was no constitutional limitation on the power of the Canadian Parliament to limit appeals.[16] (That is, Parliament could prevent appeals from being taken outside Canada to the Judicial Committee.) This carefully worded opinion did not state that the Canadian Parliament had the right to give the Judicial Committee's powers to its own creature, the Supreme Court, nor did it say that henceforth all provincial appeals should be handled by that federal institution. It did not get involved in this question because clearly the way in which Canada handled appeals was a matter for Canadians to determine. The fact that Parliament chose to transfer the authority to the Supreme Court was a matter of indifference to the Privy Council.

Were the Supreme Court to become an instrument of constitutional federalism it could no longer be the creature of the federal Parliament alone. It has been argued that, like Chief Justice Marshall's Supreme Court of the United States, it would be able to defend itself as an institution entrenched in the Constitution. This, incidentally, has been the position taken by French-Canadian scholars.[17]

The third element in imperial federalism, the legislative power of the British Parliament to amend the British North America Act, fell into disuse. Unlike the Colonial Office and the Privy Council, the British Parliament never tried to exercise its imperial authority. From 1867 on it amended the BNA Act whenever Canada asked it to do so, and acted only when requested. Nor was the Westminster Parliament prepared to act as a federal mediator. No amendments put forward by Canadian provinces were ever accepted. The British Parliament did not even "look behind" a request to see whether the provinces supported a proposed amendment. Whatever the Parliament of Canada asked for, it received.

The Canadian Parliament was successful because it was so circumspect in its requests that it did not embarrass the British. On only three occasions (1940, 1951, and 1964) did it propose that powers assigned to the provinces in Section 92 be transferred to the Parliament of Canada and then it did so with provincial consent. Consequently, except in 1930, there was no occasion when the provinces could properly challenge the convention agreed to by both Westminster and Ottawa that the

Canadian Constitution could be amended by the Parliament of the United Kingdom on the request, and only on the request, of the Parliament of Canada.

In 1930 a novel situation arose when, according to the proposed Statute of Westminster, all the legislative powers of the British Parliament were to be transferred to the Dominions. In Canada's case, this meant to the Parliament of Canada. However, the Canadian provinces were unwilling to permit the power to amend the Constitution to become the exclusive property of Ottawa, and they persuaded the federal government to leave the formal power of amendment in British hands until a domestic federal formula, including some form of provincial consent, could be agreed upon. There was thus implicit recognition that as far as control of the Constitution was concerned, imperial federalism had to be preserved until some form of constitutional federalism was agreed to.

Notwithstanding the precedent of 1930, in 1949 the Parliament of Canada, with Britain's consent, arrogated to itself the power to amend much of the BNA Act. Its reasons for doing so appear to have been based on a false analogy: that if the provincial legislatures could amend their constitutions, then Parliament should have power to amend its constitution, except for those powers assigned exclusively to the provinces. In fact, of course, the BNA Act was not comparable to a provincial constitution: it was a federal as well as a parliamentary document. Nor was the Canadian Parliament comparable to either a provincial legislature or the British Parliament. It, too, was a federal as well as a parliamentary institution, and with limited powers. While some powers belonged to the provinces and others to the federal Parliament, there were many gray areas over which Parliament had no authority to claim exclusive jurisdiction. Yet this is precisely what Parliament did, in the same year that it transferred judicial interpretation of the Constitution to the Supreme Court.

In sum, by the time the Quiet Revolution got under way, Canada had for all practical purposes dismantled the apparatus of imperial federalism, virtually ending the role of the governor general, the Judicial Committee, and the British Parliament as external umpires. These were not replaced by Canadian institutions consonant with what we have called "constitutional federalism." Instead, with power transferred from the governor general to the prime minister and Cabinet, from the British

Parliament to the Parliament of Canada, and from the Privy Council to the Supreme Court of Canada (all Ottawa institutions), it would seem that Canada was becoming a quasi-unitary or pseudofederal state.

However, most Canadians appear to have assumed, at least until the 1960s, that their federal system remained unimpaired, or even that it had been improved by a shift from "imperial federalism" to "Canadian federalism." They may even have convinced themselves that a novel form of federalism, known as "parliamentary federalism," and not imperial federalism, had been in existence since the BNA Act came into operation. They were unaware that without the imperial umpires, something was missing from Canada's federal system.

Quebec, then, was not rejecting the state of affairs established in 1867 but the quasi-unitary system that had replaced it. Symbolic of the government's power was the continuation of its control over taxation after the war ended in 1945. During the war Canada had almost become for all practical purposes a unitary state: it did not revert to its previous mode of operation just because the war was over.

In other words, the English-Canadian view, reiterated by the Royal Commission on Bilingualism and Biculturalism, that the 1867 agreement was being challenged for the first time, was not shared by French Canadians. They believed that Confederation had been intended to permit the provinces, especially Quebec, to retain their distinctive character. Instead, the spread of North American civilization had eroded provincial autonomy. Only the provinces could resist this trend. Even before the Quiet Revolution, Quebec's own Royal Commission on Constitutional Problems (the Tremblay Commission) had drawn attention to the need to return to the original principles underlying Confederation. One historian of Quebec has commented on the Tremblay Commission's report, "Significantly the proposal was a return to the past, the past of true federalism in 1867. . . . In short, federalism should sustain rather than undermine the genuine differences between provinces and peoples."[18] Dated though the report may have become by the early 1960s as an expression of Quebec nationalism, it nevertheless reflected Quebec's perennial concern about the decline of federalism in Canada.

In the light of Canada's failure to replace the external umpires of imperial federalism by an internal umpire appropriate to constitutional federalism, we can begin to understand why the emergence of political nationalism in Quebec led so quickly to the province's disillusionment with the whole political system. What began as a search for a new form of federalism deteriorated into a series of confrontations and ultimately led to the demand for political sovereignty.

We can now begin to understand why the transformation of cultural nationalism into political nationalism occurred so quickly and with such intensity in Quebec. We can also comprehend why English Canada, because it was committed to the "parliamentary federalism" it believed Canada to have pioneered in 1867, was unable quickly to respond to Quebec's demands for structural change. The Quiet Revolution cannot be examined solely in terms of the modernization of Quebec and separate from the evolution of Canada itself from imperial federalism to quasi-unitary state.

2   Background to the New Quebec Nationalism: The Decline of French Power in Ottawa, 1957–68

In retrospect, the Quebec of the Duplessis era appears to have been as strong in the defense of its "national" identity as the Quebec of the 1960s was to be aggressive in the promotion of political nationalism. Such a contrast may, however, be something of an oversimplification. While it was during the Duplessis regime that federal hegemony reached its peak in the late 1940s, it was also during the Duplessis regime in the 1950s that the federal government's hegemony began to be challenged. Ottawa was unable to retain all the power it had acquired during the Second World War or as legatee of the British Empire. Even before 1960, the relationship of Quebec with Ottawa had altered. It continued to change as conservative cultural nationalism gave way to the political nationalism of the Liberals (1960–66; 1970–76) and the temporarily revived *Union Nationale* (1966–70).

The new nationalism that began to emerge in Quebec did so against a background of weakening federal power both at home and abroad. Even before the death of Duplessis the Dominion government appeared to have lost its confident grip on Canadian affairs. At first it seemed that the disarray in Ottawa was simply the result of the overconfidence, complacency and insensitivity of St. Laurent's Liberal government. As one observer put it not long afterwards: "cracks had begun to appear in the monolithic structure of the Liberal Party."[19] To judge by the widespread opposition to the government's policies in both domestic and external affairs by the end of 1956, Liberal hegemony had already passed its high point.

On the domestic front, though Canadians were delighted that oil and gas had been discovered in large quantities in Western Canada since 1947, many of them were dismayed by the government's handling of the TransCanada Pipeline that was to transport surplus gas to the United States. So anxious was the St. Laurent government to complete the Canadian stage of construction in 1956 that it insisted on passing the bill lending the American-financed company $80 million within three weeks. For the first time in Canadian history a bill was carried through all its stages under closure. The government succeeded in its object, but there was fierce opposition in Parliament, and a loss of 10 percent in the Government's public opinion rating.

A further erosion of popular support occurred as a result of a foreign policy issue: the Suez crisis. Under St. Laurent's outward-looking policies during the "golden age" of Canadian diplomacy, the Liberals were proud of Canada's role as a middle power. They were therefore particularly pleased, at the time of the Suez invasion by Britain and France in 1956, to be able through their good offices to help resolve this contentious conflict which put the United States in opposition to its European allies. The Secretary of State for External Affairs, Lester B. Pearson, later won the Nobel Peace Prize.

However, conservative anglophile Canadians were angered by what seemed to them to be support for American policy, and especially by the Liberals' hostility to the United Kingdom. The dispute highlighted the ideological differences between the pro-British Conservatives and pro-American Liberals. To criticism in the House of Commons that the Liberals had deserted the British to become choreboys for Washington, Pearson had replied, "If it's bad to be a chore-boy for the United States, it's equally bad to be a colonial chore-boy running around shouting: 'Ready, aye, ready.' "

St. Laurent justified the intervention of the smaller powers like Canada by arguing that "the era when the supermen of Europe could govern the whole world has and is coming pretty close to an end."[20] But as the Conservatives were gleefully to point out, it was also an era when the "supermen" running the federal government were to find their days numbered. In the 1957 general election, the Canadian voters refused to renew the Liberals' mandate—the first refusal since 1930. And so, three years before the Quiet Revolution erupted in Quebec, Liberal power in Ottawa came to an end.

The decline in the Liberals' hegemony proved to be more than "cracks in the monolithic structure of the Liberal Party." The Liberals' defeat was followed by a weakening of the federal government as such. There was no transfer of federal hegemony to the new Conservative government. For one thing, in 1957 the Conservatives did not win a majority of the seats and so had to form a minority government. For another, in selecting their leader the Conservatives had tried to capture the popular mood of English Canada after the pipeline debate and the Suez crisis by appointing John Diefenbaker, an orator, a visionary, and a westerner who represented the new Canadian mosaic. Unfortunately he was not someone acceptable to the party's Quebec wing, such as it was.

Moreover, to secure the leadership Diefenbaker had to win the support of provincial Conservative leaders. Already in 1954, Duplessis had introduced personal and corporate income tax in Quebec, and had then made the federal government reduce its share of income tax by 10 percent. Now, to placate Ontario, Diefenbaker promised a new tax-sharing agreement with the provinces. The erosion of federal power in response to provincial demands had begun before the Quiet Revolution.

Moreover, despite the victory of the Conservatives there was not sufficient permanent support for the Conservative cause and the British connection to bring about a political realignment comparable to that of 1896.[21] The result was stalemate. The decline of the Liberals, the failure of the Conservatives to create a new alignment of social and political forces, and the need to choose between two leaders both of whom were anglophones with no Quebec connection, together with the elimination of the external umpire, created another vacuum that could be filled only by French-Canadian politicians, either in Ottawa or in Quebec City. For the first time in decades there was little evidence in Ottawa of French power in federal politics.

The defeat of the virtually leaderless *Union Nationale* in 1960 following the deaths of both Duplessis and his chosen successor, Paul Sauvé, had therefore been preceded by an important shift in federal Liberal Party politics, a shift that was to have a considerable impact on Quebec's relations with the rest of Canada. From the days of Laurier, the Liberals had always maintained a close association with Quebec sentiment. With Laurier as leader from 1887 to 1919 the Liberals had become firmly entrenched in Quebec, the Conservatives being labeled the party of *les anglais*. Mackenzie King continued the tradition. Possessed not only of the Mackenzie name but of the personal qualities that enabled him to preserve the Quebec connection and to revive the national party, he was able to secure as his successor in 1948 another Quebecois, Louis St. Laurent. A lawyer able to think about the Quebec civil code in French and corporate law in English, St. Laurent might not be in the *Rouge* tradition, or even be a politician, but at least he was a Quebecois. But his successor in 1957 had to be from English Canada.

While Quebec remained loyal to the aging St. Laurent in the 1957 election, many English Canadians had been swept off their feet by the rhetoric of Diefenbaker. Stung by their defeat, the Liberals had to choose a new leader. They could have selected Paul Martin, a Franco-Ontarian fluent in French, and a seasoned politician who seemed to remember the name of everyone he encountered. However, the party convention decided to elect the virtually unilingual Lester Pearson, the hero of Suez. Quebec's support, it seemed, could be taken for granted. A cosmopolitan public servant, diplomat and now minister, Pearson was admirably suited for Canada as the outward-looking middle power over which St. Laurent had presided. But Canada's role as an important middle power was coming to an end.

Pearson started out ill-equipped to deal with the turbulent Quebec of the 1960s. Without political roots in the province he was at first derisively referred to as "Monsieur Personne" (Mr. Nobody). Without a francophone at the helm in Ottawa, the Liberals could no longer rely on the Quebec vote in another election.

The election came very soon. In 1958, having broadened his support through numerous popular economic and social reforms, Diefenbaker decided to consolidate his position. This time Quebec jumped on the bandwagon and voted Conservative. Indeed, the province returned a larger number of Conservative MPs than at any time since 1887.

However, Diefenbaker was no more able to galvanize the Quebec electorate than Pearson. The prime minister was unable (or perhaps unwilling) to capitalize on his success. The large batch of fifty Quebec MPs who, to everyone's surprise, were returned from Quebec was not rewarded with the fruits of office. A golden opportunity to integrate the Quebec representatives into the Conservative Party, and to restore Macdonald's carefully constructed alliance of Tories and *Bleus,* was lost.[22] John Diefenbaker was a prairie Baptist who understood Quebec even less than he understood Ontario.

Perhaps the worst thing to befall Diefenbaker was the immense size of his victory in 1958. So great was his margin over the Liberals that even without the support of the fifty Quebec members he had a majority of twenty-five. He therefore had no need to pacify his new francophone MPs. Later, as leader of the opposition, his electoral defeats (in 1963 and 1965) did nothing to improve his relationships with the Quebecois remaining in the party. Their leader finally gave up, remarking, "There is no place for a French Canadian in the party of Mr. Diefenbaker."[23]

The limitations of Mr. Diefenbaker, and indeed of the "quasi-unitary" system that had been evolving, were becoming apparent, especially in Quebec. The Ottawa of Diefenbaker and Pearson, neither of whom seemed to be at home in French or in French Canada, became alien to many Quebecois.[24] The transformation of Quebec nationalism took place when the federal government was no longer able to reach out to Quebec.

It was at this point, with Ottawa's image so anglophone, and the *Union Nationale* a spent force, that the momentous Quebec election of 1960 took place. Jean Lesage, a former federal Cabinet Minister who had not contested the (federal) 1958 election, led the Quebec provincial Liberals to victory. His revitalized party appealed to those Quebecois alienated by Duplessis, ignored by Diefenbaker and lukewarm towards Pearson. It attracted a considerable pool of talent.[25]

Two years later, in 1962, Quebec's electors were given the opportunity of voting in both a provincial and a federal election. In the provincial election they voted even more decisively than in 1960 for the Liberals, giving them sixty-three of the ninety-five seats. In the federal election, although the Quebec voters who had supported Diefenbaker in 1958 largely abandoned him, they did not all swing back to the Liberals. Instead they divided their vote between the federal Liberals, the Conservatives and the *Créditistes,* the Quebec version of the Social Credit movement that had begun in an alienated Alberta after the Depression. The *Créditistes* appealed to the religious and nationalistic rural voters in ridings where there was industry owned and managed by *les anglais*.[26] They won twenty-six seats, the Liberals thirty-five, and the Conservatives fourteen. The *Créditistes* thus deprived the Liberals of a majority. The indecisive Diefenbaker hung on to office for a further year of minority government. Yet even when the 1963 election ended his six-year term, it gave Pearson only a minority government. Pearson failed once again to win a majority in 1965.

Between the resignation of St. Laurent in 1957 and the appointment

Table 3. Liberal Members of Parliament from Quebec in the House of Commons, 1957-68

1957	62	Conservative minority government
1958	25	Conservative majority government
1962	35	Conservative minority government
1963	47	Liberal minority government
1965	56	Liberal minority government
1968	56	Liberal majority government

of Trudeau in 1968, a time when Quebec was in upheaval and demanding a new federal system, there was no strong Liberal government in Ottawa (see table 3). English Canada was trying to carry on business much as usual. French Canadians played a subordinate role in federal politics, especially under the Tories between 1957 and 1963.

However, Pearson proved to have a more easygoing and relaxed personality than Diefenbaker and as prime minister after 1963 was able to employ his considerable diplomatic talents to prevent further erosion of Quebec support for the Liberal Party. It was Pearson who set up the Royal Commission on Bilingualism and Biculturalism on taking office. Slowly, starting with the 1962 election, the Quebec electors returned to the Liberal fold, despite the absence of a Quebec lieutenant and despite the attraction of the *Créditistes* to many Quebecois.

Although he tried to find and develop a strong Quebec lieutenant comparable to Mackenzie King's Ernest Lapointe, Pearson at first employed Lionel Chevrier, a seasoned veteran of Parliament but a Franco-Ontarian. "Clearly the Liberals expected Quebec to return automatically to the fold."[27] The scandals that swirled around several Quebec MPs in the 1960s did not improve matters.

In sum, the Quiet Revolution in Quebec needs to be viewed not only against the background of Quebec and the Duplessis regime but also in the context of a Canada in transition. In the late 1950s not only was there evidence of a central government in decline but as well a crisis over Suez, which symbolized the end of Canada's traditional special relationship with Great Britain—a relationship that Diefenbaker was unable to restore, partly because Britain began to move more towards Europe and the European Community. In addition there was the pipeline affair, one of several incidents that highlighted Canada's growing dependence on the United States. For Canada, as for Britain, geography was exerting a stronger pull than history. Yet both parties appear to have ignored Quebec in selecting their leaders, and to have given little thought to the probability of Duplessis' mortality or to the pressures for modernization that would be unleashed after his death. Neither Diefenbaker nor Pearson was primarily a party manager capable of bringing all sections of Canada together. Quebec's transformation occurred, therefore, in the context not only of its own modernization and the political lag resulting from the long tenure of the *Union Nationale,* but also in the decline of federal hegemony, especially after 1957 when there was no French Canadian at the helm in Ottawa.

3   The Transformation of a Province: L'Etat du Québec, 1960

The transformation of Quebec from a province into *L'Etat du Québec* can be interpreted as a process of decolonization, a nationalist revolt against English-Canadian "imperialism" (or majority rule) by a new generation of Quebecois. Until the end of the Duplessis regime, St. Laurent's government in Ottawa was looked to for leadership and support by those liberals in Quebec who disagreed with the conservative nationalism of the *Union Nationale,* the repressive policies of Duplessis himself, and the failure of the Quebec government to provide leadership to meet the challenge of modernization. Duplessis had permitted foreign corporations to develop, and often exploit, Quebec's economy and natural resources, but he had shown no particular interest in developing a francophone economy. He had resisted federal encroachment in fields within Quebec's jurisdiction, but he had not been concerned with extending the scope of the government of Quebec.[28] Instead he had remained committed to the preservation of his province's traditional society, one in which the protection and transmission of Quebec's distinctive culture was largely the responsibility of the Church and Church-related institutions. Jehovah's Witnesses were prosecuted for challenging the established Catholic order. Communists were attacked for promoting an alien and atheistic world view.

In addition, those within French-Canadian Catholic society who questioned the wisdom of Duplessis' policies were harassed. The President of the Episcopal Commission on Social Questions, Archbishop Charbonneau of Montreal, was exiled to British Columbia after showing sympathy for the strike of asbestos workers in 1949. Father Georges-Henri Lévesque, the outspoken dean of the School of Social Sciences at Laval

University, was forced into early retirement. Pierre Elliott Trudeau, a lawyer of independent means who had also participated in the Asbestos Strike, and who later edited *Cité libre,* an independent journal of liberal views, was denied an appointment at the University of Montreal on orders from the Premier. *Le Devoir* was now edited by Henri Bourassa's son-in-law, André Laurendeau. Unable to suppress this influential liberal newspaper, at one time all the members of Duplessis' Cabinet brought libel suits against the Montreal daily.

The demise of the Duplessis regime brought to an end the era of the "division of labor" in Quebec between a francophone culture protected by the Church and a North American civilization through which the "imperialist" *anglais* dominated the economy. Even during the *Union Nationale* regime there had been a number of strikes that indicated that the French workers were no longer docile. Quebec's "colonial" status was resented by a new generation. Numerous voices were raised against the *Union Nationale* and its defensive policies. Among them were the criticisms of Pierre Trudeau and his associates at the magazine *Cité libre;* the progressive sentiments of the liberal clergy; the teaching of Father Lévesque and his colleagues in the Faculty of Social Science at Laval University, and the leaders of voluntary organizations, trade unions and even business associations, all concerned that so little leadership was offered by the party.[29] All of these expressions of concern were indications that the dominant position of the *Union Nationale* might be challenged once Duplessis left the scene unless firm action was taken to change the party's direction.

The death of Duplessis in 1959 and of Paul Sauvé in 1960 opened the way for Lesage and the Liberals. It was now clear that neither of the two pillars on which the *Union Nationale* had relied, the anglophone business community for the promotion of Quebec's economy as part of North America, and the Church for the defense of French Canada's traditions, was capable of providing the thrust that Quebec needed to meet the twin challenges of North American civilization and French Canadian culture. Only the Government of Quebec, which the Liberals now controlled, could provide the impetus for change. Instead of the old antistatism of the cultural nationalists, Quebec was now treated to the promotion of *L'Etat du Québec*.

The attitude of liberal Quebecois to government now underwent a profound change. During the Duplessis era a generation of educated young people had grown to maturity amid political inertia and corruption. Government in Ottawa, though alien in many ways to the francophones who obtained positions there, appeared to be more open, more professional, and more responsive to the needs of contemporary society than the *Union Nationale*. The replacement in Quebec of an aging Duplessis by a dynamic Lesage, and in Ottawa of the silky St. Laurent by the prickly Diefenbaker, helped to transform this image. The negative view of Quebec City became positive. At the same time the positive view of Ottawa became negative. Just as for English Canada the imperial government had been regarded first as benign and later as alien, so for French Canadians the formerly benign federal government of St. Laurent, a haven for those opposed to Duplessis, became foreign and even imperialist. Fear that this sense of alienation could lead to separatism persuaded Mr. Trudeau and two of his friends to leave Quebec for Ottawa in 1965.

4   The Sixties in Retrospect: The End of the Old Canada

The 1960s saw not only a decline in federal hegemony and the transformation of Quebec nationalism but the end of the old Canada. English Canadians who in their search for political autonomy had regarded the United States as a useful foil against the pretensions of British imperialism began to conceive of the main threat to Canada's autonomy as coming from the United States, and from an imperialism more economic than political. As we saw earlier, the new English-Canadian nationalism was given expression by writers like George Grant, who by 1965 was lamenting the passage of Canada from a colony of the United Kingdom to a satellite of the United States. Yet the two English-Canadian prime ministers who had grown up in the earlier era failed to comprehend what was happening. Diefenbaker continued to fuss over political symbols, deploring disrespect for the Crown. The more cosmopolitan Pearson appeared at times to think Canadians were a new breed of internationalists. Appropriately enough, Diefenbaker vacationed with Lord Beaverbrook in the Bahamas, Pearson with David Rockefeller in the Virgin Islands.

The 1960s brought about a change in English Canada. Though marred by de Gaulle's outburst of *Vive le Québec libre,* the centenary of Confederation was a time for reflection, in English Canada at least, on Canada's recent emergence on the world stage as a mature and influential nation. The widely acclaimed Centennial exposition, *Expo 67,* held in Montreal, brought together people from all over Canada to celebrate the achievements of what had become an admired member of the world community. *Expo 67* was neither British nor American in concept: it was distinctively and joyously Canadian. It appeared to symbolize the transformation of Canada into a state that was part of a North American civilization and also the expression of two cultures that were partners in an exciting enterprise.

Soon a further stimulus was given to Pan-Canadian sentiment. The following year the ambitions of several English-Canadian political warhorses who sought to succeed Lester Pearson as leader of the Liberal Party and prime minister were dashed at the party convention. Instead the honor went to an interesting newcomer to federal politics, Pierre Elliott Trudeau. The ideal Canadian leader, it seemed, should be a true Pan-Canadian, at ease in both languages, at home in Quebec, and preferably of mixed parentage. (No doubt he, or she, would combine French flair and panache with English self-discipline and organizing ability!)

French Canadians had also changed their outlook. They had long wanted to be emancipated from the United Kingdom; but now they discovered that they, too, had lost the external umpire. With the departure of St. Laurent, it was clearer than ever that henceforth they were to be alone in North America among a "sea of anglophones." They, too, wanted a federal leader who was Pan-Canadian in orientation, who was bilingual, and who understood Quebec.

In the early 1960s even the nationalism of Quebec had acquired something of a Pan-Canadian quality. Quebec City was no longer regarded as a backwater away from the pressures of the modern world. Instead the Quebec government became as professional as its federal counterpart and in some respects its rival. Quebec became a full partner in North American civilization, offering new approaches to the development of social services, the adaptation of political institutions, and the encouragement of the arts and architecture. The Quebec economy was integrated into the economies of Canada and the United States, its huge hydroelectric power projects being designed with a view to the export market.

However, the pull of nationalism soon prevailed. There was still concern over the need to protect the distinctive culture of Quebec. This now focused not on the faith and the Church but on the language and the education system. Television, which at first seemed to signify Quebec's acceptance of North American civilization, soon developed as a distinctive medium, providing the Quebecois with proof that they had a lively culture of their own.[30]

As always, the Quebecois wanted the best of both worlds, to be part of North American civilization and to retain their own culture. In the 1950s they had expressed these sentiments by voting for the worldly St. Laurent as prime minister and the homespun Duplessis as provincial premier. In the 1960s they appeared to opt for the wider world at both levels of government when they voted Liberal both nationally and provincially. But as we have seen, they voted Liberal nationally with the greatest enthusiasm only when there was a Quebecois candidate for the position of prime minister (many of them electing *Créditistes* who believed in the doctrine of Social Credit first implemented in Alberta in the 1930s). Provincially, they made clear that there were limits to their Pan-Canadianism as early as 1966. In that election they not only returned the supposedly discredited *Union Nationale* to power but also began to show an interest in separatism. In 1968 Trudeau won the same number of seats in Quebec as Pearson three years earlier.

It has been suggested that provincial politics in Quebec center very much on the personality of the candidates, especially the leaders.[31] If this is so, then it helps to explain the continued success of Duplessis. After his death, there was a gradual diminution in votes cast for the *Union Nationale*. Following the emergence of the *Parti Québecois* in the 1970 election, the party rapidly declined, with support dropping from 41 percent in 1966 to 5 percent in 1973.

By the end of the sixties, the traditional picture of a "feudal" Quebec, once widely held in North America, was dated.[32] The province described by Michel Brunet as antistatist, agricultural and messianic, was no more. *L'Etat du Québec* had taken over from the Church and the English-speaking business community; an industrial and even postindustrial society was firmly established; and concern for the French language had long since replaced a belief in a spiritual mission.

The 1960s had seen the transformation of a Quebec with its traditional cultural nationalism of two solitudes, where the premier occasionally tangled with the federal government, into a society in which the government of Quebec, whatever its political color, found itself continually at war with the federal authorities over spheres of jurisdiction. In Ottawa, the hegemony of the federal government had given way to a succession of minority governments. A weakened government of Canada had to deal with the fervent new nationalism in Quebec.

Neither Diefenbaker nor Pearson was opposed in principle to the aims of the Quiet Revolution. In his own way, each attempted to recognize "the French fact." Diefenbaker appointed the distinguished soldier, General Georges Vanier, as the first French-Canadian governor general. He also ordered checks issued by the government of Canada to be printed in both languages. Pearson encouraged senior federal public servants to learn French.

Yet neither these nor other federal measures had much to do with the main concerns of the Quebec nationalists, who were preoccupied with the inferior role of the French language (and therefore of French employees), particularly in business dominated by *les anglais*. The aim of the nationalists was to establish French as the working language of Quebec.

Not that the nationalists were always as inward-looking as their critics suggested. Quebec's traditional belief in its spiritual mission had encouraged large numbers of its sons and daughters to serve in the mission field abroad. With the secularization of Quebec society, some of this zeal found its way into the political arena. There was now a considerable interest not so much in foreign missions as in Third World politics. But whereas Diefenbaker and Pearson looked to the Commonwealth as the main stage on which Canada performed its international role, Quebec's interest focussed on the French-speaking countries of the world (*francophonie*). These countries were not part of the Commonwealth. Quebec demanded the right to be represented by its own delegates at international conferences of francophone states. English Canada reacted strongly to these claims to quasi-sovereign status, claims that at least served to illustrate Canada's traditional bias towards the English-speaking world.[33] (Even university professors specializing in Canadian studies were not expected to be bilingual or to have spent any time in Quebec.)

The efforts of successive federal governments to meet the challenge of *L'Etat du Quebec* were not entirely in vain. By the end of the 1960s the old image of Canada as an "Anglo-American society" had been discarded. Gone was the old Canada from Confederation onward in which English was the language spoken by the elites and in which the legitimacy of English as the official language was sustained by the principle of majority rule. As a result of the Official Languages Act, French was in principle treated as the equal of English, at least in the federal public service. For a time after 1968 it even seemed as though a bilingual

Canadian elite was in the making, and that under Trudeau the system was capable of adaptation to meet Quebec's requirements.

5 Pan-Canadianism and Its Limitations, 1968–76

Pan-Canadian dualism replaced the principle—although not always the practice—of majority rule in the 1960s. In saying "Canada is in fact a country based on the coexistence of these two cultures, and is the better for it," James Mallory expressed the new positive approach of English-speaking Canadians to a bicultural Canada.[34] Successive reports of the Royal Commission on Bilingualism and Biculturalism kept the public aware that a new Canada had emerged.

The year 1965, when the "B & B Commission" first reported on the crisis in Canada, was a turning point in Pan-Canadianism, the year that Pierre Trudeau and his friends Gérard Pelletier and Jean Marchand decided to enter the federal Parliament and to throw in their lot with Canada. Three years later, Trudeau's appointment as prime minister signified a nationwide acceptance of a new style of politics in which French Canadians claimed to be equal in a way that had not been possible under previous prime ministers. While the voters in the Atlantic provinces, New Brunswick excepted, showed less enthusiasm for Trudeau in 1968 than for Pearson in 1965, a larger percentage of Westerners voted for Trudeau than had supported his Liberal predecessor.

When, under Trudeau, legislation was passed making French an official language, the wrong done to French-speaking Canadians after the 1837 Rebellion seemed at last to have been redressed. When in April 1970 the Liberals were returned to office once more in Quebec, it appeared that the decade that had begun with the defeat of the *Union Nationale* had ended with the party's final defeat by a Liberal Party committed to the federal system. Judging by the seventy-two seats the Liberal Party won in the Quebec legislature, Pan-Canadian dualism appeared to be as triumphant in Quebec as in Ottawa where the Trudeau regime was making it clear that French Canadians were capable of filling any portfolio in the federal government, including finance, industry, trade and commerce, and external affairs. Even the Conservatives had come to accept the new Pan-Canadian order, replacing the peppery Diefenbaker by the courtly Robert Stanfield, a man who would have no truck with those who still believed that Canada was an English-speaking country.

For a brief while in 1970 it appeared that the new Pan-Canadian dispensation might falter and that Quebec's peaceful political nationalism might give way to a new revolutionary nationalism: violence erupted once again in Montreal. The kidnapping of British Trade Commissioner James Cross and the kidnapping and murder of a Quebec Cabinet minister, Pierre Laporte, was the climax of a long period of sporadic terrorism that had begun with the bombing of mail boxes in the English-speaking part of Montreal in 1963. To some extent the violence was a reflection of the unrest that other countries had experienced in the 1960s. Some French Canadians identified with the American blacks, and others compared Quebec to Algeria where the indigenous people had ousted a million French *colons*. The *Front de Libération du Québec* (FLQ), which perpetrated the kidnappings and assassination in Montreal, was reminiscent of the organization (the FLN) that had been instrumental in forcing the French settlers to leave Algeria. (There were some who suspected that de Gaulle, having had to accept Algeria's self-determination in 1962, hoped to compensate for France's humiliation by encouraging the Quebecois to treat *les anglais* as *colons*.)

However, Quebec was not Algeria and Canada was not France. The appearance of troops on the streets of Montreal was a reminder not only of federal authority but of the fact that in normal times Canada's armed forces were invisible. Quebec was not comparable to Algeria or Ireland. It was an autonomous province that elected its own francophone government and was able to wield considerable influence over the government of Canada. Unless and until a nonviolent solution to Quebec's problems, using the electoral process, proved impossible, it seemed at the very least premature to adopt a strategy of assassination and rebellion. The "October crisis" of 1970 demonstrated that the Quebecois had not reached the stage when violence seemed to be the only way of achieving their goals.

Mr. Trudeau's handling of the crisis by invoking the War Measures Act could be (and was) criticized as an overreaction to what proved to be a small group of activists organized in separate cells. But at the time no one was sure how numerous the terrorists might be, or how sympathetic the people might become if the federal government seemed indecisive. Trudeau, like President Kennedy in the Cuban crisis two years after his election, was an untested leader. Indeed Trudeau was an intellectual with no military experience at all. His firm policy in what could have become a nasty situation won him the support of the vast majority of the population in both English and French Canada.[35] The Pan-Canadians had met their first test of leadership and passed.

However, the victory of Pan-Canadianism over the tradition of majority rule and the threat of revolutionary violence was not the whole story. Just when the Pan-Canadians appeared to be winning the battle for Canada, they began to be challenged by a new form of nationalism from Quebec. In 1966, a year after the "three wise men" had departed for Ottawa (and the Liberal government of Quebec had been defeated by the *Union Nationale*), 9 percent of the electors voted for one or the other of two separatist parties. With its defeat, the Liberal Party of Quebec became more conservative and after its 1967 party convention some of its more radical members, for whom the Quiet Revolution was only the beginning, joined the separatists. In 1968, the year of Trudeau's appointment as prime minister, the various nonviolent separatist movements came together to form the *Parti Québecois*. They chose as their leader René Lévesque, Minister of Natural Resources in the Lesage government until its 1966 defeat, and leader of those who bolted the party in 1967 when it declined to support their proposal for an independent Quebec.

Why could Quebec not be satisfied with the Pan-Canadianism of the new prime minister? Why did the Quebecois in provincial elections reject in turn the *Union Nationale* in 1970 and the Liberals in 1976, preferring instead a separatist party that had come into existence as a rival to Trudeau in 1968?

There are a number of possible explanations for the apparent inadequacy of Pan-Canadianism as a policy in English Canada and in Quebec. In the first place, though the federal government was able to declare French an official language throughout Canada, in practice its authority was confined to the federal public service, especially in Ottawa. Most Canadians, however, lived outside the national capital region and were dependent on their provincial governments. Second, in Quebec itself, the federal government was powerless to transform society, for example by curbing the power exercised by *les anglais* over private business and the language of work. Trudeau himself represented a largely English-speaking constituency in Montreal. The provincial Liberal Party had traditionally close ties with the English-speaking business community of that metropolis.

Quebec and the Rest of Canada   325

In sum, the more radical Quebecois decided that a new party was necessary, one outside the influence of the anglophone business community and willing to put the interests of *L'Etat du Québec* first. Hence the swift rise of the *Parti Québecois,* a coalition of nationalist, socialist, and separatist movements under the radical Réne Lévesque, a leader as charismatic as Trudeau himself. The policy of the *Parti Québecois* was not simply *maîtres chez nous* ("masters of our own house") or "Quebec for Quebecois" against the federal government: it was also directed against the province's anglophone community. Its aim was to transform this "psychic majority" into a minority group comparable in some ways to other groups that were not purely Quebecois. To the political nationalism of the Lesage Liberals was added a neocultural nationalism that concentrated on *Québec pour les Québécois*.

Partly in response to these developments in Quebec, the Pan-Canadian fervor, which outside Quebec had reached a climax with Expo 67 and the election of Trudeau, began to wane, thus adding force to the nationalist arguments of the *Parti Québecois*. After four years in office, Trudeau (like Diefenbaker) lost his majority. Between the election of 1972 and his return to majority government in 1974, Trudeau depended on the support of the New Democratic Party, an English-speaking social-democratic party which had little sympathy for the new Quebec nationalism. In the West there was a growing alienation from a Liberal government that appeared to be dominated by central Canada, and especially French Canada. Because the West chose to elect very few Liberals to Parliament, there were almost no Western MPs available as Liberal cabinet ministers.

In the fall of 1971 the Liberals, probably inadvertently, dealt a blow to Quebec by implementing a proposal of the B & B Commission to recognize the role of other ethnic groups. Canada, especially English Canada, was becoming very much a pluralist society. Many of the recommendations of the Royal Commission on Bilingualism and Biculturalism in support of the French-speaking minority had already been implemented, notably the recognition of French in the Official Languages Act. But although Canada then became officially bilingual, it was not yet officially bicultural. In April 1971 the Royal Commission wound up its activities without having reached an agreement on biculturalism. A few months later, partly in response to the commission's recommendations regarding other ethnic groups in Canada, and possibly in search of votes among New Canadians, the federal government announced a new policy: multiculturalism.

While this policy was well-received among those for whom it was intended, and involved modest programs by no means comparable to the expense of bilingualism, multiculturalism was regarded by many Quebecois as an indication that the cherished notion of Canada as a country of two founding peoples, of which one was French, was being abandoned by the Trudeau government. The provincial Liberal government, for its part, also appeared hesitant in meeting the demands of francophones for a wider use of the French language. The Quebec Liberals still depended on anglophone support and the English-speaking community of Montreal had retained its position partly because of the political assimilation of New Canadians into the anglophone community. Montreal's ethnic groups favored multiculturalism.

The policies of the English-speaking provinces on bilingualism also hurt the Pan-Canadian cause. The provinces remained unwilling to match the bilingualism of the federal government and Quebec, and Ontario was particularly opposed to the recognition of French through an official languages act. To many Quebecois it began to seem clear that if the other provinces remained unilingual, Article 133 of the Constitution should no longer require Quebec, alone of the provinces, to be officially bilingual. And if the federal government could establish bilingualism, making French the equal of English, then surely in areas within Quebec's own jurisdiction French should become the working language of francophones, and French culture accepted as equal to English. It was to this growing sentiment that the *Parti Québecois* appealed.

In sum, although Trudeau's successful election in 1968 appeared to symbolize the victory of Pan-Canadianism, his success was limited. By the time bilingualism was introduced the historical moment for its acceptance had passed. Pan-Canadianism turned out to be attractive to English Canada only so long as it kept Quebec pacified, encouraged French Canadians to enter the public service in larger numbers, and enabled the Quebecois to acquire an education and a secular world view that enabled them fully to participate like other Canadians in North American civilization. It was not favored when it discriminated against unilingual English Canadians, members of the country's majority. In the competition for jobs and for promotion to other jobs, English Canadians did not like to be treated as inferior because they did not speak

French; hence the widespread popular opposition to Pan-Canadianism as an attempt "to ram French down our throats." As so often before in Canada's history, the Pan-Canadians were caught in the crossfire between English and French Canada.

Nor was the October crisis of 1970 an unmixed blessing for the Pan-Canadian cause. The French-language newspapers in Quebec avoided taking sides on the issue.[36] A number of leading Quebecois, including René Lévesque and Claude Ryan, editor of *Le Devoir,* publicly endorsed negotiations with the terrorists. Trudeau and his associates were portrayed less as Pan-Canadians protecting the best interests of Quebec than as *vendus* acting on behalf of the Canadian (i.e., English-Canadian) establishment. The Quebec Liberal government of Robert Bourassa, which had requested the deployment of troops, was accused of vacillation. In any case it was caught in the middle between the nationalist intellectuals in Quebec and the Pan-Canadians who controlled the federal government.

The early 1970s did not, therefore, see the consolidation of Pan-Canadianism. Despite Trudeau's electoral victory in 1968, the Official Languages Act of 1969, the Quebec Liberals' electoral victory of 1970 and the resolute handling of the October crisis of that year, the tide was not running in favor of the Pan-Canadians. It is true that in 1971 at a First Ministers' Conference in Victoria, British Columbia, agreement was at last reached on patriation of the BNA Act and an amending formula, but when Premier Bourassa returned home his acceptance of the so-called "Victoria Charter" was overruled by his colleagues. Pan-Canadianism also received a setback with the death of André Laurendeau, cochairman of the B & B Commission, and later with the failure of the commission to reach agreement on a final report. It was because the objections to the idea of Canada as a country of only two cultures were so vociferous that in 1971 the federal government had embarked on a program of multiculturalism. Designed, its opponents suggested, to encourage "New Canadians" to remain loyal to the Liberal Party, the policy of multiculturalism was hardly attractive to French Canadians.

A third setback occurred in 1972 when Parliament's Joint Committee on the Constitution issued its report favoring reform. A minority of its members dissented from the committee's findings, and no action was taken by the federal government on the committee's recommendations. Soon afterwards an election was called and for two years the Liberals formed a minority government. Needing the support of the New Democratic Party, the Liberals played down the subject of constitutional reform.

Despite these setbacks, by the mid-1970s Trudeau's Pan-Canadianism appeared to English Canadians to be firmly established. There were no more violent incidents in Quebec, not even the sporadic bombings that had taken place between 1963 and 1970. The Quebec Liberals had won the 1973 election overwhelmingly, with 102 of the 110 seats. The leader of the *Parti Québecois,* René Lévesque, once again failed to win election. By early 1976 Quebec was becoming excited at the prospect of hosting the spectacular Olympic games that summer. Trudeau could look back on eight years of government during which French Canadians had become more conspicuous and more numerous in the federal Cabinet than ever before. The federal public service had managed to come to terms with French as an official language. Early in 1976 Trudeau went so far as to declare separatism a dead issue.

6   Toward Sovereignty-Association? 1976–80

However, by the end of 1976 the *Parti Québecois* had swept into power in Quebec. Although it downplayed the separatist issue during the election (indicating that Trudeau had not been so far off the mark), its victory persuaded many people, especially party members, that it was time to promote independence. The whole future of Canada was put into question. It may have been coincidence, but the Canadian dollar began its long slide in value. From being above par it gradually declined to under eighty cents in American currency. Pan-Canadians tried to console themselves with the fact that not all those who voted for the *Parti Québecois* were *indépendantistes:* many simply wanted a change of government after the corruption of the Liberal regime.

There were several reasons for the victory of the *Parti Québecois,* not least of which was an ominous incident that occurred in the summer of 1976. This seemed to indicate that the passage of the Official Languages Act, and the proclamation of Canada as officially a bilingual country, was just a sham. Nationalists had long pointed out that what mattered was not bilingualism in Ottawa, still less in Alberta and British Columbia, but the use of French as the working language in Quebec. In 1976 French-speaking air traffic controllers (ATC) employed by the federal government at Quebec airports complained that they were compelled to use only English, even when speaking to French-speaking pilots. Failing to obtain satisfaction they went on strike.

The ATC strike was an interesting phenomenon because it indicated the frailty of the Pan-Canadians' hold on the Canadian public. As in the conscription crisis, English Canadians forgot their differences. Faced by a francophone challenge to the status quo they rallied to the defense of English-speaking pilots and air traffic controllers, demanding that only English be used. They argued that English was the accepted language of international aviation and that the use of French as a second language was a hazard. French Canadians also forgot their differences and came together in defense of *"les gens de l'air."* It was a clear case, once again, of the English-Canadian majority confronting the French-Canadian minority.

As so often happened on such occasions, the federal government was caught in the middle, and in the end had to bow to English-Canadian pressure. It did so by issuing an order forbidding the use of French in air traffic control, thus confirming the nationalists' argument that the Official Languages Act did nothing to promote the use of French in Quebec. Citing disagreement with the government's handling of the disputes, Jean Marchand resigned his portfolio as environment minister. But as similar actions had shown in the conscription crisis of 1942, resignation from the Cabinet had no immediate effect on government policy. The federal government did, however, establish a commission of inquiry to report on the possible use of French at Quebec airports.

Some years later the commission made its report. It noted that while English was the international language of aviation it was not the only language employed. In Paris, for example, French was also used. The commission therefore recommended that French as well as English be spoken in Quebec. By the time the report was published in 1979 the Conservatives were in office. Prime Minister Joe Clark immediately accepted the report and subsequently both English and French were acceptable at Quebec airports. No accidents occurred as a result of this policy.

One consequence of the decision was that unilingual English-speaking air traffic controllers in Quebec had to be transferred to other provinces. In other words, the strike was not only over the right of francophone federal public servants to use French in their day-to-day work. It was over the right of anglophones to continue to operate unilingually in Quebec in the federal service. The bilingual francophones got their way: the unilingual anglophones lost.[37]

How far the strike influenced the Quebec electorate later in 1976 it is difficult to say, but it cannot have done the *Parti Québecois* any harm. The following year, the new *Parti Québecois* government obtained much public support for a unilingual Quebec. It sponsored Bill 101, which replaced the province's traditional commitment to bilingualism with the recognition of French as sole official language. In other words, within a decade of the federal government's becoming officially bilingual, Quebec became unilingual, in French. However, it should also be noted that this did not come about until the other provinces (except New Brunswick) had made it clear that they refused to follow the example of the federal government and Quebec: they all remained officially unilingual, in English.

The success of the *Parti Québecois* confirmed the nationalists in their belief that ultimate victory for the cause of independence was inevitable. Although the party won only seven seats in its first election in 1970, it secured 23 percent of the vote, and with only six seats in 1973 it obtained 30 percent. Finally, in 1976 it won 71 seats and received 41 percent of the votes. While older voters preferred the Liberals, the younger generation voted for the *Parti Québecois*. With time and patience the *Parti Québecois* would be acceptable not only because it provided good government (which at first it certainly did), but because it offered the possibility of independence. No doubt it was too soon to expect a clear majority of Quebecois to vote for independence, especially as 20 percent of the population were English-speaking and opposed to separation. But they might at least favor the start of negotiations with the federal government to assess the feasibility of a new political system that replaced federalism with some form of sovereignty-association.

However, just as Pan-Canadianism had received a setback when things appeared to be going well, so separatism began to encounter unexpected obstacles. For one thing, the very success of Bill 101 in establishing French as the working language in Quebec, and the acquiescence of the anglophones in the demotion of their language, reduced the tension over language (and of course jobs). The generation of anglophones born after 1960 took the new Quebec for granted and accepted the fact that they lived in a predominantly francophone society. Many of them learned to be bilingual at school.

Support for sovereignty-association was not as great as had been expected. Between the time when the date of the referendum was announced in the fall of 1979 and its execution in May 1980, Ottawa's Pan-Canadians rallied to the support of the Quebec Liberals. They pointed out that the Pan-Canadian perspective made all Quebecois citizens of a vast country. The Rocky Mountains their ancestors had explored (to say nothing of Western oil) still remained part of their heritage as Canadians. Sovereignty-association would create a separate Quebec, cutting off the Quebecois from their continental patrimony.

In the end, the Pan-Canadians won by a margin of 60 percent to 40. Families and friends had been divided on the issue, and even among the Quebecois support for remaining a part of Canada was surprisingly strong. In only 16 of the 110 ridings did a majority of voters express a preference for separation. However, nearly half of the francophone population had voted *Oui*.

7 Post-Referendum Quebec

Although the referendum was a traumatic experience not only for Quebec but for all Canadians, especially the francophones living outside Quebec, it managed to lay to rest certain ghosts of the past, notably those of 1760 and 1837 (if not 1970). Now, no one questioned the right of the people of Quebec to determine their own future. Consequently, henceforth there was no need to rebel violently against the regime. For the first time, but not necessarily for the last, Quebecois had been offered the opportunity of establishing their own political system. The nationalists could no longer take as their starting point the finality of the Conquest. Therefore they could not insist that the province's shackles could be removed only by rebellion.

In the early 1980s the *Parti Québécois* seemed to lose some of its momentum. Its aura of incorruptibility was tarnished by a number of scandals involving some of its members. Its claim to treat all Quebecois fairly was damaged not only by the harsh implementation of Bill 101 but by its draconian treatment of public servants. Salary increases promised before the referendum were withdrawn three years later. Indeed, the government rolled back some salaries by as much as 20 percent (for three months) early in 1983. A final blow to *péquiste* hopes that independence was inevitable was the discovery that some of the younger generation did not share their passionate commitment to sovereignty-association. To their surprise, the *Péquistes* found themselves labeled as an aging cohort sandwiched between an older and a younger generation. And, like the Liberals before them, they were apparently unable to remain uncorrupted by power.

Participation in Canadian government and politics continued to have certain advantages for people in Quebec. When the provincial government became too authoritarian or too corrupt Ottawa always provided escape. Moreover, the federal system provided an alternative source of patronage. Liberals out of power in Quebec could still be recipients of the patronage of the federal Liberals. (This helps to explain Bourassa's somewhat curious election slogan of "profitable federalism.")

Although the referendum took the wind out of the *Péquistes'* sails, it did not mean that Quebec had finally accepted Pan-Canadianism instead of sovereignty-association. In the 1981 provincial election, the *Parti Québecois* won no fewer than 80 of the 122 seats, leaving the Liberals with only 42 (the *Union Nationale* disappearing from view). The PQ's share of the vote continued to rise, reaching 49 percent, and it now commanded the support of a majority of the francophone voters. Quebec was still sending warning signals to the rest of Canada. Quebec remained as nationalist as ever.

One thing was certain: There was no way the government of Canada could topple the provincial government in Quebec. Such a treatment was now a thing of the past.[38] Nowadays the Quebec electorate was sufficiently politicized to be able to make up its own mind which party it wished to see in office at the federal and provincial level. In 1970 Mr. Trudeau had indicated the limitations of the federal government when he had been unwilling to deploy troops unless officially requested to do so by Quebec. And much as the federal government disliked Bill 101, it was unwilling to use its formal constitutional powers of reservation and disallowance. In this sense Canada had become more federal. People in every province now took it for granted that the composition of their provincial government was their responsibility and no one else's. They enjoyed the right to elect one party in Ottawa and another in their own provincial capital.

It would seem that many Quebecois still saw certain advantages in the federal system. For the more idealistic francophones it helped to guard their freedoms. For the realists, one level of government could be played against the other: they did not want to have to choose, and choose finally, between them. This may explain why in 1970 Quebec recoiled against the use of force by the FLQ, and why in 1980 many of the Quebecois resented being asked to make a choice between Canada and Quebec through referendum. As always, there was a preference for gradual evolution. Federalism depended on unresolved contradictions—which may help to explain why a Marxist theory based on the resolution of contradictions never took hold in federal states like Canada and the United States. Certainly most Canadians, whether English or French, preferred to keep their options open.

8 Toward a Canadian Dialectic?

The basic concept of federalism is a contradiction. It is a contradiction between unity on the one hand and diversity on the other, between nation and province. It is dialectical: the thesis and the antithesis give us a synthesis. This process is constantly with us in federalism, constantly unpredictable, but always expected and always prepared for if the federalism works.—Ray Forrester, *The Future of Federalism*

After decades of argument, Canada in the 1980s remained a "peaceable kingdom." It seemed almost to thrive on the contradictions underlying so much of its conflict. These contradictions appeared capable of continuing indefinitely, being submerged and then reemerging, with one part or another of the contradiction dominant. Canada's philosophers had long been aware of the contradictions in their environment, and had been reluctant to press arguments to their conclusions, because they knew that the contradictions could not be resolved. Hence the philosophical federalism which, as we saw in Chapter 2, characterized Canadian philosophy.

The victory of the *Parti Québecois* suggested that there might after all be a dialectical explanation of Canada's history. This was especially attractive to Quebec intellectuals. They discerned a conservative nationalism opposed after 1960 by a liberal nationalism, which in 1976 led to a resolution of this contradiction by the socialist nationalism of the PQ.

With the unprecedented decision to hold a referendum on Quebec's future in Canada, the *Parti Québecois* attempted to address one of these contradictions. In effect it asked the Quebecois to abandon federalism with its two conflicting orders of government in favor of a single, unitary system based on Quebec. The unwillingness of a majority of the voters to endorse this resolution of the Canada–Quebec conflict would seem to indicate that many Quebecois, like other Canadians, preferred an untidy federal system with two governments at loggerheads. In other words, they were comfortable with simple contradictions (or dyads) and saw no reason to transform them into complex triads of theses and antitheses that had to be resolved through a higher synthesis. They preferred to travel hopefully rather than to arrive dialectically at an unsatisfactory destination.

A good illustration of Canada's unwillingness to commit itself to a specific option is the reluctance to make any sharp change in the role of the Monarchy. For example, in 1972 the Special Joint Committee of the Senate and the House of Commons on the Constitution reported on the future of the Monarchy as follows:

> The majority of the members of the Committee would prefer a Canadian as head of state who would no longer represent a Monarch beyond the seas but would assume office for an established period of years following an affirmative vote of Parliament. We therefore support the evolutionary process by which the governor general has been granted more functions as the head of state in Canada.
>
> However, in the present climate of Canadian opinion any sharp change would probably be an unduly divisive step. As far as we are able to measure, Canadians are about equally divided between those who favor and those who oppose the Monarchy, with the proponents generally being older, and the opponents generally younger.
>
> In such circumstances, therefore, the Committee does not recommend any change in the Monarchy at the present time, but eventually the question of retaining or abolishing it will have to be decided by a clear consultation with the Canadian people.[39]

In 1980 the Quebec Liberal Party went no further. Having stated that a majority of Quebecois, including the authors of *A New Canadian Federation* themselves, favored abolishing the Monarchy, the report continued: "However, we do not consider that the issue has achieved such importance as to justify it being considered among the matters to be urgently reviewed. Furthermore, we respect the affection many Canadians have for this tradition."[40]

In a statement on the Monarchy, the government of Ontario declared its complete opposition to any change whatsoever in the status of the Crown. The government of Quebec, when putting forward its proposals for sovereignty-association in 1979, said nothing at all about the Monarchy. None of the statements made reference to the role of the Crown in the Canadian political system as a federation. Consequently there was no discussion of the extent to which the continuation of the prerogative power, traditionally associated with imperial federalism and still exercised by both orders of government, prevented Canada from adopting the principles of constitutional federalism. Since the Constitution Act of 1982, the Monarchy can be abolished, but only with the unanimous consent of the provinces. Meanwhile, Canadians will keep on traveling toward their unknown destination.

The dialectical explanation of Canada's evolution, one that is bent on resolving the country's various contradictions, appeared to have its limitations. This becomes apparent from an examination of the interaction of Canada's three successive civilizations.

When in the early 1970s it began to seem as though there might be a dialectical explanation of Canada's transformation from a British colony into an independent state and then, apparently, into an American dependency, the title of Lower's history of Canada was parodied as *From Colony to Nation to Colony*.[41] But the relationship of Canada to the three world civilizations of which it has been part cannot be explained dialectically. There were important qualitative differences in the impact of the three civilizations.

French civilization manifested itself as an absolutist and colonial *ancien régime*, a form of rule that was formally rejected by the British Government in 1791 when representative institutions were introduced. Canada's first civilization has become irrelevant as an explanation of twentieth-century Canada. As we saw in Chapter 1, all that remains of France in Quebec is its culture, not its civilization.

British civilization, its successor, remained influential throughout the nineteenth century. Indeed, it is impossible to do full justice to Canada's political development without recognizing that it was a colony and its autonomy limited, especially in external affairs. However, once the First World War brought to an end the imperialist era, Canada established its independence from the United Kingdom. Although the pace of evolution was slow, it was irreversible. Certain elements of British civilization survived, notably the Monarchy and the Westminster parliamentary tradition. But in general it was British culture, not British civilization, that persisted.

There can be little doubt that by 1950 Canada had become part of a North American civilization dominated by the United States. However, the United States lacked the political instruments to impose its will on Canada after the manner of the old colonial powers. The extent to which Canada was independent of American influence was hotly debated in Canada, but there can be no question that the country's formal political independence from the United States was regarded as important. English Canadians would not have been so concerned about the possibility of Quebec separating itself from the rest of Canada had they not regarded a declaration of independence significant. Canada's relationship with the United States was different from its relationship with France under the *ancien régime* and with Britain as part of the British Empire. It was possible to speak of the "economic imperialism" of the United States, but that imperialism was qualitatively different from the political imperialism experienced by Canada in the past. This means that it is superficial to see an imperialist dialectic at work in Canada, with the French Empire as thesis, the British as antithesis, and the American "empire" as synthesis.

The older model of Canada as emerging from colony to nation was not wrong. It was simply outmoded and inadequate. Canada had now to be explained not in terms of its relationship with the United Kingdom, the Empire, and the Commonwealth, but in terms of the role played by the United States. Moreover, whereas Canadians had been united in their goal of autonomy from the United Kingdom, they were much more divided over other more recent issues. These ranged from the challenge of continentalism (the relationship with the United States), regionalism (the relationship of central Canada with the other provinces), and dualism (the role of Quebec in the political system).[42]

It is not true that "memorable" political history came to an end between the wars with the resolution of the relationship with Britain. Canada's political development merely changed the nature of its history.

An alternative to the dialectical approach was a view of Canada's future that drew an analogy with Canada's past and to conclude that just as Canada emancipated itself from the United Kingdom, so Quebec would inevitably evolve into a separate state, independent of Canada. Then, presumably, parts or all of a partitioned English Canada would be tempted to join the United States, thus fulfilling the dreams of those who signed the Declaration of Independence. While such a view was not without its proponents, it assumed an unjustified logic of development. Instead, as we saw in Chapters 2 and 3, there was a "philosophical federalism," a willingness to stake out different positions, but a disinclination to insist on the adoption of one of them to the exclusion of the others. For example, in reviewing four very different interpretations of Canada's culture, David Bell concluded, "these four perspectives complement each other. Any one of them alone is insufficient. Yet taken together, they illuminate the complexity and richness of a political culture."[43] According to this interpretation of Canada's "development," different explanations were offered for the country's contradictions. But Canada survived because of a gentleman's agreement to live and let live, to pursue arguments but never to their logical conclusion, and to trust that in life things would somehow work out. The hallmark of a British politician was that he muddled through: a successful Canadian man of affairs possessed an ability to procrastinate.

9 Limitations of Philosophical Federalism

Were Quebec to declare its independence it would mean the end of philosophical federalism. But it would not mean that Canada had evolved dialectically. A declaration of independence would be a departure from Canada's traditional assertion of authority bit by bit. Nor would the parting with the rest of Canada be quite so amiable as Canada's gradual separation from the United Kingdom. Nor would English Canada necessarily join the United States.

Philosophical federalism may have been unable to explain Canada's contradictions. The dialectic may have its limitations when applied to Canada. Even so, Canada does seem to be a country of contradictions or dyads. It is by examining these that we may better understand the country's predicament.

The American Revolution versus Loyalty to the Crown

In this dyad, the thesis was the decision of the American colonists to revolt against the Crown. Its antithesis consisted of the unwillingness of the more remote British North American colonies to join the revolutionaries, the migration of many American Tories northwards, and the establishment in Canada of what has been called, perhaps misleadingly, a "counterrevolutionary" tradition.[44] In Canada it is called the loyalist tradition, inasmuch as it was the antithesis of the America revolutionary thesis.

There could be no synthesis of American principles and Canada's monarchical tradition. It is true that there were always some Canadians, for example those who signed the Annexation Manifesto in 1849, who were willing to contemplate absorption into the United States. But in general, Canada resisted absorption into a continental community.[45] Most Canadians remained loyal to the Crown. Insofar as there was a model for Canadian government, whether federal or provincial, it was the Parliament at Westminster.[46] In Ontario, English Canada's heartland, the Conservative Party, which became the governing party after 1943, remained fully committed to the Monarchy as an institution, retaining the Union Jack in the quarter of the provincial flag.

Yet while there could be no synthesis of the American and English-Canadian philosophical traditions—the American Revolution and its liberal ideology always being unacceptable—the loyalist tradition became attenuated. It had few roots in Western Canada or Quebec. Some, particularly Westerners, questioned the assumption that the political beliefs of Canadians were determined forever by those who had lost power in the American Revolution. Certainly, the loyalist tradition was not strong enough to determine federal policies. Even in the days of Queen Victoria's British Empire, when Sir John A. Macdonald and the Conservatives reigned in Ottawa, the pressures for Canadian autonomy were irresistible. Imperial federation was rejected. With the rise of the Liberal Party to power after 1896, and the later appointment of William Lyon Mackenzie's grandson as prime minister, the movement towards autonomy gathered further momentum.

Colonialism versus Canadian Autonomy

A second dyad consisted of Canada as a nineteenth-century British colony in conflict with the demand for political autonomy. In 1848 this contradiction seemed to be resolved by the granting of responsible government to various colonies of British North America. But the principle of responsible government contradicted the whole notion of imperial rule. Over the years, as imperialism was gradually eliminated, Canada became autonomous. However, unlike the United States, Canada never declared its independence. Instead it remained a Monarchy and a Dominion, with opinion divided over whether the Monarchy implied a vestige of colonialism. There were those who presumed that the country would one day be not only autonomous but an independent republic.

Westminster Parliamentarianism versus Constitutional Federalism

It is possible to discern both a thesis and antithesis in the Confederation settlement. The thesis was the Westminster parliamentary system with its many conventions, and the antithesis was the written constitution and the federal distribution of powers associated with constitutional federalism. It has been customary to regard Canada's "parliamentary federalism" as a synthesis of these two principles. But as we saw in Chapter 5, what was established in 1867 was really imperial federalism. While by 1982 there had been introduced a number of elements associated with constitutional federalism, it was still not clear whether the vacuum left by the removal of the external umpire was to be filled by some form of constitutional federalism.

Majority Rule versus Dualism

One element in this dyad was the "representation by population" proposed by the Grits (Liberals) in Upper Canada before Confederation. The other was the dualism of the Union period that was defended by the French Canadians in Lower Canada. Confederation was expected to provide an acceptable resolution of this conflict through federalism and the distribution of powers. It did not. Instead there were two interpretations of the federal principle. The French Canadians interpreted Confederation as a new form of dualism. English Canadians accepted federalism to the extent that it was compatible with majority rule. The English-speaking provinces did not share Quebec's notion of dualism, preferring to think of federalism as involving provincial rights and regional representation in the Senate. But Quebec had no special status.

By the 1960s there was general recognition of the claim that Confederation involved an element of dualism, and that French Canadians should be treated as equals. However, in times of crisis, whether over conscription or over the use of French at Montreal airports, English Canadians were capable of coalescing and operating on the principle of majority rule.

In other words, although dualism was acceptable as an element in the Canadian political tradition, there was no consensus on its role in determining the nature of government, especially at the provincial level. The word "dualism" continued to be applied differently depending on whether it was defined by English or French Canadians.

Conquest versus Rebellion: Dualism as Synthesis?

For a long time in Quebec the thesis from which everything else flowed was Conquest (or Cession). This seemed to be the permanent explanation of the province's position. Its antithesis in due course was the Rebellion with its rejection of British (and English-Canadian) hegemony. After the failure of the rebellions in 1837–38 there appeared to be a synthesis in the form of dualism.

This synthesis was replaced in 1867 by a Confederation in which, as we have noted, there was for a long time an unwillingness on the part of English Canadians to give more than limited recognition to the dualist principle. In the 1970s the recognition that Quebec might one day decide to secede peacefully from Canada made the possibility of rebellion or violent secession through civil war unlikely. The Rebellion antithesis was therefore eliminated. The 1980 referendum asking the people of Quebec what regime they preferred eliminated the conquest thesis also: the Quebecois could no longer view themselves as suffering permanent Conquest from which the only escape was armed struggle. The Conquest-Rebellion antithesis therefore became outmoded.[47]

The Westminster Tradition versus Dualism:
Pan-Canadianism as the Synthesis?

The Westminster tradition of majority rule was in contradiction to the dualism of French Canadians. Out of this conflict there emerged after Confederation a synthesis we have called Pan-Canadianism. One element of Pan-Canadianism was provided by the Catholic Church with its sense of a mission for all of North America. Another was provided by secular leaders from Laurier to Trudeau who promoted the interests of the French-Canadian community in the federal government. Pan-Canadianism, which began by accepting the minority position of French Canada in Confederation, was gradually transformed into the recognition of Canada as bilingual and bicultural.

However, although this synthesis was promoted by early French-Canadian nationalists such as Henri Bourassa, it was rejected as inadequate by a later generation, particularly the *Parti Québecois*. The support offered by the Quebec electorate in the referendum of 1980 and the elections of 1980 (federal) and 1981 (provincial) for both Pierre Trudeau and René Lévesque, indicated that as far as Quebec was concerned there was still no consensus on the nature of the synthesis between the Westminster parliamentary tradition of majority rule and the demand of Quebec to be treated as an equal.

One State versus Two Nations

One nationalist French-Canadian thesis has always been that Canada is an association of two nations. However, in creating the Dominion of Canada English Canadians established a single state and intended to create a single nation, the antithesis of the two-nations thesis. Those who believed that Canada formed one state and therefore one nation thought that Canadians, whether considered as British subjects or Canadian citizens, should be regarded *politically* as unhyphenated.

Over time most English Canadians and many Pan-Canadian French Canadians came to accept the fact that while Canada was indeed a single state it also represented the association of two cultures, or of nations in the cultural sense. English Canadians were reluctant to go so far as to use the term *deux nations* because of the political connotation of the term "nation." Pan-Canadians like Trudeau shared this concern.

However, in Quebec, where nationalists continued to insist that Canada was indeed a country composed of two nations, the term *deux nations* enjoyed a wider currency. Even the Quebec Liberal Party, always conscious of the role played in its affairs by the anglophone minority, felt constrained to admit that "within the Canadian political family, Quebec society has all the characteristics of a distinct national community."[48] It went on to say, "We must affirm the fundamental equality of the two founding peoples who have given, and still provide, this country its unique place in the family of nations. This basic dualism must be consecrated in the supreme document of the country."[49]

However, there was still considerable ambiguity surrounding such terms as "nation" and "sovereignty." And there was still no consensus in Quebec over the future status of the province. Consequently, there could be no synthesis that recognized Canada as a single state politically and as two nations culturally.

Summary of the Seven Dyads

Earlier we suggested that the term used by Armour and Trott to describe the historical development of philosophy as a discipline in Canada—"philosophical federalism"—might well represent the "Canadian dialectic." The outstanding characteristic of this dialectic has been that despite the contradictions in Canadian thought and practice this has rarely resulted in a higher synthesis. A summary of the seven dyads makes this clear (see table 4).

10 The Canadian "Dialectic" Reviewed

None of the seven dyads has resulted in the synthesis associated with much dialectical philosophy. The Platonic interpretation of the dialectic as the reduction of multiple ideas to a unity has no counterpart in Canadian thought, where multiplicity remains a reality. Nor can we apply to Canada the modern philosophical definition of the dialectic as a logic consisting of inseparable contradictions united by a superior category or an agreed synthesis. A more popular use of the term describes a situation where an attempt is made to resolve the conflict between opposed ideas; this use is more nearly appropriate. But it may be in the very na-

Table 4. Synthesis in the Seven Dyads

Dyad	Nature of the synthesis
1. Revolutionary-Loyalist	None. Antithesis fading
2. Colonial-autonomous	Triumph of antithesis
3. Westminster parliamentary-constitutional federalist	None as yet
4. Majority rule-dualist	Ambiguous
5. Conquest-Rebellion	Outmoded
6. Westminster-dualist	Incomplete
7. One State-Two Nations	None as yet

ture of the country's "philosophical federalism" that there is never a final solution of conflict, merely an agreement to differ.

The various traditional interpretations of the logic of the dialectic from Plato to Marx were devised in the context of a unitary state. But the "logic of federalism," a term which we noted in Chapter 5 to be commonly used in Canada, remains to be explored.[50] The nature of federalism may be such that there are conflicts and contradictions that do not result in reconciliation and synthesis. Moreover, Canadian federalism as a practical political arrangement has always been subject to outside centrifugal forces preventing unity. It was no doubt in the interest of British imperialism to have a central government in Canada, but at the same time to promote provincial autonomy. Later it was in the interest of foreign business firms to be able to play the federal and provincial governments against one another.

There was resolution of conflict in only one area, that between Canada as a colony and the United Kingdom as imperial power. In patriating their Constitution, Canadians agreed that in due course their country should become autonomous and for all intents and purposes independent.[51] Apart from that, the country was still evolving. There was no agreement on the principles of government that should govern Canada as an independent country. Despite its independent status, Canada remained tied to the United Kingdom through the Crown and had yet to modify its Westminster parliamentary form of government and to reconcile it with dualism or federalism.

After the St. Laurent era English Canadians tended to take a pessimistic view of their country's evolution. Canada's future had appeared both settled and secure, but after 1960 the horizon seemed clouded and even threatening. Perhaps the earlier optimism and confidence Canadians had in their future were unfounded. These feelings were due in large measure to economic prosperity and to concentration on the one aspect of Canada's political evolution where there was widespread agreement: the achievement of sovereign status vis-à-vis the United Kingdom. There never was agreement on many of the fundamental issues facing Canada. The views of Quebec, and the other provinces, were not given the serious consideration in the halcyon days of optimism that they were to receive after 1960.[52] When they finally were considered, the inability to reach amicable agreement on such an issue as the patriation of the Constitution was regarded as a failure of Canadians in operating their political system. Perhaps it should have been dealt with instead as a condition rooted in the imperial nature of Canadian government, a system that needed to be replaced by a form of constitutional federalism.

It is possible, therefore, to conclude that disagreement over Canada's goals was widespread throughout its history and was part of the Canadian political tradition. In the 1980s the process of evolution through conflict and compromise that had characterized the country's past continued to operate. There was sufficient modification in the world views of both English- and French-speaking Canadians to justify the prognostication of further evolution. Such an evolution could continue to follow the logic of the Canadian dialectic. Historically, there had been no synthesis of Canada's contradictions. Rather, it was expected that in time events would somehow resolve them.

However, the evolution of the relationship between English Canada and Quebec might well take a different path. In the past the imperial government was able first to dominate Canada's affairs and later to adjudicate its conflicts. In the multiracial Empire, Quebec knew its place. In an independent Canada, Quebec came to enjoy a number of advantages over the other provinces. One of these was a widely held commitment to its role as a "distinct national community," a commitment that the divided English-speaking provinces could not share. English Canada had abandoned most of its British connections, but its relations with the United States remained ambivalent. Until the emergence of an independent and indigenous cultural tradition that absorbed the British heritage and incorporated the culture of the increasing proportion of Canadians of non-British origin, fears of American cultural and economic domination would naturally be far greater in the rest of Canada than in Quebec.

Quebec had a geographical as well as an ideological advantage over English Canada. Instead of being stretched across 4,000 miles, the province occupied a compact area based on the St. Lawrence estuary, and divided English Canada in two. Whether it would be to Quebec's advantage to concentrate on the Canadian rather than the American market remained to be seen. A great deal depended on whether trade throughout Canada continued to develop in a north-south direction.

In the 1980s another unresolved issue was that of Canada's cultural identity in general. The old English-Canadian self-perception was of a Canada which, except for those French-speaking Canadians who chose to live within their francophone community, was an English-speaking society. The newer concept had been the Pan-Canadian perception of Canada as a country of two cultures where bilingual francophone and anglophone minorities could retain their cultural identity and speak their own language at home and in school. But since only New Brunswick had become officially committed to bilingualism, minorities were not protected against determined provincial governments. The vision of Canada as two nations (i.e., cultures) in one state could still be replaced by a Canada of two nations (i.e., political entities) in two states.

Much depended on public opinion in Quebec. Culturally, the Quebecois had always felt threatened by the "sea of anglophones" surround-them. Until recently, indeed, the anglophones had a firm foothold in Montreal itself. But while there were always nationalists believing that Quebec could withdraw behind its own borders, there was also general recognition that Quebec must continue to exist as part of North America.

The question remained: Would Quebec be in a better position to protect its heritage and to deal with Canada and the United States if it became a separate state? For some separatist-minded Quebecois the option of being part of a tripartite North American economic community still seemed attractive, even if it continued to be rejected by both English Canadians and Americans.

After 1976 the issue was joined between proponents of a united, federal Canada and of two successor states. The choice turned out to be not simply between the majoritarian rule and parliamentary supremacy of the BNA Act and sovereignty-association. In the whirlwind of activity preceding passage of the Constitution Act, 1982, a number of options were presented. Since the Act dealt with only some of the issues being debated, these various proposals for a renewed or restructured federalism remained important guideposts for the next round of constitutional discussions expected in the later 1980s.

Options Canada: Options Quebec

Q. *Quelle est votre position constitutionelle?*
R. *Nous devrions garder nos options à ce suject.*
—Michael Wilson, candidate for the leadership of the Conservative Party, interviewed by *Le Devoir,* May 1983.

1 The Contradiction Expressed: Keeping the Options Open

On May 20, 1980, the government of Quebec held its referendum. The following question was put to the electors of the province:

> The Government of Quebec has made public its proposal to negotiate a new agreement with the rest of Canada, based on the equality of nations.
>
> This agreement would enable Quebec to acquire exclusive power to make its laws, administer its taxes and establish relations abroad—in other words sovereignty—and at the same time to maintain with Canada an economic association including a common currency.
>
> Any change in political status resulting from these negotiations will be submitted to the people through a referendum.
>
> On these terms, do you agree to give the Government of Quebec the mandate to negotiate the proposed agreement between Quebec and Canada?

The "exclusive power" of Quebec as an "equal nation" after negotiations "between Quebec and Canada" made it clear that for all the talk of economic association the political goal was indeed independence.

Canada's contradictions—majority rule versus equality—were thus clearly exposed. The political nationalism that had emerged in Quebec after 1960 now challenged the basic assumptions on which Confederation had rested since 1867. The Westminster tradition assumed that there would be two major parties in Parliament facing each other as adversaries and alternating in power; but this tradition made no provision for the representation in government of the collective interests of a permanent ethnic minority such as the Quebecois.[1] It had been expected that the French Canadians would continue to support the policy initiated by LaFontaine and continued by Laurier and his Pan-Canadian successors, namely of representation through one or other of the two main parties.

Since 1960 the adequacy of the Westminster system with its allocation to Quebec of a steadily shrinking proportion of seats in Parliament (75 of 282 by 1980) had been increasingly questioned. But now the *Parti Québecois* went much further than its nationalist predecessors. Instead of defending or promoting Quebec's cultural sovereignty within the federal system, it sought to arrest Quebec's political decline by committing itself to a political system in which Quebec would enjoy not merely cultural but political sovereignty.

While almost 60 percent of those who gave their opinion voted *Non* in the referendum (much to the surprise and discomfiture of the *Parti Québecois*), it was unwise to conclude that those who voted against sovereignty-association were expressing a preference for the status quo. Public opinion polls had long shown that most people in Quebec were dissatisfied with the system of majority rule and expected structural change. Indeed, the prime minister and his colleagues had promised the Quebecois that if they voted *Non* the party leaders would do their best to bring this about.

Trudeau was of course a Pan-Canadian opposed to the representation or recognition of Quebec or the Quebecois as a collectivity at the federal level. But the Constitution Act patriating the BNA Act, which he persuaded the Parliament of Canada to pass in 1981, did include a charter of rights and freedoms. This purported to protect all minorities, including francophones. Such a charter, entrenched in the Constitution, could be used to challenge the practice of majority rule. Canada was perhaps embarking, once again, on a new regime.

If there was one date when Canadians appeared to be changing regimes, replacing their Westminster tradition of parliamentary supremacy by an American-style Constitution with a bill of rights and judicial review, that date was September 10, 1981, when the prime minister met the provincial premiers before the television cameras for what was to be the penultimate First Ministers Conference before the Constitution was patriated. Mr. Trudeau wanted the premiers to agree to Parliament's Constitution Act, including a formula for patriation, that is, a procedure for amending the Constitution in Canada itself. But he also insisted on the entrenchment of his charter of rights and freedoms.

During the morning's televised discussion, no fewer than seven of the provincial representatives stated their opposition to the charter. Such a charter of rights would be part of a constitutional document above the ordinary law of the land. Instead of Parliament and the provincial legislatures each being supreme in its own sphere, there would be a constitution, including the charter, to be interpreted by the courts.

In the opinion of at least one scholar, the debate was the best ever held at a federal-provincial conference, because it addressed fundamental principles.[2] Yet it was more than a debate over entrenchment; it concerned the substitution of the principle of judicial review by the courts for parliamentary supremacy. Such was the hostility to the prime minister's proposals that by the time the morning was over Mr. Trudeau had called upon two of his cabinet colleagues to state their support for the charter so that the debate would not look too one-sided. With the additional support of the premiers of Ontario, New Brunswick, and Newfoundland, the spokesmen favoring a new regime numbered six, their opponents being the other seven provincial premiers.

To judge by the nostalgic references to parliamentary sovereignty as the time-honored Canadian system, it certainly appeared as if this were the last hurrah for the Westminster doctrine of majority rule.[3] It was more than twenty years since the Quiet Revolution had erupted in Quebec, and much had happened in the intervening years to suggest that the Westminster tradition would have to be modified. Now, in September 1981 (and at the final First Ministers Conference in early November), steps were being taken to do just that. After lunch the first ministers proceeded to discuss the charter clause by clause, as though the morning debate over principle had gone in the federal government's favor.

However, events after September 10, 1981, suggested that once again the Westminster tradition might prove more resilient than had been supposed. Behind the high-toned discourse before the television cameras over the principles of parliamentary sovereignty and judicial review there lurked more specific issues over which the provinces were anxious not to lose control. The governments of western provinces were concerned lest their Indian populations use the charter to assert prior claims to the provinces' vast natural resources. They were also reluctant to extend official provincial recognition to French, a language spoken by only a small minority of their peoples. The government of Quebec, for its part, showed little interest in the fate of francophone minorities elsewhere in Canada, being more concerned to protect its majority rule in Quebec, and in particular its Bill 101, passed in 1977, establishing French as the province's sole official language.

The federal government took a Pan-Canadian stand, anxious to protect the rights of all minorities throughout the country, whether French or Indian, or the English-speaking Canadians in Quebec. Mr. Trudeau, many of whose Montreal constituents were anglophone, reminded the premiers, and the viewers, of the way minorities had been treated by the majority in Canada's past. It had been the majority which had been responsible for ". . . denying the franchise to Chinese citizens, Canadian citizens of British Columbia, for instance, abolishing the use of French in Manitoba where it has been guaranteed by the constitution or so the French thought. Stripping Japanese-Canadians of their citizenship by the federal government. Suppression of freedom of religion in Quebec."[4]

In his speech, Mr. Trudeau displayed the liberal convictions for which he had been famous long before becoming prime minister, especially in his concern for minorities and for individual rights. It was a liberalism similar to that expressed by the French intellectuals of the Enlightenment and the early French-Canadian radicals with their notion of the brotherhood of man. The thinking behind his charter of rights was also in some ways reminiscent of the liberalism that had inspired the American Bill of Rights and the French Declaration of the Rights of Man. Nor was this philosophy unknown in England, for a Bill of Rights had been passed there in 1689. And John Diefenbaker, that most anglophile of recent prime ministers, had persuaded the Parliament of Canada to pass a Canadian Bill of Rights in 1960.

There was of course a great deal of difference between the federal statute passed in 1960 and the proposed constitutional charter. The charter directly challenged the principle of legislative supremacy and majority rule. As Mr. Trudeau himself asserted, it would protect minorities and individuals from the whim of legislatures.[5]

It was clear from the debate on September 10, 1981, that most of the provincal governments preferred the traditional Canadian approach, one that favored majority rule over the rights of minorities and individuals. It was ironic that the *Parti Québecois* should have rejected the individualist *Rouge* and Enlightenment tradition in favor of a collectivist philosophy formerly associated with the Church and the *Union Nationale*.[6] It was left to the federal government to transcend the "corporatism" espoused by Quebec. The English-Canadian premiers saw themselves defending the interests of their anglophone majorities. They certainly did not share Quebec's concern for the rights of the Quebecois as a nation. Rather, they identified majority rule with the British tradition of parliamentary government, a tradition implicitly (but not explicitly) corporate in many of its manifestations, for example, the notion of the Queen-in-Parliament. The alternative, as these premiers saw it, was an American form of government based on the principle of judicial review. They expressed their opposition to this Americanization of the Canadian political system in no uncertain terms.[7]

As it turned out, "philosophical federalism" once again triumphed, or appeared to. The principles of minority rights and judicial review were accepted, but so were the principles of majority rule and legislative supremacy. At the final meeting of the first ministers in November 1981, the provincial premiers succeeded in insisting on the insertion of a clause (Section 33) that enabled Parliament or a provincial legislature to pass legislation "notwithstanding" those sections of the Charter that dealt with fundamental freedoms (2), legal rights (7 to 14), and equality rights (15).[8] However, Section 33 allowed a legislature to override the charter only when it expressly declared its intention of so doing, and then only for five years, subject to renewal. The so-called "notwithstanding" clause, which so distressed proponents of individual rights and judicial review, had the effect of preserving Canada's traditional contradictions intact. Now that these had been exposed, Canada was to have both judicial review and parliamentary supremacy.[9]

In refusing to make a choice between the British tradition of parliamentary supremacy and the American principle of judicial review, Canadians demonstrated that they preferred to leave their options open. "Philosophical federalism," as we noted earlier, reflected an unwillingness to pursue an argument to its logical conclusion. Traditionally, English Canadians had preferred to live with contradictory principles in the hope that in practice things would work out and that an acceptable compromise would be reached. If the principle of judicial review eventually proved to have more advantages than the tradition of parliamentary supremacy, then gradually the latter would be replaced.

However, there were indications during the bitter federal-provincial negotiations of 1981 that philosophical federalism might no longer be a feasible solution. When English Canadians refused to modify the Westminster system to meet Quebec's demands for equality, Quebec refused to adopt the new Constitution. There could be no gainsaying the grim fact that the compromises that led to the Constitution Act of 1982 were between the federal government and the nine English-speaking provinces. One of the conditions of agreement put forward by Quebec was that there should be constitutional recognition that Canada was composed of two founding peoples and that these peoples were equal. This condition was rejected by the federal government.

"Philosophical federalism" as a world view could now be said to exclude the Quebecois as a political collectivity, unless and until a provincial political party emerged able and willing to come to terms with the rest of Canada over the Constitution. It had always permitted French-speaking Canadians to hold a different cultural identity but had not allowed this to have constitutional recognition. While English Canadians had been willing to come to terms with official bilingualism, they had not been compelled to abandon their assumptions about majority rule. This had been demonstrated in 1976 when English Canadians united to oppose the use of French at Quebec airports. It was reaffirmed in 1981 when final agreement was reached on the Constitution Act in the night of November 4/5 without consulting the Quebec delegation to the federal-provincial conference. The new Constitution did modify the principle of majority rule by restricting its impact on individual rights. But it did not go so far as to recognize the collective rights of French Canadians or Quebecois. In political terms, philosophical federalism was a principle that enabled English Canada to maintain the status quo. Even after the turbulent events of the 1960s and 1970s, the new Constitution left the main features of the BNA Act and the whole federal system of government intact.

Indeed, if English Canadians were convinced by the passage of the Constitution Act of 1982 that the changes it brought about were adequate; and if, as the polls indicated, a large majority of the Quebecois were still committed to a political nationalism that involved further structural change in federal institutions, then the country could not easily reconcile its differences. Preservation of the status quo, even the new status quo, was not a realistic option. Either English Canada had to become more flexible in its defense of the Westminster tradition and majority rule, or Quebec had to modify its demand for collective equality. Unless there was some agreement to compromise, the ultimate partition of Canada remained a possibility.

On the other hand, a great deal had happened since the death of Duplessis and the victory of the Quebec Liberals in 1960. Before its defeat in 1976 the Quebec Liberal Party had not only modernized Quebec but had changed the world view of English Canadians. Federal hegemony had given way to a society in which French Canadians were treated more as equal partners in Confederation than ever before. Much depended on the approach taken by future governments in Quebec City and Ottawa, and their capacity to realize that most Canadians, whether French or English, still preferred to keep their options open.

2 The Limitations of "Executive Federalism":
The Unfinished Agenda

Even if Canadians decided to retain their options, it would seem that the option of the status quo was no longer feasible. The political system had changed, was changing, and would probably have to undergo even further change involving the introduction of a new regime. Before examining the options available it may be useful to consider the logic of Canadian federalism. Canada's present system of "executive federalism," to use Professor Smiley's term, is best described as a transitional form, an attempt to preserve much of the system inherited from the era of what we have called "imperial federalism." This "executive federalism" may in its turn have to give way to a form of "constitutional federalism," though not necessarily on the American model.

Federalism itself involves the acceptance of at least five principles:

(1) two orders (or levels) of government, each with its own power under the constitution;
(2) an umpire to regulate the relations between the two orders of government;
(3) a bicameral legislature, the second chamber representing geographical regions and thereby overrepresenting minorities;
(4) the consent of the various original political units to the proposed federation; and
(5) the incapacity of either order of government to change the other of its own volition. In practice, this means that formal amendments

to the Constitution require the agreement first of the central legislature (composed of a lower house representing population and an upper house representing regions), and then of the regional (i.e., provincial or state) legislatures. In other words, to change the written Constitution requires an overwhelming majority.

The United States is often cited as the classical example of federalism. Its system is a form of constitutional federalism that conforms to all five criteria. The powers of the two orders of government are laid down (and limited by) the Constitution; there is an umpire in the shape of a Supreme Court responsible to the Constitution and not to the executive or the legislature, and offering what may be called "judicial constitutional federalism"; and there is a bicameral legislature in which the Senate represents all fifty states, regardless of size, equally. Thirdly, by offering the states a role in the central legislative process the United States also provides an example of what may be called "legislative constitutional federalism." Indeed, so careful has the Senate been to protect the differing interests of the states that it has permitted minority groups of senators and even individuals to filibuster against legislation passed by the House of Representatives. While this veto power by a minority can be overridden, putting an end to a filibuster requires the votes of no fewer than 60 of the 100 senators (at one time it required 66).[10]

With regard to the fourth principle, initial unanimous consent, the introduction of the federal system in the United States obtained the consent of all the states involved. Rhode Island, which had refused to participate in the 1787 Constitutional Convention, joined the Union in 1791. Finally, the American Constitution prevented any formal changes without the overwhelming consent of both orders of government. Considering that an amendment has to receive the support not only of two-thirds of both the House and Senate but no less than three-quarters of the state legislatures, it is surprising that so many amendments (twenty-six) have in fact been possible.

The American Constitution, therefore, established a form of what we have called "constitutional federalism." Taking the analysis a step further, one may suggest that because of the powers enjoyed independently by the Supreme Court, there was also introduced a form of "judicial federalism." In addition, the powerful position of the Senate insured that there would also be "legislative federalism." Together, the Supreme Court, the Senate, and the state legislatures effectively prevented the transformation of the American system into anything like executive federalism.

In Canada, Confederation established a different form of federal system, one that was gradually transformed from imperial to executive federalism. As in other federal systems, there were two orders of government, each with its own constitutional power. But there was no Canadian umpire to regulate relations between them. The final arbiter was the imperial government, which continued to act long after the establishment of a Supreme Court of Canada. The third principle, that of a bicameral legislature, was only partially implemented. While the Canadian Senate represented in principle the various regions of the country, it was a body whose members were appointed by the federal authorities. They were not elected by the legislatures (as in the United States before 1913) or by statewide electorates (as after 1913). There was some fear in the 1960s that a powerful Senate would weaken the central government, as it was supposed to have done in the United States (where it was thought to have contributed to the outbreak of the Civil War). There was also the belief that an elected senate was incompatible with British parliamentary government in which the Cabinet was responsible not to Parliament as a whole, but solely to the House of Commons. Canada did of course accept the fourth principle: the BNA Act was to apply only to those provinces that decided to join Confederation and to accept its terms. Prince Edward Island, for example, joined in 1873.

Where Canada radically departed from federalism in 1867 was in the absence of the fifth principle, that of amendment by both orders of government. Instead, Canada was formally treated by the United Kingdom as analogous to a local government, with amendments remaining the responsibility of the imperial Parliament. In practice, of course, Westminster left it to Canada to propose whatever amendments it wished.

At first the Canadian government, for its part, did not act over amendments as if Canada was a federal system at all. It even proposed an amendment without consulting the Dominion Parliament. However, after 1895 the convention was established that as far as amendments to the BNA Act were concerned, "Canada" meant a Joint Address of both Houses of Parliament. Although from 1907 the provinces might be consulted, as late as 1930 the federal government could contemplate patriation of the BNA Act by the simple transfer of the powers of the Westminster Parliament to Ottawa.

It is tempting to conclude that the fifty years of wrangling before patriation was finally achieved reflects adversely on the capacities of federal and provincial politicians, as persons incapable of placing the national interest above their petty concern to protect their jurisdiction. The conclusion is unfair. What was at stake was not simply an amendment to the Constitution, or even a new amendment procedure, but the very nature of the Canadian political system. The use of the term "patriation" helped to disguise the fact that to transfer the BNA Act to Ottawa involved the replacement of a nineteenth-century colonial Charter (the "Provincial Treaty"), the first of its kind, by a twentieth-century Constitution for an independent state.

It was difficult enough for American states or Canadian provinces to frame a federal constitution in the first place when there was no federal government in existence to complicate matters. For Canadians to replace the Constitution already in existence for many years without the opportunity of calling a genuine constitutional convention made the task much more difficult. When one considers that Canada was attempting fundamental change through brief conferences in which the federal government was not only an active participant but was actually able to dominate the proceedings from the chair, the contentious nature of the enterprise becomes clear. It is a tribute to the diplomatic skills of successive federal and provincial politicians that they managed to evolve a new system of government, one that not only gradually replaced the principles of imperial federalism by those of constitutional federalism, but that also led to the consideration of a great many novel ideas about government.

Originally, the Canadian system was federal only in the sense that there were two orders of government, each with its powers assigned by the BNA Act. But in the absence of a Canadian umpire comparable to the American Supreme Court, or a legislative chamber comparable to the American Senate, Canada lacked the attributes of both judicial and legislative federalism. All that was left was executive federalism, initially in the form of imperial federalism. It was the imperial Judicial Committee of the Privy Council and the imperial Parliament that acted as external umpires. In the British Empire of 1867 there was no place for constitutional federalism as understood in the United States.

As the apparatus of imperial federalism was gradually removed, it was replaced by Canada's own form of executive federalism. The period after 1867 was an era in which there was a belief in the need for a strong federal government to protect Canada from the United States, to open up the West and to negotiate with the United Kingdom. Executive federalism presented few problems. Since Canadians continued to accept imperial federalism for some time, they could even imagine that, protected by the Judicial Committee and the British Parliament, they enjoyed a form of both judicial and legislative federalism. However, as we noted earlier, the Judicial Committee was in principle an arm of the imperial government and therefore an instrument of executive federalism. And while no one could question the credentials of the British Parliament as an elected legislative body, it was not a body elected by Canadians. In any case, it would have been difficult for British institutions, designed for a unitary system of government in the United Kingdom, to be an integral part of Canada's federal structure. As the authority of these British institutions waned between 1867 and 1949, their powers were inherited by the Parliament of Canada, an institution on the British model, in which the government played a leading role. The Judicial Committee and the British Parliament were not therefore replaced by federal institutions on, say, the American model. Instead, the apparatus of imperial federalism was succeeded by executive federalism.

This conclusion seems confirmed by the interpretation of the system advanced by Canadian authorities. They asserted that the representative role of the United States Senate was adequately filled in Canada by the federal Cabinet. R. McGregor Dawson noted, "The Cabinet has, in fact, taken over the allotted role of the Senate as the protector of the rights of the provinces and it has done an incomparably better job."[11]

Indeed, it was pointed out that the French-Canadian members of the Cabinet provided a bulwark for Quebec in the federal government. For example, in the fall of 1939 Maurice Duplessis called a provincial election. Concerned over his opposition to the war (which Duplessis regarded as an excuse for further centralization and assimilation by Canada), the Quebec ministers in the federal government decided that the *Union Nationale* must at all costs be beaten if the war effort was not to be endangered. They toured the province in support of the provincial Liberals and reminded their audiences that during the First World War, when the Liberals were in opposition, English Canada had been able to impose conscription for service overseas on the province.

Now, with the Liberal Party in power in Ottawa, they argued, Quebec's representatives in the federal Cabinet could prevent such action from being taken. Indeed, they would resign rather than acquiesce in such a proposal. However, if Quebec were to receive this protection it had to pay a price, that is, to vote against Duplessis and for the Liberals provincially as well as nationally. If the voters insisted on supporting the *Union Nationale* and its anti-war policies, the federal Cabinet ministers would have no alternative but to resign their portfolios. Then there would be no bulwark to prevent the imposition of conscription again. In the 1939 provincial election, the voters of Quebec, who had given the *Union Nationale* seventy-six of the ninety seats in 1936, proceeded to reverse themselves, awarding the Liberals sixty-nine seats out of a total of eighty-six.

Yet, as we observed in Chapter 8, this bulwark easily crumbled. Despite the promises given in 1939, conscription was introduced later in the war. It is true that the Quebec ministers kept their promise and opposed conscription, but they were replaced, notably by the pro-conscriptionist St. Laurent, who had of course made no pledge. When, thirty-seven years later, Jean Marchand resigned in protest against the banning of the use of French by air traffic controllers at Quebec airports, he, too, was replaced. On another occasion, a Cabinet minister from Manitoba, James Richardson, resigned in protest against the federal government's language policy, again without any apparent impact on the federal policy of bilingualism in the West.

It is therefore difficult to confirm Dawson's conclusion that the federal Cabinet has protected the rights of the provinces. To say that "it has done an incomparably better job" than the Senate merely underlines the complete inability of that body to perform the federal functions assumed by many to have been allotted to it at Confederation.

The argument that the federal Cabinet is able to represent provincial interests depends on the assumption that the two main parties are each truly national in their appeal, and that consequently each has a quota of MPs drawn from all parts of the country. For only if there is such a pool of MPs can Cabinet ministers be selected to "represent" the various provinces. However, until the 1984 election, it seemed that no party was able to win nationwide support. Almost none of the seventy or more MPs from the four Western provinces was a Liberal, thus leaving the region virtually unrepresented in the Cabinet (see table 5).

Table 5. Number of Liberal Members of Parliament Representing Western Provinces

	1972	1974	1979	1980	1983
Manitoba	2	2	2	2	1
Saskatchewan	1	3	0	0	0
Alberta	0	0	0	0	0
British Columbia	4	8	1	0	1

Clearly the Liberals could no longer claim to be a *national* party.

Nor could the Conservatives. Until 1984 their representation in Quebec was just as sparse: two MPs in 1972, three in 1974, two in 1979, and one in 1980. (In 1984 they captured fifty-eight seats.) When the Conservatives won one seat in Quebec in 1980, the Liberals took the other seventy-four. Since neither of the major parties could claim to be a truly national party with adequate representation from each of the four or five main regions of the country, any defense of Canadian federalism that rested on the representative role of the federal Cabinet was very weak indeed. A governmental system that excluded whole regions from the decision-making process was clearly inadequate for a country that claimed to be federal.

If, then, imperial federalism in the form of the imperial executive as arbiter faded away; if there were no representative senate to defend provincial interests; and if the federal Cabinet could not always be relied upon to provide a suitable alternative, then clearly there had to be some other machinery of government to fill the gap in the federal structure. This was becoming apparent by the 1950s when the growth of federal-provincial interaction began to attract attention with the proliferation of federal-provincial committees involving both civil servants and ministers.[12]

By the 1960s this apparently new method of making federalism work was dubbed "cooperative federalism." What began as meetings largely of experts became ministerial conferences. These in turn were succeeded by regular meetings of the prime minister with the provincial premiers. As constitutional conflict between the two orders of government grew, so-called "First Ministers Conferences" became an integral part of the political process. Donald Smiley has explained that this "executive federalism" came about after 1945 for six reasons: the greater role of government in the economy; the demand for nationwide standards in fields within provincial jurisdiction; the competition between governments for tax dollars; an increase in activity in subjects covered by concurrent legislation; provincial resentment against federal encroachment; and interprovincial interaction.[13]

Nevertheless, the conflict intensified and there was a qualitative change after 1960, once the first ministers were drawn into negotiations to break the deadlock over the Constitution. By the 1970s, executive federalism (as well as its extension, "cooperative federalism") began to show its limitations as a device for filling the institutional vacuum left by the impotent Senate and the demise of imperial federalism. Despite all the talk of constitutional change during the era of executive federalism no changes of consequence were made before 1982.

The 1984 election brought about a stunning change. No party had ever won as many seats as the Conservatives did in this election: 211 out of 282. It looked as though it might be a realigning election. When Mr. Diefenbaker carried Quebec in 1958, it proved a flash in the pan. In 1984, the new head of government was Brian Mulroney, a French-speaking Quebecois. Although it is too early to assess the full implications of the Conservatives' victory, for a while at least the political system had been given a reprieve.

The shortcomings of the First Ministers Conferences as constitutional devices were many. Instead of the continual interaction that takes place in a legislative body, there were sporadic "summit" conferences that lasted barely a couple of days. While there were public (and much-publicized) sessions before the television cameras, there were also secret conclaves where the main negotiations took place. Whereas in a legislative body there would have been agreed parliamentary procedures presided over by an impartial chairman, in executive federalism there were no agreed procedures and the prime minister acted as both chairman and partisan. It was he who set the agenda and determined the course of business. Instead of a secretariat responsible to the legislature as a collectivity (and controlled by the Speaker) the Federal-Provincial Relations Office, which provided the secretariat, was responsible to the federal government alone. Each premier had his own secretariat as well. Moreover, the first ministers remained responsible to their own Cabinets, party caucuses, and provincial legislatures. In some instances, notably Quebec, the premier could be repudiated by his provincial supporters and was, therefore, unable to enter into binding negotiations.

The conferences gave conflicting signals. At times they suggested that

Canada was indeed little more than a Confederacy of eleven governments with the prime minister as merely a *primus inter pares*. At other times the prime minister seemed to be the heir of nineteenth-century imperialism, acting as a sort of colonial governor and getting his own way by the traditional tactics of divide and rule.

Certainly the system was not one of constitutional federalism where the substance of debate was incorporated in the working of central institutions. The fact that the premiers flew into the capital and flew out again, maintaining an adversary position on behalf of their constituents (leaving the observer curious to know whether the federal government represented anyone at all), indicated how close Canada was to becoming a confederate political system.[14]

Of course institutions in themselves do not prevent conflict, and to suggest that new institutions would resolve all of Canada's problems would be naive. After all, the American form of constitutional federalism proved unequal to the task of preventing civil war. But it is at least arguable that Canada's old imperial federalism kept a tight rein on both orders of government, whereas executive federalism, reflecting the absence of political institutions for conflict resolution, provided no rein at all. (It is a remarkable fact that throughout twenty years of bickering by Quebec, rarely was the Canadian public made fully aware that the seventy-five MPs representing the province in the federal Parliament shared some of these concerns.)

By the end of the 1970s there was growing interest in exploring other options, in an alternative political system in which some form of constitutional federalism took the place of imperial federalism and its transitional successor, executive federalism. Among the proposals were suggestions for a new second chamber.

There was considerable disagreement over the nature and purpose of the proposed body. Some saw it simply in terms of a parliamentary institution, a place for "sober second thoughts." To these critics, the House of Commons, like the lower house in the United Kingdom and other parliamentary systems, would oppose any proposal to increase the authority of the Senate and to make it a rival of the House of Commons.[15] In any case, the principle of responsible government, on which Canadian government rested, meant responsibility to the House of Commons alone. Reform of the Senate had been in the air since the early 1870s. Opponents of change saw no reason to make the parliamentary system unnecessarily complicated.[16]

Even those who believed that some change was desirable often argued from points of departure that were anything but federal in their inspiration. Some criticized the Senate as an institution that protected the interests of the propertied classes and for this reason wished to see it reformed.[17] Others, like the New Democratic Party, believed that it should be abolished.[18]

Even those who concluded that it was time to consider an alternative chamber more comparable to the United States Senate were concerned lest Canada adopt yet another American institution. Not only would Canadians prefer to remain different, but they recognized the United States Senate as an integral part of a distinctive system of government—presidential, republican, and based on a different set of principles than pertained to Canada. Moreover, the American Senate had been established at the formation of the republic. By contrast, Canada's provincial premiers, who had a century of experience in federal-provincial relations, were unlikely to agree to the transfer of their powers to an elected Senate. Under the Constitution Act of 1982, whatever body replaced the appointed Senate would have to be acceptable to both the federal and provincial governments.

There is, then, an unfinished agenda. This must be completed if the principles of constitutional federalism are to be implemented. A federal system involves more than the first principle of federalism, namely two orders of government with constitutionally assigned powers. In Canada it also requires (1) an impartial umpire, preferably a Supreme Court entrenched in the Constitution; (2) representation of the provinces according to geography and not just population, with some provision for a veto by the francophone minority; (3) the consent and participation of the provinces, including Quebec; and (4) no change in the federal system without the agreement of the overwhelming majority.

The Constitution Act of 1982 brought about three important changes: patriation of the Constitution; an amendment formula; and the Charter of Rights and Freedoms. It did not attend to the reform of the federal government, notably the Supreme Court and the Senate, and it did not address itself to the contentious issue of the redistribution of powers between the two orders of government. It was on the rock of redistribution that earlier attempts to patriate the Constitution had failed. It is quite possible that this would once again prevent Quebec from accepting a new regime. On the other hand, after our analysis of the various facets of constitutional federalism we can perhaps better understand Quebec's recalcitrance. Not only was the method of bringing about change—the First Ministers Conference—a dubious one for such far-reaching reforms, but it was a makeshift one, which emerged following the demise of imperial federalism and before constitutional federalism appeared to be an alternative. Under the circumstances, Quebec had reason in the sixties to be concerned lest acceptance of an amendment formula prematurely freeze the transitional makeshift "federal" system instead of waiting for the development of a more orderly and legitimate arrangement.

Following the victory of the *Parti Québecois* in 1976, politicians throughout Canada were at last galvanized into action. By 1980 a number of well-thought-out proposals for structural change had been put forward. After the referendum, and still more after the passage of the Constitution Act, most English Canadians became complacent again. Yet these various options remained as important as ever. With Quebec unwilling to accept the Constitution Act in 1982, Canada had still, it must be remembered, to reach a genuine constitutional accord.

3 Options Canada: Options Quebec

A number of options were open to Canadians after the 1980 referendum.

The Status Quo

The first option was to continue the status quo. This did not mean a rejection of any change at all. It simply involved a willingness to accept the type of incremental change to which Canada had become accustomed since 1867. Excluded was the sort of regime change that Canada experienced between 1760 and 1867 at the hands of the imperial government. Preservation of the status quo seemed the preferred option of many, if not most, English-speaking Canadians.

Polls in Quebec indicated that this option had long been rejected by most French-speaking Canadians, including Pan-Canadians. The minimum price they expected English-speaking Canadians to pay for Quebec's acceptance of Canada as a viable polity was a renewed federalism that modified the Westminster parliamentary system established at Confederation and hardly changed since. Moreover, when Mr. Trudeau and other Pan-Canadians toured Quebec before the 1980 referendum they assured their listeners that if Quebec rejected the proposed sovereignty-association the alternative would not be the status quo but a renewed federalism.

Continuation of the status quo, moreover, was unlikely because the BNA Act had begun to lose legitimacy not only in Quebec but in parts of English Canada. Following the victory of the *Parti Québecois* in 1976, several proposals for a new federalism were put forward between 1978 and 1980, not only by the federal authorities but also by several provincial governments.[19]

Concern appeared to center on the inadequacy of the existing regime as a federal system. Under the Westminster tradition, power lay very much with the majority. To the French, the majority consisted of the anglophones, concentrated in Ontario. To those on the periphery, in the four Atlantic and the four Western provinces, the majority was composed of central Canada, of Ontario plus Quebec. At times it seemed as if the federal government was most responsive to the largest province alone, Ontario.

So long as Canadians accepted philosophical federalism, they could agree to disagree and could leave the formal political system untouched. They could assume that it would adjust to pressure and that, as in the past, there would be periods of centralization followed by decentralization. Time would be the great healer of Canada's divisions.

It was becoming increasingly apparent in the 1970s that many French Canadians were no longer willing to agree to disagree or to accept the theory of the swing of the pendulum. The very nature of Federal institutions became an issue. There were those like the *Parti Québecois* who did not believe it was possible to reform the federal system. But there were many others who opposed separatism and believed that the "Ottawa" government could be remodeled to reflect the federal nature of Canada and the province's concerns.

Their alternative to the status quo was therefore a renewed or restructured federalism. In 1978, Mr. Trudeau responded to the challenge of the *Parti Québecois* and its commitment to sovereignty-association by proposing a series of amendments to the BNA Act in a Constitutional Amendment Bill.

Renewed Federalism: The Constitutional Amendment Bill, 1978

"Renewed federalism" was the term frequently associated with the proposals for change put forward by Mr. Trudeau's government in

1978. The proposal incorporated several of the ideas later contained in the Constitution Act of 1982, for example, patriation, an amendment procedure, and the Charter of Rights. The importance of the bill lay in its vision of the future, of a Canada at last willing to modernize its Constitution, replacing the imperial and archaic terminology of the BNA Act by a language more appropriate to an independent state in the late twentieth century. It was the first government measure purporting to satisfy Quebec's long-expressed preference for a new political system. How far the bill actually met this demand was disputed, but it certainly contained a number of unusual ideas. Some of its proposals went further than those of the 1982 Constitution Act.

In the first place, the 1978 bill offered a virtual replacement of the British North America Act. It dealt with such matters as the institutions composing the federal government, notably the governor general, the Senate, and the Supreme Court. It began with a Preamble and a Statement of Aims that tried to match the eloquent preambles of the American and the French constitutions. Its proposed reform of the Senate, although modest, transformed it into a House of the Federation. Half of its 118 members would be selected by the legislative assemblies of the provinces, the other half by the House of Commons. Its entrenchment of the Supreme Court was straightforward, the Court being expanded from nine to eleven members, four of them from Quebec. Both these reforms were in the direction of constitutional federalism.

The Constitutional Amendment Bill fell short of meeting many of the demands made by the Quebecois, both federalists and nationalists, for a greater share in the government of Canada. The Preamble made a point of referring not only to Quebec but to French Canada, "a society centered in but not limited to Quebec." In making the Cabinet responsible only to the House of Commons it rejected a central feature of constitutional federalism and preserved the principle of representation by population (or majority rule by English Canadians). In any case, 80 percent of the members of the proposed House of the Federation would be drawn from provinces other than Quebec, giving that province an even smaller number of members than in the existing Senate (24 out of 118 instead of out of 104). Although the governor general's powers were made statutory, the Monarch was retained. A majority of judges of the Supreme Court would be common lawyers and presumably anglophones.

There were sufficient novel features to disturb the many English Canadians committed to status quo. The Privy Council of Canada would become the Council of State (*Conseil d'Etat*); executive government would be vested in the governor general, not the Queen; ministers would be permitted to address both houses; Parliament would consist of the governor general and the two houses, not the Queen-in-Parliament; and the governor general would draw his power from the Constitution, not royal prerogative.[20]

One suggestion that was to reappear in later proposals was somewhat reminiscent of the so-called "double majority" principle put forward during the Union period before 1867, a time when the French Canadians of Lower Canada often exercised a de facto veto. Any change in language legislation was to require the support of a majority of both French- and English-speaking members of the House of the Federation. However, this veto could be reduced to a suspensive veto of sixty days if two-thirds of the House of Commons voted against it. Here was a clear indication that the principle of majority rule was not to be lightly abandoned.

It was another proposal, the modest suggestion that the Senate should become an elected body, which ran into difficulties. The federal government did not expect quite the obstacle it encountered. After all, according to its interpretation of the BNA Act (No. 2), 1949, the Parliament of Canada enjoyed authority to reform its own institutions.

According to that amendment (to Section 91) Parliament had the right of "the amendment from time to time of the Constitution of Canada, except as regards matters coming within the classes of subjects by this Act assigned exclusively to the Legislatures of the provinces."

Under the parliamentary system, the British House of Commons had been able to compel the House of Lords to accept changes in its composition and acquiesce in the curtailment of its veto power. The government of Canada assumed that the Canadian House of Commons could compel the Senate to undergo even more drastic changes. But the Canadian Senate was not comparable to the House of Lords. It had not fought openly against the popularly-elected chamber to protect the rights of private property. The Senate had never blocked the legislation of the lower house in the manner of the Lords.

Just what the role of the Senate was had never been clear. Certainly it had never been an important federal institution. As we have seen, it was an appointed body, unable to represent the provinces or regions on the model of the American Senate. Its role appears to have been that of a revising chamber.[21]

The federal government's proposal to abolish the Senate as it was then constituted was challenged as unconstitutional. The government referred the matter to the Supreme Court for an advisory opinion (or "reference"). In December 1979 the Supreme Court rejected the federal government's argument that it had the power to recommend to the Commons that the Senate be replaced. The Court ruled that, "the Senate has a vital role as an institution forming part of the federal system created by the [BNA] Act. . . . A primary purpose of the creation of the Senate, as part of the federal legislative process, was, therefore, to afford protection to the various sectional interests in Canada in relation to the enactment of federal legislation."[22]

The Supreme Court examined the 1949 amendment of the Constitution that seemed to grant the Parliament of Canada jurisdiction in all matters not exclusively assigned to the provinces (except those specified). It noted that consequent to that amendment a number of changes had indeed been made by Parliament alone, including the compulsory retirement of senators at the age of seventy-five. The Court declared that such changes "might be described as federal 'housekeeping' matters."[23] Further, it argued:

> In our opinion, the power of amendment given by Section 91(1) relates to the constitution of the general Government in matters of interest only to that government. . . .
>
> In our opinion, the power given to the federal Parliament by Section 91(1) was not intended to enable it to alter in any way the provisions of Sections 91 and 92 governing the exercise of legislative authority by the Parliament of Canada and the Legislatures of the Provinces.

In other words, the wide powers assumed in 1949 were now reduced to "matters of interest only to that government." The Senate, so the Court maintained, was an institution of interest to the provinces. It was part of the federal, as well as the parliamentary, system.

The Court had somehow to convince Canadians that the Senate, an appointed body with a poor track record of defending the interests of minorities, regions, or even provinces, was not after all a body like the Lords which defended the interests of the few, but was in fact an integral part of the federal system. Ignoring the conventional view of the upper house as a rather ineffective but perhaps harmless revising chamber, the Court boldly concluded, ". . . it is clear that the intention was to make the Senate a thoroughly independent body which would canvass dispassionately the measures of the House of Commons. This was accomplished by providing for the appointment of members of the Senate with tenure for life. To make the Senate a wholly or partially elected body would affect a fundamental feature of that body."[24]

Did this extraordinary conclusion mean that an appointed upper house was an essential feature of the Canadian federal system? Some observers appear to have drawn that inference: "The Supreme Court implies that direct election would impair the function of the Senate as a 'thoroughly independent body.' "[25] A moment's reflection, however, suggests that the Court may simply have been making a logical argument: that whereas in a unitary parliamentary system such as Britain's the popular chamber could force the reform of the hereditary Lords, in a federal system such as Canada's, where the Senate's *raison d'être* was not heredity or property (or even merit) but regional representation, then something more than Parliament was involved. Canada's federal structure was being tampered with.[26] The Court, however, did not address the question of who had the authority to abolish the Senate. It merely noted that Parliament was not competent to act unilaterally.

Two aspects of the Supreme Court's decision in the Senate reference were to be of significance in the future. One was the Court's unwillingness to base its interpretation of the Constitution solely on the written document, i.e., the precise wording of the BNA Act (No. 2), 1949. Instead, after the manner of the American Supreme Court, it referred to the interpretation of the Constitution offered in the federal government's 1965 white paper (introduced by Prime Minister Lester B. Pearson and signed by Minister of Justice Guy Favreau). Published in the wake of the Quiet Revolution in Quebec with its assertion of provincial jurisdiction, the white paper appeared to recognize a provincial role in amendments to the BNA Act beyond those matters exclusively assigned to the provinces. It said, in part, "The fourth general principle is that the Canadian Parliament will not request an amendment directly affecting federal-provincial relations without prior consultation and agreement with the provinces. . . . *The nature and the degree of provincial participation in the amending process, however, have not lent themselves to easy definition*" (my italics).[27]

The other important feature of the Court's judgment was its apparent willingness to enter the political arena and to assert its authority, even when this was not perhaps necessary. The reference to the Court was made by Mr. Trudeau's Liberal government. By the time the Court was prepared to rule in December 1979 the government had been defeated and its proposed Constitutional Amendment Bill had lapsed. There was therefore no pressing need for the Court to take any action at all. McWhinney has commented, "The Court . . . has contributed to its own subsequent difficulties by rushing to judgment in cases perhaps better left to the ordinary political process for resolution."[28] Certainly in this case, and in a number of others, the Court was not behaving like a court in the British tradition of parliamentary supremacy. It appeared to model itself more on the American Supreme Court where the justices were expected to act as guardians of the Constitution. But the movement towards constitutional federalism, as we have seen, depended not only on the willingness of the Supreme Court to take a broad view of its responsibilities but first of all on the establishment of its constitutional authority so to act. John Marshall had been able to point out first, that the U.S. Supreme Court was entrenched in the Constitution, and secondly, that the Constitution had been ratified by representatives of the American people at the Constitutional Convention in Philadelphia as well as in thirteen state conventions. Had the Constitutional Amendment Bill been passed, it would have provided for the entrenchment of the Canadian Supreme Court in the Constitution. Failure to pass the measure meant that the Court remained, as it had been since its establishment in 1875, the creature of the federal Parliament, its members appointed by the government of the day.

The 1978 bill to amend the BNA Act represented more of a watershed than was realized at the time. It was probably the last instance when the federal government acted solely on the principle of parliamentary supremacy to bring about constitutional change. Soon after its proposals were published, the government of Canada discovered that the powers that the federal authorities had arrogated to themselves under Louis St. Laurent in 1949 could no longer be exercised unilaterally. The Supreme Court of Canada had its own views on the Constitution, and it was these that won the acceptance of public opinion. Parliament was not even allowed to determine the nature of its own institution, i.e., to reform the Senate. The practice of judicial review triumphed over the principle of parliamentary supremacy.

Yet this transformation of the system only added to the contradictions as Canada attempted to fulfill the promise of a renewed federalism without embarking on a regime change. Canada's was traditionally a parliamentary system, with a Constitution similar in principle to that of the United Kingdom as stated in the Preamble of the BNA Act. Presumably, the Parliament of Canada, like the British Parliament, could make changes in its own governmental institutions. This had been taken for granted by those who amended the Act in 1949. The Senate in those days was assumed to be a parliamentary, not a federal, institution. Yet, thirty years later, Canada was regarded primarily as a federal system, so that Parliament could not act alone except in "housekeeping" matters. The importance of the Supreme Court's decision lay in this insistence that the Canadian system was primarily federal.

The Court's decision also indicated the ambiguity attendant on a constitution in transition. By its attention to the 1965 white paper of Guy Favreau, the Court revealed its sympathy for a provincial role in the constitutional process, i.e., for structural change. The Court also assumed that it already had the legitimate authority to declare the proposals of the federal Parliament to change the Senate to be *ultra vires,* even though, until such structural change involving the Court as well as the Senate took place, the Court itself lacked the constitutional legitimacy to act as an independent branch of government.

Moreover, the Constitutional Amendment Bill had been criticized in some quarters for not going far enough in its proposals for structural change, and in others for going too far in the direction of constitutional federalism. The second view was held by many English Canadians, including several provincial premiers who, at the First Ministers Conference called in February 1979, expressed misgivings over the proposed modification of the Westminster tradition. But the bill was relatively conservative in its major objectives. It left intact the notion of a government being responsible only to the House of Commons; the institution of a Monarchy; and the distribution of powers between the two orders of government.

Restructured Federalism: A Future Together, 1979

Early in 1979 a second document was produced which proposed further constitutional change. This was *A Future Together,* the report of the Task Force on Canadian Unity, established by the federal government in 1977 to review the options for Canada following the victory of the *Parti Québecois*. The report was often referred to by the names of its cochairmen, Jean-Luc Pépin, a former Liberal Cabinet minister, and John P. Robarts, the former Conservative Premier of Ontario.[29]

Perhaps not surprisingly, the Task Force went further than the federal government in its 1978 bill toward meeting the demand for structural change. Its composition (particularly the appointment of John Robarts as cochairman) reflected provincial as well as federal concerns. One of its most controversial proposals was the replacement of the Senate by a sixty-member Council of the Federation, which would consist entirely of delegates nominated by the provinces. The federal government had proposed that only half of its proposed House of the Federation be selected by provincial legislatures. The Task Force argued that the new body should be entirely provincial. The rationale behind its proposal can perhaps be summarized as follows:

1. The Senate had failed to defend provincial interests.
2. This failure left a vacuum in Ottawa.
3. The vacuum had in due course been filled by federal-provincial conferences. But these were held infrequently, often reached no agreement, and were no substitute for a permanent ongoing deliberative body.
4. The Council of the Federation would supplement the federal-provincial conference. It would help to reduce federal-provincial tensions and combat the popular belief that the federal and provincial governments were always at loggerheads.
5. The Council would also replace the Senate. And unlike the Senate it would be given real power.

In short, by incorporating the provincial perspective in a federal institution, Canada would make its parliamentary system truly federal.

A second novel proposal was inspired by the failure of the House of Commons to adequately represent the provinces. The "first past the post" electoral system of single-member constituencies had resulted in Alberta returning Conservatives and Quebec, Liberals. In each province, when the voters preferred opposition parties they were virtually unrepresented in government. The Task Force suggested that an additional sixty seats, using proportional representation and ranked lists drawn up before the election, be made available to redress the imbalance in the Commons. (The elections of 1980 highlighted the problem more clearly than ever before. Alberta returned twenty-one Conservatives for twenty-one seats, Quebec seventy-four Liberals out of seventy-five members.)

A third proposal was to increase the number of Quebec civil law judges on an expanded Supreme Court from three out of nine to five out of eleven. In addition, the Court would be divided into three benches. There would be one of provincial jurisdiction with a Quebec law section composed of the civil law judges, and a common law section composed of common law judges; one of federal jurisdiction with a quorum of seven or nine judges; and one of constitutional jurisdiction composed of the full court.

In these three proposals, for the Senate, the House of Commons, and the Supreme Court, the Task Force was guided by two federal principles: the recognition that Canada was a country of different regions, and the recognition that it comprised two cultures. As a result of these assumptions, the report appears to have been well received in both the West and Quebec.

True to its principles, the task force went much further than the Constitutional Amendment Bill in the direction of curbing the powers of the federal government and the Parliament, and recommended the transfer of some of these powers to the provinces. Certain powers were assumed to be obsolete, for example, the federal power to reserve and disallow provincial legislation. These were to be formally abolished. Others, such as the emergency power and the spending power, would require the concurrence of the Council of the Federation. But another important federal power, known as the declaratory power because it enabled the federal government to declare provincial public works as being of advantage to Canada as a whole and therefore within federal jurisdiction, was to require the concurrence of the provinces themselves.

It was the task force proposals specifically designed for Quebec that most aroused the federal government's hostility. One was the notion of "asymmetrical federalism," that is the formal recognition that all provinces were not the same. The task force avoided the *de jure* recognition of special privileges or a special status for Quebec. Instead, it recognized this *de facto* by offering special status to all the provinces, but on the understanding that on most issues only Quebec would take advantage of the opportunity to opt out of particular federal programs (as it had when setting up its own Quebec Pension Plan in 1964).

An even more controversial proposal recognized the right of each province to determine its language policies. This meant acceptance of the English-language policy of most of the provinces, and the replacement of bilingualism in Quebec by French as the provincial language (as had already been accomplished by Quebec's Bill 101 in 1977). This proposal for provincial control over language policy recognized the reality of the Canada of the 1970s, but it was interpreted in Ottawa as confining bilingualism to federal institutions, and as rejecting the Pan-Canadian perspective with its concern for minority rights.

The tone of the Pépin-Robarts report was one of accommodation with the provinces rather than confrontation. It criticized the federal government for its arrogance and asserted that federalism meant the recognition that there were two equal *orders* of government, not two levels, one of which, the federal, was superior. Unlike the federal government in 1978, the task force did not present its suggestions in the form of a specific bill. Its aim was to change the climate of opinion throughout Canada. By stressing the federal principles of regionalism and dualism, *A Future Together* attempted to meet the concerns of both alienated Westerners and nationalist Quebecois. Even members of the *Parti Québecois* government of Quebec professed to be impressed (though confident that the federal government would not act upon its recommendations).

If ever there were proposals that challenged the federal government to reexamine the federal system from a different perspective, that of a society where regionalism and dualism played increasingly important roles, they were those of the Pépin-Robarts report *A Future Together*. More than any previous document it recognized, implicitly at least, the importance of the principles of constitutional federalism. In arguing that there were two orders, not levels, of government it attacked the "imperialism" of successive federal governments. In recognizing that the new upper house would have to be a realistic supplement to First Ministers Conferences and therefore composed of delegates from the provincial governments, it provided an interesting alternative to executive federalism. In its recommendations for a special amendment procedure for basic changes in the Constitution it ensured that there would be a considerable, and perhaps overwhelming, majority for reform. Not only would basic amendments require the support of a majority of the House of Commons and the Council of the Federation (i.e., of provincial governments), but they would need the acceptance of a majority of the Canadian people in each of the country's four main regions, through a referendum. Consequently, the people of Quebec, but not their government, would have a veto.

If there were to be a compromise between the separate state demanded by the government of Quebec and the executive federalism practiced by the federal government, notice would have to be taken of *A Future Together,* the product of a federally-appointed task force that had traveled throughout Canada before making its report. That report firmly rejected the separatist option, but reflected the regional concerns of Western Canada and the dualist philosophy taken for granted in much of Quebec. It tried to meet the demands of the more moderate Quebec nationalists for provincial autonomy, for provincial control over language policy, for an upper house responsible to the provinces, and for recognition of Quebec's special position in Confederation.

Committed as it was to its own Constitutional Amendment Bill, and unwilling to accept still more provincial autonomy, the federal government had little use for its task force's recommendations. It was careful not to reject the report outright, but did what the government of Quebec said it would: it ignored the report. Instead, a few weeks later, the Liberal government dissolved Parliament, in March 1979. On May 22 it was defeated in the general election.

Nor was the report taken up by the new Conservative government under Joe Clark, though the new prime minister was sympathetic to Quebec's demands for reform of the country's federal structure. A minority government that lacked representation in Quebec had more pressing concerns than a reform of the Constitution which could divide the Conservative Party. By the time the date of Quebec's referendum was announced in November 1979, much time had been lost. By then the Constitutional Amendment Bill had lapsed with the defeat of the Liberal government, and *A Future Together* was in limbo. The Quebec Liberal Party had to respond to the one document on the table as government policy: The government of Quebec's white paper proposing sovereignty-association.

Sovereignty-Association: Québec-Canada: A New Deal, 1979

The proposals of the government of Quebec in preparation for its referendum were of course quite different from the federal government's "renewed federalism" and the "restructured federalism" of the Pépin-

Robarts report. Basing its demands on what may be called the "Quebec nationalist" view of history, *Québec-Canada: A New Deal* argued for the replacement of the present system by a "Community" structure in which nine provinces would form "Canada" and the tenth would be Quebec, a separate state.[30] (We shall distinguish this truncated "Canada" by the use of quotation marks.) The report did not explain how the remaining nine provinces were to work together, but it presumably expected them to continue as the "Canadian" federation with Ottawa as its capital. Quebec would not be represented. There would be no common Parliament for "Canada" and Quebec.

Because Quebec would be politically sovereign it would be able to ignore all political decisions made for Canadians in "Canada" by simply regarding them as applying only to its neighboring state. However, because there would be an economic association with the new "Canada" (comprising English Canada and the francophone minorities in the various provinces), Quebec would not be totally free to make economic decisions. The economic association was carefully defined as something more than a free trade zone (such as the European Free Trade Association) or a customs union (such as the nineteenth-century German *Zollverein*). It would include a common market with free mobility for goods, people, and capital. But it would also include a monetary union, thus going a step further than the European Community.

Four institutions were proposed to organize the "Canada"-Quebec economic community. One would be a Council of Ministers, and another a Commission of Experts (as Secretariat). A third would be a Court of Justice, with equal representation for "Canada" and Quebec. Lastly there would be a Central Monetary Authority. Here there would not be equality. "Canada" would be permitted to play a greater role. There would not be, it bears repeating, a common legislature or Parliament.

The basic assumption explicitly stated to be behind these proposals was that federalism was an outmoded concept. It had been designed for an eighteenth-century America and adopted by nineteenth-century Canada because the obvious alternative, a unitary system, was clearly unsuitable. In the twentieth century, on the other hand, there were alternatives. Several of the more advanced countries had sought a new cooperative system that would also insure the preservation of their political sovereignty. The relevant model, according to *Québec-Canada: A New Deal,* was the European Community, a pattern that could be adopted by "Canada" and Quebec. (The document did not explore the problems that might arise in a community of only two members.)

The justification for the withdrawal of Quebec from Canada's federal system was spelled out in a historical introduction. According to the white paper, Quebec had suffered conquest and had learned survival. It had borne with colonial rule, and had tried rebellion. A form of government called "dualism" had then been imposed by the 1840 Act of Union, replaced by a system called "Confederation" in 1867. But it was a Confederation in name only. Since 1867, Quebec had experienced English-Canadian hegemony; it had been without special status; and it was treated as a minority. The federal system had not prevented constant pressure for centralization. There had been continual invasion of Quebec's provincial rights. The history of Quebec, and of Canada, clearly proved the need for fundamental change.

The authors of the white paper assumed that Quebec was the homeland of the French-Canadian people, and that French Canadians living elsewhere would ultimately be assimilated. Quebec, and Quebec alone, could, by taking appropriate action, remain French-speaking and could enjoy a special status, even political sovereignty.

In its polemical and one-sided treatment of Canada's history, this document was very different from the proposals made by those Canadians who accepted Confederation. While its language of discourse was lucid, its message was deceptive. Instead of a complex picture of Canada there was a clear vision of Quebec. The interpretation of federalism in Canada was different: Confederation was identified with English-Canadian hegemony, not only in Parliament but on vital matters affecting Quebec.

Québec-Canada: A New Deal had a number of attractive features for Quebec nationalists. In the first place it promised to end all arguments with Canada. Once independence was obtained, Quebec would have all the responsibilities it wanted. The new institutions proposed for "Canada" would pertain to the nine provinces; Quebec would have only those powers freely granted by Quebec. The aggrandizement of the federal government would finally be stopped. The Quebecois would be able to establish their own political system, presumably a republic headed by a president. An independent Quebec would be able to negotiate with foreign powers, including the United States and France, and would become a member of the United Nations.

The document even had some attractive features for those English-speaking Canadians outside the province who had become frustrated by Quebec's refusal to cooperate within the federal system and by the steady attrition of the British parliamentary tradition. With separation, the pressure on English Canadians to abandon their British heritage would stop. The Monarchy could be preserved indefinitely; a truly national educational strategy could be planned; and a genuine "Canadian" political culture could be developed. Instead of two riders uneasily astride a single horse, there would be a horse for each rider, as it were. Or, to use René Lévesque's expression, there would no longer be two scorpions in a bottle. In a word, equality would have been achieved.

Not all Quebecois were convinced that Confederation was as insufferable as the *Parti Québecois* insisted, and that a sovereign Quebec would be better off. The plans for sovereignty-association received a setback when they were rejected by almost 60 percent of the voters in the provincial referendum. One may speculate whether the perceived socialist leanings of some members of the *Parti Québecois* played a role in influencing the more conservative voters. Certainly an independent Quebec with socialist leanings would have upset the emerging francophone business community, and might have created problems for relations with both English Canada and the United States.[31]

There was no way in which sovereignty-association, as proposed, could be made palatable to English Canada. Canada would be partitioned. On this issue the vision of most *indépendantistes* did not extend beyond the boundaries of Quebec. Few gave much thought to the damage that Quebec's sovereignty would inflict on the rest of Canada, with the Atlantic provinces separated from the rest. English Canadians would hardly be compensated by knowing that they could have a common national policy for education, retain the Monarchy, and promote their own anglophone culture unilingually.

Nor was the analogy of the European Community at all appropriate for "Canada" and Quebec. There was a great deal of difference between six (and later a dozen) European countries drawing closer together (and electing a common Parliament) and a united Canada being dismembered. An economic association of only two partners, and two very unequal partners, was hardly comparable to a voluntary association of six or more.

If it did nothing else, the publication of *Québec-Canada: A New Deal* should have laid to rest the complacent assumption that Canada could continue to agree to disagree. Yet some English Canadians continued to assume that the status quo was still an option. Many of those who defeated the Liberal government in the 1979 election concluded that the constitutional issues raised by Trudeau's Constitutional Amendment Bill were dead and buried. At the other extreme were those Quebec nationalists who were persuaded that Quebec and "Canada" could reach a modus vivendi analogous to the European Community. They assumed that if they chose independence and partitioned Canada, they could still amicably negotiate such delicate matters as the adjustment of the Labrador boundary, division of the country's assets, control over the St. Lawrence Seaway, membership in NORAD and NATO, and the position of the minorities on both sides of the border.

At the end of 1979 there were some who asked whether the Quebec government's white paper would be the only option put forward on behalf of Quebec. Was there no alternative to satisfy those Quebecois who, though nationalists in their defense of Quebec's cultural sovereignty and committed to structural change in the political system, nevertheless remained attached to Canada? The Quebec Liberal Party under Claude Ryan tried to give an answer, and offered its own alternative to sovereignty-association.

The Confederal Option: A New Canadian Federation, 1980

The Quebec government's white paper clearly called for a response from the Liberal Opposition before the referendum took place. But if the federal Liberals were able to offer "renewed federalism" through a Constitutional Amendment Bill, and the Task Force on Canadian Unity a "restructured federalism," was there anything left for the Quebec Liberals themselves to propose as an alternative to sovereignty-association? It could not be a replica of the two Pan-Canadian proposals, and it could hardly contemplate political sovereignty: like *A Future Together* it had to offer something in between.

In January 1980 the Quebec Liberal Party authorized the publication of what was called a "beige paper" entitled *A New Canadian Federation*. Its opening pages displayed pro-Canadian sympathies, which immediately attracted favorable notice in English Canada. In its foreword it rejected the negativism of *Québec-Canada: A New Deal* and instead radiated optimism, a willingness to cooperate, and even a vision of the future, not only of Quebec but of Canada as a whole. It recommended a renewed, if modified, federation, not the destruction of Canada, a country it described as having a fine tradition of political liberty and long experience of economic interdependence.[32] Quebec was declared to be a mature entity, whose people shared a profound attachment not only to their provinces but to Canada. *A New Canadian Federation* appeared to be a document in the best Pan-Canadian tradition.

However, these early pages were deceptive. For the beige paper offered a vision of Canada very different from that traditionally taken for granted by English Canadians and Pan-Canadians like Trudeau. The proposed "new Canadian federation" was to allocate far more power to the provinces (and especially Quebec) than either of the Pan-Canadian proposals. The new Canada was viewed not from an Ottawa but from a Quebec perspective. If the political system the Quebec Liberals had in mind was not simply a Confederacy, it was certainly sufficiently confederal to be very different from present-day Canada.

The beige paper reflected the profound desire in Quebec for structural change. It asserted, even in the foreword, that there had to be a redistribution of powers between the federal and provincial governments. It argued that an amendment formula and patriation could come only after this redistribution. (In fact the Constitution Act, 1982, was passed without a redistribution of powers, a clear victory for the federal government.)

It is arguable that in their proposals, and in their qualifications, the Quebec Liberal party was putting the very federal structure of Canada in question. The political system was declared to be acceptable only if "federalism can prove itself capable of adapting to Quebec's legitimate aspirations."[33] Among these aspirations were: the desire for a modern written Constitution made in Canada; popular approval of the change; explicit agreement between the communities comprising Canada; and the affirmation of the equality of the two founding peoples (something the federal Liberals remained unwilling to recognize).[34] The Quebec Liberals wanted the guarantees to Quebec to be spelled out, and not confined to cultural questions. There should be recognition that in Canada there were two sovereign jurisdictions. While admitting that the government of Canada should retain power over defense and the economy, the beige paper recommended the transfer of many other powers to the provinces. The provinces themselves would be linked by an intergovernmental body called The Federal Council.

A careful reading of the presentation indicated that the document alternated its moods between the warm and the chilling. In its warmer moments it asked Canadians to consider themselves as partners, not adversaries, and as people willing to negotiate publicly and in good faith. In its more frigid passages it insisted that there were certain fundamental values and principles that were accepted in Quebec, including its sovereign jurisdiction. These could not be bargained.

At the institutional level, the beige paper accepted the parliamentary system and paid tribute to the role played by the House of Commons. It was less positive toward the Crown and the upper house. It gave its opinion that the Monarchy would disappear, and it proposed the abolition of the Senate. All MPs should be elected by proportional representation. If Canadians were confused by the two alternatives already proposed for the Senate (the 118-member *House of the Federation* proposed by Mr. Trudeau, half of which would be elected by provincial legislatures, and the 60-member *Council of the Federation* suggested by the Task Force, all of whose members would be nominated by provincial governments), they may have been confused even further by the beige paper's proposal. This called for a provincially-appointed upper house of members with yet another name: the *Federal Council*.

The Federal Council was to remain an instrument of the provincial government. To prevent manipulation by the federal government, it was not to be treated as a federal institution at all. Though located in Ottawa it would be a provincially-appointed body, with its own source of funds. As such it would appear to inject an element of confederacy into the system. It would seem appropriate to describe the proposal as confederal.

This provincially-appointed Federal Council would have four functions: ratifying; advisory; dualist; and federal-provincial. As a ratifying body it would have some of the powers associated with the American Senate, for example, the approval of senior federal appointments and the ratification of those treaties which affected the provinces. It would also have the power to prevent unilateral federal action through the use of the emergency power and Parliament's spending power. As an advisory body the Federal Council would proffer counsel in a number of areas, notably in fiscal, monetary and transportation policy. In its dualist role it would operate on the "double majority" principle first put forward by the federal government for the handling of language legislation. The beige paper suggested that in its resolution of cultural problems, the Federal Council should appoint a committee on which French- and English-speaking Canadians were equally represented. Twenty percent of the francophone representatives should be drawn from the minorities outside Quebec. Finally, in its fourth role, that of federal-provincial relations, the Federal Council would incorporate the responsibilities at present exercised at federal-provincial conferences.

On a number of issues the beige paper went beyond both the Constitutional Amendment Bill and *A Future Together*. Approval of the emergency and spending powers of the federal government would require the assent not of a simple majority of the Federal Council but of a two-thirds majority. The declaratory power, which the task force thought should be curbed, would be abolished. Provincial lieutenant governors, at present appointed by the federal government alone, would be appointed by the provinces themselves. In sum, the Quebec Liberals were prepared to meet the *Parti Québecois* almost halfway, at a point between federalism and sovereignty-association, a position that we have called confederal.

The beige paper revealed the dilemma faced, at least before the referendum, by those Quebecois who wished to combine federalism and nationalism. Despite the warm welcome it received from English Canadians who had recently read *Québec-Canada: A New Deal* with its litany of complaints, the document indicated that even federalist Quebecois were moving away from the position of philosophical federalism. If Quebec were to remain in Confederation, it was on the understanding that Canada was ultimately to become a republic, a view diametrically opposed to that of the government of Ontario. Moreover, the proposed Federal Council representing the provinces was not even to be part of the federal structure. The confederalism that Ontario had feared in the 1860s was now being put forward as a serious option by moderate Liberals in Quebec.

The beige paper was yet another challenge to the assumptions underlying the federal government's Constitutional Amendment Bill. Whatever Mr. Trudeau might assert, the options being seriously considered in Quebec, which would ultimately decide for itself the form that its relationship with the rest of Canada would take, included not only his renewed federalism but even more the restructured federalism of *A Future Together,* the confederalism of *A New Canadian Federation,* and the *Parti Québecois'* proposals for sovereignty-association.

All the proposals for change between 1978 and 1980 owed much of their inspiration to French Canadians, Pierre Trudeau, Jean-Luc Pépin (who appears to have been more influential than his cochairman John Roberts), René Lévesque, and Claude Ryan. The three federalist proposals responded to the demand for a Canada based more on the principle associated with constitutional federalism than heretofore. All curbed the power of the anglophone majority. Gradually over the decades the principles of Canadian government were being changed. The bilingualism and biculturalism that had seemed too avant-garde when promoted by Henri Bourassa had become the conventional wisdom of the 1960s. The new Constitution with its Charter of Rights that had at first appeared to challenge Canada's parliamentary tradition was slowly being absorbed into the system in the 1980s. There seemed to be recognition that sooner or later the Senate would have to be replaced by an upper house representing the provinces and that the Supreme Court would have to be entrenched in the Constitution.

In this section we have described five options facing Canada in the 1980s. Of course they do not exhaust all the possibilities. Were Ottawa and Quebec to reach a complete stalemate over further reform, Canada's tradition of incremental change, which we have called the status quo, could be replaced by a refusal on both sides to make any change at all. The result might be what the French call *immobilisme,* or immobility. Alternatively, were the Quebecois in general to feel strongly that no further negotiations with English Canada were possible, they might opt for sovereignty without association, a policy proposed by members of the *Parti Québecois* in 1982. If Quebec seceded from Canada completely, the result would be the partition of English Canada. Such a divided "Canada" would find it difficult to retain its present federal structure. At some point the Maritimes or the Western provinces might wish to explore union with the United States. In other words, one consequence of Quebec's demand for independence could very well be not partition but disintegration. This was a possibility few people in Quebec or elsewhere dared openly to contemplate, and yet it may have been one reason for the reluctance of the Quebec electorate to embark on an uncharted course by committing itself to sovereignty-association.

In terms of the degree of change involved, the possibilities we have so far considered can be listed as follows:

1. Immobility
2. Status quo

3. Renewed federalism
4. Restructured federalism
5. Confederalism
6. Sovereignty-association
7. Partition (with Quebec's sovereignty)
8. Distintegration

Leaving aside the extremes of immobility and disintegration, we can discern six options. Of these, continuation of the status quo and renewed federalism as proposed in the federal government's Constitutional Amendment Bill of 1978 have been regarded as inadequate by public opinion in Quebec. Conversely, the Quebec government's options of sovereignty-partition and sovereignty-association, together with the Quebec Liberal Party's confederalism have been declared unacceptable to English Canada and the federal government. This leaves some form of restructured federalism as the only negotiable option. With the passage of the Constitution Act in 1982, and the tentative acceptance of the principle of constitutional federalism rather than the Westminster tradition of parliamentary supremacy, Canadians might be expected to begin to think seriously about new structures for their federal institutions, with particular emphasis on the Supreme Court and the Senate.

A Further Option: Constitutional Federalism

If Canadians decided to restructure their federal system to meet the demands of the more moderate elements in Quebec (as many thoughtful Canadians were beginning to think they should once the 1980 referendum was over), probably the most difficult decision would be to determine the form that constitutional federalism would take. While over time Canadians had replaced imperial rule with what they called the "logic of federalism," the logic to which they referred was the constitutional federalism explained by Chief Justice Marshall in *Marbury v. Madison* in 1803. This was the logic of a judicial review by a Supreme Court established by a Constitution framed by the representatives of the people and ratified by state conventions. For opponents of the judicial review proclaimed by Marshall the only alternative was the notion of legislative supremacy. But the American Revolution had rejected the doctrine of British parliamentary supremacy. Moreover, since the new federal system required an umpire, there was a logic to American federalism. However, it was the logic not of the federal principle per se but of the type of constitutional federalism which the Americans introduced.

The American form of constitutional federalism involved a fundamental principle alien to the Westminster tradition of the Crown-in-Parliament. It explicitly maintained that government was dependent on the popular will: the people were sovereign. From this fundamental principle followed a number of practical applications. A constitution was a document framed by representatives of the people elected to a constitutional convention. It was later ratified by the people either through a referendum (the procedure followed for French constitutions since 1946) or by regional conventions (as in the United States after 1787 when the thirteen states ultimately agreed to its terms.)

This world view would probably encounter little opposition in Quebec. Since the decline of the Church the notion of popular sovereignty has become more attractive than parliamentary sovereignty. The idea of ratifying constitutional change by referenda was put forward during the 1981 negotiations over the Constitution, after the Quebec government had debated the proposed Constitution in the National Assembly before the television cameras.

Such a constitutional federalism would be difficult for many English Canadians to accept. The idea of a popular referendum to determine the future of Canada was opposed by all nine English-Canadian provincial premiers in 1981 when it was mooted by Trudeau and accepted by Lévesque.[35] A referendum was widely thought to conflict with the Westminster tradition of parliamentary supremacy. In fact, in none of the English-speaking provinces was the Constitution Act debated in the Legislative Assembly. Instead, in accordance with the principle of executive federalism, negotiations were left in the hands of the provincial governments. Moreover, as the visit of the Queen to sign the Proclamation of the Constitution Act into law demonstrated, a vital element of the legitimacy of Canadian government remained the role of the Monarch as sovereign.

It should be pointed out that constitutional federalism does not require the abolition of the Monarchy. Nor does it necessarily involve either a constitutional convention or a referendum to determine the nature of the federal system, provided the governments involved in the negotiations are able to reach agreement. In Canada it would be premature to conclude that such agreement is impossible.

However, the two orders of government do face a number of obstacles.

1. A federal system is already in being; it is not being established de novo as in the United States.
2. The federal government plays such a dominant role that it would be difficult for the provinces to obtain a redistribution of power.
3. There are conflicting views on the nature of constitutional federalism: (a) English Canadians believe it should be based on negotiation between governments, i.e., on the principle of parliamentary supremacy; (b) French Canadians are willing to consider an element of popular sovereignty, e.g., a referendum or even a constitutional convention.

The calling of a constitutional convention in Canada, basing the future political system on the principle of popular sovereignty, would be novel, if not alien. The very idea of a constitutional convention would suggest that Canada was adopting not only the principle underlying American constitutional federalism but the very liberal and republican system which traditional Canadians, whether British, Loyalist and conservative or French, Catholic and conservative, had always opposed. English Canadians would no doubt prefer to continue to try and resolve problems through the parliamentary system, federal-provincial conferences, and the procedures introduced in the Constitution Act, 1982. Such procedures might not, however, be flexible enough to produce a new regime. In that case, a constitutional convention and/or referendum might be the best alternative—if they did not seem so un-Canadian and un-British.

But are they? In 1689 the English had to call together a Convention Parliament to give legitimacy to the new regime installed after the flight of King James II. In 1864 the Canadian provinces came together in a sort of constitutional convention. As for referenda or plebiscites, these, too, are not unknown to the Westminster tradition. In 1942 the Canadian government conducted a plebiscite to help determine its policy on conscription. Quebec adopted the referendum to discover the views of the electorate in 1980. (In doing so it used as its model the British referendum on entry to the European Community in 1975.) In other words, were negotiations for a new federalism unsuccessful, it would not be "unconstitutional" to proceed by constitutional convention and/ or referendum.

It has often been noted in Quebec that Canada used to manage changes of regime in the old days. However, on each occasion (1774, 1791, 1849, and 1867), there was no federal system and it was the imperial Parliament that made the decision. Even in 1867 it was imperial participation that helped to bring about Confederation. Since then, the imperial Parliament has not been available, and no change of regime has taken place. Were the Constitution Act to prove inadequate to bring about structural change in the system, a fresh approach might be necessary.

Under the Constitution Act of 1982, Canadians still elect both federal and provincial legislatures, each with its own jurisdiction and vested interests. By contrast, when a new regime is organized (except under imperial federalism) the people may have to take back, temporarily, the power they have previously distributed among these bodies. During a specific regime the people in a federal system enjoy the luxury of watching the two orders of government struggle between themselves like hockey teams in an arena. Having two sets of government adds to the freedom that citizens in such a system enjoy. But when fundamental questions arise regarding the size of the political arena and the rules of the game, then the sovereign people may be unable to delegate that responsibility to two sets of decision-makers. This is particularly true of contemporary Canada, where the federal government has often been at odds with the government of Quebec. Each claims, with justice, that it enjoys the support of the electorate. In 1980 the voters in Quebec elected 74 Liberals to the 75 Quebec seats in the House of Commons. In 1981 they elected 80 members of the *Parti Québecois* to an *Assemblée Nationale* of 122 members.

Moreover, as the principles of constitutional federalism become more accepted, the legitimacy of the two other branches of government, the judiciary and the legislature, becomes an issue. The Supreme Court has to become an impartial federal tribunal entrenched in the Constitution. Because of the extraordinary importance of regionalism in many parts of English Canada and of dualism among French-speaking Canadians, the composition of the Court will have to reflect the nature of Canadian society even more carefully than the American Supreme Court has come to reflect various important elements in the United States. Particular care will have to be given to insuring that the Court is considered in Quebec to be a symbol of "judicial federalism" and not the creature of executive federalism.

The third branch of government, the legislature, is of particular importance because only if this body had legitimacy (and power) could the executive and judiciary properly perform their federal functions. In any political system based on the principles of constitutional federalism, the upper house is a vital element. Not surprisingly, those who presented the various federalist options between 1978 and 1980 were preoccupied with a reform of the Senate that would transform it into a legitimate federal institution.

It is doubtful whether agreement on a new regime, one based on constitutional federalism, would be reached if it depended on the concurrence of two such diverse representative bodies as the governments of Canada and Quebec, the one committed to federalism and the other to a form of confederalism. The obvious alternative, a constitutional convention, would not necessarily provide a solution either, though it might have to be tried.[36]

In sum, constitutional federalism requires the replacement of the external umpire of imperial federalism by a set of domestic political institutions that embody the federal principle. In making the transition to constitutional federalism, the two orders of government in Canada could conceivably reach agreement without an American-style constitutional convention or a French-style referendum on the acceptability of the new regime. However, if the governments could not agree on the replacement of the existing system, and if public opinion still favored a new regime, then one or both of these might prove to be acceptable alternatives.

Constitutional federalism will come about when agreement has been reached on the legitimacy of federal institutions. In Canada, after imperial federalism lost its legitimacy it was replaced by executive federalism. This in turn began to lose its legitimacy when both main political parties, and therefore the federal Cabinet or executive, were unable to represent major regions of the country. In any case, executive federalism alone could not fulfill the requirements of constitutional federalism.

If there is to be another federal institution representing provinces rather than populations, and if its members are not to be popularly elected on the American pattern of legislative federalism, then there will have to be a body representative of the provincial governments themselves. Consequently, there will be an institution quite separate and different from the House of Commons: a "Council of the Provinces."

Such an organization would have certain disadvantages. Provincial delegates would probably bring the obstreperousness that has come to characterize federal-provincial conferences. The task of the federal Cabinet, now directly responsible only to the House of Commons, would be complicated. On the other hand, no one could dismiss the Quebec delegates as *vendus:* they would be representatives of the Quebec government and the nationalist tradition. Moreover, while it is true that ministers have been directly responsible only to the lower house, in practice they have had to take account of the views of provincial governments. The debate over the Constitution Act made this very clear. After the bill was passed by Parliament it was submitted to the provinces for debate at two First Ministers Conferences in September and November 1981; then certain revisions were made and it was resubmitted to Parliament for final passage. In other words, the First Ministers Conference acted in place of the upper house in a federal system. A Council of the Provinces would merely regularize this process.

The advantage of a Council of the Provinces would be that, unlike First Ministers Conferences, its proceedings would conform to normal parliamentary procedure: it would represent legislative, not executive, federalism. It is difficult to imagine an occasion arising when members of the Council would meet without informing one of the provincial delegations that they were intent on resolving a fundamental issue. Yet at the Federal-Provincial Conference of November 4–5, 1981, representatives from nine provinces reached agreement with the federal government in the absence of a Quebec representative. There was no independent speaker and no parliamentary procedure to insure that legislative proprieties were observed.

The Council of the Provinces would represent provinces and not populations. Would it, like the American Senate, represent the provinces (or states) equally, with perhaps ten senators from each jurisdiction, or would it continue to represent the large regions of Canada, with twenty-four senators each from the Maritimes, Quebec, Ontario, and the Western provinces (plus six from Newfoundland and two from the Territories)? From the perspective of the eight "peripheral" provinces, equal representation of provinces would seem desirable, thus reducing the representation of central Canada from nearly 50 percent to less than 20 percent.

The two central Canadian provinces, with over 60 percent of the population, have, of course, dominated the House of Commons, with 170 of the 282 seats. They have controlled successive federal cabinets. It seems unnecessary for them to add to their already overwhelming influence domination of the Council of the Provinces. It so happens that a representation of 20 out of about 100 would simply reflect their current representation at First Ministers Conferences, with two out of ten premiers, an arrangement they seem to have been comfortable with. In sum, equal provincial representation, a novelty for Canada, would help to redress the balance of Canadian politics in favor of the Western and Atlantic provinces. That is long overdue.

Even if this were accomplished, it would not resolve the problem of Canadian dualism. As chief representative of one of Canada's two main cultures, the province of Quebec would still be in a minority of one. Yet it might be possible to meet Quebec's demand for equality by confirming that Canada has historically been bicultural, and by asserting that on cultural issues French Canada, represented mainly by Quebec, was to be the equal of the rest of Canada. For cultural matters the Council of the Provinces could be represented by a special committee composed of equal numbers of English- and French-speaking Canadians. This would recall the days of the old Province of Canada when there was a demand for a "double majority." In other words, there could be a committee of twenty-four members, twelve of whom would be francophones. Ten of these could be the Quebec delegation, and the other two, nominees of the francophone minorities. Were such a committee to be established, there would have been some attempt made to recognize Canada as a country of ten equal provinces and two equal cultures.

Nothing like this has ever been seriously proposed in the United States. There the blacks have no special representation as a community and remain a minority everywhere, except in a number of local jurisdictions. On the other hand, the United States, despite the victory of the North in the War between the States, did make provision for the white South in Congress. Among the protective devices available was the filibuster or veto. Traditionally in Canada the provinces have also assumed that they have some sort of veto, at least over constitutional amendments vital to their interest. That veto was preserved in the Constitution

Act of 1982 through the provision for unanimous consent for certain amendments. It would seem desirable to give Quebec special recognition of its distinctiveness as a minority by permitting a veto on certain issues vital to its interests. Such a veto would provide a better defense against decisions taken by English Canada in the heat of emotion, for example, the imposition of conscription or the banning of French in Quebec airports, than has been available to the French minority in times of crisis. Membership of the federal Cabinet or the governing party caucus has too often failed.

Only by finally recognizing the legitimacy of Quebec's demands to be treated as an equal can that province (or *L'Etat du Québec*) be expected to accept the Constitution. Without its acceptance the document will never acquire full legitimacy. Unless it becomes part of the new Canada, Quebec could continue to drift away from Confederation.

The passage of the Constitution Act in 1982 indicated that a new dialectic was about to get under way, between Parliament on the one hand, with its "notwithstanding" clause that enabled Parliament and the provincial legislatures to override sections of the Charter of Rights, and on the other, the Supreme Court, which would have to interpret the Charter. In other countries such a dialectic had already begun. In the United Kingdom, the sovereignty of Parliament was being challenged by the courts of the European Community. In India the courts and Parliament have for some time been engaged in conflict over the sections in the Indian Constitution dealing with Directive Principles and Fundamental Rights. Canada was therefore by no means the only parliamentary country where the courts appeared to be steadily enlarging the scope of their activities.

The Supreme Court of Canada's constitutional interventions had for the most part been welcomed, especially its declaration in September 1981 that for the federal government and Parliament to patriate the Constitution unilaterally would be legal but not constitutional. But despite these initial successes it was still possible that at some point there would be a disastrous intervention like the 1857 Dred Scott case over slavery in the United States. Then the legitimacy of the Supreme Court, long discussed in the abstract, could become a political issue unless entrenchment had already occurred.

In the past it was possible for Canada to live with its contradictions and to practice philosophical federalism through incremental change. That option was no longer available after 1980. The Quebecois, and some English Canadians, were determined to convince the people of Canada that their existing political institutions, notably the BNA Act, the Senate and the Supreme Court, inherited from the days of imperial federalism, lacked legitimacy, and that parliamentary tradition based on convention was inadequate for a federal system like Canada. Instead, they wanted the principles associated with constitutional federalism, though not necessarily those of the American variety, to be accepted and implemented.

11
Conclusion: Toward a New State Structure?

1 Introduction

In accordance with the principle of dualism, Canadians have made a number of important concessions in recent years to minorities, notably to the French-speaking Canadians. Throughout the federal public service, French has become an official language, and it is being increasingly accepted at the provincial level of government. To complement the new language policy there is a national program promoting multiculturalism that recognizes the distinctive character of the mosaic that is modern Canada. To update the archaic BNA Act a new Constitution has been proclaimed. And two prime ministers in succession, both fluently bilingual, have come from Quebec. The principle of dualism would seem to have been fully accepted and the major obstacles to a renewed federalism overcome.

Although these changes are certainly significant, it would be shortsighted and unwise not to recognize their limitations. Overall, they do not depart from the tradition of philosophical federalism with its reliance on an incremental change that appears to keep options open but which in fact does not disrupt the established order. Yet the most important lesson of the victory of the *Parti Québecois* in 1976, and of the 1980 referendum on sovereignty-association, is the desire for structural change.

In practice there have been almost no structural changes in the institutions of government. Imperial federalism might have been dispensed with, and with it the various imperial umpires. But a vacuum has been left. One umpire, the governor general, has become more of a cipher than ever. Another, the Judicial Committee of the Privy Council, has been replaced by a Supreme Court that is still a creature of Parliament and not the Constitution. The third, the British Parliament, has been replaced by a Canadian Parliament dominated by a Cabinet that is responsible only to the House of Commons, a body elected on the basis of population. Far from representing the interests of Quebec and the smaller provinces, the Senate remains a bastion of privilege, whose members are appointed by the prime minister on the basis of political patronage. In sum, instead of the balanced Constitution of imperial federalism of 1867, there is the concentration of power in the Cabinet and the House of Commons, and a dependence on majority rule.

Canada's federalism can therefore be described as pseudofederalism. The attitude of many Canadians to their system of government has in many ways resembled that of people elsewhere (e.g., Britain), who have accepted majority rule. It is an attitude appropriate to an established homogeneous society for which the state is assumed (often incorrectly) to represent a single dominant nation. It is not suitable for the new Canada in which the state has to implement bilingualism, accept multiculturalism, and recognize the role of native peoples.

Structural change means more than an ability to adapt to the impact of successive civilizations through a philosophical federalism that results in incremental changes to the existing regime. It requires the replacement of pseudofederalism by a truly constitutional federalism with institutions appropriate for a balanced constitution. Even more, it involves a transformation of the whole concept of the state: the replacement of the notion that Canada is a nation-state and thereby implicitly identifying the state with its majority "nation." It requires the acceptance of a secular state in the broadest sense, one that insures the rights of both founding peoples as well as New Canadians and the country's original inhabitants.

We shall deal with each of these issues in turn.

2 Canada's Response to Successive Civilizations

Canada's various political traditions, while reflecting the impact of successive civilizations, have never completely accepted any of them. There has always been a desire to be different, along with a refusal to be imprisoned by the past.

Although French Canadians retained the language, religion, and civil law of Bourbon France, and a strong sense of being an isolated and threatened community, the limitations of the civilization of the *ancien régime* from the point of view of government were all too apparent after the Conquest. In those fields where British civilization appeared to offer a superior alternative—for example, in representative institutions and

Conclusion: Toward a New State Structure?

the criminal law—Quebec (like India in the following century) adopted British traditions. Chief among these was the Westminster form of parliamentary government.

Nor did Canadians show much of a disposition to remain a colony of the United Kingdom. Responsible government proved to be incompatible with imperialism. Indeed, it set the stage for the ultimate emergence of an independent Commonwealth. British civilization in its turn was found to be inadequate for Canada's needs as a dual society. When English-speaking Canadians had to choose whether to support the Imperial authorities in their attempt to assimilate French Canada into *British* North America or to cooperate with the French Canadians against Whitehall in order to achieve *Canadian* political autonomy, they made a momentous choice: they selected as their partners the French Canadians, not the British government and its representatives. Soon after the Act of Union of 1840, therefore, the Imperial authorities had to abandon their aim of making English Canada's sole official language. By 1848, the governor general was reading the Speech from the Throne in both English and French.

The *Canadiens* of Lower Canada proved willing to cooperate with the Upper Canadians. Instead of remaining outside the party system like the Irish in the United Kingdom, they took office in coalition governments during the Union era (1840–67). During this period, the Province of Canada's political culture differed sharply from that of the Mother Country. Its guiding principle was dualism.

Dualism involved two separate administrative structures: an English-speaking public administration in Upper Canada and a francophone administration in Lower Canada. There were therefore two sets of ministers who collaborated under the leadership of two first ministers. One (who might be francophone) was first minister by British convention; the other was co-first minister by Canadian convention. The capital alternated between Upper and Lower Canada. Every four years, politicians and civil servants set sail either upstream to Toronto or downstream to Quebec City, the old capital of New France. Twenty years' experience of French-English cooperation made possible the federation of the Province of Canada (divided into two equal sections, henceforth to be called Ontario and Quebec) with the other British North American provinces.

After Confederation, the principle of dualism meant different things to the two communities. To the English-speaking Canadians, the French-speaking Catholic minority had been given control of Quebec, where they formed a majority. "Dualism" now meant collaboration between a national (English) majority and a provincial (French) majority, with both Ontario and Quebec providing for the education of their religious minorities. The French-speaking Canadians, on the other hand, hoped that the principle of dualism would mean the equality of the two languages and cultures across Canada, regardless of size. They regarded the West, which they had pioneered, as the joint patrimony of the two founding peoples. Instead, English-speaking Canadians assumed that the Dominion Government, which they controlled, was taking over Canada from England—and Western Canada from the Hudson's Bay Company. This apparent abandonment of the principle of dualism as equality enabled the seeds of French-Canadian discontent to grow once more, just when the English-speaking Canadians thought that with Confederation the relationship had been finally resolved to everyone's satisfaction.

For about a century, the two principles of majority rule and dualism were to be in conflict. Not until the 1960s, and the emergence of the threat of separatism, were English Canadians prepared to accept the principle of two founding peoples and two official languages—and French culture treated not as *Québecois* but as *Canadian*. This has meant a new Canada.

The acceptance of the principle of dualism has still to be translated into appropriate political institutions. For although after much argument Canadians have remained together—unlike Britain and Ireland—in one state, their two cultures remain different, with the French-speaking Canadians a declining minority. English-speaking Canadians have always regarded the individual voter (together with the Crown) as the basis of sovereignty and rule by the majority as the source of the federal government's legitimacy. By contrast, the francophone minority has not been able to look at the individual voter (or the Crown, now that it is domiciled in Canada and is no longer an external umpire) for adequate support. Instead, the francophones look to their community to provide the basis of sovereignty. Ultimately, therefore, dualism involves a reappraisal of the role of French-speaking Canadians, and particularly Quebec, in the federal political system. It means the modification of the Westminster form of parliamentary government so that the government of the day is no longer responsible only to the House of Commons, elected solely on the basis of population (i.e., majority rule).

The conflict between the principles of majority rule and dualism

Conclusion: Toward a New State Structure? 395

reached a climax just as British civilization was being eclipsed. Indeed, it may have been no accident that the emergence of a strong sentiment throughout Quebec in favor of Canada becoming a dualist society, recognizing two official languages, should have occurred with the decline of British influence and its replacement by that of the United States.

The impact of this third civilization is still being assessed. Canadians have always found much of American civilization agreeable, ever since the days when they were able to use their friendship with the United States as a counter to British domination. American science and technology, the hallmark of the twentieth century's dominant civilization, have been particularly admired. This explains why Canada looks so American to first-time visitors.

As it has become obvious that Canada is destined to be part of a North American civilization, Canadians have once again shown their determination to be different. There has developed considerable concern over American cultural penetration. Nationalists who a generation earlier resented the teaching of British history now feared a "continentalist" approach to the subject, and they insisted that attention be devoted to a distinctive Canadian history, in which the Westminster political tradition played an important role. They also began to draw a distinction between Canadian and American literature.

The American social sciences have presented the greatest challenge to Canadian intellectuals. It is one thing to argue in favor of Canadian history and Canadian literature, which are humane studies, but another to question the methods of the social sciences. These methods have been presented as scientific, and therefore of universal applicability. Only gradually has it become apparent to Canadians that the social sciences are different from the natural sciences. As Charles Taylor has noted, natural science theory cannot be used as a model for social theory: it is part of a significantly different activity. American social and political theories, even in the form of empirical theory, have cultural overtones. They are based on certain philosophical assumptions, which we have suggested are similar to those of the pragmatists whose philosophy Canadians long ago rejected.[1] Instead, Canadian intellectuals have preferred a tolerant world view of keeping options open, which has been called philosophical federalism.

In sum, after the Conquest (1760), Canada retained much of French culture, but replaced French civilization with British parliamentary institutions. After the Rebellions (1837–38), the Province of Canada rejected a British imperialism that demanded English supremacy. Instead, despite the worldwide dominance of British civilization, for over twenty years governments in Canada depended on a modification of British parliamentary government that made provision for dualism. Later, the acceptance of two cultures gave rise to the notion of philosophical federalism. This was accommodated to the practice of majority rule that characterized the Dominion of Canada after Confederation.

Philosophical federalism persisted, even as British civilization gave way to American (though much of the British political culture was retained). On the one hand Canadians accepted the scientific and technological know-how of the United States; on the other they attempted to resist American economic and cultural penetration (or "imperialism"). They were not always successful: the Canadian economy became increasingly dependent on the American, the United States accounting for an estimated $69 billion of the $86 billion of Canadian imports in 1984.[2] At the level of popular culture, American films, magazines, and TV programs predominated: for every Canadian popular drama shown on TV in 1984, there were twenty-four American ones. Nevertheless, at the level of high culture, with which this study has been concerned, the attempt to protect and promote an indigenous culture has continued to show some success. Few Canadian intellectuals have been willing to let themselves be absorbed into a uniform continental culture.

3 The Interaction of the Two Cultures:
From Philosophical Federalism to Regime Change

Even so, by the 1980s philosophical federalism was no longer feasible as a solution to Canada's political contradictions. It is true that concessions had been granted by the English Canadian majority; a new constitution was put into operation. It was also true that the separatist movement was in disarray; indeed, early in 1985 the *Parti Québecois* abandoned its policy of working toward sovereignty-association.

It did not follow, however, that Canada could expect to bring about further reforms through incremental change. The practice of majority rule, with the federal government responsible to the House of Commons, still held good. If dualism was to be implemented, there had to be structural changes in the institutions of government. It was for this reason that the French-speaking Canadians had threatened to leave Confederation and might do so again, if the principle was not implemented. After

Conclusion: Toward a New State Structure? 397

all, in early 1985 Quebec still had not signed the 1982 Constitution Act, and therefore had refused to give it the legitimacy it needed. And just when the *Parti Québecois* was abandoning separatism and giving English-speaking Canadians hope for the future, a new separatist movement was under way. Camille Laurin, previously a leading minister in the *Parti Québecois* government of Quebec, announced he was leaving the party and forming a movement called *Rassemblement démocratique pour l'indépendance,* or RDI. This held its founding convention on March 30, 1985, and committed itself to a platform favoring outright independence.

If past experience is any guide, it is just when Canadians become complacent about their future as one state that a constitutional crisis erupts. For example, in 1976, after Pierre Trudeau had confidently declared separatism to be dead, Quebec was suddenly up in arms over the right of air traffic controllers to speak French with francophone pilots. The issue was ultimately resolved to Quebec's satisfaction, but not before the *Parti Québecois* had been swept into power. The demand for structural change became more insistent than ever. After 1976 philosophical federalism was dead.

Similarly, in the later 1980s, with the intensity of separatist feeling on the wane, and a new government supported by the Quebec voters in power, it was tempting for English-speaking Canadians to believe that a new consensus had emerged. On the contrary, a constitutional crisis could once again erupt and reveal to Quebec the might of the English-speaking majority. Next time around, it is probable that the nationalist option available will not be the *deux nations* proposal of the *Union Nationale* in the 1960s, or the sovereignty-association rejected in 1980, but outright independence. While this option is hardly likely to be immediately attractive to an electoral majority, it could prove significant in the future. Although support for separatism had abated in the early 1980s, it would be misleading to conclude that the fundamental belief in the desirability, and indeed the justice, of structural change had been jettisoned.

4   From Pseudofederalism to Constitutional Federalism

Whatever may have been the merits of philosophical federalism as a mechanism (or paradigm) to hold Canadian intellectuals together throughout the British connection, after 1976 its inadequacies became obvious. The principle underpinning the Canadian governmental system had become majority rule. At Confederation, when a form of federalism *was* introduced, it was one we have called imperial federalism. It was federal because it provided umpires for each of the three branches of government. It was imperial because the institutions that acted as umpires were British, not Canadian: the governor general in Ottawa, representing the executive; Parliament in Westminster acting as the legislature; and the Judicial Committee of the Privy Council in Whitehall performing the role of final court of appeal.

When these three external umpires were discarded and not replaced, the vacuum that was created was concealed by the fiction that Canada enjoyed "parliamentary federalism." Yet without a constitutionally recognized internal umpire (or umpires), Canada's imperial federalism was transformed into the pseudofederalism of majority rule—as Quebec discovered. Canada has yet to fill the vacuum. To do so, all three branches of government will have to conform to the federal principle, thus replacing the postimperial system by constitutional federalism. It is not enough for the various institutions of government to act (as they do) *as if* Canada were truly federal: they must become federal. That is why the present system must be recognized for what it really is: pseudofederal and not as an expression of something called "cooperative federalism" or "executive federalism," still less "legislative federalism" or "judicial federalism."

Canada is *not* governed according to what is euphemistically described as "executive federalism." The meetings of first ministers, or their associates, are certainly meetings of executives. But they do not have a federal character in the proper sense of demonstrating a coordinate relationship. The prime minister assumes he may chair all the sessions, set the agenda, control the Secretariat and assess the sense of the meeting—as though the First Ministers Conference were a parliamentary Cabinet. However, unlike the Cabinet, the other members cannot by opposing the prime minister cause his resignation, nor he theirs. There is no doctrine of collective responsibility or responsible government. The First Ministers Conferences remain what they always have been: ad hoc arrangements to keep the system working.

Were executive federalism to be introduced, the chairperson would be determined by all eleven first ministers: the Secretariat would be federal-provincial and not an arm of the federal government, and the agenda would have no bias in favor of Ottawa. Decisions would be formally

Conclusion: Toward a New State Structure?

taken. It is by no means certain that if executive federalism *were* introduced, Quebec would be mollified. However, it might help to remove a sense of the prime minister and other premiers "ganging up on Quebec." If the federal government could not accept the replacement of its convenient "parliamentary conventions" by federal rules of procedures, then the myth of "executive federalism" would be exposed. In any case, a federal system does not require First Ministers Conferences. These represent a transitional stage before legislative federalism is introduced.

Legislative federalism involves the replacement of government responsible to the lower house by responsibility to both chambers. The upper house has to be elected, but on a different principle from the lower. It must also be able to exercise a veto on behalf of the minority, perhaps like the American Senate. Alternatively, as in Sweden from 1866 to 1970, disagreement between the houses can be resolved through a joint vote in which the lower house preponderates.[3]

It may be difficult to envisage the Canadian House of Commons becoming enthusiastic about sharing its considerable powers with a rival elected Senate, or to imagine the government of Canada being persuaded to accept responsibility to two Chambers. It is certainly unlikely that the provincial premiers will permit the powers they wield by "executive federalism" to be exercised by senators through legislative federalism. However, it is demonstrable that the House of Commons has arrogated powers to itself not envisaged in the Confederation debate. Moreover, the First Ministers Conferences, with their inevitably infrequent ad hoc meetings, have proved their limitations for resolving questions that require the careful debate and analysis only a legislature can provide. Nor is there any reason why a reformed Senate should be modeled after any other body, particularly the unique United States Senate. Instead, it could satisfy the provincial premiers by acting as the direct expression of official provincial sentiment, that is, the sentiments of provincial governments whose premiers or other designated officials would lead the delegations.

It is certainly possible for the government of Canada to be responsible to both Houses, one representing the provinces. In effect something like this has already happened. During the 1981 debates, the Constitution Act had to be acceptable to both Parliament and the (extraconstitutional) First Ministers Conferences. Under federalism, the first ministers' informal executive veto would become a legislative veto exercised through the Senate.[4]

If legislative federalism is a prerequisite of constitutional federalism, then so is judicial federalism. Though the Canadian Supreme Court conducts itself *as if* it were analogous to the American Supreme Court, it is not. The Canadian court has not yet been entrenched in the Constitution, and remains a creature of the Parliament of Canada. Even so, it has pronounced on a number of controversial constitutional questions, among them Senate reforms in 1979, the constitutional amendment procedure in 1981, and Quebec's language legislation in 1984. In 1984 the new chief justice, R. G. B. Dickson, is reported to have stated that "the days of the British tradition in which judges left it to the politicians to change laws no longer applied. The Charter imposed a 'duty' upon judges to strike down laws that violated constitutional guarantee."[5]

Now that it has been made clear that the court rejects the doctrine of parliamentary supremacy, it may be much more difficult for the Canadian Supreme Court to persuade Parliament to give it enhanced constitutional status. Chief Justice Marshall did not directly attack either Congress or the president in *Marbury v. Madison,* even though his was a constitutionally entrenched court. In sum, it may be as difficult to introduce judicial federalism as it is to institute legislative federalism.[6]

5 From Nation-State to Broad Secular State

One of the most important decisions facing Canada is the recognition that it is no longer a nation-state reflecting the interests of the dominant (British) majority. Rather, it is becoming a secular state of a quite distinct character. In the ordinary, and narrow, sense, the term "secular state" is usually interpreted to mean a political system that does not afford official recognition to a particular religion or religious denomination. Strictly speaking, the United Kingdom is not entirely a secular state even in this narrow sense. It has an established Church of England, and its political leaders still refer to Britain as a Christian country. Official documents may require a person's "Christian name." Nevertheless, citizens of all religions in Britain are equal under the law, have the same political rights, and in the absence of religious political parties can always aspire to being part of the ruling majority.[7]

Canada has long been a secular state in the narrow sense. It is certainly more secular than the United Kingdom because there is no Established Church in Canada. It is perhaps less secular than the United States, which has insisted on a constitutional separation of church and

Conclusion: Toward a New State Structure?

state. In this aspect, as in so many others, Canada was long thought to be a halfway house between the United Kingdom and the United States—or the apex of a North Atlantic triangle of "Anglo-American democracies."

But the new Canada is no longer a halfway house. Indeed, it is becoming different from both the United Kingdom and the United States. It is secular in a much broader sense than that implied by *religious* toleration. As a "broad secular state" Canada now displays *linguistic* toleration as well. Canada does not demand that to be a full Canadian one must speak English. A "broad secular state" is one that does not officially establish a single religion or a single language.

In some ways, Canada is more comparable to non-Anglo-American democracies. An interesting comparison, for example, can be made with India, a state renowned for its variety of religions and religious tolerance. Although 80 percent of Indians are Hindus, minority religions are treated as equal, although they stand outside the formal state structure. This is despite the fact that for up to a thousand years the Hindus were subject to harassment by Muslim or Christian conquerors.[8]

India is also a *broad* secular state because it displays a toleration not only for religions but also for languages. There are many different cultures within Indian society, as well as several officially recognized regional languages, each spoken by many millions of people. Culturally and linguistically it is as diverse as the continent of Europe. To be Indian does not mean to be Hindu. Nor do Indians have to speak Hindi. They can be Kerala Christians, speaking only Malayalam; Hyderabadi Muslims conversant with Urdu; or Gujerati-speaking Jains from Ahmedabad. All are equally Indian. India is very much a state, but it is not a nation-state in the conventional sense. To be an Indian does not involve adherence to a common religion or an ability to speak a shared language. It is secular in the broad sense of religious *and* linguistic toleration.

Similarly, but in a far less complex manner, to be a Canadian does not involve a common language or a common religion. Canada, like India, is multicultural, and a secular state in the same broad sense. It is no longer a British Dominion, or even an English-speaking country, despite a reluctance to recognize this development because of the impact of European and American modes of thought.

The European tradition, after the French Revolution, favored the nation-state. Regional cultures, whether Provençal or Catalan, Welsh or Breton, were discouraged. There was fear that recognition of a distinctive culture would encourage the assertion of nationality, and that this in turn could lead to the demand for a separate nation-state.

By the 1920s Europe was a patchwork of new nation-states from Norway and Finland to Hungary and Bulgaria. Only a few, notably Czechoslovakia or Yugoslavia, were multicultural. With the disintegration of the Austro-Hungarian Empire, the prime example of a multicultural state, there disappeared the theories of nationality to which it had given rise.

The British Empire, though even more complex than the dual monarchy of Austria-Hungary, was thought to be different. England had formed the United Kingdom of Great Britain and Ireland by adopting "British" as the generic term for the English, Welsh, Scots, and Irish, thus maintaining the fiction that the United Kingdom, like England under the Tudors, was a nation-state. The term "British" was also applied to the Dominions, though it was most appropriate in those lands where the English, Welsh, Scots, and Irish had settled.

With Dominion autonomy a common British nationality ultimately proved impractical. English-speaking people in Canada preferred their own Canadian nationality and abandoned the use of the term "British subjects." It was only a matter of time before the United Kingdom came to be regarded by many Canadians as a foreign country.

At first, as in most of the successor states of the Austro-Hungarian Empire, it was assumed that Canada was a nation-state. However, this notion implied that there was a dominant nationality. Unlike the English nation in the unitary state of Great Britain (though not in Ireland), English-speaking Canadians had never been able to exercise hegemony. They had never shown a disposition to form an English Canadian state separate from the French.

Canada therefore in practice long ago abandoned the doctrine of the nation-state. In doing so, it showed itself willing to join the ranks of a number of countries, from Yugoslavia to India, that have become broad secular states in the sense of being multinational.

There are signs that this multinational doctrine will become increasingly attractive not only in Canada but elsewhere as well. Its adoption by the larger European states, which have found difficulty in absorbing the immigration of non-Christians and non-Europeans (often with very different cultures) into their nation-states, would be helpful. The problems facing countries like Canada, where the commitment to the nation-state has been periodically challenged, are much less severe. The transformation of the European Community, which most western European states have now joined, into a continental secular state on the lines of Canada or India may do much to reduce social tensions, but such change will be more difficult to achieve.

Citizens in federal states have, however, an initial advantage in the transformation from nation-states into broad secular states. Following the American example, they already exercise a double sovereignty, being responsible for both federal and regional governments, often of different parties. What they next have to learn, and without the Americans to guide them, is to tolerate a separate cultural identity within the federal system, and not to regard its political expression as a cause for instability like the "ramshackle" Austro-Hungarian Empire.

Canada long ago demonstrated that it could rise above those confines of the nation-state which made England's relationship with Ireland so difficult. The Union period, 1840–67, gave the lie to the dictum that Canada comprised two nations warring in the bosom of a single state. Instead the foundations were laid for a distinctive state in which the two cultural communities cooperated. The country's experience since 1840 has also proved another dictum to be false—that Canada is composed of two solitudes. Politically at least there has not been solitude: French- and English-speaking Canadians belong to the same federal political parties.

Of course there have always been those who remain committed to an extremist position. At one extreme there have been United Empire loyalists unwilling to have any truck with the French. At the other end of the spectrum there has been an equally recalcitrant group of separatists unwilling to be called Canadians. In normal times, however, the most significant feature of Canadian politics has not been colorful extremism, but rather the moderation displayed by members of both language groups. They have been able to reach accommodation. Initially, this was through a tentative manifestation of the secular state that we have called philosophical federalism.

Normal times have had a way of suddenly coming to an end in Canada, and extremists have had a habit of exploiting crises to expose raw nerves. "Loyalty to the Crown" has been the rallying point of numerous conservative English-speaking Canadians; the proclamation of *deux nations* has been the cry of nationalists in Quebec. The replacement of a tolerant philosophical federalism, which leaves options open, by a commitment to a broad secular state, which officially recognizes differences, could help to eliminate some of these traditional latent hostilities. If francophones could separate the nation from the state, English-speaking Canadians could then constitutionally recognize the existence of *deux nations* without the fear that separatism was implied. And were English-speaking Canadians to separate the Crown from practical politics, allowing French-speaking Canadians to swear allegiance to the Canadian Constitution instead of to the Queen, then the latter might come to terms with the Crown. While each side would think it was making a great concession of principle, it would not change the polity. Such a compromise would be the sort of trade-off taken for granted in the flexible 1840s.

Today the fears of the past are much less in evidence. "French Canada" no longer threatens *les anglais* with a high birthrate and a religious mission. English-speaking Canadians no longer try to assimilate the francophones, refuse to let French be spoken, or compel the young Quebecois to fight on the side of the British Empire. Instead there is widespread acknowledgment of a secular state with two founding peoples, New Canadians and native peoples (or "First Nations"). All have their cultural heritage and all are having to adopt to pressures from the United States.

If worse came to worst, and the existing Canadian political system proved unable to adapt to the demand for structural change and a truly constitutional federalism, Canada might have to take the ultimate step of calling a constitutional convention. Here the issues discussed in this book would all be debated. For the deeper significance of over twenty years of constitutional debate has still to be understood. Canada has seen American civilization replace British. It has seen the limitations of philosophical federalism once the *Parti Québécois* voiced opposition to the status quo. It has begun to realize that imperial federalism gave way to a vacuum that "executive federalism" never filled. Pseudofederalism has to be replaced by constitutional federalism.

With the end of the Empire a new and independent Canada has emerged, whose inhabitants are no longer British subjects but Canadian citizens. As an autonomous country Canada has never really been a nation-state. Only if Canadians are able to accept the concept of Canada as a broad secular state will they begin to carry out the institutional changes that are needed to resolve the country's political contradictions.

Notes

1 American in Civilization, Canadian in Culture

1 Herbert Marshall McLuhan, *The Gutenberg Galaxy* (Toronto: University of Toronto Press, 1962), p. 31 and *Understanding Media* (Toronto: University of Toronto Press, 1964). See also Donald V. Smiley, "Must Canadian Political Science Be a Miniature Replica?" *Journal of Canadian Studies* 9, no. 1 (Feb. 1974): 31–42.
2 Richard J. Barnet and Ronald E. Muller, *Global Reach* (New York: Simon and Schuster, 1974), p. 14. Professor Lars Ingelstam has asked, "Can Cultural Diversity Be Preserved or Are We Heading for a Uniform Global Culture?" in "The End of an Epoch?" *Current Sweden,* Sept. 1976, 1.
3 Fernand Braudel, *The Mediterranean and the Mediterranean World in the Age of Philip II* (London: Collins, 1973), 2:763.
4 Norbert Elias, *The Civilizing Process* (New York: Urizen, 1978), 4.
5 Daniel J. Boorstin, *The Republic of Technology* (New York: Harper & Row, 1979), 3, 4, 5, 10.
6 See, for example, the essays in Robert Laxer, ed., *Canada Ltd.* (Toronto: McClelland & Stewart, 1973) and in Leo Panitch, ed., *The Canadian State* (Toronto: University of Toronto Press, 1977).
7 Karl Marx and Friedrich Engels, *The German Ideology* (New York: International Publishers, 1947), 26, 56, 57, 60.
8 Shlomo Avineri, *The Social and Political Thought of Karl Marx* (Cambridge: Cambridge University Press, 1970), 168–69.
9 A. L. Kroeber and Clyde Kluckhohn, "Culture: a Critical Review of Concepts and Definitions," *Papers of the Peabody Museum of American Archaeology and Ethnology* 47, no. 1 (1952): 181.
10 Karl Marx, preface to *A Contribution to the Critique of Political Economy,* translated by Melvin Rader, in *Marx's Interpretation of History* (New York: Oxford University Press, 1979), 11.
11 Karl Marx, *Grundrisse,* trans. Martin Nicolaus (New York: Vintage, 1973), 111.
12 R. T. Naylor, "The Rise and Fall of the Third Commercial Empire of the St. Lawrence" in Gary Teeple, ed., *Capitalism and the National Question in Canada* (Toronto: University of Toronto Press, 1972), 2.
13 Ibid., 36.

14 Joseph S. Nye, Jr., "Transnational Relations and Interstate Conflicts: An Empirical Analysis," *International Organization* 28, no. 4 (1974): 961–96.
15 Marx and Engels, *The German Ideology*, 39.
16 Frank Underhill, *The Image of Confederation* (Toronto: CBC, 1964), 68–69.
17 The classic works are Harold A. Innis, *The Fur Trade in Canada* (New Haven: Yale University Press, 1930) and C. B. Macpherson, *The Theory of Possessive Individualism* (Oxford: Clarendon Press, 1962).
18 Quoted in Carl Berger, *The Writing of Canadian History* (Toronto: University of Toronto Press, 1976), 95.
19 Milton M. Gordon, *Assimilation in American Life* (New York: Oxford University Press, 1964).
20 *The Shorter Oxford English Dictionary* defines "civilize" as "to enlighten and refine." Culture is "improvement or refinement." *Webster's New Collegiate Dictionary* defines "civilization" as "a relatively high level of cultural and technological development" and gives as one definition of culture "a particular stage of advancement in civilization." Incidentally, even the restrictive expression "high culture" is often assumed to be synonymous with "civilization."
21 Bissell has forecast a gradual withdrawal from what he calls the "continental pattern." Claude T. Bissell, "The Place of Learning and the Arts in Canadian Life" in Richard A. Preston, ed., *Perspectives on Revolution and Evolution* (Durham, N.C.: Duke University Press, 1979), p. 210.
22 C. P. Snow, *The Two Cultures and the Scientific Revolution* (Cambridge: Cambridge University Press, 1962), especially 19.
23 A separate Department of Sociology was established at the University of Toronto in the mid-1960s. In 1975, there were still no chairs of sociology at either Oxford or Cambridge. This may explain why Snow, a Cambridge scientist, contrasts scientists with "literary intellectuals."
24 *Report* of the Royal Commission on Bilingualism and Biculturalism (Ottawa: Queen's Printer, 1967), General Introduction, xxv.
25 Ibid., xxxi–xxxii.
26 Ibid., xlix.
27 Gabriel A. Almond and Sidney Verba, *The Civic Culture* (Princeton, N.J.: Princeton University Press, 1963), 493, 496.
28 See, for example, Alan Cairns, "Political Science in Canada and the Americanization Issue," *Canadian Journal of Political Science* 8, no. 2 (June 1975): 191–234. George Radwanski, *Trudeau* (New York: Taplinger, 1978), 185, has referred to Trudeau's "selective intervention."
29 Braudel, *The Mediterranean*, 2:764.
30 Bissell developed this theme in "The Place of Learning and the Arts in Canadian Life," 186ff.
31 "Understanding England is important for the study of comparative politics, because England is a deviant case." Richard Rose, *Politics in England*, 2d ed., (Boston: Little, Brown, 1974), 1. "The South and the Negro are the great 'deviant cases' in American life." Donald R. Mathews and James W. Prothro,

Negroes and the New Southern Politics (New York: Harcourt, Brace, & World, 1966), 10.

2 Pragmatism and Canada's "Philosophical Federalism"

1. See, for example, Paul Edwards, ed., *The Encyclopedia of Philosophy*, 8 vols. (New York: Macmillan & Free Press, 1967), passim.
2. T. H. B. Symons, *To Know Ourselves* (Ottawa: Association of Universities and Colleges of Canada, 1975), 1:99 and 102. The *Swedish Encyclopedia of Philosophy* devotes six columns to Plato, six to Aristotle, ten to E. G. Geijer and fifteen to C. J. Boström. See Alf Ahlberg, ed., *Filosofiskt Lexikon* (Stockholm: Natur och Kultur, 1925).
3. According to the editor of the five volumes of his published papers. See Charles Sanders Peirce, *Collected Papers* (Cambridge, Mass.: Harvard University Press, 1931–58), 1:iii.
4. Andrew M. Scott, *Political Thought in America* (New York: Rinehart, 1959), 7.
5. Particularly Gunnar Myrdal. See his *An American Dilemma* (New York: Harper, 1944), chap. 1.
6. For a critical appraisal of pragmatism, see Bernard Crick, *The American Science of Politics* (London: Routledge & Kegan Paul, 1959), 92–93.
7. John Dewey, *Reconstruction in Philosophy* (New York: Henry Holt, 1920), 75–76.
8. Richard Hofstadter, *The Progressive Historians* (New York: Knopf, 1968), xii.
9. Charles Morris, *The Pragmatic Movement in American Philosophy* (New York: Braziller, 1970), 4–6.
10. Peirce, *Collected Papers*, 5:212.
11. William James, *Pragmatism* (New York: Longmans Green, 1907), 45, 51, and 75.
12. John Dewey, *Democracy in Education* (Chicago: University of Chicago Press, 1916), iii.
13. For example, Talcott Parsons, *The Structure of Social Action*, 2d ed. (New York: Free Press, 1949), vi.
14. Charles Edward Merriam, *New Aspects of Politics* (Chicago: University of Chicago Press, 1925), 100.
15. Ibid., 18–19.
16. Thomas Kuhn would seem to imply this in such observations as "scientists . . . never learn concepts, laws and theories in the abstract and by themselves" and "to reject one paradigm without simultaneously substituting another is to reject science itself." *The Structure of Scientific Revolutions*, 2d ed. (Chicago: University of Chicago Press, 1970), 46 and 79.
17. Merriam, *New Aspects of Politics*, 7.
18. Ibid., 102.
19. See Crick, *The American Science of Politics*, chap. 3.
20. According to Professor Thomas Goudge (personal communication) on the

basis of Dewey's discussion in *Human Nature and Conduct* and *Democracy and Education*.
21 Morris, *The Pragmatic Movement*, 9.
22 Ibid., 8–9.
23 W. L. Morton, *The Canadian Identity*, 2d ed. (Toronto: University of Toronto Press, 1972), 84–85.
24 Leslie Armour and Elizabeth Trott, *The Faces of Reason* (Waterloo, Ont.: Wilfrid Laurier University Press, 1981), 4.
25 Ibid., 457.
26 Ibid., 431–32.
27 John A. Irving, adapted by A. H. Johnson, "Philosophical Literature to 1910" in Carl F. Klinck, ed., *Literary History of Canada: Canadian Literature in English*, 2d ed. (Toronto: University of Toronto Press, 1976), 1: 455.
28 Ibid., 460.
29 Morton White, *Social Thought in America* (New York: Oxford University Press, 1976), 8.
30 Ibid., 24.
31 Thomas A. Goudge, *The Thought of C. S. Peirce* (Toronto: University of Toronto Press, 1950), 3ff.
32 See, for example, Henryk Mehlberg, *The Reach of Science* (Toronto: University of Toronto Press, 1958), and Charles Taylor, *The Explanation of Behaviour* (London: Routledge & Kegan Paul, 1964).
33 Northrop Frye is an ordained minister of the United Church. Marshall McLuhan made no secret of his Catholicism.
34 Watson Kirkconnell and Louis-M. Regis, in Mason Wade, ed., *Canadian Dualism/La Dualité Canadienne* (Toronto: University of Toronto Press, and Quebec: Laval University Press, 1960).
35 George Grant, *Lament for a Nation: The Defeat of Canadian Nationalism* (Toronto: McClelland & Stewart, 1965) and *Technology and Empire: Perspectives on North America* (Toronto: House of Anansi, 1969).
36 Grant, *Lament for a Nation*, 43.
37 Ibid., 54.
38 Ibid., 76.
39 Ibid., 8.
40 Ibid., 37.
41 Leslie Armour, personal communication.
42 James, *Pragmatism*, 8–9.
43 Ibid., 32.
44 Ibid., 42.
45 Ibid., 45.
46 Ibid., 46.
47 Ibid., 58–59.
48 Wade, *Canadian Dualism*, 64.
49 Until the 1950s, despite the high standards of its scholarship, Canadian philosophy is said to have been limited and conservative, dedicated to the

study of the thought of the past. Thomas A. Goudge, "Philosophical Literature, 1910–1960" in Klinck, ed., *Literary History of Canada,* 2:96, 103.
50 V. V. Mshvenieradze, "Early Canadian Philosophers: A Soviet View," *The Marxist Quarterly* (Toronto), 1962, 65n. (Translated from *Istoria filosofii,* V, 1961.)
51 John A. Irving, *The Social Credit Movement in Alberta* (Toronto: University of Toronto Press, 1959), ix–x.
52 Armour and Trott, *The Faces of Reason,* 980.
53 Klinck, ed., *Literary History of Canada,* 3:323.
54 But see David V. J. Bell, "Nation and Non-Nation" (Ph.D. diss., Harvard University, 1969).
55 See, for example, F. E. Sparshott, "National Philosophy," *Dialogue* 16, no. 1 (March 1977): 3–21.
56 Stanley G. French, ed., *Philosophers Look at Confederation* (Montreal: The Canadian Philosophical Association, 1979), 17.
57 Bruce Hunter, "Nation, State and History," in French, ed., *Philosophers Look at Confederation,* 167–71.
58 Isaiah Berlin, "An Introduction to Philosophy" in Bryan Magee, ed., *Men of Ideas* (London: BBC, 1978), 24.

3 The Americanization of the Social Sciences

1 Even the most recent edition of George H. Sabine's standard work is almost exclusively devoted to European thought. See *A History of Political Theory,* 4th edition, revised by Thomas Landon Thornson (Hinsdale, Ill.: Dryden, 1973).
2 For example, Charles E. Merriam's *A History of American Political Theories* (New York: Macmillan, 1903) and *American Political Ideas, Studies in the Development of American Political Thought, 1865–1917* (New York: Macmillan, 1920).
3 For some figures see Charles Morris, *The Pragmatic Movement in American Philosophy* (New York: Braziller, 1970), 170.
4 Parsons, *The Structure of Social Action,* 2d ed. (New York: Free Press, 1949), v.
5 The American Political Science Association Report of 1950 was the last of its kind.
6 Charles E. Merriam, "The Meaning of Democracy," *Journal of Negro Education* 10, no. 3 (July 1941): 309. It is not surprising that Merriam's article was cited as "a contemporary exegesis" by Gunnar Myrdal when the latter was assembling his illustrations of an "American Creed . . . centered in the belief in equality and the rights to liberty" (*An American Dilemma* [New York: Harper, 1944], 8). For the American Creed very much reflected the ideals of the philosophical pragmatists, ideals that were to carry Americans through the next generation of social reform, particularly in education. Myrdal avowed that Dewey had turned the philosophy of pragmatism into a theory of education (p. 882).

7   Alan Cairns, "Political Science in Canada and the Americanization Issue," *Canadian Journal of Political Science* 8, no. 8 (1975): 205.
8   Macdonald was familiar with Madison's Debates and favored some of Hamilton's proposals that were defeated at Philadelphia. William Bennett Munro, *American Influences on Canadian Government* (Toronto: Macmillan, 1929), 18–20.
9   Cairns, "Political Science in Canada," 195ff.
10 For the debate between Seymour Martin Lipset and C. B. Macpherson, see *Canadian Forum*, vol. 34, November and December 1954 and January 1955.
11 Heinz Eulau, "Understanding Political Life in America: the Contribution of Political Science," *Social Science Quarterly* 57, no. 1 (June 1976): 112n.
12 Commenting on the older tradition, Allen Kornberg has written, "Political science, then, had some of the qualities of a first-rate men's club." See Allen Kornberg and Allen Tharp, "The American Impact on Canadian Political Science and Sociology," in Richard A. Preston, ed., *The Influence of the United States on Canadian Development: Eleven Case Studies* (Durham, N.C.: Duke University Press, 1972), 92.
13 It is interesting to compare the different textbooks on the government and politics of Canada. See Alan Cairns, "Alternative Styles in the Study of Canadian Politics," and the replies of the authors, reviewed in *Canadian Journal of Political Science* 8, no. 1 (March 1974): 101–34.
14 G. Bruce Doern and Peter Aucoin, eds., *Public Policy in Canada* (Toronto: Macmillan, 1979), 303.
15 Pierre Elliott Trudeau, "Federalism, Nationalism and Reason," in P. A. Crépeau and C. B. Macpherson, eds., *The Future of Canadian Federalism* (Toronto: University of Toronto Press, 1965), 34.
16 Barry D. Karl, "Charles Merriam," *International Encyclopedia of the Social Sciences* (1968), 10:257.
17 Darnell Rucker, *The Chicago Pragmatists* (Minneapolis: University of Minnesota Press, 1969), 154.
18 Charles E. Merriam, *Political Power* (1934; reprint, Glencoe, Ill.: Free Press, 1950), 301.
19 Charles E. Merriam, *New Aspects of Politics,* 3d ed. (Chicago: University of Chicago Press, 1970), xiv.
20 Karl, "Charles Merriam," 10:257.
21 Robert A. Dahl, "The Behavioral Approach in Political Science: Epitaph for a Monument to a Successful Protest," *American Political Science Review* 55, no. 4 (Dec. 1961): 763ff. Among Dahl's other works are *Preface to Democratic Theory* (1956), *Who Governs?* (1961), *Modern Political Analysis* (1963), *Democracy in the United States* (1967), and *Polyarchy* (1971).
22 Karl, "Charles Merriam," 10:259.
23 *International Encyclopedia of the Social Sciences* (1968), "Introduction," xxv.
24 Barry D. Karl, *Charles E. Merriam and the Study of Politics* (Chicago: University of Chicago Press, 1974), x. By the 1930s, pragmatism was on the wane at Chicago, its demise hastened by the appointment of Robert

Hutchins as the university's president. See Gabriel Almond, *APSA News,* no. 28 (Winter 1981): 4.
25 On Merriam and Weber, see Avery Leiserson, "Charles Merriam, Max Weber and the Search for Synthesis in Political Science," *American Political Science Review* 69, no. 1 (1975): 175–85.
26 Karl, *Charles E. Merriam,* 96.
27 J. A. Corry and J. E. Hodgetts, *Democratic Government and Politics,* 3d ed. (Toronto: University of Toronto Press, 1959).
28 Paul Fox, ed., *Politics: Canada,* 4th ed. (Toronto: McGraw-Hill Ryerson, 1977).
29 Richard Van Loon and Michael Whittington, *The Canadian Political System: Environment, Structure and Process,* 2d ed. (Toronto: McGraw-Hill Ryerson, 1976).
30 Harry Eckstein and David E. Apter, eds., *Comparative Politics: A Reader* (New York: Free Press, 1963).
31 Edward Shils, "On the Comparative Study of the New States," in Clifford Geertz, ed., *Old Societies and New States* (New York: Free Press, 1963), 25–26.
32 Lucien W. Pye and Sidney Verba, *Political Culture and Political Development* (Princeton, 1965), 512. For a Canadian caveat regarding its applicability to public administration, see Robert H. Jackson, "The Analysis of the Comparative Public Administration Movement," *Canadian Public Administration* 9, no. 1 (1966): 108ff.
33 Eckstein and Apter, *Comparative Politics,* 25.
34 Gabriel Almond and James S. Coleman, *The Politics of Developing Areas* (Princeton, N.J.: Princeton University Press, 1960), 576. (Almond was later elected to the National Academy of Sciences.)
35 Ibid., 63.
36 Ibid., 64.
37 David Easton, *The Political System* (New York: Knopf, 1953), 105.
38 Ibid., 194n.
39 Talcott Parsons, *The Social System* (New York: Free Press, 1951), vii.
40 Ibid., 555.
41 Ibid., 486.
42 Ibid., 485.
43 Ibid., 537.
44 Samuel Huntington, *Political Order in Changing Societies,* passim.
45 See Richard J. Bernstein, "The Use and Abuse of Thomas Kuhn: Truman, Almond, Wolin," in his *The Restructuring of Social and Political Theory* (Philadelphia: University of Pennsylvania Press, 1978), 93ff.
46 Parsons, *Structure of Social Action,* v–vi.
47 Parsons, *The Social System,* 111.
48 Ibid., 193.
49 Ibid.
50 Talcott Parsons and Edward A. Shils, *Toward a General Theory of Action* (Cambridge, Mass.: Harvard University Press, 1951), 185.

51 Parsons, *The Social System*, 111.
52 Ibid.
53 Parsons and Shils, *Towards a General Theory of Action*, 185.
54 "The author has been greatly sensitized to the special features of this type of social structure and its culture by Dr. Florence Kluckhohn, in many oral discussions, and in her *Los Atarquenos,* unpublished Ph.D. dissertation, Radcliffe College." Parsons, *The Social System*, 199.
55 Ibid., 191.
56 In *Towards a General Theory of Action,* a book of nearly 500 pages, the pattern variables are disposed of in a short paragraph.
57 Parsons, *The Social System*, 183, 186, 188.
58 Ibid., 184.
59 Ibid., 191.
60 Ibid., 107-8.
61 Parsons and Shils, *Towards a General Theory of Action*, 185.
62 Parsons, *The Social System*, 108.
63 Pragmatism is indexed.
64 It was widely assumed that some political systems were more developed than others and that countries evolved through various stages. Using quantitative data, Russett classified 107 countries into five major types: Traditional; Primitive civilizations; Transitional societies; Industrial Revolution societies; and High mass-consumption societies. Bruce Russett et al., *World Handbook of Political and Social Indicators* (New Haven: Yale, 1961), 293ff. See also Russett, *Trends in World Politics* (New York: Macmillan, 1965), 127.
65 Almond and Coleman, *The Politics of Developing Areas,* 533.
66 Ibid., 576.
67 S. M. Lipset, "Anglo-American Society," *International Encyclopedia of the Social Sciences* (1968), I:290ff. Lipset also deals with this theme in *The First New Nation* (New York: Basic Books, 1963), chap. 7, "Value Differences, Absolute or Relative: The English-Speaking Democracies." See also his *Revolution and Counterrevolution* (New York: Basic Books, 1968), chap. 2, "Revolution and Counterrevolution: The US and Canada."
68 Lipset, "Anglo-American Society," 290.
69 Ibid.
70 Ibid.
71 Ibid.
72 Ibid., 296.
73 Ibid., 291.
74 Ibid., 290.
75 Ibid., 299.
76 Ibid., 294.
77 Robert A. Dahl, *A Preface to Democratic Theory* (Chicago: University of Chicago Press, 1956), 63.
78 Ibid., 31-32.
79 Ibid., 51.
80 Ibid., 83.

81 Ibid., 63.
82 Ibid.
83 Ibid., 71.
84 Ibid., 75.
85 Ibid.
86 Ibid., 73-74.
87 Ibid., 74.
88 Ibid.
89 Ibid., 75.
90 Ibid., 76. In *Polyarchy, Participation and Opposition* (New Haven: Yale University Press, 1971), Dahl applied his notion of polyarchy (i.e., participation and competition) to a number of countries on a more systematic basis. He provided lists of polyarchies. But he still had problems. His concluding chap. 10, "The Theory: Summary and Qualifications," was a mere five pages and asked: "Why have I not tested the theory?" His answer was because of weaknesses in the data. Nevertheless, he felt able to add a postscript of 19 pages as chap. 11: "Some Implications for Strategies of Change."
91 Dahl, *Preface*, 145.
92 Ibid., 149-51.
93 Quentin Skinner, "The Empirical Theorists of Democracy and Their Critics," *Political Theory* 1, no. 3 (Aug. 1973): 303.
94 Clifford Geertz, "The Judging of Nations," *Arch. Europ. Sociol.* 18 (1977): 261.
95 Anthony King, "Ideas, Institutions and the Policies of Governments: A Comparative Analysis," *British Journal of Political Science* 3 (1973), parts 1 and 2, 291-313; part 3, 409-23.
96 Jürgen Habermas, *Knowledge and Human Interests* (Boston: Beacon, 1968), 91.
97 Heinz Eulau, "Understanding Political Life in America," *Social Science Quarterly,* June 1976, 131.
98 Ibid., 144-45.
99 Ibid., 145.
100 Clifford Geertz, *The Interpretation of Cultures: Selected Essays* (New York: Basic Books, 1973).
101 The quotations are from Seymour Martin Lipset, rev. of *Democracy in Alberta* by C. B. Macpherson, part I, *Canadian Forum* 34 (Nov. 1954): 175-77; part II, *Canadian Forum* 34 (Dec. 1954): 196; and C. B. Macpherson, "Democracy in Alberta: A Reply," *Canadian Forum* 34 (Dec. 1955): 223-25. Quotations that follow are from Macpherson's reply, unless otherwise indicated.
102 Richard J. Van Loon and Michael S. Whittington, *The Canadian Political System: Environment, Structure and Process,* 2d ed. (Toronto: McGraw-Hill Ryerson, 1976).
103 The quotations are from John Meisel, rev. of *Elite Accommodation in Canada* by Robert Presthus, *Canadian Forum* 54 (May-June 1974): 44-46; and

Robert Presthus, "Mr. Meisel Stands on Guard: Nationalism and the Academic Elite," *Canadian Forum* 54 (Nov.–Dec. 1974): 11–12.
104 Robert Presthus, *Elite Accommodation in Canadian Politics* (Toronto: Macmillan, 1973), 352.
105 Ibid., 360.
106 John Meisel, "The Fear of Conflict and Other Failings," *Government and Opposition* 15, nos. 3–4 (Summer/Autumn 1980): 439.
107 Donald Smiley, "Must Canadian Political Science Be a Miniature Replica?" *Journal of Canadian Studies* 9, no. 1 (Feb. 1974): 40.
108 Gabriel Almond and C. Bingham Powell, *Comparative Politics: A Developmental Approach* (Boston: Little, Brown, 1966), 1–2.
109 Ibid., 300.
110 Ibid., 330.
111 Ibid., 327.
112 Gabriel Almond and C. Bingham Powell, eds., *Comparative Politics Today: A World View*, 2d ed. (Boston: Little, Brown, 1980), 3.
113 Ibid., 31.
114 Ibid., 140.
115 Abraham Rotstein, "Binding Prometheus," in Ian Lumsden, ed., *Close the 49th Parallel etc.: The Americanization of Canada* (Toronto: University of Toronto Press, 1970), 181.
116 Ellen and Neal Wood, "The American Science of Politics," in Lumsden, ed., *Close the 49th Parallel etc.*, 181.

4 Taking Tradition for Granted: English Canada's Attachment to Westminster

1 Arend Lijphart, *The Politics of Accommodation* (Berkeley: University of California Press, 1969), and Robert V. Presthus, *Elite Accommodation in Canadian Politics*.
2 Macdonald's nickname was "Old Tomorrow." King believed that the real secret of political leadership lay more in what was prevented than in what was accomplished. See J. W. Pickersgill, *The Mackenzie King Record* (University of Toronto Press, 1960), 1:10.
3 *Confederation '79* (Calgary: Canada West Foundation, 1979), 1.
4 *Canadian House of Commons Debates*, 19 February 1925, 337.
5 Carl Berger, *The Writing of Canadian History* (Toronto: Oxford University Press, 1976), 53.
6 Ibid., 32.
7 Ibid., 33.
8 R. MacGregor Dawson, *The Government of Canada*, rev. by Norman Ward (University of Toronto Press, 1970), 9. In later editions, chap. 3 was titled "Dominion and Nation."
9 For example, "The shift, however, is a pendulum swing rather than a consistent trend." R. I. Cheffins and R. N. Tucker, *The Constitutional Process in Canada*, 2d ed. (Toronto: McGraw-Hill Ryerson, 1976), 2.

Notes to Chapter Four   415

10 Professor Smiley seems to have some doubts about the reconciliation, to judge by his subheading, "The Reconciliation(?) of Federal and Parliamentary Principles," *Canada in Question* (Toronto: McGraw-Hill Ryerson, 1980), 11.
11 Cheffins and Tucker, *The Constitutional Process in Canada*, 10.
12 *The Globe and Mail* (Toronto), 13 January 1981.
13 Quoted by Edward McWhinney in his *Judicial Review*, 4th ed. (Toronto: University of Toronto Press, 1969), 33.
14 For various models of the Westminster system, see Anthony H. Birch, *The British System of Government*, 4th ed. (London: Allen & Unwin, 1980), chap. 2: "The Nature of the Constitution."
15 Gerald M. Craig, ed., *Lord Durham's Report* (Toronto: McClelland & Stewart, 1963), 20.
16 Berger, *The Writing of Canadian History*, 36.
17 Dawson, *The Government of Canada*, 12.
18 *Parliamentary Debates*, 3rd Session, 8th Provincial Parliament of Canada, 1865, 8.
19 Quoted by Frank H. Underhill, *In Search of Canadian Liberalism* (Toronto: Macmillan, 1960), 16.
20 Quoted by R. A. Mackay, *The Unreformed Senate of Canada*, rev. ed. (Toronto: McClelland & Stewart, 1963), 11.
21 *Parliamentary Debates*, 88.
22 Ibid., 29.
23 F. A. Kunz, *The Modern Senate of Canada, 1925–1953: A Reappraisal* (Toronto: University of Toronto Press, 1965), 317.
24 Ibid., 316–36.
25 B. L. Strayer, *Judicial Review of Legislation in Canada* (Toronto: University of Toronto Press, 1968), 3.
26 Peter Hogg, *Constitutional Law of Canada* (Toronto: Carswell, 1977), 198.
27 Cheffins and Tucker, *Constitutional Process in Canada*, 32.
28 Ibid., 42.
29 Hogg, *Constitutional Law of Canada*, 198.
30 Ibid., 200.
31 McWhinney, *Judicial Review*, quoting A. L. Goodhart's *English Law and the Moral Law* (1953), 23ff.
32 *Re Regulation and Control of Aeronautics* (1932), A.C.54. Quoted in Peter H. Russell, ed., *Leading Constitutional Decisions*, rev. ed. (Toronto: McClelland & Stewart, 1973), 138.
33 See, for example, *Citizens Insurance Co. v. Parsons; Queen Insurance Co. v. Parsons* (1881), quoted in Russell, *Leading Constitutional Decisions*, 76ff.
34 Smiley, *Canada in Question*, 49.
35 R. MacGregor Dawson, *Constitutional Issues in Canada 1900–1933* (London: Oxford University Press, 1933), 11.
36 J. L. Hammond, *Gladstone and the Irish Nation* (London: F. Cass, 1964), 619.

37 Guy Favreau, *The Amendment of the Constitution of Canada* (Ottawa: Queen's Printer, 1965), 15–16.
38 Letter of 10 September 1930. Reprinted in Dawson, *Constitutional Issues in Canada 1900–1933*, 29.
39 Quoted by Carl Berger in *The Writing of Canadian History*, 46.

5 The "Reconciliation" of Parliamentary Supremacy and Federalism

1 Edward McWhinney, *Judicial Review*, 4th ed. (Toronto: University of Toronto Press, 1958), 74–75.
2 See, for example, House of Commons, First Report from the Foreign Affairs Committee, Session 1980–81: *British North American Acts: The Role of Parliament*, 1:ix. Also *Minutes of Evidence* (London: HMSC, 1980–81), 87:105.
3 Statement by Dr. G. Marshall, *Minutes of Evidence*, 85ff.
4 H. Peter Russell, ed., *Leading Constitutional Decisions*, 3d ed. (Ottawa: Carleton University Press, 1982), xi–xii.
5 Supreme Court of Canada: Judgement, 28 September 1981.
6 R. I. Cheffins and R. N. Tucker, *The Constitutional Process in Canada* (Toronto: McGraw-Hill Ryerson, 1976), 8.
7 Russell, *Leading Constitutional Decisions*, xi.
8 Ibid., xi–xii.
9 McWhinney, *Judicial Review*, 14.
10 K. C. Wheare, *Federal Government*, 4th ed. (London: Oxford University Press, 1963), 10.
11 Quoted by Carl Brent Swisher, *Historical Decisions of the Supreme Court* (Princeton: Van Nostrand, 1958), 8–12.
12 Peter Hogg, *Constitutional Law of Canada* (Toronto: Carswell, 1977), 43.
13 Barry L. Strayer, *Judicial Review of Legislation in Canada* (Toronto: University of Toronto Press, 1968), 25.
14 Russell, *Leading Constitutional Decisions*, xiii.
15 In 1935 the Judicial Committee stated: "The Irish Free State is, in their Lordships' judgment, bound by the Acts of the Imperial Parliament in the same way as any other of the Dominions." *Moore v. Attorney-General of the Irish Free State* (1935), summarized in R. MacGregor Dawson, ed., *Development of Dominion Status, 1900–1936* (London: Oxford, 1937), 372.
16 *Parliamentary Debates*, 1865, 896–97.
17 Ibid., 576.
18 Strayer, *Judicial Review of Legislation in Canada*, 22.
19 McWhinney, *Judicial Review*, 62.
20 Ibid., 16–17.
21 Ibid., 20.
22 D. V. Smiley, *Canada in Question*, 3d ed. (McGraw-Hill Ryerson, 1980), 20.
23 Dawson, *Development of Dominion Status*, 122.
24 ". . . the recent vogue of enlarging the national status has emphasized the

Notes to Chapter Six

futility of pretending to have self-government while such a fundamental matter remains unchanged." R. MacGregor Dawson, *Constitutional Issues in Canada 1900–1931* (London: Oxford, 1933), 3.
25 Smiley, *Canada in Question*, 32.
26 Canada had purported to abolish appeals to the Privy Council in criminal cases in an act of 1887. This act had been declared *ultra vires* by the Privy Council in the case of *Nadan v. The King* (1926, A.C.482). However, Parliament passed a further act in 1933. This was upheld by the Privy Council in *British Coal Corporation v. The King* (1935, A.C.500).

6 From Conquest via Rebellion to Dualism

1 Gérard Bergeron has interpreted 1867 as "the end of adolescence" for English Canadians in *Le Canada français après deux siècles de patience* (Paris: Editions de Seuil, 1967), 70.
2 Ibid., 16.
3 Ibid., 11.
4 For example, Louis M. Sabourin, ed., *Le Système politique du Canada* (Ottawa: Université d'Ottawa, 1969).
5 There is a study of school textbooks in Marcel Trudel and Geneviève Jain, *Canadian History Textbooks: A Comparative Study*, Study No. 5 for the Royal Commission on Bilingualism and Biculturalism (Ottawa: Information Canada, 1970).
6 Peter W. Hogg, *Constitutional Law of Canada* (Toronto: Carswell, 1977), 298–99.
7 See Marcus Van Steen, *Governor Simcoe and His Lady* (Toronto and London: Hodder & Stoughton, 1968).
8 All of the above quotations can be found in the appendix to the report of the Task Force on Canadian Unity, *Coming to Terms*, 1979, 87–88.
9 Daniel Johnson, *Egalité ou indépendance* (Montreal: Renaissance, 1965), 34.
10 It was reported that forty-three of fifty-five doctoral theses in progress in history at Laval University, Quebec, in 1974 related to the history of Quebec. Carl Berger, *Writing of Canadian History* (Toronto: University of Toronto Press, 1976), 260.
11 Fernand Ouellet, *Lower Canada 1791–1840: Social Change and Nationalism* (Toronto: McClelland & Stewart, 1980), 11.
12 Ibid., 2.
13 Denis Monière, *Ideologies in Quebec: The Historical Development* (Toronto: University of Toronto Press, 1981), 69ff.
14 Ramsay Cook, *Canada and the French-Canadian Question* (Toronto: Macmillan, 1967), 120. Even for the French-Canadian clergy "it was natural for the notion to emerge that the Conquest had been a stroke of providence." Ouellet, *Lower Canada 1791–1840*, 43.
15 Edward McWhinney, *Judicial Review*, 4th ed. (Toronto: University of Toronto Press, 1969), 245.

16 Ramsay Cook, *Canada and the French-Canadian Question*, 24.
17 Note the 1907 translation of André Siegfried's book as *The Race Question in Canada*.
18 Note the many references to the Conquest in the writings translated in Ramsay Cook's anthology *French-Canadian Nationalism* (Toronto: Macmillan, 1969).
19 The Treaty of Paris also settled other outstanding claims between the two empires. In 1757, Clive's victory at Plassey had made the British masters of Bengal and, in due course, of all India.
20 Gerald M. Craig, ed., *Lord Durham's Report* (Toronto: McClelland & Stewart, 1963), 28.
21 By 1784, 43 percent of the revenues from ownership of seigneurial lands was received by English-speaking individuals. (Ouellet, *Lower Canada 1791–1840*, 3).
22 Pierre Elliott Trudeau, "Quebec on the Eve of the Asbestos Strike," in Cook, *French-Canadian Nationalism*, 33.
23 "The Catholic Church was also regarded as a national institution, even by certain agnostics . . ." Ouellet, *Lower Canada 1791–1840*, 324.
24 See for example the view of the *habitants* as "insubordinate" according to Monière, *Ideologies in Quebec*, 70, 75, 80.
25 André Siegfried, *The Race Question in Canada* (1907; rpt. Toronto: McClelland & Stewart, 1966), 19.
26 Henri Bourassa, "French-Canadian Patriotism: What It Is, And What It Ought To Be," in Cook, *French-Canadian Nationalism*, 123.
27 Mason Wade, *The French Canadians 1760–1967* (Toronto: Macmillan, 1968), 1:103.
28 Ibid., 104.
29 Ouellet, *Lower Canada 1791–1840*, 170.
30 Jean-C. Bonenfant and Jean-C. Falardeau, "Cultural and Political Implications of French-Canadian Nationalism," in Cook, *French-Canadian Nationalism*, 21.
31 Quoted by Monière, *Ideologies in Quebec*, 101.
32 Ibid.
33 Ibid.
34 Reproduced in W. P. M. Kennedy, *Documents of the Canadian Constitution 1759–1915* (Toronto: Oxford University Press, 1918), 366–88.
35 James Morris, *The Pax Britannica Trilogy* (London: Faber & Faber), vol. 1, *Heaven's Command* (1973), 132; vol. 2, *Pax Britannica* (1968), 499.
36 Compare the heading of the chapter on Lower Canada ("A National-Democratic Revolution") in Stanley Ryerson, *Unequal Union: Confederation and the Roots of Conflict in the Canadas 1815–1873* (Toronto: Progress Books, 1968) with "The Rising in Upper Canada."
37 Ouellet, *Lower Canada 1791–1840*, 327.
38 Ryerson, *Unequal Union*, 69.
39 Jacques Monet, "La Fontaine," *Dictionary of Canadian Biography* (Toronto: University of Toronto Press, 1976), 9:443.

Notes to Chapter Six

40 Ouellet, *Lower Canada 1791–1840,* 314. In November 1837, Papineau was 51 years old.
41 Ibid., 218.
42 Ibid., 326.
43 J.-C. Bonenfant, "Cartier," *Dictionary of Canadian Biography,* 9:142.
44 "By 1840 he (Papineau) had come to hate all things British and stood by waiting for the great moment when Lower Canada must inevitably become the thirty-fourth state of the American Union." Jacques Monet, *The Last Cannon Shot: A Study of French-Canadian Nationalism 1837–1850* (Toronto: University of Toronto Press, 1969), 395.
45 According to Greg Keilty some 25,000 refugees from Upper Canada crossed into the United States. Keilty, *1837: Revolution in the Canadas* (Toronto: NC Press, 1974), 224.
46 Monière, *Ideologies in Quebec,* 133. "Popular university" is too strong a term.
47 Ibid., 136.
48 Hence the sponsorship by the Social Science Research Council of Canada, after a considerable period of gestation, of *Canadian Dualism/La Dualisme canadienne,* ed. Mason Wade (Toronto: University of Toronto Press, and Quebec: Laval University Press, 1960).
49 Quebec's Eastern Townships, established as part of the plan to assimilate the French, were ultimately settled by the French Canadians themselves.
50 Monet, *Last Cannon Shot,* 72ff.
51 The result of the application of the dualism of equal representation was that French Canadians "turned against its authors the plan that was meant to hold them in check." *Quebec-Canada: A New Deal* (Quebec Government's White Paper on Sovereignty-Association, 1979), 6.
52 For a Marxist interpretation of French-English relations during this period, see Ryerson, *Unequal Union.*
53 André Bernard, *La Politique au Canada et au Québec* (Montréal: L'Université du Québec, 1977), 166.
54 J. E. Hodgetts, *Pioneer Public Service: An Administrative History of the United Canadas 1841–1867* (Toronto: University of Toronto Press, 1956), 57 and 275.
55 The double-majority principle received greater notice in later books. See, for example, the eight references in Careless, *Union of the Canadas.*
56 After the establishment of the Tremblay Commission in Quebec in 1953, there was more interest in the notions of a double majority and a compact between the races, notions summarily dismissed by those English-Canadian scholars who had taken hegemony over the French for granted. See for example, G. F. G. Stanley, "Act or Pact? Another Look at Confederation," *Canadian Historical Association Report* 9 (1956), and William Ormsby, *The Emergence of the Federal Concept in Canada 1839–1845* (Toronto: University of Toronto Press (1969), 123. See also Elizabeth Nish's two articles, "LaFontaine and the Double Majority" *Centre d'Etudes du Québec Revue* 1 (1967): 9–17, and "La Double Majorité: L'Union et la Réaction,"

loc. cit., 31–46. For the original proposal by D.-B. Viger, see Monet, *Last Cannon Shot*, 204–6.

57 Described in detail by Paul G. Cornell, *The Alignment of Political Groups in Canada 1841–1867* (Toronto: University of Toronto Press, 1962). Note especially figure V, p. 62.

58 The population of Lower Canada increased between 1841 and 1851 from 650,000 to 890,000. In Upper Canada, the increase was from 450,000 to 952,000. The birth rate and infant mortality were high in both sections. "But the greater net growth in the West was obviously the result of immigration . . . more than forty percent of the Upper Canadian population in 1851 were still British-born." Careless, *Union of the Canadas*, 150.

59 Ibid., 171.

60 Monière, *Ideologies in Quebec*, 132.

61 Canada, *Parliamentary Debates* (1865), 30.

62 The ability of the French Canadians to learn the rules of parliamentary government was made clear by Helen Taft Manning in *The Revolt of French Canada 1800–1835* (London: Macmillan, 1962). She gave an early example of how they learnt to humor the English, pp. 36–37.

63 Léon Dion, *Quebec: The Unfinished Revolution* (Montreal and London: McGill-Queen's University Press, 1976), 115.

64 Quoted by Dion in *Quebec*, 125. The word "place" might have been better translated as "spectrum." See Dion's original French work, *Nationalismes et politique au Québec* (Montreal: Hurtubise HMH, 1975), 53.

65 For an example, see Conrad Black, *Duplessis* (Toronto: McClelland & Stewart, 1977), 193.

66 See the widely read popular history of the 1960s, Léandre Bergeron, *Petit Manuel d'histoire du Québec* (Editions Québecoises, n.d.), 115ff.

67 As the Quebec Government's White Paper on Sovereignty-Association put it in 1979, the French Canadians were able "to hamper Anglophone territorial and commercial expansion" (p. 6).

7 Dualism versus Majority Rule

1 For confirmation, see Kenneth McRoberts & Dale Posgate, *Quebec: Social Change and Political Crisis*, rev. ed. (Toronto: McClelland & Stewart, 1980), 3–8.

2 The Maritime Provinces, conquered from the French before Quebec was taken, had been known as *L'Acadie*.

3 For details, see A. I. Silver, *The French-Canadian Idea of Confederation, 1864–1900* (Toronto: University of Toronto Press, 1982), 3ff.

4 "Nevertheless, Quebec and its many aspirations constitute only one of several dimensions of Canadian unity and diversity. If Quebec disappeared tomorrow, most of what we have to say about Canadian political parties and regions would remain valid." David J. Elkins and Richard Simeon, *Small Worlds: Provinces and Parties in Canadian Political Life* (Toronto: Methuen, 1980), vii.

Notes to Chapter Seven

5 The changes in boundaries are portrayed in D. G. G. Kerr, *A Historical Atlas of Canada*, 3d ed. (Toronto: Nelson, 1975), 67.

6 Pierre Berton, *The National Dream: The Great Railway, 1871–1881* (Toronto: McClelland & Stewart, 1970), and its sequel, *The National Dream: The Last Spike* (Toronto: McClelland & Stewart, 1974).

7 "Both men [George Brown and William McDougall] wanted to make the West an extension of English Canada, with a view to dominating French Canada. Quebec, whose interest in the West had been stirred by the reports of the missionaries whom it supported and largely supplied, naturally opposed the program, which increased its chronic sense of insecurity." Mason Wade, *The French Canadians, 1760–1967* (Toronto: Macmillan, 1968), 1:395.

8 D. G. Creighton argued cogently against the notion that Confederation was based on a bilingual and bicultural compact between two nations in "John A. Macdonald, Confederation and the Canadian West" reprinted in Ramsay Cook, Craig Brown, and Carl Berger, *Minorities, Schools and Politics* (Toronto: University of Toronto Press, 1969), 1–9.

9 Canada, *Parliamentary Debates* (1865), 60.

10 W. L. Morton, *The Critical Years: The Union of British North America, 1857–1873* (Toronto: McClelland & Stewart, 1964), 177.

11 "The whole idea of a national spirit or 'national sentiment,' to use the phrase of the day, was under suspicion as being slightly treasonous." Berton, *The National Dream*, 24.

12 This argument formed the basis of Quebec's *Report of the Royal Commission of Inquiry on Constitutional Problems* (1956).

13 Ramsay Cook, *Provincial Autonomy, Minority Rights and the Compact Theory, 1867–1921* (Ottawa: Queen's Printer, 1969), 1.

14 "Mill suggests that political tyranny of the majority may take the form of oppression of a racial, religious or sectional minority, but the form he discusses in most detail is the violation of the rights of a wealthy minority by a poorer majority. Presumably, he does so because class was, as it is now, the most serious division in England." Dennis F. Thompson, *John Stuart Mill and Representative Government* (Princeton, N. J.: Princeton University Press, 1976), 69.

15 A. R. M. Lower, *Colony to Nation* (Toronto: Longmans, 1946).

16 Silver, *The French-Canadian Idea of Confederation*, 41.

17 Hugh MacLennan, *Two Solitudes* (Toronto: Collins, 1945).

18 Léon Dion, *Quebec: The Unfinished Revolution* (Montreal and London: McGill-Queen's University Press, 1976), 218 n. 2.

19 Madame St. Laurent refused to leave her home in Quebec City when her husband accepted a Cabinet post in Ottawa.

20 The French immigrants believed that "the French Canadians were a people chosen by Providence to carry on the true French and Catholic tradition, uncorrupted by liberalism and republicanism." Mason Wade, *The French Canadians*, 1:352.

21 See Ramsay Cook, "Church, Schools and Politics in Manitoba, 1903–1912," reprinted in Cook et al. *Minorities, Schools and Politics,* 19–41.
22 One can hardly imagine a Mercier or a Lévesque addressing young Liberals as Laurier did: "Let your convictions be always calm, serene . . ."
23 Not that French Canadian MPs were reluctant to express their opposition in private. When Mackenzie King in 1946 proposed a new Canadian flag, still displaying the Union Jack in the quarter, Jean Lesage and about ten other Quebec members threatened to vote against the design even if it meant bringing down the government. See Dale C. Thomson, *Louis St. Laurent: Canadian* (Toronto: Macmillan, 1967), 192.
24 Canada, House of Commons, Debates, March 17, 1886, 195.
25 Letter from John A. Macdonald to John Rose, February 23, 1870. Reprinted in Sir Joseph Pope, *Correspondence of Sir John A. Macdonald* (Toronto: Oxford University Press, 1921), 128.
26 Reprinted in Sir Joseph Pope, *Memoirs of the Right Honorable Sir John Alexander Macdonald* (London: Edward Arnold, 1894), 339. Quoted by Donald V. Smiley, *The Canadian Political Nationality* (Toronto: Macmillan, 1967), 10–11.
27 Smiley, *The Canadian Nationality,* 10 n. 12.
28 By 1980, Quebec's share of MPs had dropped to 75 of 282, although in absolute figures the number was ten above the number allotted before and after 1867.
29 Quoted from the French edition of Mason Wade, *The French Canadians,* 456, by Denis Monière, *Ideologies in Quebec: The Historical Development* (Toronto: University of Toronto Press, 1981), 170.
30 "En tout cas, durant cette période [1945–1960], la croissance de la productivité au Quebec a été telle qu'elle a permis, depuis, à cinq gouvernements successifs de poursuivre une considerable expansion." Roch Bolduc, in a review of *L'Etat du Québec en devenir,* by G. Bergeron and R. Pelletier, in *Canadian Public Administration* 24, no. 3 (1981): 498.
31 Silver, *The French-Canadian Idea of Confederation,* 221.
32 D. V. Smiley, *Canada in Question,* 3d ed. (Toronto: McGraw-Hill Ryerson, 1980), 292.
33 According to Monière, the *Rouges'* ideology "was the expression of an increasingly limited element of the petty bourgeoisie." *Ideologies in Quebec,* 136.
34 André Siegfried, *The Race Question in Canada* (1907; rpt. Toronto: McClelland & Stewart, 1966), 184.
35 Mason Wade, *The French Canadians,* 1:370.
36 Barry Gough, *Canada* (Toronto: Prentice-Hall, 1975), 99.
37 Jean-Claude Robert, *Du Canada français au Québec libre* (Paris: Flammarion, 1975), 147–48.
38 The classic statement of this perspective, no doubt shaped by the Duplessis regime, is that of Pierre Elliott Trudeau, "Some Obstacles to Democracy in Quebec," first published in the *Canadian Journal of Economics and Political Science* 24, no. 3 (1958), and later included in his collection of es-

Notes to Chapter Eight 423

says, *Federalism and the French-Canadians* (Toronto: Macmillan, 1968), 103–23.
39 For an analysis of the application of theories of change to Quebec, see McRoberts and Posgate, *Quebec,* Chapter 1, "Analyzing Change: Theories and Concepts."
40 Herbert F. Quinn, *The Union Nationale: Quebec Nationalism from Duplessis to Lévesque,* 2d ed. (Toronto: University of Toronto Press, 1979), xii.
41 When Laval University built a new campus it included a chapel. On a wall inside the entrance was a large map of North America. The original American colonies were in red, Spanish territories in yellow, and the rest of the continent was in green, signifying French sovereignty.
42 Thomson, *Louis St. Laurent,* 499. St. Laurent was accustomed, between the wars, to crossing the Atlantic at least once a year to plead cases before the Privy Council.
43 Silver, *The French-Canadian Idea of Confederation,* 223.
44 Brian Young, *George-Etienne Cartier: Montreal Bourgeois* (Kingston and Montreal: McGill-Queens University Press, 1981), 16.
45 At Cartier's funeral, the casket was placed on a large base inscribed with the words, "Homme sincère, Homme droit, Homme firme, Homme honnête." Alastair Sweeny, *George-Etienne Cartier* (Toronto: McClelland & Stewart, 1976), 322. Despite Wolseley's dislike of Cartier, the general wrote of him: "His greatest enemy dares not question his honesty." Ibid., 218.
46 Ibid., 180.
47 Young, *Cartier: Montreal Bourgeois,* 77, 142.
48 Quoted by Sweeny, *Cartier,* from the *Report of the Select Committee on the Causes and Difficulties in the North-West Territories in 1861–1870* (1874).
49 Cartier had been defeated in Montreal East twice before, in 1857 and 1861, but had then been elected from Verchères, near his family home.
50 Sweeny, *Cartier,* 120.
51 Ibid., 276.
52 Paul G. Cornell, *The Great Coalition, June, 1864* (Ottawa: Canadian Historical Association Booklets, no. 19, 1966), 19.

8 French Canada and the Triumph of Majority Rule

1 The Constitutional Amendment Bill, 1978, Section 4.
2 When the bilingual Constitution Act was sent to Westminster in 1982, a question was raised in London regarding the constitutionality of the British Parliament passing legislation in a language other than English.
3 "It is nevertheless true that increasingly in English Canada the principle of majority rule took precedence over minority rights. Macdonald's tolerant belief that there were at least two ways of being Canadian was replaced by a rigid, even intolerant, adherence to the letter of the British North America Act." Ramsay Cook, quoted by Lovell Clark, ed., *The Manitoba School*

Question: Majority Rule or Minority Rights? (Toronto: Copp Clark, 1968), 12.
4   W. L. Morton, *The Critical Years* (Toronto: McClelland & Stewart, 1964), 209–10.
5   Some historians have insisted that before D'Alton McCarthy came from Ontario to stir Manitobans up, relations were amicable. See the selections from the works of W. L. Morton and Mason Wade quoted by Clark, *The Manitoba School Question,* 26, 68.
6   Morton, *The Critical Years,* 208.
7   Ibid., 213.
8   United Kingdom, *Parliamentary Debates* (Lords), 3d Series, vol. 185, 19 February 1867, 565–66.
9   Morton, *The Critical Years,* 204.
10 Quoted by A. I. Silver in *The French-Canadian Idea of Confederation, 1864–1900* (Toronto: University of Toronto, 1982), 90.
11 Ibid., 92.
12 Ibid., 92.
13 *Toronto Mail,* 23 and 25 November 1885. Quoted by Mason Wade, *The French Canadians, 1760–1967* (Toronto: Macmillan, 1968), 1:419. Cf. Peter B. Waite, *Canada, 1874–1896* (Toronto: McClelland & Stewart, 1971), 170, for another interpretation.
14 G. F. S. Stanley, in *The Birth of Western Canada* (Toronto: University of Toronto Press, 1963), quotes a statement of the provisional government of Manitoba, 22 March 1870, that the French- and English-speaking elements were equally divided (112). He notes, however, that the provisional government was established "with the approval of a majority of the different racial elements in the colony" (115). The results of the first provincial elections in December 1870 refutes "any charge that the insurrection was entirely a minority movement, the work of Louis Riel and a few French-speaking adherents" (142).
15 Kenneth McNaught, *The Pelican History of Canada,* 2d ed. (Harmondsworth: Penguin, 1978), 64.
16 According to the 1871 census, the population was as follows:

by race		by religion	
French half-breeds	5,720	Roman Catholics	6,240
English half-breeds	4,080	Protestants	5,720
Whites	1,600		
Indian householders	560		
	11,960		11,960

Reproduced by M. S. Donnelly, *The Government of Manitoba* (Toronto: University of Toronto Press, 1963), 17n.
17 Morton, quoted in H. Bowsfield, ed., *Louis Riel: Rebel of the Western Frontier or Victim of Politics and Prejudice?* (Toronto: Copp Clark, 1969), 3.
18 There had been some speculation that when Cartier broached the subject

of Confederation in London in 1858 he had made it clear that the West was not to be regarded as a colony of Canada West. (See Bowsfield, *Louis Riel*, 24).
19 Stanley, *The Birth of Western Canada*, 130, 132.
20 Silver, *The French-Canadian Idea of Confederation*, 21.
21 Morton, *The Critical Years*, 191.
22 Clark, *The Manitoba School Question*, 2.
23 Silver, *The French-Canadian Idea of Confederation*, 187ff.
24 Clark, *The Manitoba School Question*, 5.
25 As Cartier discovered. When Taché, en route to the 1870 Vatican Council, informed him of what might happen at the Red River, Cartier snubbed him. When Taché returned to Canada from Rome he was "taken fully and unreservedly into the government's confidence." Stanley, *Birth of Western Canada*, 64, 108.
26 John W. Dafoe, *Sir Clifford Sifton in Relation to His Times* (Toronto: Macmillan, 1931), 40.
27 Lovell Clark has argued that some "favoured purely secular education from which religion would be entirely eliminated." But "the largest group seemed to be composed of Protestants who insisted upon Christian religious education in the schools and yet were adamant that none of it must be Roman Catholic." *Manitoba School Question*, 6.
28 "This ill-defined—and difficult to define—relationship is peculiarly Canadian. Perhaps it can be best described in three words—legally disestablished religiosity." John S. Moir, *Church and State in Canada, 1627–1867* (Toronto: McClelland & Stewart, 1967), xiii.
29 In his "A Roman Catholic View of the Public Schools," Archbishop Taché wrote: "I cannot help being convinced that the actual public schools of Manitoba are nothing else but the continuation of the Protestant public schools. . . ." Reprinted in Clark, *The Manitoba School Question*, 73.
30 Donnelly, *The Government of Manitoba*, 34–35n.
31 Ibid., 35.
32 W. L. Morton, *Manitoba: A History*, 3d ed. (Toronto: University of Toronto Press, 1967), 245.
33 At that time there appears to have been more concern about religious education than about the official use of French.
34 The federal government had fought Manitoba unsuccessfully over disallowance of its railway legislation. Macdonald believed that the government of Manitoba would merely "summon the legislature again, and carry the Bill over again and then dissolve and go to the country." He had no doubt that the Public Schools Act of Manitoba was unconstitutional and concluded that the courts would "finally dispose" of the question. See Sir Joseph Pope, *Correspondence of Sir John A. Macdonald* (Toronto: Oxford University Press, 1921) 466.
35 Clark, *The Manitoba School Question*, 119.
36 For a discussion of the appeals to the courts and excerpts from the various judgments, see ibid., 98–117.

37 There were four Conservative prime ministers between Macdonald's death in 1891 and Laurier's Liberal victory in 1896. Among them were figures as diverse as Sir John Thompson (1892-94), a Roman Catholic, and Sir Mackenzie Bowell (1894-96), a former Grand Master of the Orange Order.

38 However, to conclude that the American system of constitutional federalism would have helped the Manitoba Catholics, on the assumption that the judges would have done what legislatures were unwilling to do, is probably to misjudge the nature of American federalism in the 1890s. As *Plessy v. Ferguson* (1896) showed, the rights of minorities were not at that time defended by the courts.

39 Peter Oliver, *G. Howard Ferguson: Ontario Tory* (Toronto: University of Toronto Press, 1977), 41.

40 *Report of the Royal Commission on Bilingualism and Biculturalism, Book II: Education* (Ottawa: Queen's Printer, 1968), 47-51.

41 Quoted by Oliver in *G. Howard Ferguson*, 41.

42 J. W. Dafoe, *Laurier: A Study in Canadian Politics* (Toronto: McClelland & Stewart, 1963), 94.

43 This used to be a favorite description of Canada. Note William Kilbourn, ed., *Canada: A Guide to the Peaceable Kingdom* (Toronto: Macmillan, 1970). But see also Judy Torrance, "The Response of Canadian Governments to Violence," *Canadian Journal of Political Science* 10, no. 3 (1977): 473-96.

44 Silver has drawn attention to the frustration felt by French Canadians after Confederation. See, for example, *The French-Canadian Idea of Confederation*, 219-20.

45 J.-C. Bonenfant, "Cartier," *Dictionary of Canadian Biography*, X, 145.

46 These famous words were first uttered by Sir George Foster in 1896, and were later repeated by Arthur Meighen in a speech delivered in 1922.

47 For Cartier, see fn. 48; for Lapointe, fn. 52; for Taché, p. 75, in Clark, *The Manitoba School Question*.

48 This sensitivity toward Quebec helps to explain his otherwise puzzling unwillingness in 1926 to deflect the wrath of the Conservatives by taking firmer action in the customs scandal (largely centered in Montreal) that led to constitutional crisis of 1926.

49 Canada, House of Commons, Second Session, 1939, 65.

50 When St. Laurent argued that "The will of the majority must be respected, and it must prevail," he was referring to the majority of Canadians (who supported conscription), not to the Quebecois (who were very much opposed to it). Dale C. Thomson, *Louis St. Laurent: Canadian* (Toronto: Macmillan, 1967), 157.

51 "In short, English-speaking Canadians enlist in much smaller numbers than the newcomers from England because they are more Canadian; French-Canadians enlist less than English-Canadians because they are totally and exclusively Canadian." Henri Bourassa, *Canadian Nationalism and the War* (Montreal: no publisher, 1916), 29.

52 Commenting on the 1942 conscription crisis, J. L. Granatstein has written: "Perhaps the most important result of the crisis was that French Canada felt itself betrayed. Even Mackenzie King, the heir of Laurier, had let the Quebecois down. After this no federal leader would even be regarded with total confidence by French Canada. *Conscription in the Second World War 1939-1945* (Toronto: McGraw-Hill Ryerson, 1969), 48.

53 St. Laurent blandly told Parliament that the right to use French in the House of Commons, despite Section 133 of the BNA Act, could be abolished by an ordinary act of Parliament, but that because of the goodwill of the majority this would never happen. See Thomson, *St. Laurent,* 189.

54 D. W. Brogan once wrote a critical account of those countries which had experienced revolution, and called his book *The Price of Revolution* (London: Hamish Hamilton, 1951). The student of the Canadian political system, by contrast, is aware of the price that may be paid for evolution.

55 In 1982, when Canada became independent in constitutional as well as international law, the government of Canada distributed to every household a leaflet containing the words: "We are now, in law as well as in fact, a fully sovereign country."

56 According to Conrad Black, Duplessis' nationalism was "conservative of traditions, of the French language, the Catholic religion, and the distinct status of Quebec." As for *Le Chef* himself, "He was a legitimist, a nationalist, a conservative—in a word an autonomist. When he died, legitimacy, conservatism, and autonomy in Quebec died with him." Black, *Duplessis* (Toronto: McClelland & Stewart, 1977), 448, 496.

57 Thomson, *St. Laurent,* 114.

58 See above, note 53.

59 The willingness of St. Laurent to abandon Canada's earlier support for Quebec over the Labrador dispute when Newfoundland joined Confederation tends to be glossed over. See, for example, the references in Thomson, *St. Laurent,* and S. J. R. Noel, *Politics in Newfoundland* (Toronto: University of Toronto Press, 1971).

60 See the discussion in Kenneth McRoberts and Dale Posgate, *Quebec: Social Change and Political Crisis,* rev. ed. (Toronto: McClelland & Stewart, 1980), Chapter 5.

61 Pierre Elliott Trudeau, "Federal Grants to Universities," reprinted in Trudeau, *Federalism and the French Canadians* (Toronto: Macmillan, 1968), 79–102.

62 In *Duplessis* (especially Chapter 20), Conrad Black describes the nature of the hold Quebec's premier held over his associates and supporters.

63 For example, Léon Dion, *Nationalismes et politiques au Québec* (Montreal: Hurtubise, 1975).

64 Jean-Guy and Pauline Vaillancourt have added a fifth type, the extreme left, to these four (which they attribute to Dion). See their "Contemporary Quebec Nationalism and the Left," *The Australian and New Zealand Journal of Sociology* 14, no. 3, pt. 2 (1978): 330.

9 Quebec and the Rest of Canada

1. Inferred from statements in *The Amendment of the Constitution of Canada* (1965), 11–16.
2. K. C. Wheare described Canada's system as "quasi-federal" in law. Wheare, *Federal Government,* 4th ed. (London: Oxford University Press, 1963), 19–21.
3. In 1965, sixty-one percent of Canadian respondents to a Gallup poll expressed the opinion that the monarchy's importance in Canada was decreasing. By 1981 the percentage had risen to 74. Paul Fox, ed., *Politics: Canada,* 5th ed. (Toronto: McGraw-Hill Ryerson, 1982), 426.
4. Dawson, *The Government of Canada,* 5th ed. (Toronto: University of Toronto Press, 1970), 43.
5. Ibid., 134.
6. J. R. Mallory, "The Five Faces of Federalism," in P.-A. Crépeau and C. B. Macpherson, eds., *The Future of Canadian Federalism* (Toronto: University of Toronto Press, 1965), 5.
7. Dawson, *Government of Canada,* 49.
8. "When populism went too far . . . it was curbed by the old imperial remedies of reservation and disallowance." Mallory, "Five Faces of Federalism," 5.
9. J. R. Mallory, *The Structure of Canadian Government* (Toronto: Macmillan, 1971), 42.
10. Ibid., 45–46.
11. Ibid., 46.
12. "There is no basis for the claim that the court has been biased in favor of the federal interest in constitutional litigation." P. W. Hogg, "Is the Supreme Court of Canada Biased in Constitutional Cases?" *Canadian Bar Review,* December 1979, 739.
13. Mallory, *Structure,* 330.
14. Ibid., 330–31.
15. Ibid., 331.
16. Ibid., 339.
17. Ibid., 398.
18. Susan Mann Trofimenkoff, *The Dream of Nation: A Social International History of Quebec* (Toronto: Macmillan, 1982), 275.
19. Peter C. Newman, *Renegade in Power: The Diefenbaker Years* (Toronto: McClelland & Stewart, 1963), 32.
20. Quoted in ibid., 44.
21. Ibid., 49.
22. Although Diefenbaker tended to identify himself with Macdonald.
23. *Canadian Annual Review* (1965), 97.
24. Yet it was a Conservative minister Davie Fulton, a Roman Catholic from British Columbia, who attracted bilingual Montrealers like Michael Pitfield and Marc Lalonde to Ottawa.

Notes to Chapter Nine

25 Thirty-seven Liberal MPs, defeated in the election, returned to Quebec in 1958.
26 J. M. Beck, *Pendulum of Power: Canada's Federal Elections* (Toronto: Prentice-Hall, 1968), 344-45.
27 Ibid., 341.
28 Possibly because "it was bound to develop the kind of social leadership which would destroy him." Mallory, "The Five Faces of Federalism," 12.
29 Kenneth McRoberts and Dale Posgate, *Quebec: Social Change and Political Crisis,* rev. ed. (Toronto: McClelland & Stewart, 1980), chap. 5: "The Duplessis Regime: Resistance to State-Building."
30 Trofimenkoff, *The Dream of Nation,* 285.
31 Arthur Siegel, *Politics and Media in Canada* (Toronto: McGraw-Hill Ryerson, 1983), 225.
32 "Feudalism and liberalism confront one another as 'nations' in Canada." Louis Hartz, *The Founding of New Societies* (New York: Harcourt, Brace & World, 1964), 16n.
33 In 1979-80, 25 percent of official bilateral development assistance went to francophone Africa compared to 23 percent to Commonwealth Africa. Margaret Doxey, "Canada and the Evolution of the Modern Commonwealth," *Behind the Headlines* (Canadian Institute of International Affairs) 40, no. 2 (1982), 16.
34 Mallory, "Five Faces of Federalism," 15.
35 Whereas Riel had been hanged, those responsible for Laporte's death were exiled. Unlike the 1837 rebels, they were flown to Cuba, not transported to Australia.
36 Siegel, *Politics and Media,* 218.
37 As so often in the past, having lost the battle, the francophones won the war. For an account of this affair, see Sanford F. Borins, *The Language of the Skies* (Montreal: McGill-Queen's University Press, 1983).
38 "Ottawa could not use party structures to influence or even control Quebec as had been the case in the nineteenth century, when federal Conservative leaders regularly chose the Quebec premier, or during this century, when Laurier imposed Simon-Napoleon Parent as premier of Quebec and Mackenzie King forced the resignation of Taschereau in 1936." McRoberts and Posgate, *Quebec,* 89.
39 *Report of the Special Joint Committee of the Senate and House of Commons on the Constitution* (Ottawa, 1972), 32.
40 Quebec Liberal Party, *A New Canadian Federation,* 46.
41 This title was at one time used as a course description for an introductory course in political science at York University. It was based on A. R. M. Lower, *From Colony to Nation* (Toronto: Longmans Green and Company, 1946).
42 See, for example, the articles contributed to John H. Redekop, ed., *Approaches to Canadian Politics,* 2d ed. (Scarborough, Ont.: Prentice-Hall, 1983).

43 David V. J. Bell, "Political Culture in Canada," in Michael S. Whittington and Glen Williams, eds., *Canadian Politics in the 1980's* (Toronto: Methuen, 1981), 122. Bell's four perspectives were those of Louis Hartz, Seymour Martin Lipset, Karl Marx, and Harold Innis.

44 Seymour Martin Lipset, *Revolution and Counterrevolution* (New York: Anchor, 1970).

45 See Naomi Black, "Absorptive Systems Are Impossible: The Canadian-American Relationship as a Disparate Dyad," in Andrew Axline et al., *Continental Community?* (Toronto: McClelland & Stewart, 1974), 92–108.

46 Quebec National Assembly, *Le parlementarisme britannique: anachronisme ou réalité moderne? Documents et débats.* (Québec: Assemblée nationale du Québec, 1980).

47 Even before the referendum this may have been true. Early in 1980 the Quebec Liberal Party stated: "Quebec knows that from now on no possibility is forbidden, that it alone must define the frontiers of its own future." *A New Canadian Federation*, 122.

48 Ibid., 13.

49 Ibid., 22.

50 For example, "It is in examining the bases of the various accommodations which have been arrived at over time that one can begin to understand the logic of Quebec's relations to Canada." Reginald A. Whitaker, "The Quebec Cauldron," in Whittington and Williams, *Canadian Politics in the 1980's*, 29.

51 It used to be said that whereas the Conservatives wanted the unity of the Empire and the autonomy of Canada, the Liberals wanted the autonomy of Canada and the unity of the Empire. The possibility that in Quebec the difference between conservatives and radicals is really of the same order has long worried English Canadians.

52 Thus the Statute of Westminster was long regarded as a landmark. The provinces' vigorous objections to the federal government's proposals for patriation of the BNA Act at that time tended to be glossed over.

10 Options Canada: Options Quebec

1 In the United Kingdom, the collective interests of one permanent minority, the rich (and especially the landed rich), were safeguarded before the Parliament Act of 1911 by the House of Lords. In Canada, as Sir John A. Macdonald had observed, protection of property rights was provided by the Senate.

2 David Milne, *The New Canadian Constitution* (Toronto: Lorimer, 1982), 67.

3 See the remarks on behalf of the governments of Manitoba, Alberta, Saskatchewan, British Columbia, and Nova Scotia in verbal transcript of the Federal-Provincial Conference of First Ministers on the Constitution, morning session, September 10, 1981, 477, 492, 497, 558, 570. Cited below as "verbal transcript."

4 "Verbal transcript," 474. Trudeau was speaking extempore.

Notes to Chapter Ten   431

5   "Verbal transcript," 473–74.
6   The Quebecois are sometimes said to vote as individuals in provincial elections and collectively in federal contests.
7   "Verbal transcript," 477, 482, 483, 490, 511, 560.
8   Section 33(1) states: "Parliament or the legislature of a province may expressly declare in an Act of Parliament or of the legislature, as the case may be, that the Act or a provision thereof shall operate notwithstanding a provision included in section 2 or sections 7 to 15 of this Charter."

    The equality of women could not be overridden. Women's groups had successfully insisted on the insertion of Section 28, which read: "Notwithstanding anything in this Charter, the rights and freedoms referred to in it are guaranteed equally to male and female persons."
9   "The notwithstanding clause, however, provides a political escape-hatch for the results of the litigious process. Such a mechanism is a boon to the courts and to democratic principles. . . . It is perhaps unfortunate that in the long constitutional debate this democratic principle was so often equated with 'Parliamentary sovereignty.'" Milne, *The New Canadian Constitution,* 175.
10 Until 1975 it took a two-thirds vote of the senators present to cut off debate. Since then, cloture requires the vote of three-fifths of the entire membership.
11 Dawson, *The Government of Canada,* 5th ed. (Toronto: University of Toronto Press, 1970), 46–47.
12 According to Gérard Veilleux, in 1957 there were five federal-provincial ministerial liaison agencies and 59 at the administrative level. By 1977 there were 31 ministerial groups and 158 involving appointed officials. See D. V. Smiley, *Canada in Question,* 3d ed. (Toronto: McGraw-Hill Ryerson, 1980), 94.
13 Ibid., 92–94.
14 The Task Force on Canadian Unity was critical of executive federalism and concluded that it was partly responsible for the crisis of Canadian unity. "Some observers have regarded it with suspicion as a weakening influence on Canadian democratic life." *A Future Together,* 95.
15 "In short, anything the House of Commons would pass, the provincial legislatures would spew out of their mouths; anything the legislatures would pass, the House of Commons wouldn't look at." Eugene Forsey, letter to *The Globe and Mail,* 26 March 1983.
16 After examining the proposals to make the Senate more representative of the provinces, two scholars commented on the idea of a Canadian upper house like the German *Bundesrat* as follows: "If it is stimulated by the belief that the appointment of those familiar with provincial interests will promote a higher quality of legislation, it should be viewed with suspicion." Robert J. Jackson and Michael M. Atkinson, *The Canadian Legislative System,* 2d ed. (Toronto: Macmillan, 1980), 207. (They did acknowledge that there was an argument in favor of strengthening Parliament's integration, representation, and legitimation functions.)
17 ". . . the public may wonder if it is well served by senators, particularly

those on the committee on banking, trade and commerce, who have extensive corporate interests . . ." John McMenemy, "Business Interests and Party Organizers in the Senate Imperil the Independence of Parliament," in Paul Fox, ed., *Politics: Canada,* 5th ed. (McGraw-Hill Ryerson, 1982), 548. The Special Joint Committee of the Senate and of the House of Commons on Senate Reform made no mention of this criticism when discussing the arguments for reform in its 1984 report, chap. 3.

18 "I believe it is proper for the laws of the country to be made by persons elected by the people of Canada. That is what we are in this House." Stanley Knowles, MP, House of Commons, *Debates,* October 17, 1974, 491. Quoted in Fox, *Politics: Canada,* 4th ed., 474. Mr. Knowles and the New Democratic Party do not appear to think of Parliament as a federal institution.

19 Those discussed below are: *The Constitutional Amendment Bill,* Government of Canada, June 1978; *A Future Together,* The Task Force on Canadian Unity, January 1979; *Québec-Canada: A New Deal,* Gouvernement du Québec, November 1979; *A New Canadian Federation,* The Constitutional Committee of the Quebec Liberal Party, January 1980.

20 "The important, in fact the crucial point for Ontario, is that the powers and authority are those of the Queen, not of the Governor General. . . . The modern monarch stands for all those beliefs we deeply hold, but cannot easily articulate. In our view, it is imperative that the position of the Crown remain exactly as it is. This view was unanimously endorsed by all premiers at our recent Conference held in Regina." Premier William Davis, "Monarchy: A Statement to the Federal-Provincial Conference of First Ministers on the Constitution," October 31, 1978.

21 "Reform should not be so radical as to impair the effective working of parliamentary government as it has developed in Canada." Robert A. Mackay, *The Unreformed Senate of Canada,* rev. ed. (McClelland & Stewart, 1963), 188.

22 Quoted by Edward McWhinney, *Canada and the Constitution, 1979–1982,* (Toronto: University of Toronto Press, 1982), 185.

23 Ibid., 185.

24 Ibid., 188.

25 Ibid., 21.

26 Whether the British House of Commons could further reform the reformed House of Lords is a moot point.

27 Canada, *The Amendment of the Constitution of Canada,* 1965, 15.

28 McWhinney, *Canada and the Constitution,* 18.

29 The total report consisted of three volumes. The volume titled *Coming to Terms* offered an excellent analysis of the terms commonly used in Canadian political debate.

30 The official title in the English version was *Québec-Canada: A New Deal. The Quebec government proposal for a new partnership between equals: sovereignty-association.*

31 While the *Parti Québecois* was widely viewed outside Quebec as "socialist,"

Notes to Chapter Eleven 433

it was more of a social-democratic party akin to the British Labor movement. Quebec socialists regarded it as petit bourgeois at best. The FLQ wanted the overthrow of capitalism and "the total independence of Quebecers, reunited in a free society purged of its clique of voracious sharks." *Manifesto,* October 1970. Quoted in M. Patricia Marchak, *Ideological Perspectives on Canada* (Toronto: McGraw-Hill Ryerson, 1975), 92.
32 *A New Canadian Federation,* 12.
33 Ibid., 17.
34 "We must affirm the fundamental equality of the two founding peoples. . . . This basic dualism must be consecrated . . . b) by the granting to Quebec of guarantees. . . . These guarantees should not be narrowly confined to cultural policy." *A New Canadian Federation,* 22.
35 Edward McWhinney (*Canada and the Constitution, 1979–1982,* 46) touches on the Canadian dilemma over the use of the referendum. "A legally unimpeachable, popular source of sovereignty would thus have been established (in place of or as a supplement to the older imperial basis, now presumably fallen into disuse), just as it had been in the United States and France. But to Trudeau, 'it would represent a "revolutionary" step, involving too sharp a break with the original British basis of Canada's constitutional system.' "
36 For one thing, the composition of Quebec's delegation at a constitutional convention would prove controversial. For another, Quebec might insist on equality (i.e., equal representation) or a veto.

11 Conclusion: Toward a New State Structure?

1 Charles Taylor, *Social Theory as Practice* (Delhi: Oxford University Press, 1983), 2–3.
2 *Financial Post* (Toronto), *Canada: Outlook '85,* 39.
3 For details see Douglas V. Verney, *Parliamentary Reform in Sweden, 1866–1921* (Oxford: Clarendon Press, 1957).
4 In *Democracies: Patterns of Majoritarian and Consensus Government in Twenty-One Countries* (New Haven: Yale University Press, 1984), Arend Lijphart has contrasted the Westminster model of majoritarian government with the "consensus" model in much of Western Europe.
5 *Canadian News Facts* (1984), 3055.
6 Some federalist Quebecois seem prepared to accept the present Court's legitimacy. See Clause Ryan's two articles in *Le Devoir,* 3 and 4 August 1984.
7 Nevertheless, in subtle ways to be a non-Christian (and even a non-Anglican not so long ago) could involve certain social disabilities.
8 According to Ashis Nandy, Mahatma Gandhi's assassin, N. V. Godse, saw the one thousand years of domination of India by rulers who were Muslims or Christians as a humiliation of the Hindus that had to be redressed. Nandy, *At the Edge of Psychology: Essays in Politics and Culture* (Delhi: Oxford University Press, 1980), 83.

Bibliography

Ahlberg, Alf, ed. *Filosofiskt Lexikon*. Stockholm: Natur och Kultur, 1925.
Almond, Gabriel, and James S. Coleman. *The Politics of Developing Areas*. Princeton: Princeton University Press, 1960.
Almond, Gabriel, and C. Bingham Powell. *Comparative Politics: A Developmental Approach*. Boston: Little, Brown, 1966.
———, eds. *Comparative Politics Today: A World View*. 3d ed. Boston: Little, Brown, 1984.
Almond, Gabriel, and Sidney Verba. *The Civic Culture*. Princeton: Princeton University Press, 1963.
Armour, Leslie, and Elizabeth Trott. *The Faces of Reason*. Waterloo, Ontario: Wilfrid Laurier University Press, 1981.
Avineri, Shlomo. *The Social and Political Thought of Karl Marx*. Cambridge: Cambridge University Press, 1970.
Axline, A., et al. *Continental Community? Independence and Integration in North America*. Toronto: McClelland & Stewart, 1974.
Barnet, Richard J., and Ronald E. Muller. *Global Reach*. New York: Simon & Schuster, 1974.
Beck, J. N. *Pendulum of Power: Canada's Federal Elections*. Toronto: Prentice-Hall, 1968.
Bell, David V. J. "Nation and Non-Nation." Ph.D. dissertation, Harvard University, 1969.
Berger, Carl. *The Writing of Canadian History*. Toronto: University of Toronto Press, 1976.
Bergeron, Gérard. *Le Canada français après deux siècles de patience*. Paris: Editions de Seuil, 1967.
Bergeron, Léandre. *Petit Manuel d'histoire du Québec*. Editions Québecoises, n.d.
Bernard, André. *La Politique à Canada et au Québec*. Montreal: L'Université du Québec, 1977.
Bernstein, Richard J. *The Restructuring of Social and Political Theory*. Philadelphia: University of Pennsylvania Press, 1978.
Berton, Pierre. *The National Dream: The Great Railway, 1871–1881*. Toronto: McClelland & Stewart, 1970.
———. *The National Dream: The Last Spike*. Toronto: McClelland & Stewart, 1974.

Birch, Anthony H. *The British System of Government.* 4th ed. London: Allen & Unwin, 1980.
Black, Conrad. *Duplessis.* Toronto: McClelland & Stewart, 1977.
Boorstin, Daniel J. *The Republic of Technology.* New York: Harper & Row, 1979.
Borins, Sandford F. *The Language of the Skies.* Montreal: McGill–Queen's University Press, 1983.
Bourassa, Henri. *Canadian Nationalism and the War.* Montreal: N.p., 1916.
Bowsfield, H., ed. *Louis Riel: Rebel of the Western Frontier or Victim of Politics and Prejudice?* Toronto: Copp Clark, 1969.
Braudel, Fernand. *The Mediterranean and the Mediterranean World in the Age of Philip II.* 2 vols. London: Collins, 1973.
Brogan, D. W. *The Price of Revolution.* London: Hamish Hamilton, 1951.
Cairns, Alan. "Alternative Styles in the Study of Canadian Politics." *Canadian Journal of Political Science* 7, no. 1 (March 1975): 101–34.
———. "Political Science in Canada and the Americanization Issue." *Canadian Journal of Political Science* 8, no. 2 (June 1975): 191–234.
Canada. *The Amendment of the Constitution of Canada.* 1965.
Canada. *The Constitutional Amendment Bill.* 1978.
Canada. *Parliamentary Debates,* 3d Session, 8th Provincial Parliament of Canada, 1965.
Canada. *Report* of the Royal Commission on Bilingualism and Biculturalism. Ottawa: Queen's Printer, 1967.
Canada. *Report* of the Royal Commission on Bilingualism and Biculturalism. Book II: Education. Ottawa: Queen's Printer, 1968.
Canada. *Report* of the Select Committee on the Cause and Difficulties in the North-West Territories in 1861–1870. 1874.
Canada. *Report* of the Special Joint Committee of the Senate and the House of Commons on the Constitution. 1972.
Canada. *Report* of the Special Joint Committee of the Senate and of the House of Commons on Senate Reform. 1984.
Canadian Annual Review of Politics and Public Affairs. Toronto: University of Toronto Press.
Canadian News Facts. Toronto, 1967– .
Cheffins, R. I., and R. N. Tucker. 2d ed. *The Constitutional Process in Canada.* Toronto: McGraw-Hill Ryerson, 1976.
Clark, Lovell, ed. *The Manitoba School Question: Majority Rule or Minority Rights?* Toronto: Copp Clark, 1968.
Confederation '79. Calgary: Canada West Foundation, 1979.
Cook, Ramsay. *Canada and the French-Canadian Question.* Toronto: Macmillan, 1967.
———. *Provincial Autonomy, Minority Rights and The Compact Theory, 1867–1921.* Ottawa: Queen's Printer, 1969.
———, ed. *French-Canadian Nationalism.* Toronto: Macmillan, 1969.
Cook, Ramsay, Craig Brown, and Carl Berger. *Minorities, Schools and Politics.* Toronto: University of Toronto Press, 1969.

Cornell, Paul G. *The Alignment of Political Groups in Canada 1841–1867.* Toronto: University of Toronto Press, 1962.
———. *The Great Coalition, June, 1864.* Ottawa: Canadian Historical Booklets (no. 19), 1966.
Corry, J. A., and J. E. Hodgetts. *Democratic Government and Politics.* 3d ed. Toronto: University of Toronto Press, 1959.
Craig, Gerald M., ed. *Lord Durham's Report.* Toronto: McClelland & Stewart, 1963.
Crépeau, P. A., and C. B. Macpherson, eds. *The Future of Canadian Federalism.* Toronto: University of Toronto Press, 1965.
Crick, Bernard. *The American Science of Politics.* London: Routledge & Kegan Paul, 1959.
Dafoe, J. W. *Laurier: A Study in Canadian Politics.* Toronto: McClelland & Stewart, 1963.
———. *Sir Clifford Sifton in Relation to His Times.* Toronto: Macmillan, 1931.
Dahl, Robert A. *A Preface to Democratic Theory.* Chicago: University of Chicago Press, 1956.
———. "The Behavioral Approach in Political Science: Epitaph for a Monument to a Successful Protest." *American Political Science Review* 55, no. 4 (December 1961): 763–72.
———. *Polyarchy, Participation and Opposition.* New Haven: Yale University Press, 1971.
Dawson, R. MacGregor. *Constitutional Issues in Canada, 1900–1933.* London: Oxford University Press, 1933.
———. *The Government of Canada.* 5th ed., rev. by Norman Ward. Toronto: University of Toronto Press, 1970.
———, ed. *Development of Dominion Status, 1900–1936.* London: Oxford University Press, 1937.
Dewey, John. *Democracy in Education.* Chicago: Chicago University Press, 1916.
———. *Reconstruction in Philosophy.* New York: Henry Holt, 1920.
Dictionary of Canadian Biography. Toronto: University of Toronto Press, 1966– .
Dion, Léon. *Nationalismes et politique au Québec.* Montreal: Hurtubise HMH, 1975.
———. *Quebec: The Unfinished Revolution.* Montreal and London: McGill-Queen's University Press, 1976.
Doern, G. Bruce, and Peter Aucoin, eds. *Public Policy in Canada.* Toronto: Macmillan, 1979.
Donnelly, M. S. *The Government of Manitoba.* Toronto: University of Toronto Press, 1963.
Doxey, Margaret. "Canada and the Evolution of the Modern Commonwealth." *Behind the Headlines* (Canadian Institute of International Affairs) 40, no. 2 (1982).
Easton, David. *The Political System.* New York: Knopf, 1953.
Eckstein, Harry, and David E. Apter, eds. *Comparative Politics: A Reader.* New York: Free Press, 1963.

Edwards, Paul, ed. *The Encyclopedia of Philosophy*. 8 vols. New York: Free Press, 1967.
Elias, Norbert. *The Civilizing Process*. New York: Urizen, 1978.
Elkins, David J., and Richard Simeon. *Small Worlds: Provinces and Parties in Canadian Political Life*. Toronto: Methuen, 1980.
Eulau, Heinz. "Understanding Political Life in America: The Contribution of Political Science." *Social Science Quarterly* 57, no. 1 (June 1976): 112–53.
Favreau, Guy. *The Amendment of the Constitution of Canada*. Ottawa: Queen's Printer, 1965.
Fox, Paul, ed. *Politics: Canada*. 5th ed. Toronto: McGraw-Hill Ryerson, 1982.
French, Stanley G., ed. *Philosophers Look at Confederation*. Montreal: The Canadian Philosophical Association, 1979.
Geertz, Clifford. *The Interpretation of Cultures: Selected Essays*. New York: Basic Books, 1973.
———. "The Judging of Nations." *Arch. Europ. Sociol.* 18 (1977): 245–61.
———, ed. *Old Societies and New States*. New York: Free Press, 1963.
Gordon, Milton M. *Assimilation in American Life*. New York: Oxford University Press, 1964.
Goudge, Thomas A. *The Thought of C. S. Peirce*. Toronto: University of Toronto Press, 1950.
Gough, Barry. *Canada*. Toronto: Prentice Hall, 1975.
Granatstein, J. L. *Conscription in the Second World War, 1939–1945*. Toronto: McGraw-Hill Ryerson, 1969.
Grant, George. *Lament for a Nation: The Defeat of Canadian Nationalism*. Toronto: McClelland & Stewart, 1965.
———. *Technology and Empire: Perspectives on North America*. Toronto: House of Anansi, 1969.
Habermas, Jürgen. *Knowledge and Human Interests*. Boston: Beacon, 1968.
Hammond, J. L. *Gladstone and the Irish Nation*. London: F. Cass, 1964.
Hartz, Louis. *The Founding of New Societies*. New York: Harcourt, Brace & World, 1964.
Hodgetts, J. E. *Pioneer Public Service: An Administrative History of the United Canadas, 1814–1867*. Toronto: University of Toronto Press, 1956.
Hofstadter, Richard. *The Progressive Historians*. New York, Knopf, 1968.
Hogg, Peter W. *Constitutional Law of Canada*. Toronto: Carswell, 1977.
———. "Is the Supreme Court of Canada Biased in Constitutional Cases?" *Canadian Bar Review*, December 1979, 721–39.
Huntington, Samuel. *Political Order in Changing Societies*. New Haven: Yale University Press, 1968.
Ingelstam, Carol. "Can Cultural Diversity Be Preserved or Are We Heading for a Uniform Global Culture?" *Current Sweden*, September 1976.
Innis, Harold A. *The Fur Trade in Canada*. New Haven: Yale University Press, 1930.
Irving, John A. *The Social Credit Movement in Alberta*. Toronto: University of Toronto Press, 1959.

Jackson, Robert H. "The Analysis of the Comparative Public Administration Movement." *Canadian Public Administration* 9, no. 1 (1966): 108-30.
Jackson, Robert J., and Michael M. Atkinson. *The Canadian Legislative System.* 2d ed. Toronto: Macmillan, 1980.
James, William. *Pragmatism.* New York: Longmans Green, 1907.
Johnson, Daniel. *Egalité ou indépendance.* Montreal: Renaissance, 1965.
Karl, Barry D. "Charles Merriam." *International Encyclopedia of the Social Sciences.* 1968.
―――. *Charles E. Merriam and the Study of Politics.* Chicago: University of Chicago Press, 1974.
Keilty, Greg. *1837: Revolution in the Canadas.* Toronto: NC Press, 1974.
Kennedy, W. P. M. *Documents of the Canadian Constitution, 1759-1915.* Toronto: Oxford University Press, 1918.
Kerr, D. G. G. *A Historical Atlas of Canada.* 3d ed. Toronto: Nelson, 1975.
Kilbourn, William, ed. *Canada: A Guide to the Peaceable Kingdom.* Toronto: Macmillan, 1970.
King, Anthony. "Ideas, Institutions and the Policies of Governments: A Comparative Analysis." *British Journal of Political Science* 3 (1973): parts 1 & 2, 291-313; part 3, 409-23.
Klinck, Carl F., ed. *Literary History of Canada: Canadian Literature in English.* 2d ed. Toronto: University of Toronto Press, 1976.
Kroeber, A. L., and Clyde Kluckhohn. "Culture: A Critical Review of Concepts and Definitions." *Papers of the Peabody Museum of American Archaeology and Ethnology* 47, no. 1 (1952).
Kuhn, Thomas. *The Structure of Scientific Revolutions.* 2d ed. Chicago: University of Chicago Press, 1970.
Kunz, F. A. *The Modern Senate of Canada, 1925-1963: A Reappraisal.* Toronto: University of Toronto Press, 1965.
Laxer, Robert, ed. *Canada Ltd.* Toronto: McClelland & Stewart, 1973.
Leiserson, Avery. "Charles Merriam, Max Weber and the Search for Synthesis in Political Science." *American Political Science Review* 69, no. 1 (1975): 175-85.
Lijphart, Arend. *Democracies: Patterns of Majoritarian and Consensus Government in Twenty-one Countries.* New Haven: Yale University Press, 1984.
―――. *The Politics of Accommodation.* Berkeley: University of California Press, 1969.
Lipset, S. M. *The First New Nation.* New York: Basic Books, 1963.
―――. Review of *Democracy in Alberta* by C. B. Macpherson. *Canadian Forum* 34 (November 1954): 175-77; (December 1954): 196. (Reply by Macpherson in *Canadian Forum* 35 (December 1955): 223-25.)
―――. *Revolution and Counterrevolution.* New York: Basic Books, 1968.
Lower, A. R. M. *Colony to Nation.* Toronto: Longmans, 1946.
Lumsden, Ian, ed. *Close the 49th Parallel etc.: The Americanization of Canada.* Toronto: University of Toronto Press, 1970.
Mackay, Robert A. *The Unreformed Senate of Canada.* Rev. ed. Toronto: McClelland & Stewart, 1963.

MacLennan, Hugh. *Two Solitudes.* Toronto: Collins, 1945.
McLuhan, Herbert Marshall. *The Gutenberg Galaxy.* Toronto: University of Toronto Press, 1962.
———. *Understanding Media.* Toronto: University of Toronto Press, 1964.
McNaught, Kenneth. *The Pelican History of Canada.* 2d ed. Harmondsworth: Penguin, 1978.
Macpherson, C. B. *The Theory of Possessive Individualism.* Oxford: Clarendon Press, 1962.
McRoberts, Kenneth, and Dale Posgate. *Quebec: Social Change and Political Crisis.* Rev. ed. Toronto: McClelland & Stewart, 1980.
McWhinney, Edward. *Canada and the Constitution, 1979–1982.* Toronto: University of Toronto Press, 1982.
———. *Judicial Review.* 4th ed. Toronto: University of Toronto Press, 1969.
Magee, Bryan, ed. *Men of Ideas.* London: BBC, 1978.
Mallory, J. R. *The Structure of Canadian Government.* Toronto: Macmillan, 1971.
Manning, Helen Taft. *The Revolt of French Canada, 1800–1835.* London: Macmillan, 1962.
Marchak, M. Patricia. *Ideological Perspectives on Canada.* Toronto: McGraw-Hill Ryerson, 1975.
Marx, Karl. *Grundrisse.* Trans. by Martin Nicolaus. New York: Vintage Books, 1973.
———. *Marx's Interpretation of History.* New York: Oxford University Press, 1979.
Marx, Karl, and Friedrich Engels. *The German Ideology.* New York: International Publishers, 1947.
Matthews, Donald R., and James W. Prothro. *Negroes and the New Southern Politics.* New York: Harcourt, Brace & World, 1966.
Mehlberg, Henryk. *The Reach of Science.* Toronto: University of Toronto Press, 1958.
Meisel, John. "The Fear of Conflict and Other Failings." *Government and Opposition* 15, nos. 3–4 (Summer/Autumn 1980): 435–45.
———. Review of *Elite Accommodation in Canadian Politics* by Robert Presthus. *Canadian Forum* 54 (May–June 1974): 44–46. (Reply by Presthus in *Canadian Forum* 54 (November–December 1974): 11–12.)
Merriam, Charles E. *American Political Ideas; Studies in the Development of American Political Thought, 1865–1917.* New York: Macmillan, 1903.
———. *A History of American Political Theories.* New York: Macmillan, 1903.
———. "The Meaning of Democracy." *Journal of Negro Education* 10, no. 3 (July 1941): 309–52.
———. *New Aspects of Politics.* 1925. Reprint. Chicago: University of Chicago Press, 1970.
———. *Political Power.* 1934. Reprint. Glencoe, Ill.: Free Press, 1950.
Milne, David. *The New Canadian Constitution.* Toronto: Lorimer, 1982.
Moir, John S. *Church and State in Canada, 1627–1867.* Toronto: McClelland & Stewart, 1967.

Monet, Jacques. *The Last Cannon Shot: A Study of French-Canadian Nationalism, 1837–1850.* Toronto: University of Toronto Press, 1969.
Monière, Denis. *Ideologies in Quebec: The Historical Development.* Toronto: University of Toronto Press, 1981.
Morris, Charles. *The Pragmatic Movement in American Philosophy.* New York: Braziller, 1970.
Morris, James. *The Pax Britannica Trilogy.* London: Faber & Faber. Vol. I: *Heaven's Command* (1973); vol. II: *Pax Britannia* (1968); vol. III: *Farewell the Trumpets* (1980).
Morton, W. L. *The Canadian Identity.* 2d ed. Toronto: University of Toronto Press, 1972.
———. *The Critical Years: The Union of British North America 1857–1873.* Toronto: McClelland & Stewart, 1964.
———. *Manitoba: A History.* 3d ed. Toronto: University of Toronto Press, 1967.
Mshvenieradze, V. V. "Early Canadian Philosophers: A Soviet View." *The Marxist Quarterly* (Toronto), 1962. Translated from *Istoria Filosofii* 5 (1961).
Munro, William Bennett. *American Influences on Canadian Government.* Toronto: Macmillan, 1929.
Myrdal, Gunnar. *An American Dilemma.* New York: Harper, 1944.
Naylor, R. T. "The Rise and Fall of the Third Commercial Empire of the St. Lawrence." In Gary Teeple, ed., *Capitalism and the National Question in Canada.* Toronto: University of Toronto Press, 1972.
Newman, Peter C. *Renegade in Power: The Diefenbaker Years.* Toronto: McClelland & Stewart, 1963.
Nish, Elizabeth. "LaFontaine and the Double Majority." *Centre d'Etudes du Quebec Revue* 1 (1967): 9–17.
———. "Document: La Double majorite: Union et la reaction." *Centre d'Etudes du Quebec Revue* 1 (1967): 31–46.
Noel, S. J. R. *Politics in Newfoundland.* Toronto: University of Toronto Press, 1971.
Nye, Joseph S. "Transnational Relations and Interstate Conflicts: An Empirical Analysis," *International Organization* 28, no. 4 (1974): 961–96.
Oliver, Peter. *G. Howard Ferguson: Ontario Tory.* Toronto: University of Toronto Press, 1977.
Ormsby, William. *The Emergence of the Federal Concept in Canada, 1839–1845.* Toronto: University of Toronto Press, 1969.
Ouellet, Fernand. *Lower Canada, 1791–1840: Social Change and Nationalism.* Toronto: McClelland & Stewart, 1980.
Panitch, Leo, ed. *The Canadian State.* Toronto: University of Toronto Press, 1977.
Parsons, Talcott. *The Social System.* New York: Free Press, 1951.
———. *The Structure of Social Action.* 2d ed. New York: Free Press, 1949.
Parsons, Talcott, and Edward A. Shils. *Towards a General Theory of Action.* Cambridge, Mass., Harvard University Press, 1951.
Peirce, Charles Sanders. *Collected Papers.* Cambridge, Mass.: Harvard University Press, 1931–58.

Pickersgill, J. W. *The Mackenzie King Record.* 4 vols. Toronto: University of Toronto Press, 1960–71.
Pope, Sir Joseph. *Correspondence of Sir John A. Macdonald.* Toronto: Oxford University Press, 1921.
———. *Memoirs of The Right Honourable Sir John Alexander Macdonald.* London: Edward Arnold, 1894.
Preston, Richard A., ed. *The Influence of the United States on Canadian Development: Eleven Case Studies.* Durham, N.C.: Duke University Press, 1972.
———. *Perspectives on Revolution and Evolution.* Durham, N.C.: Duke University Press, 1976.
Presthus, Robert. *Elite Accommodation in Canadian Politics.* Toronto: Macmillan, 1973.
Pye, Lucien W., and Sidney Verba. *Political Culture and Political Development.* Princeton: Princeton University Press, 1965.
Quebec, Government of. *Québec-Canada: A New Deal.* Quebec Government's White Paper on Sovereignty-Association, 1979.
———. *Report* of The Royal Commission of Inquiry on Constitutional Problems, 1956.
Quebec Liberal Party. *A New Canadian Federation.* The Constitutional Committee of the Quebec Liberal Party, 1980.
Quebec National Assembly. *Le Parlementarisme britannique: Anachronisme ou réalité moderne? Documents et débats.* Quebec: Assemblée nationale Québec, 1980.
Quinn, Herbert F. *The Union Nationale: Quebec Nationalism from Duplessis to Lévesque.* 2d ed. Toronto: University of Toronto Press, 1979.
Radwanski, George. *Trudeau.* New York: Taplinger, 1978.
Redekop, John H., ed. *Approaches to Canadian Politics.* 2d ed. Scarborough, Ontario: Prentice-Hall, 1983.
Robert, Jean-Claude. *Du Canada français au Québec libre.* Paris: Flammarion, 1975.
Rose, Richard. *Politics in England.* 2d ed. Boston: Little, Brown, 1974.
Rucker, Darnell. *The Chicago Pragmatists.* Minneapolis: University of Minnesota Press, 1969.
Russell, Peter H., ed. *Leading Constitutional Decisions.* 3d ed. Ottawa: Carleton University Press, 1982.
Russett, Bruce. *Trends in World Politics.* New York: Macmillan, 1965.
———, et al. *World Handbook of Political and Social Indicators.* New Haven: Yale University Press, 1961.
Ryerson, Stanley B. *Unequal Union: Confederation and the Roots of Conflict in the Canadas, 1815–1873.* Toronto: Progress Books, 1968.
Sabine, George H. *A History of Political Theory.* 4th ed., rev. by Thomas Landon Thorson. Hinsdale, Ill.: Dryden, 1973.
Sabourin, Louis M., ed. *Le Système politique du Canada.* Ottawa: Université d'Ottawa, 1969.
Scott, Andrew M. *Political Thought in America.* New York: Rinehart, 1959.

Siegel, Arthur. *Politics and Media in Canada*. Toronto: McGraw-Hill Ryerson, 1983.
Siegfried, André. *The Race Question in Canada*. 1907. Reprint. Toronto: McClelland & Stewart, 1966.
Silver, A. I. *The French-Canadian Idea of Confederation, 1864–1900*. Toronto: University of Toronto Press, 1982.
Skinner, Quentin. "The Empirical Theorists of Democracy and Their Critics." *Political Theory* 1, no. 3 (August 1973): 287–306.
Smiley, D. V. *Canada in Question*. 3d ed. Toronto: McGraw-Hill Ryerson, 1980.
———. *The Canadian Political Nationality*. Toronto: Macmillan, 1967.
———. "Must Canadian Political Science be a Miniature Replica?" *Journal of Canadian Studies* 9, no. 1 (February 1974): 31–42.
Snow, C. P. *The Two Cultures and the Scientific Revolution*. Cambridge: Cambridge University Press, 1962.
Sparshott, F. E. "National Philosophy." *Dialogue* 16, no. 1 (March 1977).
Stanley, G. F. S. "Act or Pact? Another Look at Confederation," *Canadian Historical Association Report* 9 (1956).
———. *The Birth of Western Canada*. Toronto: University of Toronto Press, 1963.
Steen, Marcus Van. *Governor Simcoe and His Lady*. Toronto and London: Hodder & Stoughton, 1968.
Strayer, Barry L. *Judicial Review of Legislation in Canada*. Toronto: University of Toronto Press, 1968.
Sweeny, Alastair. *George-Etienne Cartier*. Toronto: McClelland & Stewart, 1976.
Swisher, Carl Brent. *Historical Decisions of the Supreme Court*. Princeton: Van Nostrand, 1958.
Symons, T. H. B. *To Know Ourselves*. Ottawa: Association of Universities and Colleges of Canada, 1975.
Task Force on Canadian Unity. *A Future Together: Coming to Terms*. Ottawa: Information Canada, 1979.
Taylor, Charles. *The Explanation of Behaviour*. London: Routledge & Kegan Paul, 1964.
———. *Social Theory as Practice*. Delhi: Oxford University Press, 1983.
Teeple, Gary, ed. *Capitalism and the National Question in Canada*. Toronto: University of Toronto Press, 1972.
Thomson, Dale C. *Louis St. Laurent: Canadian*. Toronto: Macmillan, 1967.
Thompson, Dennis F. *John Stuart Mill and Representative Government*. Princeton: Princeton University Press, 1976.
Torrance, Judy. "The Response of Canadian Governments to Violence." *Canadian Journal of Political Science* 10, no. 3 (1977): 473–496.
Trofimenkoff, Susan Mann. *The Dream of Nations: A Social International History of Quebec*. Toronto: Macmillan, 1982.
Trudeau, Pierre Elliott. *Federalism and the French-Canadians*. Toronto: Macmillan, 1968.
Trudel, Marcel, and Geneviève Jain. *Canadian History Textbooks: A Comparative Study*. Ottawa: Information Canada, 1970.

Underhill, Frank H. *The Image of Confederation.* Toronto: CBC, 1964.

———. *In Search of Canadian Liberalism.* Toronto: Macmillan, 1960.

United Kingdom. House of Commons, First *Report* from The Foreign Affairs Committee, session 1980–81: British North America Acts: The Role of Parliament.

United Kingdom. *Parliamentary Debates,* House of Lords, 3d Series, 185, 19 February 1867.

Vaillancourt, Jean-Guy, and Pauline Vaillancourt. "Contemporary Quebec Nationalism and the Left." Part 2. *The Australian and New Zealand Journal of Sociology* 14, no. 3 (1978): 329–39.

Vallières, Pierre. *Nègres blancs d'Amérique.* Montreal: Parti Pris, n.d.

Van Loon, Richard J., and Michael S. Whittington. *The Canadian Political System: Environment, Structure and Process.* 3d ed. Toronto: McGraw-Hill Ryerson, 1981.

Verney, Douglas V. *Parliamentary Reform in Sweden, 1866–1921.* Oxford: Clarendon Press, 1957.

Wade, Mason. *The French Canadians, 1760–1967.* 2 vols. Toronto: Macmillan, 1968.

———, ed. *Canadian Dualism/La Dualité canadienne.* Toronto: University of Toronto Press; Quebec: Laval University Press, 1960.

Waite, Peter B. *Canada, 1874–1896.* Toronto: McClelland & Stewart, 1971.

Wheare, K. C. *Federal Government.* 4th ed. London: Oxford University Press, 1963.

White, Morton. *Social Thought in America.* New York: Oxford University Press, 1976.

Whittington, Michael S., and Glen Williams, eds. *Canadian Politics in the 1980's.* Toronto: Methuen, 1981.

Young, Brian. *George-Etienne Cartier: Montreal Bourgeois.* Kingston and Montreal: McGill–Queen's University Press, 1981.

Index

Acadia. *See* Nova Scotia
Acadians/*Acadiens*, 211, 217, 255, 258
Act of Union, 31, 126, 129, 174, 176–77, 205, 206
Aeronautics case (1932), 136
A Future Together (1979). *See* Task Force on Canadian Unity
Air Traffic Controllers' strike, 328–29
Alberta, 98–100, 328. *See also* Social Credit
Algeria, 323
Allan, Sir Hugh, 247
Almond, G. A., 72, 73, 74, 80–81, 107–8
A New Canadian Federation (1980), 377–82
"Anglo-American society," 63–81, 105, 114, 296, 401; Lipset on, 82–88, 110; obsolescence of, 299, 300, 321
Annexation Manifesto, 338
Aquinas, Thomas, 94
Archibald, Adams, 214
Aristotle, 18, 69, 71, 93, 94
Armour, Leslie, 48, 54, 342
Army Act, 144
Austin, John, 49
Australia, 82–84, 155, 191
Austria-Hungary, 223–24
Avineri, Shlomo, 15

Bagehot, Walter, 69
Baldwin, Robert, 117, 127, 198, 200, 202–3
Bank of Montreal, 240
Barrett v. Winnipeg, 270, 275
"Beige Paper." *See A New Canadian Federation*
Bell, David, 337
Berger, Carl, 142

Bergeron, Gérard, 173
Bilingualism, 252–53, 279, 300, 322, 326
Bilingualism and Biculturalism, Royal Commission on, 235, 301–2, 309, 315, 322, 325, 327
Bill of Rights: American, 151, 152; Canadian, 135, 136, 215, 349
Bill 101, 330, 331, 349
Bissell, Claude, 25
Bleus, 193, 203, 204, 235, 247, 258, 278
Blewett, George, 49
Boer War. *See* War
Bonham's case, 132
Boorstin, Daniel, 12–13
Bourassa, Henri, 185, 233–35, 279, 281, 282–83, 300
Bourassa, Robert, 127
Bourget, Bishop Ignace, 195, 238, 239, 247
Braudel, Fernand, 10, 31, 106
Brett, George, 48, 54
British Empire, 2, 3, 47, 55, 110, 114, 116, 117, 118, 121, 127, 128, 144, 183, 185; Canada's pride in, 219–23; and Canadian nationalism, 227; Canadian support for, 281–87; decline of, 22, 51; end of, 289–92, 301–10; evolution into Commonwealth, 140, 173; and French Canada, Chapter 6 passim; lack of ideology, 190; Merriam's admiration of, 67
British North America Act (BNA Act, 1867), 19, 31, 113, 120, 127, 131, 133, 136, 146–47, 148, 151, 153, 156, 157, 159, 161, 162, 163, 169, 215, 217, 222–23, 254, 277, 279–80,

British North America Act (BNA Act, 1867) (Cont.)
301, 326, 338, 348; a British document, 253–54; and Constitutional Act (1982), 351; and Constitutional Amendment Bill (1978), 363–69; "declaratory power" in, 145; and education, 216–17, 221; English-Canadian view of, 174; French-Canadian view of, 279; legitimacy of, 389–90; power to amend, 137–43; Preamble to, 127–28; provinces and, 138–39; role of British Parliament, 134, 140, 151, 152, 157; Sections of: no. 47, 159; no. 55, 144, 304; no. 56, 144, 304; no. 85, 137; no. 91, 136, 137, 302, 365, 366; no. 92, 136, 137, 147, 214, 215, 216, 217, 302, 366; no. 93, 214, 215, 216, 217, 254, 255–56, 268–69 (provisions of), 270, 273, 274, 280, 302
British North America Act (1871), 267–68
British North America Act (No. 1, 1949), 291
British North America Act (No. 2, 1949), 139–40, 147, 169, 291, 365, 367
Brokerage theory of politics, 63
Brophy v. Attorney-General of Manitoba, 275

Cabinet, Canadian, 356, 357
Canada: character of, 31–34, 54, 95; criticism of, 102–3; end of the old, 318–22; independence of, 142–43; a Middle Power, 287, 301, 311; quasi-unitary, 301–10; response to scientific empiricism, 98–107
Canada, Dominion of (1840–67), 6, 8, 113, 116, 128, 162, 166, 172, 174, 177, 178, 185, 211, 219, 230, 231, 236, 263, 265, 289
Canada, East and West (1840–67), 126, 196, 197, 199, 202, 206
Canada, French. *See* French Canada
Canada, Province of (1840–67), 8, 128, 129, 203
Canada, Upper and Lower (1791–1840), 7, 124, 126, 130, 190, 191; established, 176

Canadian dialectic. *See* Dialectic
Canadian Forum, 98–107
Canadian Philosophical Association, 55
Canadiens, 172, 182, 183, 184, 185, 187, 190, 196, 206, 211, 255
Cape Breton, 180
Capital, selection of, 201–2
Cardin, P. J. A., 285–86
Carnarvon, Henry, fourth earl of, 129, 256–58, 273
Caron, Adolphe, 229
Cartier, George-Etienne, 130, 168, 192, 193, 210, 233, 234, 240, 243, 260, 261, 279, 282, 294; career of, 244–51; after Confederation, 232; death of, 211; and Judicial Committee, 161–62; and majority rule, 254, 257–59; and Manitoba, 214, 215; and Manitoba Act (1870), 264–65, 273, 274; a Pan-Canadian, 229; and Sulpician Order, 239; and two nations, 218–19
Cartier, Jacques, 250
Castors. *See* Ultramontanes
Castro, Fidel, 52
Cauchon, Joseph, 246–47
Charbonneau, Archbishop Joseph, 316
Charter of Rights and Freedoms, 348, 364, 389
"Charter races," 179
Chateau Clique, 125, 189, 192, 198, 206
Cheffins, R. I., 133
Chevrier, Lionel, 315
Chicago, University of, 22, 41, 66–67, 68, 70
Cicero, 71, 94
Cité libre, 208, 317
Citizenship, 20, 282. *See also* Nationality
City of Fredericton v. The Queen (1880), 160
Civil law, 175, 216, 245
Civil liberties, 114, 175, 178
Civil rights, 175
Civil War. *See* War
Civilization: American, 11–12, 21, 30, 32, 100; British, 12–34, 52, 100, 196, 220, 223, 241, 273; Canadian response to, 111, 234, 335, 392–96; and culture, 29–30; defined, 10–11;

Index

French, 11–12, 180–81, 335; North American, 5, 9, 10, 52, 62, 63, 173, 177, 262, 317, 320, 395
Clark, Joe, 329, 373
Coke, Edward, 132
Colborne, Sir John, 191
Coleman, James, 72, 73, 74, 80–81
Colonialism, 5, 16, 106, 157, 175, 338–39
Colonial Laws Validity Act, 140–41
Colonial Office, 47
Commission on Canadian Studies, 36
Common Schools Act, 258–59, 281
Commonwealth, 22, 140
Compact theory, 173, 179, 218–26, 255, 258, 279–80
Comparative politics, 58, 107–8
Confederacy, 128, 220, 360, 377–82
Confederation, 112, 113, 116, 117, 120, 127, 128, 131, 132, 172, 174, 179, 202, 206; challenges to, 302; debates about, 204; extension of, 213; Fathers of, 153–54, 177; philosophers and, 55; as victory for English Canada, 219
Connolly, Archbishop Thomas Louis, 256, 266
Conquest, 2, 172–79, 180, 201, 207, 208, 261, 331, 340
Conscription, 119, 282, 284, 285–86, 293
Conservatism, 6, 55, 116–17, 296
Consociationalism, 106
Constitution: American, 19, 46, 141, 144, 150–51, 155, 158, 159, 215, 347; British, 114, 120, 133, 144; Canadian, 114, 141, 143; supremacy of, 149. *See also* Parliamentary supremacy; Supreme Court; Westminster
Constitutional Act (1982), 8, 335, 345, 348, 351, 361, 362, 364, 378, 385; Quebec and, 397; Queen and, 383; provisions of, 350
Constitutional Amendment Bill (1978), 252, 363–69, 377
Constitutional convention, 355, 383–84
Continentalism, 9–24, 336
Contradictions. *See* Dialectic
Conventions, parliamentary, 145–48, 221, 255, 384

Cook, Ramsay, 178–79, 221
Cooperative Commonwealth Federation, 32, 115. *See also* New Democratic Party
Corry, J. A., 70
Council of the Federation, 370–73
Council of the Provinces, 387–88
Covenant, 38, 47
Créditistes, 298, 314–15, 320. *See also* Social Credit
Creighton, Donald, 1
Cross, James, 323
Crown, 12, 21, 22, 34, 117, 132, 144, 145, 161, 164, 166, 167, 168, 189, 197, 198, 221, 261, 336, 337–38, 343, 403; changed role of, 288; and the Constitution, 364, 383, 394; in Europe, 224; and French Canadians, 279, 283; and Judicial Committee, 150; loyalty to, 230; and Parliament, 124–28; and parliamentary joint committee, 334–35; and Quebec, 298–99, 376, 379
Culture, 2, 3, 4, 9, 344–45; American, 5, 6, 12, 396; civic, 28; defined, 10, 15–16; derivative, 18; French-Canadian, 28–29, 218, 254–55, 345; indigenous, 51; interpretation of, 24–30; and *kultur,* 11; political, 18, 27–28, 63

Dahl, Robert, 58, 68, 69, 70, 86, 87, 88–94, 95
Darwin, Charles, 43
Dawson, R. MacGregor, 119, 126, 166, 178, 221, 356
Declaration of Independence, 38, 46, 47, 54, 188, 289, 337
Declaration of the Rights of Man, 188, 349
Declaratory power, 371, 380
de Gaulle, Charles, 52, 318
Dependency theory, 14, 16, 17
Depression, Great, 140
Descartes, René, 42, 46
Deux nations, 218–24, 297, 341–42
Deviant cases, 33, 85, 296
Dewey, John, 13, 37, 39, 41, 48–50, 51, 60, 67, 79, 86, 95
Dialectic, Canadian, 333–38, 342–45
Dicey, A. V., 122, 147

Dickson, R. G. B., 400
Diefenbaker, John, 115, 297, 312–16, 318, 321, 322, 325, 359
Dion, Léon, 172, 207, 224
Disallowance, 144, 216, 274, 304, 371
Dorion, A. A., 250
Double majority principle, 201–2, 209, 365, 379, 388
Dred Scott, 167, 389
Dualism, 202–4, 212–36, 253, 254, 373, 391
Duplessis, Maurice, 234, 244, 250, 285, 292, 293–99, 310, 316–18, 320
Durham, John Lambton, first earl of, 7, 125, 181, 199, 205, 253
Durham Report, 19, 125, 181, 196
Dyads. *See* Dialectic

Eastern Townships, 183, 196–97
Easton, David, 33, 62, 68, 70, 74, 100
Eckstein, Harry, 70, 71
Education, 186, 256–59, 272
Education Act (1801), 186
Egypt, 22
Einstein, Albert, 43–44
Elgin, James Bruce, eighth earl of, 193, 199
Elias, Norbert, 11
Emergency powers, 136–37
Empire, British. *See* British Empire
Empirical theory. *See* Scientific empiricism
L'Etat du Québec, 316–18, 325. *See also* Quebec
Eulau, Heinz, 94–98
European Community, 22, 374–75, 376, 384, 389
Expo 67, 318–19, 325

Fackenheim, Emil, 50
Family Compact, 125, 192, 198
Favreau, Guy, 367, 369
Federal Council, 378–79
Federalism: American, 20, 353, 382–83; asymmetrical, 371; Canadian, 200, 204, 354–56, 358–62; constitutional, 151, 153, 155–59, 165, 303, 307, 339, 344, 353, 361, 372, 382–90; defined, 123, 352; executive, 352–62; imperial, 116, 146–47, 151, 159–62, 288, 301–10, 338, 339; judicial, 353, 386; legislative, 353, 386; logic of, 115, 121, 153–59, 163, 167, 343, 382; outmoded, 374; parliamentary, 20, 31, 121, 153, 165, 339; profitable, 332; pseudo-, 392, 397–400; quasi-, 160, 332–33; quasi-imperial, 157; renewed, 363–69; restructured, 209, 369–73, 377–82; types, 397–400. *See also* Philosophical federalism
Federalists, 252, 253. *See also* Pan-Canadianism
Federal Judiciary Act (1789), 158
Federal principle, 130, 132, 136
Federal-Provincial Conference, 131. *See also* First Ministers Conferences
Federal-Provincial Relations Office, 359
Ferguson, Howard, 141, 143
Filibuster, 353
First Ministers, 200, 206
First Ministers Conferences, 327, 347–48, 358, 359–60, 362, 369, 387–88, 398–99
Forrester, Ray, 333
Founding Fathers, 60, 154
Fourth York, 323
Fox, Paul, 70
France, 3, 7, 20, 31, 173–74, 187, 189, 242, 243, 323
Franchise, 129
Francophonie, 321
French Canada, 183–85, 202–5, 209, 211, 218, 221, 223, 225, 237–38, 280, 299, 364; criticism of, 178, 181–82; historical sense of, 172–74; resists assimilation, 196–200, 223–24; vision of North America, 242–44
French language, 199, 215, 216, 276, 277–81, 319–20, 328–29, 349
French Revolution, 183, 185, 237
Front du Libération du Québec, 323, 333

Galbraith, John K., 22
Galt amendment, 236
Geertz, Clifford, 94, 97
Genesis, Book of, 44
Germany, 76–77
Gettysburg Address, 18
Gilson, Etienne, 50
Gladstone, W. E., 129

Index

God Save the King, 222
Gordon, General Charles, 223
Goudge, Thomas, 50
Governor general, 1, 153, 221, 239, 249, 270, 303–5, 321, 365
Grant, George, 1, 51, 52, 55, 110, 318
Great Coalition, 206, 250
Grits, Clear, 194, 195, 203, 204, 339

Habermas, Jürgen, 96
Hailsham, Quinton Hogg, Lord, 252
Hartz, Louis, 106
Hegel, G. W. F., 15, 18, 42, 43, 49, 94
Hobbes, Thomas, 43, 55
Hodge v. The Queen, 133
Hodgetts, J. E., 70
Hogg, Peter, 145, 156, 162
Holmes, O. W., 49
Houde, Camillien, 295
House of the Federation, 364–65, 370
Hudson, Henry, 263
Hudson's Bay Company, 263, 265
Hunter, Bruce, 56
Huntington, Samuel H., 74

Ideals, 37, 38, 45–46, 61, 85, 88
Immigration, 196–97, 202, 277–78, 280
Imperial Conference, 289, 304
Imperialism, 4, 32, 34, 234, 236, 318–22, 335
Indépendantistes, 8, 208, 252, 328. See also Separatism; Sovereignty-association
Independence, 330, 336–37, 346, 373–77
India, 11, 15, 155, 176, 201, 389, 401
Indians, 2, 27, 180, 263
Innis, Harold, 14, 22, 54, 106
Institut Canadienne, 194–95, 239
Instituts Nationaux, 194, 239
International Business Machines, 9, 51
International Encyclopedia of the Social Sciences, 68
Intra vires, 157–58
Inuit, 2, 27
Ireland, 151, 161
Irish, 164, 182, 205, 266
Irving, John, 48, 53, 54

Jacksonian democracy, 128, 189
James, William, 37, 41, 52

Jefferson, Thomas, 18
Jehovah's Witnesses, 178, 316
Jesuits, 237, 240
Johnson, Daniel, 177, 209, 250
Johnson, Harry, 22
Joint Address, 354
Joint Committee on the Constitution (1972), 327
Judicial Committee of the Privy Council, 114, 121, 122, 131, 134, 140, 151, 153, 156, 159, 160, 161, 162, 163, 355–56; abolition of appeals to, 133, 143, 166, 168; Canadian views of, 161, 162–63; described, 150, 164, 169; judgments of, 136, 137, 166, 239, 258–59, 260, 269–76; replaced, 149, 290, 305–7

Karl, Barry, 69
Kennedy, John F., 323
Key, V. O., 68
Keynes, J. M., 44
King, Anthony, 96
King, W. L. M., 110, 113, 116, 235, 284–85, 288, 294
Kluckhohn, Clyde, 15
Kroeber, A. L., 15
Kuhn, Thomas, 44, 74, 75, 166
Kunz, F. A., 131

Lachine rapids, 250
LaFontaine, Hippolyte, 7, 191, 192, 193, 198, 200, 202–3, 205, 210, 244, 245, 246, 294
Langevin, Hector, 256, 257, 259
Language policy, 372
Languages of discourse, 172–74, 224, 228
Lapointe, Ernest, 283, 285
Laporte, Pierre, 323
Lartigue, Bishop Jean-Jacques, 191–92
Laski, Harold, 69
Laskin, Bora, 160
Lasswell, Harold, 68, 94
Laurendeau, André, 235, 317, 327
Laurier, Wilfrid, 114, 116, 229, 233, 244, 250, 273, 275, 283
Laurin, Camille, 397
Laval University, 240
Le Devoir, 235, 317, 327
Lenin, V. I., 67

Lépine, Ambroise, 26
Lesage, Jean, 314, 318
Lévesque, Georges-Henri, 316
Lévesque, René, 115, 244, 250, 297, 298-99, 324, 325, 327, 328, 376
Liberalism, 207, 210, 237, 279
Liberal Party, 283, 310-16, 338
Lieutenant governors, 380
Ligue Nationaliste, 233-36, 279
Lijphart, Arend, 113
Lincoln, Abraham, 18, 60
Lindsay, A. D., 70
Linton, Ralph, 75
Lipset, Seymour M., 6, 58, 63, 82-88, 95-96, 98-100, 104-6, 109
Literary History of Canada, 25
Livingston, W. S., 210
Locke, John, 18, 42, 43
Lodge, Rupert, 49
London School of Economics and Political Science, 105
"Loose fish," 207-8
Louisburg, 180
Louisiana, 185
Lower, A. R. M., 222, 335
Loyalists, 37, 47, 124, 128, 166, 176, 177, 193, 197, 228, 403; committed, 116; as losers, 182-83

McDougall, William, 214
Machiavelli, Nicolo, 18, 69, 94
McGee, D'Arcy, 149
McGibbon, Pauline, 183
McGill University, 220, 229
Mackenzie, Alexander, 138, 247, 260
Mackenzie, W. L., 63, 190, 203, 261, 338
MacLennan, Hugh, 181
McLuhan, Marshall, 9
Macpherson, C. B., 6, 21, 63, 98-100, 104-6, 109
McWhinney, Edward, 155, 162, 178, 368
Madison, James, 86, 94
Madisonian democracy, 88-89, 93
Majority: psychic, 325; rule of, 135-36, 145, 253, 262-81, 292-94, 300, 301, 348-50
Mallory, James, 322
Manitoba, 248, 249, 251, 253, 254, 260, 262-81

Manitoba Act (1870), 260, 264-65, 267, 268-75
Marbury v. Madison, 150, 154, 156, 166, 170
Marchand, Jean, 322, 329, 357
Maritime provinces, 130, 180, 183, 232, 256-59
Marshall, John, 150, 154-59, 166, 167, 368, 382
Martin, Chester, 126
Martin, Paul, 313
Marx, Karl, 13-17 passim, 43, 49, 67, 94, 97-99, 104, 106, 109, 245, 343
Mason-Dixon line, 262
Mayflower, 38, 47
Meade, George H., 46, 67
Meighen, Arthur, 114, 116, 161
Meisel, John, 6, 100-107
"Memorable history," 6, 166, 167, 288, 336
Mercier, Honoré, 131, 233, 240, 244, 250, 262
Merriam, Charles E., 39, 41, 42, 58, 59, 60, 61, 64, 66-72, 86
Merriam, John, 69
Métis, 211, 214, 217, 255, 259-62, 263-65, 272
Michels, Robert, 69
Militia Bill (1862), 204, 281
Mill, John Stuart, 13, 18, 49, 59
"Miniature replica," 2
Minorities, 253, 257
Monck, Charles Stanley, Lord, 231
Monière, Denis, 188
Montesquieu, Charles, Baron de, 43
Montreal, 197, 201, 245-46, 323, 326; University of, 239-40
Moore, G. E., 48
Morris, Charles, 39, 44
Morton, W. L., 141, 257, 258
Mosaic, cultural, 23
Mosca, Gaetano, 69
Mshvenieradze, V. V., 53
Mulroney, Brian, 359
Multiculturalism, 3, 23, 325-26, 327, 392
Murray, John Clark, 49

Napoleon Bonaparte, 185
Napoleon III, 19, 238
National anthem, 222, 225

Index

National Dream, The, 221
Nationalism, 9–24, 32, 207, 210–11, 218, 226–27, 234, 281; development in Quebec, 232–36; Duplessis' defensive, 295–99, 316–17; political, 300
Nationality, 218–19, 230, 341, 440–404
NATO, 64, 143, 290, 294
Navy, 233–34
Naylor, R. T., 17
Nelson, Robert, 192
Neo-Marxism, 14, 16
New Brunswick, 180, 211, 251, 252–59, 267, 322, 330
"New Deal," Canadian, 166
New Democratic Party, 32, 325, 328, 361
Newfoundland, 143, 172, 287, 290, 294
New France, 180
Ninety-Two Resolutions, 189
NORAD, 64
North West Rebellion, 259–62
Norway-Sweden, 224
"Notwithstanding" clause, 389
Nova Scotia, 119, 124, 180, 211

Oath of Allegiance, 23
October crisis (1970), 323, 327
Ogdensburg, 246
Official Languages Act (1969), 235, 300, 301, 321, 325, 327, 328–29
Ontario, 113, 116, 118, 119, 124, 130, 137, 139, 140, 176, 201, 214; and bilingualism, 253; and Crown, 338; in Dominion cabinet, 232; education in, 216–18, 257, 276–81; and 1885 rebellion, 260–62; and Manitoba, 248–49, 262–64
Ontario, Lake, 183
Orange Order, 183, 248, 260–62, 264
Ottawa, 120, 278, 310–16
Ouellet, Fernand, 188, 192

Pacific Scandal, 247–48
Pan-Canadianism, 226–36, 242–44, 252, 262, 283, 287, 300, 329, 347, 349, 378; limitations of, 322–28
Papacy. *See* Vatican
Papineau, Louis-Joseph, 63, 188, 190–93, 246, 261
Parish Schools Act (1824), 186
Parliament: of Canada, 126, 138; of United Kingdom, 133, 141, 142, 307–8
Parliament Act (1911), 129
Parliamentary government, 143–44
Parliamentary supremacy, 112, 122–37, 144, 145, 146, 147, 308, 348–50
Parnell, C. S., 138
Parsons, Talcott, 6, 13, 14, 44, 58, 60, 61, 72–82, 88, 90, 91, 99
Parti Canadien, 188
Parti National, 233–36, 240, 262
Parti Patriote, 188. See also Patriotes
Parti Québecois, 32, 170–71, 208, 233–34, 306, 333–34, 350, 362–63, 372; and Constitutional Amendment Bill, 368–69; promotes sovereignty-association, 328–31; and referendum, 346–47
Party labels, 204
Patriation, 142, 168, 327, 343
Patriotes, 186, 187, 189, 190–91, 193, 210, 232
Pattern variables, 72–88
"Peaceable kingdom," 112, 301, 333
Pearson, L. B., 311, 313, 316, 318, 319, 320, 321, 322, 367
Peirce, C. S., 5, 37, 40, 41, 50, 96
Pelletier, Gérard, 322
Pépin, Jean-Luc, 370
Philosophical federalism, 47–57, 99, 105, 108, 121, 165, 169, 201, 256, 333, 337–42, 350–51, 363, 391, 395–97, 404
Philosophy, 35–38, 42–44, 53, 56, 57
Plains of Abraham, 180, 298
Plato, 18, 42, 59, 71, 343
Pledge of Allegiance (U.S.), 38, 46
Political economy, 14, 22
Polyarchy, 87
Popular sovereignty, 383
Population, changes in, 22, 202, 206, 209, 212
Populism, 88–89, 93
Positivists, 39
Powell, C. Bingham, 107–8
Power, C. G., 285, 286
Pragmatism, Canadian, 153
Pragmatism, philosophy of, 5, 37–46, 52–54, 59–98
Prerogative, 132, 144, 160, 167. *See also* Crown

Prince Edward Island, 354; attorney general of, 122, 145
Privy Council. *See* Judicial Committee
Progressives, 39
Protestantism, 182, 183, 186, 194, 198, 205, 207, 214–21 passim, 227–28, 237–38, 254, 257, 262–81
Provinces, role of, 289, 290–91
"Provincial Treaty," 141, 143, 355

Quebec, 6, 124, 130, 131, 177, 183, 201, 313, 319, 321, 328; before 1837, 172–87; demand for equality, 389; education in, 216–18; elections in 1980 and 1981, 385; flag, 189; nationalism, 232–44, 296–98, 309–10; and Quiet Revolution, 319; referendum, 331, 346–47; and Riel, 260–62; and Royal Commission on Constitutional Problems, 309; violence in, 328
Quebec Act (1774), 8, 174–76, 199
Quebec-Canada: A New Deal (1979). *See* Sovereignty-association
Quebec City, 236
Quebec Liberal Party, 234, 295, 298, 314, 320, 322, 324, 327, 328, 358; "Beige Paper" and, 377–82
"Quebec lieutenant," 202, 285, 286, 292, 315
Queen. *See* Crown; Victoria, Queen
Queen's University, 49, 101
Question Time, 135
Quiet Revolution, 22, 115, 173, 179, 301, 315–16

Radicals, Quebec, 178, 184, 187, 192, 193–94. *See also* Rouges
Railways: the Canadian Pacific, 213, 220, 248; Cartier and, 244–51; the Grand Trunk, 245–47, 250; the Intercolonial, 213, 248; Manitoba and, 262–64; the St. Lawrence & Atlantic, 246
Rassemblement democratique pour l'indépendance, 397
Rebellions (1837–38), 19, 117, 119, 125, 192, 208, 248, 322, 331, 340; forgotten, 6, 126, 179; significance of, 187–95
Red River, 248

Referendum (1980), 330–33, 347, 376, 383; terms of, 346
Reform Bill, 189
Reformers, 193, 197
Regime change, 31, 174–79, 385
Regionalism, 19, 214, 336
Régis, Louis-M., 53
Regulation 17, 277–79
Remedial laws, 216, 258, 270, 275
Representation by population, 130, 207, 339
Representative government, 124
Republic, 339; of Letters, Science and Technology, 12–13
Reservation, 144, 304, 371. *See also* Disallowance
Responsible government, 20, 126, 129, 130–31, 193, 338–39
Revolution, 20; American, 19, 38, 116, 124, 337–38, 382; of 1848, 127. *See also* Quiet Revolution
Richelieu Valley, 190
Rimouski, 198
"Rise of Liberty" school, 173
Robarts, John P., 370
Robinson, James Harvey, 49
Rockefeller Foundation, 69
Roman Catholic Church, 31, 42, 176, 177; in Canada, 226–29, 256–59; in Quebec, 182, 184, 191–92, 194, 197, 207, 236–37, 295–96, 298
Rossiter, Clinton, 47
Rouges, 178, 193, 194, 195, 203, 228, 239, 258, 350
Rousseau, Jean-Jacques, 43
Royal Commission on Bilingualism and Biculturalism. *See* Bilingualism and Biculturalism
Royal Proclamation (1763), 174, 175, 180; supremacy of, 187. *See also* Prerogative
Royce, Josiah, 52
Russell, Bertrand, 48
Russell, Lord John, 190, 193
Russell, Peter, 153–56, 162
Ryan, Claude, 327
Ryerson, Egerton, 203

Saint Jean Baptiste Society, 246
St. Laurent, Louis, 114, 115, 158, 229, 243, 244, 251, 291, 318, 319, 320,

Index

343; career of, 292–94; policies in 1950s, 310–16; prime minister, 288; Quebec lieutenant, 286, 357
St. Lawrence River, 2, 16, 176, 177, 201, 211, 246, 250, 344
Sankey, Lord, 133
Sarnia, 246
Sauvé, Paul, 294–96, 312, 317
Schools, "separate," 203, 204, 216, 237, 266, 270–72
Science of politics, 5, 58
Scientific empiricism, 39–42, 44, 48; Canadian response to, 98–107; and comparative politics, 107–11; successor to Pragmatism, 59–98
Scott, Thomas, 248–49, 260, 261
Selkirk, Thomas, Lord, 263
Senate: Canadian, 129, 131, 132, 232, 354, 360–61, 364–73, 378–79; U.S., 130, 131, 353, 361
Separatism, 7, 328. *See also Indépendantistes;* Sovereignty-association
Severn v. The Queen (1878), 160
Shils, Edward, 60, 70–71, 74, 94
Siegfried, André, 1, 8, 184, 238
Sills, David, 68
Simcoe, Sir John Graves, 176
Simon, Herbert, 68
Skinner, Quentin, 91, 92
Smiley, Donald V., 106, 162, 165–66, 231–32, 352, 358–59
Smith, T. V., 67
Snow, C. P., 25–27
Social Credit, 53, 98, 115, 320. *See also Créditistes*
Social science, 5, 13, 14, 25, 29, 33, 54, 58, 62
Social Science Research Council: of Canada, 50, 52; U.S., 69
Sons of Liberty, 191
Sovereignty-association, 209, 297, 328–31, 346–47, 373–77, 396. *See also* Separatism; *Indépendantistes*
Soviet Union, 95
Spencer, Herbert, 13, 44–45, 49
Stanfield, Robert, 322
Stanley, G. F. S., 265
Star Chamber, 132, 163
State, secular, 400–404
Statute of Westminster, 119, 140, 141, 144, 147, 164, 166, 168, 289, 308

Strachan, Bishop John, 116
Stratford Festival, 24
Strayer, Barry, 162
Suez crisis, 22, 116, 311–12
Sulpician Order, 237, 239, 246, 247
Supreme Court: of Canada, 150–62 passim, 165, 167–71, 178, 294; legitimacy of, 306–7; reform of, 364–71; and Senate, 366–69; of the U.S., 133, 136, 149–66 passim, 307, 353, 368
Sweeny, Alastair, 249
Swing of compass and pendulum, 120, 135, 363

Taché, Bishop Alexandre, 264, 273–74, 276, 283
Taché, Sir Etienne-Pascal, 127
Taschereau, Archbishop Elzéar-Alexandre, 238, 240
Task Force on Canadian Unity, 369–73
Taylor, Charles, 395
Television, 319–20, 347–50, 396
Ten Resolutions, 190, 193
Terrebonne, 198
Test Act, 175
Thomism, 50, 52
Tocqueville, Alexis de, 18, 19, 59, 273
Tönnies, Ferdinand, 75
Tories, 183, 197, 198, 338
Toronto, 197, 264
Toronto, University of, 31, 105, 142
Toronto *Globe,* 203
Trans-Canada Pipeline, 311
Tremblay Commission. *See* Bilingualism and Biculturalism; Quebec
Tricolor, 189
Trott, Elizabeth, 48, 54, 342
Trudeau, Pierre Elliott, 65–66, 115, 178, 229, 244, 251, 286–87, 291, 318–28 passim; and constitutional reform, 363–69; on French Canada, 181–82; in 1950s, 295–96; a Pan-Canadian, 252–53; and sovereignty-association, 347–49
Truman, David B., 68
Tucker, R. N., 133
Turner, Frederick Jackson, 38
Two nations. *See Deux nations*
Two solitudes, 224

Ultramontanes, 194, 237–40
Ultra vires, 133, 150, 157–58, 166, 216, 269, 274, 368
Umpire *ab extra,* 121, 134, 150, 152, 160, 164, 273, 319, 339; end of, 287, 288, 291, 303
Underhill, Frank H., 21, 113
Union Nationale, 115, 189, 233–36, 285, 292, 312, 322
Union period (1940–67), 7, 19, 202, 204–7. *See also* Canada
United Church of Canada, 35
United Kingdom, 206. *See also* British Empire; Westminster
Unproblematic issues, 37–46, 54, 61, 79

Vanier, Georges, 321
Van Loon, Richard, 70
Vatican, 238, 240
Veblen, Thorstein, 49
Verba, Sidney, 71–72
Veto, 388–89
Victoria, Queen, 128, 183, 192, 201, 223, 229, 232, 243, 338. *See also* Crown
Victoria Charter, 327

Walgreen Foundation, 93
War: Boer, 117, 230, 233, 279, 282; Civil (U.S.), 18, 38, 112, 113, 128, 204; of 1812, 182, 281; First World, 2, 58, 67, 117, 277, 282, 335; of Independence (U.S.), 47, 127, 183; Second World, 2, 5, 13, 22, 32, 34, 60, 67, 117, 120, 140, 282
War Measures Act, 323
Washington, George, 190
Watson, John, 49
Weber, Max, 60, 69, 71, 82, 94
Western expansion, 203, 248–49
Western provinces, 130, 139, 172, 219–20, 241, 264, 304, 322, 325, 338, 388; and new constitution, 348–49; representation in cabinet, 357–58; and Task Force on Canadian Unity, 373
Westminster, 22, 144, 157, Chapter 4 passim; model, 105, 116, 122–43, 146, 166, 338; parliamentary system, 6, 12, 66, 148, 153, 189–90, 339, 343, 394; tradition, 20–21, 100, 104, 132, 195–96, 206–8, 230, 243, 273, 287, 288, 336, 340–41, 346–47, 369, 383
Wheare, K. C., 155
Whitehall, 144, 146, 155, 164, 166, 230, 287, 288
Whittington, Michael, 70
Wilson, Michael, 346
Winks, Robin, 9, 10
Winnipeg, 264–65
Wolseley, General Garnet, 245
Wrong, George, 142

Library of Congress Cataloging-in-Publication Data
Verney, Douglas V.
Three civilizations, two cultures, one state.
 (Duke University Center for International Studies publication)
Bibliography: p.
Includes index.
1. Canada—Politics and government—19th century.
2. Canada—Politics and government—20th century.
3. Federal government—Canada—History. I. Title.
II. Series.
JL15.V47 1985 320.971 85-25313
ISBN 0-8223-0654-9